# Butterworths Expert Guide to the European Union

# Butterworths Expert Guide to the European Union

*Editors*

**Dr Jörg Monar**
Professor of Politics and Director of the
Centre for European Politics and Institutions,
University of Leicester

**Dr Nanette Neuwahl**
Professor of European Law,
International and European Law Unit,
Faculty of Law, University of Liverpool

**Professor David O'Keeffe** BCL, LLM(NUI), LLM (Yale)
Doctorandos (Leyden), Solicitor,
Professor of Law and
Director, Centre for the Law of the European Union,
University College, London

**William Robinson**
Legal Secretary, European Court of Justice, Luxembourg,
Honorary Research Fellow, Centre for the Law of the
European Union, University College, London, Solicitor

**Butterworths**
London, Edinburgh, Dublin
1996

| United Kingdom | Butterworths, a Division of Reed Elsevier (UK) Ltd, Halsbury House, 35 Chancery Lane, LONDON WC2A 1EL and 4 Hill Street, EDINBURGH EH2 3JZ |
| --- | --- |
| Australia | Butterworths, SYDNEY, MELBOURNE, BRISBANE, ADELAIDE, PERTH, CANBERRA and HOBART |
| Canada | Butterworths Canada Ltd, TORONTO and VANCOUVER |
| Ireland | Butterworth (Ireland) Ltd, DUBLIN |
| Malaysia | Malayan Law Journal Sdn Bhd, KUALA LUMPUR |
| New Zealand | Butterworths of New Zealand Ltd, WELLINGTON and AUCKLAND |
| Singapore | Reed Elsevier (Singapore) Pte Ltd, SINGAPORE |
| South Africa | Butterworths Publishers (Pty) Ltd, DURBAN |
| USA | Michie, Charlottesville, VIRGINIA |

A CIP Catalogue record for this book is available from the British Library.

ISBN 0 406 04839 8

Typeset by Doyle & Co, Colchester
Printed and bound in Great Britain by Clays Ltd, St Ives plc

# Preface

The European Union has developed a political and legal system which has added to the complex reality of any of the nation-states which are its constituent members. It also requires study in its own right. The provisions of the Paris, Rome and Maastricht Treaties and the Single European Act, which are often described as forming the basis for a European constitution, comprise no fewer than 920 Articles. They provide for a plethora of different legal principles, decision-making rules and policy-making aims. In addition, the Community institutions have adopted tens of thousands of acts of secondary legislation which have shaped Union/Community policies and have had an impact on almost every area of national legislation. The thousands of decisions of the Court of Justice of the European Communities have also had a major influence on the development of not only the legal but also the political system of the Union.

Without being exhaustive – an impossible task for a work of this kind – the purpose of this book is to provide reliable guidance for anyone working in this area. The entries have been written by experts in the field, who have condensed often vast and complicated subjects in short but substantive summaries, intended to present the reader with the essence of the subjects covered. Many authors have found that it can sometimes be as difficult to distil this essence into a few carefully-balanced sentences as it is to provide an in-depth analysis of the subject in a lengthy article or report.

The main-entry words have been selected with the needs of professional users in mind. They represent the core of the terminology used within the European Union. A comprehensive system of cross-references should help the reader not only to find his or her way in the labyrinth of European law and politics, but also to access relevant information about issues closely related to the subject for which he or she is looking. The bibliographic indications at the end of the entries refer to books, articles or official documents which provide more detailed information and/or a comprehensive analysis of the subject.

This guide is as much a result of team-work as any academic work can possibly be. We would like to thank, first of all, the 98 authors who took precious hours out of their busy schedules to write these entries. We would also like to thank Angela Ward (European University Institute) for her co-operation. We are very grateful to our publishers, Butterworths, for their assistance and patience throughout.

Jörg Monar    Nanette Neuwahl    David O'Keeffe    William Robinson
Leicester    Liverpool    London    Luxembourg

# Contributors

| | |
|---|---|
| Anthony Arnull | Wragge Professor of European Law, University of Birmingham |
| Mark Baldwin | Solicitor, Macfarlanes, London |
| Catherine Barnard | Lecturer in Law, Trinity College, Cambridge |
| Philip Bastos Martin | Barrister, Stanbrook and Hooper, Brussels and Stanbrook & Henderson, 2 Harcourt Buildings, London |
| Brian Bercusson | Professor of Law, University of Manchester and Director of the European Law Unit, Thompsons Solicitors |
| Carl Fredrik Bergström | Institute for European Law, Stockholm University and European University Institute, Florence |
| Fiona Beveridge | Lecturer in Law, International and European Law Unit, Faculty of Law, University of Liverpool |
| Patrick Birkinshaw | Professor and Director of the Institute of European Public Law, University of Hull |
| D L Booton | Lecturer in Law, International and European Law Unit, Faculty of Law, University of Liverpool |
| Patricia Boyle | Solicitor, Brussels |
| Kieran St C Bradley | Legal Secretary, Court of Justice of the European Communities |
| Adrian Briggs | Barrister, Fellow and Tutor in Law, St Edmund Hall, University of Oxford |
| Simon Bulmer | Professor of Government and Director of the European Policy Research Unit, University of Manchester |
| Maria Byström | Research Associate, European University Institute, Florence |
| Elinor Campbell | City Solicitor's Educational Trust Lecturer in European Law, University of Nottingham |

*Contributors*

| | |
|---|---|
| Robin R Churchill | Reader in Law, Cardiff Law School, University of Wales |
| Marise Cremona | Senior Fellow, Centre for Commercial Law Studies, Queen Mary and Westfield College, University of London |
| Bruno de Witte | Professor of Law, University of Maastricht |
| Veerle Deckmyn | Head of Library and Publications, European Institute of Public Administration, Maastricht |
| Monica den Boer | Senior Lecturer, Justice and Home Affairs, European Institute of Public Administration, Maastricht |
| Eileen Denza | Barrister and Senior Research Fellow, University College London |
| Rasmus Dilling | PhD Researcher, European University Institute, Florence, Advocate |
| Janet Dine | Professor, University of Essex |
| Christopher Docksey | Legal Service, European Commission |
| T Anthony Downes | Professor and Head of the Department of Law, University of Reading |
| Dr Rose M D'Sa | Barrister and Professor of European Law, University of Glamorgan, European Consultant, Morgan Bruce |
| Andrew Duff | Director, Federal Trust, London and Vice-President of the Liberal Democrats |
| D R R Dunnett | European Investment Bank, Luxembourg |
| Baroness Elles | House of Lords Select Committee on the European Communities |
| Evelyn Ellis | Barrister and Professor of Public Law, University of Birmingham |
| Frank Emmert | Lecturer in Public International and European Union Law, Europainstitut, University of Basle |
| Emer Finnegan | Legal Secretary, Court of First Instance of the European Communities |
| John Fitzmaurice | European Commission |

| | |
|---|---|
| James Flynn | Barrister, Brick Court Chambers, London, formerly Solicitor and Legal Secretary, Court of Justice of the European Communities |
| Nicholas Forwood QC | Brick Court Chambers, Brussels and London |
| Andrew Geddes | Department of Politics, University of Liverpool |
| Elspeth Guild | Solicitor, Baileys Shaw & Gillett and Chair of the Immigration Law Practitioners Association's European Group |
| Tamara K Hervey | Lecturer in Law, University of Manchester |
| Jane Holder | Lecturer in Law, Centre for the Law of the European Union, University College London |
| Margot Horspool | Senior Lecturer in Laws, Centre for the Law of the European Union, University College London |
| Mark Hoskins | Barrister, Brick Court Chambers, London, formerly Legal Secretary, Court of Justice of the European Communities |
| Stephen Hyett | Solicitor, Department of Trade and Industry |
| Hans Ulrich Jessurun d'Oliveira | Professor of Migration Law, University of Amsterdam, Partner, Van den Biesen, Prakken, Böhler |
| David T Keeling | Member of the First Board of Appeal, Office for Harmonisation in the Internal Market (Trade Marks and Designs), formerly Legal Secretary, Court of Justice of the European Communities |
| Robert Lane | Senior Lecturer in Law, Europa Institute, University of Edinburgh |
| K P E Lasok QC | Monckton Chambers, 4 Raymond Buildings, London |
| Koen Lenaerts | Judge, Court of First Instance of the European Communities, Professor of European Law, University of Leuven |
| Jeremy Lever QC | Fellow and Senior Dean of All Souls College, University of Oxford, Bencher of Gray's Inn |
| Garth Lindrup | Solicitor, Partner, Addleshaw Sons & Latham |

*Contributors*

Marjorie Lister      Lecturer in EU-Developing Country Relations, University of Bradford

Anna Lixi      Researcher, European University Institute, Florence

Nicolas Lockhart      Legal Secretary, Court of Justice of the European Communities

Julian Lonbay      Director, Institute of European Law, University of Birmingham

Philip Lynch      Deputy Director, Centre for European Politics and Institutions, University of Leicester

Robert M Maclean      Solicitor, Stanbrook and Hooper, Brussels

Marc Maresceau      Professor and Director, European Institute, University of Ghent

Epaminondas Marias      Professor, National Centre for Public Administration, Athens

Alfonso Mattera      Director, European Commission, Professor, College of Europe, Bruges and Professor, LUISS University, Rome

Philip Mead      Barrister, Old Square Chambers

Timothy Millett      Barrister, Legal Adviser for Administrative Affairs, Court of Justice of the European Communities

Jacqueline Minor      Head of Unit, Regulated Professions, DG XV, European Commission

Jörg Monar      Professor of Politics and Director of the Centre for European Politics and Institutions, University of Leicester

Gillian More      Pupil barrister, Old Square Chambers, London

Roger Morgan      Visiting Professor of Political Science, University of Bonn

Peter-Christian Müller Graff      Professor of Law, Director of the Institute for Economic and European Law, University of Heidelberg

Fiona Murray      Barrister, Stanbrook and Hooper, Brussels

| | |
|---|---|
| Nanette Neuwahl | Professor of European Law, International and European Law Unit, Faculty of Law, University of Liverpool |
| L Neville Brown | Professor Emeritus of Comparative Law, University of Birmingham |
| Simon Nuttall | Professor, College of Europe, Bruges, Visiting Fellow, Centre for International Studies, London School of Economics and Political Science |
| Sundhya Pahuja | Solicitor, Clayton Utz, Melbourne and Research Assistant, European University Institute, Florence |
| Nicholas Paines | Barrister, Monckton Chambers, 4 Raymond Buildings, London |
| Robin Philip | Attorney-at-Law, Hjejle, Gersted & Mogensen, Copenhagen |
| Timothy Pratt | Counsel to the Speaker, House of Commons |
| G Wyn Rees | Deputy Director, Centre for European Politics and Institutions, University of Leicester |
| William Robinson | Legal Secretary, Court of Justice of the European Communities, Luxembourg, Honorary Research Fellow, Centre for the Law of the European Union, University College London, Solicitor |
| Malcolm G Ross | Jean Monnet Chair and Senior Lecturer in EC Law, University of Leicester |
| Andrew Scott | Jean Monnet Senior Lecturer in Economics of the European Union, Europa Institute, University of Edinburgh |
| Joanne Scott | Lecturer in European Community Law, Queen Mary and Westfield College, University of London |
| Jo Shaw | Professor of European Law, University of Leeds, Holder of Jean Monnet Chair of European Law and Integration |
| Francis Snyder | Professor of EC Law, European University Institute, Florence, Professor, College of Europe, Bruges, Honorary Visiting Professor of Law, University College London |

Stephen O Spinks            Partner, Coudert, Brussels

Robert Strivens             Solicitor, Partner, Allen & Overy

E Susan Singleton           Solicitor, Principal, Singletons, Solicitors

Akos G Toth                 Professor of European Law, University of
                            Strathclyde, Glasgow

Patrick Twomey              Lecturer in Law, University of Nottingham

John Usher                  Salvesen Professor of European Institutions,
                            Director, Europa Institute,
                            University of Edinburgh

Ronald van Ooik             Lecturer, Europa Institute, University of
                            Utrecht

Paulette Vander Schueren    Partner, Coudert, Brussels

Paolo Vergano               Procuratore legale, Stanbrook and Hooper,
                            Brussels

Ellen Vos                   Researcher, Centre for European Law and
                            Policy, University of Bremen

Angela Ward                 Solicitor, Assistant Director, Centre for
                            European Legal Studies, University of
                            Cambridge

Martin Westlake             Head of Unit, Institutional Relations, DG X,
                            European Commission and Associate Member,
                            Centre for Legislative Studies, University
                            of Hull

Richard Whish               Solicitor, Partner, Watson, Farley & Williams,
                            London and Professor of Law, King's College
                            London

Robin White                 Professor of Law, University of Leicester

Elaine Whiteford            Lecturer in Law, University of Nottingham

Rhodri Williams             Barrister, European Commission

John Woodliffe              Dean, Faculty of Law, University of Leicester

John Young                  Solicitor, Partner, Lovell White Durrant,
                            London

**ABUSE OF A DOMINANT POSITION** See **monopolies.**

**ACCESSION** The 'original' Community was composed of six Member States (France, Federal Republic of Germany, Italy and the Benelux countries). In 1973 a first accession wave led to membership of the United Kingdom, Ireland and Denmark. Greece joined the Community in 1981, while Spain and Portugal acceded to the Community in 1986. Since the entry into force of the **Treaty on European Union** (TEU), Sweden, Finland and Austria have joined the European Union (1995).

The rules and procedure governing accession to the **European Union** are contained in Article O TEU. This provision is identical to the former Article 237 EEC Treaty which, since the entry into force of the TEU, has been repealed.

'Any European State' may apply for membership of the Union. No further specifications are given in Article O about other substantive conditions of membership. The qualification 'European State' is from a legal point of view difficult to define and political, geopolitical, geographic, cultural and other considerations may well intervene in the definition 'European State'. In the **association agreement** with Turkey (1963) it was held that the agreement 'will facilitate the accession of Turkey to the Community at a later date', implicitly admitting that notwithstanding the fact that 95% of Turkey is in Asia, Turkey satisfied the condition of a 'European State'. However, Turkey's formal application (1987) to join the Community was rejected (1989) on the basis that Turkey would find it hard to cope with the adjustment constraints with which it would be confronted in the medium term if it acceded to the Community. In the current policy of the Community towards Central and Eastern Europe the dividing line between possible membership and non-membership is the distinction between '**Europe Agreements**' and 'Partnership and Co-operation Agreements'. This policy implies that European republics of the former USSR, such as Belarus, Moldavia and Ukraine are not included in the enlargement strategy of the Community. The same holds true for Russia, whose political and geopolitical centre is situated in Europe. On the other hand, the Central and Eastern European countries of the former COMECON, the Baltic States and Slovenia are incorporated in the enlargement perspectives of the Europe Agreements. All states with whom Europe Agreements have been signed have submitted applications for membership. Cyprus also applied for membership and its application will be considered after the 1996 Intergovernmental Conference. Malta applied for membership, but as a result of the elections of 26 October 1996, this application has been 'frozen'.

Morocco made a formal application to become a member of the European Community in 1987. This was rejected on the ground that Morocco is not a 'European State'. Therefore, in this case, there

1

was no need to follow the procedure laid down in Article 237 EEC Treaty. It is not because Article O itself does not stipulate conditions and criteria for membership that these do not exist. Any application is considered on its own merits and the applicant state will have to respect Article F TEU, which refers to the principles of democracy and the European Convention for the Protection of Human Rights. Accession implies acceptance of the **acquis communautaire**, that is to say the whole set of rights and obligations, actual and potential, resulting from Community legislation and case law. This condition does refer to substantive as well as to the institutional rules and mechanisms as they have been established by the Treaties, including the Treaty on European Union. This implies, inter alia, that an applicant state should also accept and implement the rules as established under the second and third Pillars of the Treaty on European Union.

There are no ready-made pre-accession models for accession. In the past, some states joined the Community having only a trade agreement with the Community, while others, such as the countries with whom Europe Agreements have been concluded, have embarked on a long and complex pre-accession stage incorporating vast **approximation** of laws programmes, gradual establishment of structured relations with the **institutions of the European Union**, answering a very detailed Commission questionnaire, etc. The accession by Sweden, Finland and Austria was also preceded by a far-reaching agreement (Agreement establishing a **European Economic Area**) integrating the EFTA countries (except Switzerland) in the **Internal Market**. Accession was therefore considerably facilitated for these countries. Once membership is accepted, the new Member State will generally need a transitional period to take the necessary legislative measurers resulting from membership. These transitional periods must be limited in time.

Accession to the European Union today has become more complex than accession to the Community in the 1970s and 1980s. The completion of the Internal Market and the Treaty on European Union, incorporating, inter alia, an economic and monetary union and a single currency, co-operation in the fields of foreign affairs and security and co-operation in the fields of justice and home affairs, make accession a very demanding challenge for the applicant country. However, accession is not only an issue for the applicant countries but also for the Union itself. Accession of new Member States will necessarily lead to a greater diversity inside the Union and this in turn could adversely affect its homogeneity. These considerations have provoked the debate on 'deepening and widening' and on the need to take measures to safeguard the Community's effectiveness. Further **enlargement** of the Union must therefore necessarily lead to adaptations and modifications of the Union's institutional framework.

Article O lays down the procedural rules for enlargement. The applicant state shall address its application to the **Council**. The Council will invite the opinion of the **Commission**. The opinion itself consists of two stages: first a comprehensive analysis is formulated, and, second, once the negotiations are completed, the final opinion is addressed to the Council. Only when the first opinion is favourable will further steps be taken. In case of a negative opinion by the Commission (see application by Turkey) the Council endorses the Commission's conclusions.

The role of the **European Parliament** is essential in the enlargement process. Article O requires assent of the European Parliament, which assent shall be given by an absolute majority of its component members. After having received the favourable opinion of the Commission and the assent of Parliament the Council shall act unanimously.

The conditions of admission and adjustments to the Treaties resulting from membership shall be subject to an agreement between the Member States and the applicant state. This agreement shall be submitted for ratification to all the states concerned in accordance with their respective constitutional requirements or practices. Thus, in the accession procedure with the EFTA countries the question of accession was also subject to the referendum in all the applicant countries. It was on this occasion that a majority of the population in Norway rejected accession. So far no referendum on enlargement has been organised in the Member States of the Union.

MARC MARESCEAU

*Recommended reading*
Michalski & Wallace *The European Community: The Challenge of Enlargement* (1992) Royal Institute of International Affairs.
Redmond (ed) *Prospective Europeans: New Members for the European Union* (1994) Harvester Wheatsheaf.

**ACQUIRED RIGHTS** See **employment protection**.

*ACQUIS COMMUNAUTAIRE* The *acquis communautaire* is an amorphous phenomenon. It constitutes the body of objectives, substantive rules, policies, laws, rights, obligations, remedies and case law which are fundamental to the development of the Community legal order.

The **Treaty on European Union** makes two references to the *acquis communautaire*. Neither of these references falls within the jurisdiction of the **Court of Justice**. Article B, which sets out the objectives of the Union, provides for the maintenance in full of the *acquis communautaire* and the building upon it with a view to revising the Treaties in order to ensure the effectiveness of the mechanisms and the institutions of the Community. Article C states that the Union shall be served by a single institutional framework which shall respect and build upon the *acquis communautaire*. These references clearly indicate the progressive and constructive role of the *acquis communautaire*, from which derogation is only envisaged by Treaty amendment. Despite the ability of the Court of Justice to depart from earlier rulings (see **precedent**), the *acquis communautaire* can, by its very nature, seemingly only develop in one direction.

As forming the substance of the Community legal order, Member States are required to subscribe to the *acquis communautaire* on **accession**. This obligation is explicitly stated in Accession Agreements. The result is that acceding Member States are placed on a level playing field with existing Member States and are bound – by the principles of Community law as interpreted by the Court of Justice. On the United Kingdom's accession in 1973, for example, the principles of direct effect and supremacy of Community law were already clearly established and the United Kingdom was bound by them.

Although Accession Agreements do not, as a rule, set out the contents of the *acquis communautaire*, a useful guide to those legislative acts which formed the *acquis communautaire*, as at 2 May 1992, was provided by Annexes I-XXII to the **European Economic Area** Agreement. During the negotiations it was necessary to agree which legislative acts would be adhered to as part of the *acquis communautaire*. Each Annex to the Agreement covers the *acquis communautaire* in a specific sector. In total, 1,600 **legislative acts** are referred to in the Annexes.

WILLIAM ROBINSON

*Recommended reading*
Gialdino 'Some Reflections on the *acquis communautaire*' (1995) CMLRev 1089.
Pescatore 'Aspects Judiciaires de l'*acquis communautaire*' (1991) 17 RTDE 617.

**ACTION FOR FAILURE TO ACT** Various provisions of the EC Treaty impose upon the Community **institutions** a positive obligation to act, a duty to adopt certain measures by the appropriate procedures and within a given period of time. Where an institution fails in this duty, the EC Treaty provides in Article 175 a means by which this failure can be raised before and censured by the **Court of Justice**. It is therefore a mirror of the **action of annulment**, its purpose being to compel a Community institution to do something which it is, under Community law, legally obliged to do. It is in British terms analogous to a writ of mandamus or, in Scotland, a petition for an order requiring the specific performance of a statutory duty.

According to the EC Treaty, the action for failure to act may be raised against the **European Parliament**, the **Council**, the **Commission** and the **European Central Bank** (and so provisionally the European Monetary Institute) (Article 175(1) and (4), Article 109f(9)); but applying the Court's case law on the action of annulment by analogy, it ought also to be available to pursue any other Community body which is under a duty to act. The action may be raised as of right by a Member

State or any of the five Community institutions (Article 175(1)), by the ECB (and the EMI) in areas falling within its field of **competence** (Article 175(4)), or by a natural or legal person who can show that an institution had a duty to address an act to him – that is, adopt a decision against which he would have **locus standi** to raise an action of annulment under Article 173 (Article 175(3); Case 246/81 *Bethell v Commission* [1982] ECR 2277; Case T-3/90 *Prodiforma v Commission* [1991] ECR II-1).

The action for failure to act can be raised only if the defaulting institution has first been called upon to act and thereafter has failed to 'define its position' – essentially a statement of its views and proposals for action or reasons justifying the taking of no action – within a two-month period. The action must be raised within the following two months (Article 175(2)). Because it is not easy to establish that an institution is under an obligation to act, particularly where it is accorded a wide power of discretion, and because an institution will usually be able to discharge its obligations by defining its position (which need not be in the form of an act subject to annulment under Article 173; Case 48/65 *Lütticke v Commission* [1966] ECR 19), and even if it does so after the lapse of the two-month deadline, any subsequent action may be dismissed as the subject matter has ceased to exist (Case 377/87 *European Parliament v Council* [1988] ECR 4017; Case C-41/92 *Liberal Democrats v European Parliament* [1993] ECR I-3153), it is a most difficult action successfully to pursue. This is especially so for natural or legal persons who have great difficulty in showing sufficient locus standi (eg Case T-32/93 *Ladbroke Racing v Commission* [1994] ECR II-1015). The principal exceptions are actions raised against the Commission in its administrative capacity (eg Case C-107/91 *ENU v Commission* [1993] ECR I-599 (an action under the equivalent provision in the Euratom Treaty)), and particularly in the sphere of the competition rules of Articles 85 and 86, in which a complainant under Regulation 17 is entitled to the adoption of an act by the Commission and so may raise an action if the Commission fails to act (Case T-28/90 *Asia Motor France v Commission* [1992] ECR II-2285; Case T-74/92 *Ladbroke Racing (Deutschland) GmbH v Commission* [1995] ECR II-115) (see **complaints to the Commission**). In only one case has an institution been found to have failed in an obligation to legislate in a general policy-making field (Case 13/83 *European Parliament v Council* [1985] ECR 1513). If the action is successful, the institution is required to take the necessary means to comply with the judgment (Article 176(1)), and must do so within a reasonable period of time (Case 13/83 *European Parliament v Council* [1985] ECR 1513).

ROBERT LANE

*Recommended reading*
Due 'Legal Remedies for the Failure of European Community Institutions to Act in Conformity with EEC Treaty Provisions' (1990-91) 14 Fordham International Law Journal 341.
Brealey & Hoskins *Remedies in EC Law* (1994) Longman.

**ACTION FOR FAILURE TO FULFIL AN OBLIGATION** An action for failure to fulfil a Treaty obligation may be brought before the **Court of Justice**, the administrative phase having been exhausted, in order to seek a declaration of such failure by a Member State. Actions may be brought by the **Commission** (generally under Article 169 EC) or by another Member State (Article 170 EC). The most significant and most frequently used of these procedures is the action under Article 169 by the Commission, due to the overtly political nature of an action being brought by one Member State against another under Article 170.

As the guardian of the Treaties, the Commission has a discretion to take action against a Member State under Article 169 if it considers that that Member State has failed to fulfil almost any obligation under the Treaty. The Court of Justice has held that an individual may not challenge a decision by the Commission not to initiate the Article 169 procedure (see Case 247/87 *Star Fruit v Commission* [1989] ECR 291). The Article 169 procedure consists of an administrative and a judicial phase.

As to the administrative phase, the Commission will address to the Member State the alleged breach, invite its observations and then, if necessary, in a reasoned opinion (*avis motivé*), set a reasonable period in which the alleged breach must be remedied. The arguments in law of the Commission and the state of national law are crystallised at the expiry of that reasonable period. Subsequent action by the Member State may not avail it of the judicial phase or a judgment of the Court of Justice. In the absence of a remedy to the alleged breach within the specified period, the Commission may bring an action directly before the Court of Justice.

If a declaration of a failure to fulfil a Treaty obligation is granted by the Court, and the Member State concerned has not taken the necessary measures to comply with that judgment, the Commission may, after a further administrative phase, bring a further action before the Court of Justice under Article 171 EC. The Treaty on European Union amended Article 171, at the initiative of the United Kingdom government, in order to provide that the Court of Justice may impose a lump-sum payment or penalty payment on a defaulting Member State. The Commission is required to propose the amount of the penalty. It has adopted the seriousness of the breach, the duration of the breach and the need to have a dissuasive effect as the criteria for determining the level of the proposed penalty (*Agence Europe* 6.6.96). However, as the Commission has not, to date, brought an action under this provision, there remains no practical guidance as to the level of the penalty, either to be proposed by the Commission or imposed by the Court of Justice.

WILLIAM ROBINSON

*Recommended reading*
Mastroianni 'The Enforcement Procedure under Article 169 of the EC Treaty and the Powers of the European Commission: Quis Custodiet Custodes?' (1995) European Public Law 535.
Brealey & Hoskins *Remedies in EC Law* (1994) Longman.

**ACTION OF ANNULMENT** All Community **institutions** are bound to act within the limits of the powers conferred upon them by the Treaties (Article 3b(1) EC). From time to time an institution may exceed its powers, or purport to adopt legislation which is in some other way unlawful. The EC Treaty therefore provides a number of mechanisms by which the legality of Community legislation may be challenged before the **Court of Justice**. The most direct means, and the principal avenue of judicial protection in Community law, is the action of annulment under Article 173 EC.

In British terms, the action of annulment is analogous to an application for judicial review: its purpose is to request the Court to quash (in Scotland, reduce) a legislative or administrative act of a Community institution, to deprive it of its legal effect. The action may be raised (a) as of right by the **Council**, the **Commission** or a Member State, (b) by the **European Parliament** or the **European Central Bank** in certain circumstances, or (c) by any natural or legal person, but in only very narrow circumstances (see **locus standi; direct and individual concern**). Where a person lacks the necessary title and interest under Article 173 he must rely upon other, indirect means of challenging acts of an institution (see **plea of illegality; preliminary rulings**). But in some (as yet not fully defined) circumstances, where a person clearly has title and interest under Article 173 but fails to make use of it, he may be barred from seeking judicial review through other means (Case C-188/92 *TWD Textilwerke Deggendorf* [1994] ECR I-833, Case C-178/95 *Wiljo*, pending). Under present rules the action of annulment falls within the jurisdiction of the Court of Justice if raised by a Community **institution** or a Member State and within the jurisdiction of the **Court of First Instance** if raised by a natural or legal person. In the interests of legal certainty the action must be raised within two months of publication or notification of the measure in question (Article 173(5)). This time-bar is rigorously enforced. An act not challenged within that period of time is thereafter immune from annulment.

Article 173(1) provides that the lawfulness of the following may be challenged: acts, other than recommendations and opinions, of the European Parliament and the Council (ie, measures adopted by the co-decision procedure), of the Council, of the Commission, of the European Parliament and of the European Central Bank. Subsequent Treaty provisions and legislation provide expressly for review of acts adopted by the **European Investment Bank** (Article 180), the European Monetary Institute (Article 109f(9)), the **European Investment Fund** (Protocol on the Statute of the EIB, Article 30(6)), the Board of Appeal of the Community Trade Mark Office (Council Regulation (EC) 40/94, (OJ L11 14.1.94 p 1), art 63) and the Community Plant Variety Office and its Board of Appeal (Council Regulation (EC) 2100/94 (OJ L227 1.9.94 p 1), arts 73–74). However, the Court of Justice has said that an act of *any* Community institution or body is liable to annulment (Case 294/83 *Parti Ecologiste 'Les Verts' v European Parliament* [1986] ECR 1339), whatever its nature or form, so long as it is capable of producing legal effects (Case 22/70 *Commission v Council* (ERTA) [1971] ECR 263; Case C-316/91 *European Parliament v Council* [1994] ECR I-625; Case C-327/91 *France v Commission* [1994] ECR I-3641). A Community act (see **legislative acts**) produces legal effects if it is binding upon, and capable of affecting the interests of, a person by bringing about a distinct change in his legal position (Case 60/81 *IBM v Commission* [1981] ECR 2639). Recommendations and opinions are expressly excluded because in principle they produce no binding force (Article 189 EC); but the Court always considers the substance of an act rather than its form, and so, although it has yet to do so, the Court may well examine such measures so as to discover if they are in truth acts which *do* produce legal effects and so are liable to annulment (see on this point Case 322/88 *Grimaldi* [1989] ECR 4407). Acts adopted by the Member States meeting in the Council are not liable to annulment (Cases C-181 & 248/91 *European Parliament v Council* (Bangladesh) [1993] ECR I-3685).

Article 173 provides four grounds by which an act of a Community institution may be annulled: lack of competence; infringement of an essential procedural requirement; infringement of the Treaty or of any rule relating to its application; and misuse of powers. The first ground is analogous to substantive ultra vires in British administrative law, that the institution has no power to do what it purports to have done. The second ground is analogous to procedural ultra vires, that the institution failed to comply with a mandatory procedural requirement in the adoption of the act (eg an act of the Council absent prior consultation with the Parliament where it is required (Case 138/79 *Roquette Frères v Council* [1980] ECR 3333; cf Case C-65/93 *European Parliament v Council* [1995] ECR I-643) or an act adopted without proper regard to the adopting institution's rules of procedure (Case C-137/92P *Commission v BASF* (PVC) [1994] ECR I-2555)). The third ground applies where prescriptive or normative rules of the Treaty are not complied with or some other pre-emptive rule of Community law is breached – for example the requirement of Article 190 to provide a recitation of reasons justifying the adoption of the measure (Case T-38/92 *All Weather Sports Benelux v Commission* [1994] ECR II-211), the adoption of a measure founded upon an incorrect legal base in the Treaty (Case C-300/89 *Commission v Council* (Titanium Dioxide) [1991] ECR I-2867), or the adoption of a measure which offends a **general principle of Community law** (Case 331/88 *R v Minister for Agriculture, Fisheries and Food, ex p FEDESA* [1990] ECR I-4023); however, in some circumstances an infringement of a general principle leads to annulment only if it can be established that, had it not been for the irregularity, the outcome of the procedure would have been different (Case 142/87 *Belgium v Commission* [1990] ECR I-959). The fourth ground (*détournement de pouvoir* in French administrative law), which arises only rarely, applies where an institution has acted in bad faith or where it has adopted a measure with the purpose of achieving an end other than that stated or evading a procedure specifically prescribed by the Treaty for dealing with the circumstances of the case (Case 105/75 *Giuffrida v Council* [1976] ECR 1395; Case T-106/92 *Frederiksen v European Parliament* [1995] ECR SC II-99; Case C-248/89 *Cargill v Commission* [1991] ECR I-2988; Case C-156/93 *European Parliament v Commission* [1995] ECR I-2019).

An act of an institution which is found to be unlawful upon any of these grounds is annulled (declared 'void'; Article 174(1)) by declaration of the Court, and the institution which adopted it is required to take all necessary measures to comply with the judgment (Article 176(1)). In principle, annulment means that the act is deprived of all legal effect, past, present and future. However, prior to such declaration the measure is presumed to be valid and must be given full force and effect (Case 101/78 *Granaria* [1979] ECR 623), unless the Court in which the action is raised has suspended its operation by interim order or the measure is tainted with such serious and manifest defects as to render it 'non-existent' (Case C-137/92P *Commission v BASF* [1994] ECR I-2555). Having annulled an act, the Court may none the less, 'if it considers this necessary', declare all or some of its provisions to be operative (Article 174(2)). Circumstances which justify use of this declaratory power are, for example, compelling reasons of legal certainty or legitimate expectation (eg Case 45/86 *Commission v Council* [1987] ECR 1493; Case C-295/90 *European Parliament v Council* (Students) [1992] ECR I-4193; Case C-388/92 *European Parliament v Council* [1994] ECR I-2067; Case C-21/94 *European Parliament v Council* [1995] ECR I-1827). Annulment of an unlawful act does not deprive persons who have suffered consequential injury of the right to raise an action seeking **damages** (Article 176(2); see **non-contractual liability**).

ROBERT LANE

*Recommended reading*
Albors-Llorens *Private Parties in European Community Law: Challenging Community Measures* (1996) Clarendon Press.
Schermers & Waelbroeck *Judicial Protection in the European Communities* (5th edn, 1992) Kluwer, pp 157-246.

**ADVOCATES GENERAL** Article 166 EC states that the **Court of Justice** shall be assisted by a number of Advocates General (originally two, at present nine). It is 'the duty of the Advocate General, acting with complete impartiality and independence, to make, in open court, reasoned submissions on cases brought before the Court . . .'. 'Submissions' is an inaccurate translation of the French *conclusions* and has in practice been replaced by the expression 'opinion'.

The Advocates General have the same status as the judges, and their terms of appointment are identical. They must be chosen from persons whose independence is beyond doubt and who possess the qualifications required for appointment to the highest judicial offices in their respective countries or who are jurisconsults of recognised competence. They are appointed by common accord of the governments of the Member States for a term of six years (Article 167 EC). They may be reappointed.

The **Court of First Instance** does not have permanent Advocates General. One of the judges may, however, be called upon to exercise the functions of Advocate General if the legal difficulty or factual complexity of the case so requires (CFI Rules of Procedure, Article 18). An Advocate General is compulsory when the Court of First Instance sits in plenary session (ibid, Article 17).

The office of Advocate General was introduced at the suggestion of the French delegation when the **European Coal and Steel Community** was founded. Its direct precursor is the office of *commissaire du gouvernement* in the French *Conseil d'Etat*.

The post of First Advocate General was introduced by the Court's Rules of Procedure in 1974 (CJ Rules of Procedure, Article 10). In practice it is held by the Advocates General in rotation for one year each. The primary duty of the First Advocate General is to assign each case to one of the Advocates General.

The Advocate General liaises with the judge rapporteur when the latter is preparing the report for the hearing and preliminary report and is consulted on a wide variety of procedural issues. The Advocate General participates in the hearing (if one is held), sitting to the right of the judges, and is entitled, like the judges, to put questions to counsel. His opinion is normally delivered several weeks after the hearing and constitutes the starting point for the judges' deliberations. The Advocate General takes no part in these deliberations and the parties have no opportunity to comment on his opinion (unless, exceptionally, the oral procedure is reopened). The opinion is not binding on the Court. It is estimated that the Advocate General is followed in about 70% of cases.

A typical opinion sets out the background to the case, discusses relevant legislation and case law, defines the issues, summarises the arguments of the parties, states in considerable detail how the Advocate General considers that the issues should be resolved, and finally proposes a course of action to the Court. Formerly, the Advocate General read out the full text of the opinion in open court in person; since 1990, only the concluding paragraph, which sets out the decision proposed by the Advocate General, is read out. This is done by the Advocate General who happens to be sitting on the day in question. The full written text is distributed among the judges and is published in the Reports of Cases before the Court (the ECR), together with the judgment (see **publications of the EU**).

The justification for the office of Advocate General lies in the importance of the task assigned to the Court. It is vital that the Court should dispense justice of the highest technical quality; it stands at the apex of the Community's judicial system and has exclusive power to rule authoritatively on the interpretation of Community law provisions and on the validity of acts of the other institutions. There is no other body to which aggrieved parties may turn if they consider that the Court has erred. In most cases the Advocate General enhances the efficiency of the Court and reduces the likelihood of judicial errors, while at the same time helping the Court to build up a consistent body of case law. It must be remembered that the Court's judgments are not always produced in the easiest of circumstances. The collegiate nature of those judgments does not lend itself to coherent legal analysis and detailed exegesis of previous case law, especially where complex or novel issues are raised, or where the existing authorities are unclear or conflicting. The judge rapporteur often has the handicap of working in a foreign language, occasionally has to produce a judgment with which he disagrees and constantly has to bear in mind drafting suggestions from colleagues, who may agree as to the result but differ as to the reasoning. The Advocate General, who has the privilege of presenting his own personal view of the law in his own language, is in a better position to accomplish a coherent and exhaustive exposition of the law which, if the Court finds it persuasive, will greatly simplify the task of drafting the judgment and, in many cases, improve its quality.

DAVID T KEELING

*Recommended Reading*
Dashwood 'The Advocate General in the Court of Justice of the European Communities' (1982) Legal Studies 202-216.
Borgsmidt 'The Advocate General at the European Court of Justice: A Comparative Study' (1988) 13 ELRev 106-119.

**AMENDMENT OF THE TREATIES** Amendment of the Treaties on which the European Union is founded may be made in accordance with Article N(1) TEU, which has replaced the similar provisions of the original Treaties (ie Articles 96 ECSC, 236 EEC, 204 Euratom). According to Article N(1), proposals for amendment may be submitted to the **Council** by the government of any Member State or the **Commission**. If the Council, after consulting the **European Parliament** and, where appropriate, the Commission, delivers an opinion in favour of calling an **Intergovernmental Conference**, the conference must be convened by the President of the Council. By virtue of Article 148(1) EC, such opinion may be reached by a simple majority. The conference must then determine 'by common accord' the amendments to be made. The **European Central Bank** is also to be consulted in the case of institutional changes in the monetary area. To enter into force, the amendments must be ratified by all the Member States in accordance with their respective constitutional requirements. Under Article 95 ECSC, minor amendments may be made to the ECSC Treaty without ratification.

The **Court of Justice** has emphasised on several occasions that the Treaties can only be amended by means of the above procedure (see eg Case 43/75 *Defrenne* [1976] ECR 455 at 478), and that resolutions and similar measures which express the political will of the Council or of the Member States cannot prevail over the rules contained in the Treaties (ibid, Case 59/75 *Manghera* [1976] ECR 91 at 102). In particular, the Member States or the institutions cannot change the voting rules laid down in the Treaties (Case 68/86 *United Kingdom v Council* [1988] ECR 855 at 900).

In accordance with Article N(2) a special Intergovernmental Conference has been convened in 1996 'to examine those provisions of this Treaty for which revision is provided' (see eg Article B or J.4(6)). This conference, although convened for a limited purpose, can deal with any other matter provided the procedure in Article N(1) is followed.

AKOS G TOTH

*Recommended reading*
Hartley *The Foundations of European Community Law* (3rd edn, 1994) Oxford University Press, p 99.
Lasok & Bridge *Law and Institutions of the European Union* (6th edn, 1994) Butterworths, p 107.

**ANTI-DUMPING**  Anti-dumping duties are additional charges imposed on goods imported into the Community which have been found, after investigation, to have been sold at dumped prices. The European Community has full responsibility for conducting anti-dumping investigations and imposing duties as part of the **Common Commercial Policy**. Individual Member States can no longer carry out such investigations or enact legislation for this purpose. The Community's main anti-dumping legislation is Council Regulation (EC) 384/96 (OJ L56 6.3.96 p 1).

The use of these measures has also been extensively regulated at the international level, first in Article VI of the **GATT** and now under the **World Trade Organization** Anti-Dumping Agreement. International standards have been prescribed for carrying out investigations and imposing duties. These obligations have been imposed on the Community as a member of both the GATT and the WTO.

In the European Community an anti-dumping investigation is triggered by a complaint from an EC industry claiming to have sustained injury as a consequence of dumped imports. The complaint must be lodged by producers representing more than 50% of the production of the goods in the Community. The complaint itself is lodged with the **European Commission**, which is responsible for investigating the allegations made in the submission.

The European Commission compares the price of the goods sold in the country of production against the price charged in the Community. Goods are deemed to have been dumped if the price charged in the country of origin (termed the 'normal value') is higher than the price charged in the EC market (termed the 'export price'). It is important to note that, in the calculation of dumping, it is the respective prices of the goods in the country of origin and in the EC that are being compared and not the price of the foreign goods and EC-produced goods in the EC market.

The normal value is the price of the product under investigation when sold in the country of manufacture. In many cases, this is the actual price paid for the goods, but where this is considered to be unrepresentative two alternative methods are employed to establish normal value, namely 'third market value' or 'constructed value'.

The export price of goods is the price at which the goods are sold for export to arm's-length customers inside the customs territory of the Community. It is either the actual price paid or, in certain circumstances, a price artificially constructed as a price which would have been paid had the sale been made to a purchaser at arm's length.

To ensure a fair comparison, the Commission is permitted to make due allowances, again in the form of adjustments, for differences affecting price comparability between the normal value and the export price. There are ten different grounds for which adjustments can be made. The main ones are for differences relating to physical characteristics, import charges/indirect taxes, discounts, rebates, transport, insurance, sales costs and commissions.

The margin of dumping is calculated by the Commission in a three-stage process. First, a single weighted average 'normal value' is calculated for each exporter, usually for a period of one year. Second, each exporter's export prices are compared, on a transaction-by-transaction basis, with the weighted average normal value. Finally, an average of all the individual dumping margins for that exporter is taken and applied to all its exports during the period of investigation. The dumping margin is then expressed as a percentage of the CIF ('cost, insurance, freight') value of the goods.

An affirmative determination of dumping can only occur if the alleged dumped imports are actually causing injury, or threatening to cause material injury, to an established EC industry. In an investigation into injury, the Commission is required to consider a number of economic factors, including the volume of dumped imports, the prices of dumped imports and the consequent impact on the industry concerned as indicated by actual or potential trends in relevant economic factors such as: production; utilisation of capacity; stocks; sales; market share; prices (ie the pressure of prices on prevention of price increases which would otherwise have occurred); profits; return on investment; cash flow and employment.

Anti-dumping duties cannot be imposed if the Commission finds the existence of dumping and of injury to an EC industry but the cause of injury to the EC industry is not the foreign imports. The EC's anti-dumping legislation provides that injury caused by other factors must not be attributed to the dumped products.

Before provisional or definitive anti-dumping measures can be imposed, or a complaint withdrawn, Community anti-dumping law requires the Commission and the Council to confirm that the interests of the EC call for intervention to prevent injury to an EC industry. The task for the Commission in applying the test of EC interest is to balance these various and competing interests and to adopt the necessary measures if, on balance, intervention is in the Community interest.

Where dumping, injury and causation have been established by the Commission, and if EC interests call for the adoption of measures, a Commission Regulation is issued imposing provisional anti-dumping duties. In fact, no actual duties are imposed at this stage. Collection of provisional duties only occurs if the final definitive determination is affirmative. Preliminary measures are valid for six months, although these measures may be extended for an additional three-month period.

The order for collection of provisional duties is made if, after the continuation of an investigation, the Council of Ministers decides to impose definitive duties. Definitive duties are imposed after the Commission has conducted a more thorough investigation into the existence of dumping, injury to an EC industry and causation. During this period the Commission verifies the data collected from importers, exporters and EC producers and recalculates its provisional findings.

Definitive duties normally take the form of an ad valorem duty, which is imposed as a percentage of the CIF price of the goods at the Community frontier. When setting definitive measures, the Community also establishes residual duty rates for producers that were not parties to the investigation. These residual duties are set at the highest level of dumping found to exist among those foreign manufacturers held after investigation to have been engaged in dumping.

Anti-dumping measures can be reviewed at the request of a Member State or after the lapse of a period of one year, at the request of an exporter or importer. Measures automatically expire after a period of five years unless renewed after a review.

Foreign companies whose goods are subject to anti-dumping duties are entitled to appeal the measure imposing duties to the **Court of First Instance** and thereafter to the **Court of Justice** itself. In the vast majority of cases, no such appeal is made.

ROBERT M MACLEAN

*Recommended reading*
Stanbrook & Bentley *Dumping and Subsidies* (1996) Kluwer.
Van Bael & Bellis *Anti-Dumping and Other Trade Protection Laws of the EEC* (1990) CCH Editions Ltd.

**ANTI-TRUST** See **competition policy** and, in particular, **cartels** and **concerted practices**.

## APPEALS AGAINST JUDGMENTS OF THE COURT OF FIRST INSTANCE

The rules applicable to appeals against judgments of the **Court of First Instance** may be found at Article 168a EC; Articles 49-54 Statute of the Court of Justice of the EC; Articles 110-123 Rules of Procedure of the Court of Justice; Articles 117-121 Rules of Procedure of the Court of First Instance.

The decisions of the Court of First Instance are subject to an appeal to the **Court of Justice** on points of law only. Appeals lie on three grounds: lack of competence of the Court of First Instance; a breach of procedure before the Court of First Instance which adversely affects the interests of the appellant; and infringement of Community law by the Court of First Instance.

An appeal may be brought against final decisions of the Court of First Instance and against decisions disposing of the substantive issues in part only or disposing of a plea of incompetence or inadmissibility, an application to intervene or an application for interim measures. On the other hand, appeals do not lie against purely procedural matters, such as costs.

Appeals may be brought by the principal parties and interveners in the first instance proceedings, provided that where the intervener is not a Member State or a Community **institution** the decision of the Court of First Instance must directly affect him. Appeals may also be brought by Member States and Community institutions which did not intervene at first instance, subject to certain safeguards.

An appeal must be lodged within two months of notification of the decision appealed against (two weeks in the case of a decision dismissing an application to intervene).

An appeal has no suspensory effect. The operation of the decision appealed against can be suspended only if the Court of Justice so orders on a separate application for interim relief.

The appeal may seek the setting aside of the decision of the Court of First Instance, in whole or in part, and grant of the same relief, in whole or in part, as that sought at first instance. The relief sought by the appellant may not be different from that sought at first instance and the subject matter of the proceedings before the Court of First Instance may not be changed in the appeal.

The language of the appeal is the language of the decision appealed against, unless the Court of Justice authorises otherwise.

Where the appeal is clearly inadmissible or clearly unfounded, in whole or in part, the Court of Justice may at any time dismiss it, in whole or in part, by reasoned order.

The procedure on appeal is basically similar to that in a direct action before the Court of Justice but it is more expeditious in a number of respects (see **written procedure** and **oral procedure**). The two-month period for lodging an appeal and the two-month period for the opposing party to lodge a response may not be extended. Basically, there is only one round of written pleadings, and further pleadings

15

may be lodged only with the express authorisation of the President of the Court of Justice. Furthermore, the Court of Justice may dispense with the hearing of oral argument from the parties, unless one of the parties objects on the grounds that the written procedure did not enable him fully to defend his point of view.

If an appeal is well founded, the Court of Justice quashes the decision of the Court of First Instance. Thereupon it may either give final judgment itself, where the state of the proceedings so permits, or refer the case back to the Court of First Instance for judgment.

Where the Court of Justice dismisses the appeal, or where it upholds it and gives final judgment itself, the Court of Justice makes the decision as to the costs. Where the case is referred back to the Court of First Instance, the latter decides on the costs.

TIMOTHY MILLETT

*Recommended reading*
Vaughan (ed) *Law of the European Communities* Butterworths, ch 2.
Lasok *The European Court of Justice: Practice and Procedure* (2nd edn, 1994) Butterworths, ch 15.

**APPROXIMATION** Chapter 3 of Title V of the EC Treaty (Common Rules on Competition, Taxation and Approximation of Laws) deals with the 'Approximation of Laws'. Article 100, for instance, provides for the circumstances when the **Council** may issue Directives 'for the approximation of such laws, regulations or administrative provision of the Member States as directly affect the establishment or functioning of the common market'. However, the term 'approximation' is not defined. The terms 'approximation' and **'harmonisation'** are sometimes used interchangeably. Approximation means replacing national rules by uniform Community provisions when this is required (eg by Article 100 EC) for the establishment and functioning of the **Internal Market**. This is a daunting task, in view of the considerable diversity among the Member States.

It is not surprising, therefore, that approximation is not the sole method by which the Community can attain this objective: Article 100b(1) also provides for the mutual acceptance of standards or **'mutual recognition'**, ie 'The Council, acting in accordance with the provisions of Article 100a, may decide that the provisions in force in a Member State must be recognised as being equivalent to those applied by another Member State'. In addition, Article 100a(4) permits states (under defined procedures) the possibility, despite the adoption of a harmonisation measure by the Council, of continuing to apply national provisions 'on grounds of major needs referred to in Article 36, or relating to protection of the environment or the working environment . . .'. This may therefore allow the preservation of national law despite its possible obstructive effect if Community standards are considered inadequate.

In some instances, the Community has also opted to establish only a minimum standard, leaving Member States free to choose a stricter regime if they wish. For example, in the Commission's 'New approach to technical harmonization' (COM(85)19, adopted by the Council in its Resolution of 7 May 1985; OJ C136 4.6.85 p 1) the Commission proposed to set basic rules governing health and safety of products, but left manufacturers with flexibility outside that area. Article 130t EC dealing with the **environment** also provides that measures adopted 'shall not prevent any Member State from maintaining or introducing protective measures compatible with this Treaty'. A similar pattern is followed by Article 129a EC in relation to consumer protection (see **consumer policy**).

Approximation for the purposes of the objectives set out in Article 7a EC (completion of the Internal Market) does not apply, by virtue of Article 100a(2), to 'fiscal provisions, to those relating to the **free movement of persons** nor to those relating to the rights and interests of employed persons'.

Approximation is not a precondition for the applicability of directly effective rights (Case 193/80 *Commission v Republic of Italy* [1981] ECR 3019). Nor can a Member State rely on the non-transposition of a harmonisation Directive to deny Treaty rights (eg Case 2/74 *Reyners v Belgian State* [1974] ECR 631; Joined Cases C-6/90 & C-9/90 *Francovich* [1991] ECR I-5357).

ROSE D'SA

*Recommended reading*
Mathijsen *A Guide to European Union Law* (6th edn, 1995) Sweet & Maxwell, pp 262-266.
Weatherill & Beaumont *The Essential Guide to the Legal Workings of the European Community* (1993) Penguin, pp 420-422.

**ARTICLE 37** See **State monopolies**.

**ARTICLE 85** See **competition policy** and, in particular, **cartels** and **concerted practices**.

**ARTICLE 86** See **competition policy** and, in particular, **monopolies**.

**ARTICLE 90** See **State monopolies**.

**ARTICLE 113** See **Common Commercial Policy**.

**ASSOCIATION AGREEMENTS** Pursuant to Article 238 EC and Article 206 ECSC, association agreements are agreements concluded between the Community and one or more states or international organisations which give rise to reciprocal rights and obligations, common action and special procedures. It is not necessary for these agreements to yield an exact balance of rights and obligations among the contracting parties.

The conclusion of an association agreement is either the basis towards full accession to the Community (eg the agreements with Turkey or the Visegrad counties), an alternative to full membership (eg the agreement establishing the **European Economic Area**) or a form of assistance to the development of the contracting party (the agreement with the ACP countries).

Some association agreements target the liberalisation of reciprocal trade through the progressive establishment of either a free trade area or a **customs union**. Other agreements concluded with developing countries, like the ACP states, are less ambitious and only provide for preferential entry into the Community of products originating in these countries. Contrary to the commercial agreements under Article 113 EC, the scope of the association agreements is not restricted to commercial issues. On the contrary, they may include economic, political, technical, financial, cultural and/or environmental co-operation. The obligation to respect human rights, democracy and the principles of a market economy is a common feature of these agreements.

The association agreements provide for an institutional framework allowing joint decision making and dispute settlement such as, for example, an association council (at ministerial level), an association committee (at senior civil servant level) and a parliamentary committee.

In accordance with Article 228 EC, association agreements are negotiated by the **European Commission** upon a specific mandate issued by the **European Council** which subsequently concludes these agreements after having obtained the assent of the **European Parliament**.

PAULETTE VANDER SCHUEREN

*Recommended reading*
Smith & Herzog *The Law of the European Economic Community: A Commentary on the EEC Treaty* (1995) Matthew Bender.
Louis & Brückner 'Relations exteriéures' in Mégret & Others *Le droit de la Communauté Economique Européenne* 12 (1980) Université Libre de Bruxelles.

**ASYLUM** Asylum is the grant by a state of admission to or residence on its territory to a person who is not a national of that state on the ground that the person is a refugee within the definition of the UN Convention on the Status of Refugees 1951 and its 1967 Protocol (the Geneva Convention), or for humanitarian reasons normally related to the state's obligation not to return a person to a country where he or she will suffer torture, inhuman or degrading treatment or punishment contrary to Article 3 of the **European Convention on Human Rights.** All Member States are parties to both conventions.

Refugees are the subject of a **Council** Declaration (OJ L78 22.5.64) evidencing the intention of Member States to facilitate access for refugees recognised under the Geneva Convention in one Member State to residence in another. Refugees, as defined by the Geneva Convention, are also included within the personal scope of Council Regulation (EEC) 1408/71, as amended and updated by Council Regulation (EEC) 2001/83 (OJ L230 22.8.83 p 6) relating to the **approximation** of **social security** systems in the Community. Refugees are not included within the personal scope of Articles 48, 52 and 59 EC relating to the **free movement of persons** for economic activities.

Article 7a EC, introduced in 1986, provides for a Union area without internal borders. This accentuated the issue of asylum seekers, resulting in common work on asylum policy outside the institutional framework of the Community. The first product was the Dublin Convention determining the state responsible for examining applications for asylum lodged in one of the EC Member States tabled by the 1989 French Presidency, signed on 15 June 1990 and which entered into force on 1 November 1996. This Convention identifies the Member State which must consider an asylum application, bearing in mind that without internal borders the applicant may well be present on the territory of any Member State.

The Work Programme on asylum policy approved by the **European Council** in December 1991 (SN 4038/91(WGI 930)) included the application and implementation of the Dublin Convention, **harmonisation** of substantive asylum law; harmonisation of expulsion policy; setting up a clearing house on legislation; policy; case law; countries of origin; legal examination of applications and reception conditions. These matters continue to form the basis of Union action on asylum.

In November 1992, acting intergovernmentally but with the approval of the European Council, the Member States adopted a series of measures of uncertain legal nature relating to asylum policy, variously entitled resolutions or conclusions, defining a common approach to manifestly unfounded asylum applications, the principle of the first country of asylum and countries in which there is generally no risk of persecution.

Asylum policy formally became a matter of common interest for the Union by virtue of Article K.1 of the Treaty on European Union. It appears in Title VI, **Co-operation in the Fields of Justice and Home Affairs,** the so-called Third Pillar.

As acts taken under the Third Pillar are not subject to the jurisdiction of the **Court of Justice** (Article L TEU) and are not binding under Community law, and in view of the importance of asylum issues to some Member States, a **declaration** on asylum was attached to the Final Act of the Treaty on European Union whereby the Member States agreed to consider the possibility of transferring asylum policy to the First Pillar by the end of 1993. Reviewing progress on asylum policy within the Third Pillar, the Commission's report of 4 November 1993 (SEC(93) 1687) indicates that in view of delays in ratification of the Treaty on European Union it was too soon to consider transfer of asylum policy. The issue can be expected to arise again.

ELSPETH GUILD

*Recommended reading*
Barwig, Brinkmann, Huber, Lorcher & Schmumacher *Asyl nach der Anderung des Grundgesetzes* (1994) Nomos Verlagsgesellschaft.
d'Oliveira 'Expanding external and shrinking internal borders: Europe's defence mechanisms in the areas of free movement, immigration and asylum' in O'Keeffe & Twomey (eds) *Legal Issues of the Maastricht Treaty* (1994) Wiley Chancery.

**BANKING** See **financial services**.

*BARBER* Case 292/88 *Barber v Guardian Royal Exchange* [1990] ECR I-1889 concerned the application of Article 119 EC on **equal pay** to **pensions**.

**BORDER CONTROLS** The regulation of border controls in the **European Union** divides neatly into two interconnected parts: controls on internal borders between Member States and controls on Member States' external borders with third countries.

As regards internal borders, Article 7a EC provides that by 1 January 1993 an **Internal Market** shall be achieved. This market comprises an area without internal frontiers in which the free movement of goods, persons, services and capital is ensured. Accordingly, internal border controls between the Member States in the four areas are a matter of **Community law** and should have been abolished by the end of the transitional period. However, a **declaration** appended to the **Single European Act** 1986, which introduced Article 7a into the Treaty, states that the setting of the date does not create an automatic legal effect. The interpretation of Article 7a and the declaration by the Court of Justice has yet to occur.

The abolition of internal customs controls on goods, services, and capital has been largely achieved. However, passport or identity controls on persons at internal EU borders continue to exist.

In a Communication to the **Council** and **European Parliament** dated 8 May 1992 the **European Commission** gave its opinion as to the meaning of Article 7a EC (SEC (92) 877). As regards goods, once released for free circulation in the Community they must be treated in the same way as products originating in the Member States. In the Commission's view, the phrase 'free movement of persons' refers to all persons, whether or not they are economically active and irrespective of their nationality. However, the United Kingdom does not accept that third country nationals travelling within the Union are entitled to benefit from Article 7a EC and are thereby exempt from passport or identity checks at internal EU borders.

The control of external borders of the Union is an area of mixed competence. As regards goods and services, the Community has entered into a wide variety of agreements with third countries which provide a framework of common rules for access of some goods and services to the Union territory from those states. Further, common standards on products introduced through Community legislation and applicable in all Member States constitute a controlling mechanism on access to the Union territory of goods and services across external borders.

As regards access by persons to the Union territory across external borders, the Member States have chosen to rely primarily on intergovernmental instruments outside Community **competence** but now within Title VI TEU **Co-operation in the Fields of Justice and Home Affairs**. However, as Article 100c EC provides for a common format visa for citizens of an agreed list of countries whose nationals require a visa to enter the territory of the Member States, there is an element of mixed Community and Member State competence.

In June 1991 the Immigration Ministers of the Member States reached political agreement on a draft Convention between the Member States of the European Communities on the Crossing of their External Frontiers. The draft Convention, which was laid in both Libraries of the United Kingdom Parliament in July 1992, sets out the common rules for the crossing by third country nationals of Member States' external borders. This convention is foundering on a dispute between the United Kingdom and Spain as to its territorial application to Gibraltar. On 10 December 1993 the Commission proposed under Article K.3(2) TEU an amended version of the Convention which avoids the problem of the territorial application and introduces jurisdiction to the **Court of Justice** as regards the Convention's interpretation (COM(93)684).

The conclusion of an agreement on the crossing of external EU borders by persons is considered by many Member States as a prerequisite for the abolition of passport or identity checks at internal borders.

ELSPETH GUILD

*Recommended reading*
House of Lords Select Committee of the European Communities *Visas and Control of External Borders of the Member States* (Session 1993-94, 14th Report, 19 July 1994) HMSO.
Schermers, Flinterman, Kellermann, Haersolte & van de Meent *Free Movement of Persons in Europe, Legal Problems and Experiences* (1991) Martinus Nijhoff.

**BRUSSELS CONVENTION** The Convention on Jurisdiction and the Enforcement of Judgments in Civil and Commercial Matters ('the Convention') was signed at Brussels by the six original Member States of the EC on 27 September 1968. It was amended and extended with the **accession** of new Member States. As acceded to by the United Kingdom it appears in the Civil Jurisdiction and Judgments Act 1982, Sch 1; and as amended in SI 1990/2591. The states which join the EU in 1995 will accede to the Convention at a later date.

The Convention, foreshadowed by Article 220 EC, is designed to create a free market in judgments from the civil courts of Member States. A judgment in a civil or commercial matter from any such court may, in principle, be freely enforced in any other state. The automatic recognition of judgments is the corollary of a detailed statement of the rules under which these courts may exercise original jurisdiction: these limit the provisions which may be relied against defendants domiciled in a Contracting State. To achieve uniformity of application, a Protocol (Luxembourg, 1971) gives the **Court of Justice** jurisdiction to interpret the Convention. In addition, a parallel Convention (Lugano, 1988) brings the states of the EFTA within a system of jurisdiction and recognition of judgments which is closely similar.

The point of departure for the Convention is that a defendant is entitled to defend itself in its own courts. But there are numerous particular exceptions. For example, an additional jurisdiction is given for contract and tort claims; and for claims against multiple defendants, and for third party claims (amongst others). Insurance and consumer contracts have special rules which suppose that the insured or the consumer merits broad jurisdictional privileges against the stronger opponent. Written agreements on choice of court are generally effective to exclude the jurisdiction of other courts; and a defendant who elects to appear in a court confers jurisdiction by his submission. But in a few cases (disputes concerning title to land, dissolution of companies, validity of patents, etc), a strictly exclusive jurisdiction is given to a particular court.

The recognition and enforcement of judgments has been much simplified. Though grounds are given upon which recognition may be opposed, these do not generally permit the objection that the court which gave judgment should not have taken jurisdiction in the first place. Accordingly, a defendant who considers that he should not be sued where proceedings have been commenced, must generally make that objection to the court which is hearing the case, not to a different court later called upon to recognise and enforce the judgment. Strikingly, the recognition provisions apply regardless of whether the defendant was domiciled in or a national of a Contracting State. This has undoubtedly made the position of non-European defendants sued in a Contracting State more difficult.

The Convention, in its original form, was drafted by civil lawyers. Though amended on the accession of the United Kingdom, the changes made were not structural. In some places the Convention does not easily accommodate English concepts. In particular, it is no part of the Convention that a court should have a discretion to decline to hear a case on the ground that another court elsewhere is better placed to do so. Instead, the Convention states that the first court seised of a dispute may (and courts seised later may not) hear a case; a rush to commence proceedings before one's opponent does so is the predictable result.

ADRIAN BRIGGS

*Recommended reading*
Collins *Civil Jurisdiction and Judgments Act 1982* (1983) Butterworths.
Briggs & Rees *Civil Jurisdiction and Judgments* (1993) Lloyd's of London Press.

**BUDGET (STRUCTURE)** Overall provisions on the **European Union** budget are found in Articles 199–209 EC (Financial Provisions). According to the introductory Article, 'all items of revenue and expenditure of the Community, including those relating to the **European Social Fund** shall be included in estimates to be drawn up for each financial year and shall be shown in the budget'. In the same provision it is explained that the budget shall cover also expenditures relating to the institutions' involvement in European Union co-operation outside the strict Community field (cf Articles J.11(2) and K.8(2) TEU). One may thus safely refer to the budget as that of the European Union.

In order for the Treaty's financial provisions to be given substance, the **Council of Ministers**, acting on a proposal from the **European Commission**, has been assigned with the task of making Financial Regulations (Article 209 EC). The present Financial Regulation was adopted in 1977 (OJ L356 21.12.77 p 1). It has been modified a number of times for various reasons, most recently in 1995 (OJ L312 23.12.95 p 1).

The general budget of the European Union for the financial year 1996 (OJ L22 29.1.96 p 1) encompasses, on the one hand, a general statement of revenue of the Community, and on the other, separate sections for the different institutions (plus a section on the **Economic and Social Committee** and **Committee of the Regions**). Within each section statements of revenue and expenditure are classified into subsections, titles, chapters, articles and, finally, items. For the budget to be transparent, the Financial Regulation prescribes, inter alia, that the general statement and the separate sections must include estimated revenue and revenue for the preceding year. Notable also is that appropriations under the different sections are classified into commitments and payments. Quite naturally, the official unit of the general budget is the ECU.

The most important section, encompassing 98.3% of all Community expenditure, is that concerning the European Commission. Appropriations are here divided into those relating to administration (Part A), and those relating to operation (Part B). The sections dealing with the European Parliament (including the Ombudsman), the Council of Ministers, the **Court of Justice** and the **Court of Auditors** are almost exclusively concerned with administrative budgets. Their largest expenditure comprises appropriations for personnel and buildings, especially for rents. Also significantly high are expenditures relating to translation services and business travels.

The expenditures change every year, especially when new political goals are envisaged by the Community. Definitions and distribution of the different budget headings (the budgetary nomenclature) is drawn up during the budgetary procedure. Reading the budget as a 'reflection of Europe in development' a new field of commitment for 1996 is that of action against fraud in the field of structural action (Chapter B2-1 5). Nevertheless, once appropriations are entered into the budget they are as a general rule, binding. In compliance with the principles of budgetary discipline (Article 201a EC) and of sound financial management (Article 205 EC) the Commission may not engage in any activities unless resources to finance them are available in the budget. Some flexibility in Commission operation is, however, guaranteed by a monetary reserve available for in accordance with procedures laid down in the Financial Regulation. In the general budget for 1996 this monetary reserve amounts to 500 million ECU. As this reserve is primarily directed against deadlocks between the Council of Ministers and the European Parliament, flexibility is also served by some expenditures which are recognised without any specific amount entered under their subject heading. As with the monetary reserve, the use of these so-called 'token entries' have been made subject to procedures in the Financial Regulation.

CARL FREDRIK BERGSTRÖM

*Recommended reading*
Walder *The Budgetary Procedure of the European Economic Community* (1992) Böhlau.
Zangl 'The Interinstitutional Agreement of Budgetary Discipline and Improvement of the Budgetary Procedure' (1989) 26 CMLRev 675.

**BUDGETARY PROCEDURE** The main provisions on Community finance are Articles 199–209a EC. For the budgetary procedure,

Article 203 is of particular relevance, coupled with Rule 85 of the Rules of Procedure for the **European Parliament** and Annex IV to these rules.

Following the adoption of the Budgetary Treaties of 1970 and 1975, the European Parliament was given significant powers for the control over the Community's budget. The two Treaties replaced the original budgetary procedure and the powers granted to the Parliament should be seen in context of the adoption of a system to fund the Community through own resources.

The budgetary procedure is initiated by the **Commission**, which is responsible for drawing up a preliminary draft budget on the basis of estimates of expenditure submitted by each institution. The preliminary draft budget, which also must contain an estimate of revenue, shall be placed before the Council no later than 1 October for the following financial (calendar) year. Acting on qualified majority and being free to make amendments, the Council then establishes the draft budget, which shall be forwarded to the European Parliament for its first reading not later than 5 October.

Within the following 45 days, the Parliament has the power to accept the budget, to amend it, or to reject it. If it gives its approval the budget stands as finally adopted. Likewise, if the Parliament takes no action within the stipulated period, the budget shall be deemed adopted. Usually, however, the Parliament will exercise its powers to make changes in the budget. The extent of these powers varies according to the classification of the expenditure in question. The distinction is made between expenditure necessarily resulting from Treaty obligations or secondary Community legislation ('compulsory expenditure') and other kinds of expenditure ('non-compulsory expenditure').

The Parliament can amend the parts of the budget relating to non-compulsory expenditure, whereas, for the parts relating to compulsory expenditure, the Parliament's powers are limited to proposals for modifications only. Given the inherent difference in the type of control to be exercised by the Parliament depending on whether it is amending the budget or just proposing modifications, the voting rules differ. Amendments have to be passed by a vote of the majority of all members of Parliament, whereas a majority of the members who actually vote is sufficient for proposals to modifications.

If the Parliament makes amendments or proposes modifications, the draft budget is returned to the Council, but the procedure in the Council depends on whether it is dealing with an amendment or a proposed modification. In case of an amendment (non-compulsory expenditure), the Council may within 15 days modify or reject the amendment in question by an act of qualified majority. Otherwise, the amendment is deemed to have been accepted.

When it comes to proposed modifications (compulsory expenditure), the procedure is more complicated. If the modification implies an increase of compulsory expenditure, it is deemed rejected unless the Council have accepted it by a vote of a qualified majority, which must be taken within 15 days. On the other hand, if the proposed modification implies a reduction (or standstill) of compulsory expenditure, a qualified majority of the Council has 15 days to reject it. Otherwise, it will stand as accepted. Instead of merely rejecting a proposed modification, the Council is free to fix another amount and is thus not obliged to retain the amount shown in the draft budget for the Parliament's first reading.

Since the Council rarely agrees with the Parliament on every change to the draft budget, the budget is usually returned to the Parliament for a second reading. At this point, the Parliament has no power to change provisions relating to compulsory expenditure. However, for the parts of the budget dealing with non-compulsory expenditure, the Parliament has 15 days to reject or amend the Council's 'modifications' to its original amendments. In order to do so, the Parliament must act by a majority of its members and in addition three-fifths of the votes cast. The budget must then be adopted by the Parliament. This happens automatically if the Parliament does not observe the stipulated time-limit.

Instead of adopting the budget, the Parliament has the alternative of rejecting it as a whole. To do so, a majority of its members and two-thirds of the votes cast must be in favour. The Parliament has used its power to reject the 1980 budget and the 1985 budget. In this situation, a new draft must be submitted to the Parliament. If no budget has been adopted by the beginning of a new financial year, the previous year's budget continues to operate on a one-twelfth basis for each month without a formally adopted budget. Thus, Community expenditure will be limited to that of the previous year. However, the Article 204 EC provides a legal basis for an increase of both types of expenditure, conditioned on the approval of the Council and the Parliament respectively.

Although substantial with regard to non-compulsory expenditure, the powers of the Parliament are limited by Article 203(9) EC, which proscribes certain restrictions on the annual increase of this kind of expenditure. Furthermore, since the classification of an expenditure plays a decisive role to the question of control, the Parliament, the Commission and the Council have in a Joint Declaration from 1982 (OJ C194 28.7.82 p 1) sought to clarify the definition of a compulsory expenditure. Finally, two interinstitutional agreements on budgetary discipline and improvement of the budgetary procedure have been concluded in 1988 and in 1993 (OJ L185 15.7.88 p 33 and OJ C331 7.12.93 p 1).

ROBIN PHILIP

*Recommended reading*
Brouwer et al *Do We Need a New EU Budget Deal?* (1995) Philip Morris Institute
    for the Public Policy Research.
Walder *The Budgetary Procedure of the European Economic Community* (1992) Böhlau.

**BULLETIN OF THE EC** See **publications of the EU**.

*CABINETS* The private offices of senior members of the Community **Institutions** are commonly known by the French term *cabinets*. Commissioners, Judges, **Advocates General** and, to a lesser extent, Members of Parliament may appoint and retain at their discretion a secretariat and professionally qualified staff. Appointments are generally made for a period of three to five years, and frequently include national or Community civil servants on secondment. *Cabinet* members often later develop significant careers in their own right, founded upon the experience gained in the *cabinet*.

Commissioners have *cabinets* of between six to eight senior political advisers. *Cabinets* function as an extension of the Commissioner for whom they work. They provide policy advice; represent the Commissioner at Commission meetings (without a right to speak or vote); supervise and control the work of the Community administration; and, perhaps most importantly, ensure the smooth operation of the Commission by co-ordinating policy between cabinets. Policy co-ordination occurs informally and, more formally, at weekly meetings of the *Chef de Cabinets* in anticipation of the Commission's meeting.

Judges and Advocates General at the **Court of Justice** may appoint three legal secretaries, or *référendaires*, to assist in the preparation of cases. Judges in the **Court of First Instance** may appoint two. Legal secretaries are usually either qualified lawyers in one or more Member States or experienced academics. Similarly, they usually have a specialisation in **Community law**. The concept of legal secretaries was borrowed from the French *Cour de Cassation* and has its closest analogy in the common law world with law clerks in the American Supreme Court.

The '*cabinets*' of members of the **European Parliament** – a term rarely used in this context – are smaller than those of Commissioners and judges. MEPs frequently employ researchers to assist in their political and constituency workload.

WILLIAM ROBINSON

*Recommended reading*
Brown & Kennedy *The Court of Justice of the European Communities* (4th edn, 1994) Sweet & Maxwell.
Donnelly & Ritchie 'The College of Commissioners and their *Cabinets*' in Edwards & Spence (eds) *The European Commission* (1995) Cartermill.

**CARTELS** In competition law the word 'cartel' generally refers to an arrangement between competitors (at the same level of supply) to fix purchase or sales prices, set production or sales quotas, allocate customers or markets, boycott certain suppliers or prevent other competitors from entering or selling in the market.

When they engage in a cartel, competitors seek to organise economic resources so as to manipulate output and maintain or increase prices, particularly in the event of market downturns. Circumventing market forces in this way is considered to be particularly harmful to consumers and to the general well-being of the economy. It can also hinder market integration, a primary objective of the European Community.

For these reasons cartels constitute particularly blatant and serious violations of EC competition laws (see Article 85(1) EC and Article 65(1) ECSC). They have led in recent years to the imposition of very large fines of millions of **ECU**, with 'ringleaders' generally receiving the largest fines. As part of its **competition policy**, the European **Commission** has set up a special unit to try to uncover cartels. Given the Commission's difficulty in obtaining adequate proof of clandestine cartels or **concerted practices** in the absence of admissions by the parties, it has recently introduced, as part of its **competition procedure**, a fining policy to encourage participants voluntarily to 'blow the whistle' on secret cartels in exchange for the non-imposition or substantial reduction of fines and to co-operate in cartel investigations in exchange for a significant reduction of fines (see Commission notice (96/C 207/04) on the non-imposition or reduction of fines in cartel cases (OJ C207 18.7.96 p 4)).

Cartels are virtually per se violations of EC competition law, as they are highly unlikely to qualify for exemption if notified to the Commission. They are most unlikely to produce 'exemptible' benefits outweighing the negative effects on competition, unless they take the form of so-called 'crisis' cartels complying with certain strict conditions established by the Commission in its decisional practice.

Cartels usually consist of formalised, but hidden organisations, involving, over a long period of time, regular meetings and systematic exchanges of information on production capacities, output levels, costs and prices. However, formal cartel structures are not necessary for a violation of EC competition law. Even occasional exchanges by competitors of competitively sensitive information could give rise to a serious violation, particularly if such exchanges lead to significant modifications of market behaviour. As a rule, competitors may not exchange sensitive, individualised data normally regarded as being confidential, such as market shares, production capacities, output, quantities sold, prices, discount terms, credit notes and terms of sale, delivery and payment.

Joint sales ventures between competitors are considered to have the same effects as classic cartels. Similarly, joint purchasing ventures are often an instrument for obtaining uniform purchase prices and conditions and may also be used as a basis for purchase quotas.

STEPHEN O SPINKS

*Recommended reading*
Guerrin & Kyriazis *Cartels: Proof and Procedural Issues,* Annual Proceedings of the Fordham Corporate Law Institute (1992), International Antitrust Law and Policy (1993) Kluwer.
Joshua *Attitudes to Anti-Trust Enforcement in the EU and US: Dodging the Traffic Warden, or Respecting the Law?* Fordham Corporate Law Institute 22nd Annual Conference on International Antitrust Law & Policy (1995).

*CASSIS DE DIJON* Case 120/78 *Rewe-Zentral AG* [1979] ECR 649 is commonly known as *Cassis de Dijon* after the subject matter of the case. The case is considered under the **free movement of goods** and **discrimination.**

**CAUSES OF ACTION FOR DAMAGES FOR BREACH OF COMMUNITY LAW** National courts are under an obligation to provide effective protection for Community law rights. In the absence of any Community **harmonisation** or ruling by the **Court of Justice,** they are entitled to apply their own procedural, evidential and substantive rules, provided that these rules do not treat Community law rights less favourably than national law rights and do not make it excessively difficult to protect those rights (Case 33/76 *Rewe* [1976] ECR 1989; Case 45/76 *Comet* [1976] ECR 2043; Case C-312/93 *Peterbroeck* [1995] ECR I-4599; Joined Cases C-430/93 & 431/93 *van Schijndel* [1995] ECR I-4705).

In the United Kingdom, actions for damages against private parties were considered by the House of Lords in *Garden Cottage Foods v Milk Marketing Board* [1984] 1 AC 130. The majority believed that damages were available for breach of Article 86 EC (see **monopolies**) and that the appropriate cause of action was breach of the statutory duty imposed by section 2(1) of the **European Communities Act** 1972. Section 2(1) of the 1972 Act provides that Community law rights and obligations are 'without further enactment' to be given legal effect within the United Kingdom and enforced accordingly. The idea that it was necessary to invent new causes of action ('innominate torts') was rejected.

*Garden Cottage Foods* was a decision on an interlocutory matter. As s 2(1) of the 1972 Act does not contain any indication of the conditions of liability applicable to damages claims under EC law (eg remoteness, causation), it may be inappropriate to treat breach of statutory duty as a 'catch-all' cause of action, unless the Court of Justice has itself established detailed conditions of liability for a particular type of claim. In each case, a plaintiff should consider whether there is an existing cause of action in English law which is better suited to the circumstances of the case (for example, the tort of unlawful interference with trade or business in the context of competition law). In any event, until the position has been definitively settled, any claim for private damages should be based in the alternative on (a) an existing cause of action, such as the tort of unlawful interference (if available); (b) breach of statutory duty under s 2(1) of the 1972 Act; (c) breach of duty arising under Community law (in effect, a sort of 'innominate tort').

Actions for damages against the state were considered by the Court of Appeal in *Bourgoin v MAFF* [1986] 1 QB 716. The majority held that a mere breach of Article 30 EC could not in itself give rise to liability in damages on the part of the state. The only remedy for breach of Community law by the state acting in a legislative or executive capacity should be misfeasance in public office, under which it is necessary to show that the relevant public officer acted maliciously or with knowledge that his actions were unlawful and could injure the plaintiff.

*Bourgoin* can no longer be considered as good law, in so far as it states that damages may only be obtained against the state where the plaintiff can establish a claim based on misfeasance. This is because, in a succession of cases (Joined Cases C-6/90 & 9/90 *Francovich* [1991] ECR I-5357; Joined Cases C-46/93 & C-48/93 *Brasserie du Pêcheur and Factortame* [1996] ECR I-1029; Case C-392/93 *R v HM Treasury, ex p British Telecommunications* [1996] ECR I-1631; Case C-5/94 *R v MAFF, ex p Hedley Lomas* judgment of 23 May 1996; Joined Cases C-178-179, 188-189, 190/94 *Dillenkofer*, judgment of 8.10.96), the Court of Justice has established conditions for state liability which are more widely drawn than the ingredients of the tort of misfeasance. Indeed, in *Brasserie du Pêcheur/ Factortame* (para 73 of the judgment), the Court of Justice expressly stated that, if English law were to impose a condition on state liability requiring proof of misfeasance, this would make it impossible or extremely difficult in practice to obtain damages where there was a breach of Community law by the national legislature (see also the Opinion of Advocate General Léger in *Hedley Lomas* (paras 138-141 and 206-207).

Until the English courts have an opportunity to reconsider the appropriate cause of action for state liability in light of the Court of Justice's new case law, a plaintiff should plead his case as a breach of statutory duty under s 2(1) of the 1972 Act and, in the alternative, as a breach of duty arising under Community law (in effect, a sort of 'innominate tort').

MARK HOSKINS

*Recommended reading*
Brealey & Hoskins *Remedies in EC Law* (1994) Longman, ch 6.
D'Sa *European Community Law and Civil Remedies in England and Wales* (1994) Sweet & Maxwell, chs 8–10.

**CITIZENSHIP AND NATIONALITY** Union citizenship has been established and defined by the **Treaty on European Union**. It finds its place mostly in a new Part Two of the Treaty establishing the European Community, Articles 8-8e.

Article 8 confers Union citizenship to 'every person holding the nationality of a Member State'; therefore, non-nationals seem to be excluded from Union citizenship, although they may possess some of the rights (and duties) which together form the content of the concept of Union citizenship. Indeed, Article 8(1) states that Union citizens 'shall enjoy the rights conferred by this Treaty and shall be subject to the duties imposed thereby'. It is worthwhile noting that this section does not refer to Part Two but to the whole 'Treaty', which may imply that there are rights and duties to be found elsewhere in the Treaty pertaining to Union citizenship, and furthermore that it is not fully clear which Treaty is meant: the Treaty on European Union or the EC Treaty, and this may have consequences for the first-mentioned implication. The inclusion of 'duties', which are not to be detected in Part Two, reinforce the suggestion that one may look beyond this part of the EC Treaty for elements of Union citizenship.

According to Part Two, the following rights belong to Union citizenship:

- the right to move and reside freely within the territory of the Member States, 'subject to the limitations and conditions laid down in this Treaty and by the measures adopted to give it effect' (Article 8a[1]);
- the right to vote and to stand as a candidate in municipal elections in the Member State of residence, under the same conditions as nationals of that state (Article 8b[2]), see also Council Directive (EC) 93/109 (OJ L329 6.12.1993 p 34);
- entitlement to diplomatic protection by the diplomatic or consular authorities of any Member State in the territory of a third country where the own country is not represented (Article 8c);
- the right to petition the European Parliament (Article 8d[1]);
- the right to apply to the Ombudsman, established by Article 138e (Article 8d[2], see also Decision EP of 9 March 1994, OJ L133 pp 15-18).

These rights do only partially differentiate between citizens and non-citizens. Thus, **free movement of persons** is, on the one hand, not fully granted yet to Union citizens, and, on the other hand, available for large categories of non-citizens, ie non-nationals of Member States, such as nationals of **European Economic Area** Member States, nationals of states which have concluded **association agreements** with the EC, etc. The same goes for most other rights conferred in Part Two and elsewhere, especially the fundamental rights mentioned in Article F of which 'everyone' can avail him or herself.

As Union citizenship is a dynamic, although still somewhat hollow, concept, Article 8e lays down the procedure for the Council to adopt provisions to strengthen or to add to the rights laid down in Part Two of the EC Treaty.

Although the logic of EC law would suggest that *nationality*, as a key to Union citizenship and other rights, is a **Community** law term, to be defined more or less autonomously according to Community law canons and principles, this is not the case. The overriding argument which prohibits making nationality a Community term is the fact that nationality is central to the existence of the Member States. **Competence** of the Union to define nationality of the Member States would be tantamount to dissolving the Member States. There is little doubt that Member States have jealously guarded their competence to define their own nationals. This position is clearly expressed in an important Declaration annexed to the Treaty on European Union:

> 'The Conference declares that, wherever in the Treaty establishing the EC reference is made to nationals of the Member States, the question whether an individual possesses the nationality of a Member State shall be settled solely by reference to the national law of the Member State concerned. Member States may declare for information, who are to be considered their nationals for Community purposes by way of a declaration lodged with the Presidency and may amend any such declaration when necessary.'

In the same vein, the **Court of Justice** held in Case C-369/90 *Micheletti* [1992] ECR I-4239 that '. . . the definition of conditions governing acquisition and loss of nationality are, according to international law, matters which fall within the competence of each Member State, a competence which has to be exercised in compliance with Community law', with the effect that the provisions of Community law on freedom of establishment preclude a Member State from denying a national of another Member State who possesses at the same time the nationality of a non-member country entitlement to that freedom on the ground that the law of the host state regards him as a national of the non-member country. It is not clear which restrictions Community law might impose in the eyes of the Court of Justice on national legislators in the area of nationality law, and which sanctions could be brought to bear on infringement. **Subsidiarity** is the key word in this reserved domain.

HANS ULRICH JESSURUN D'OLIVEIRA

*Recommended reading*
Jessurun d'Oliveira 'Union Citizenship: Pie in the Sky?' in Rosas & Entola *A Citizen's Europe* (1995) Sage Publications.
O'Leary *The Evolving Concept of Community Citizenship* (1995) Graham & Trotman.

## CO-DECISION PROCEDURE  See **decision making**.

## COHESION
It has been said that 'the extent to which the 1992 programme can attract economic and social cohesion around it will be key to its chances of success' (Cecchini *The Benefits of a Single Market* (1988) Wildwood House, p 105). As such, the **Single European Act**

introduced a new title into the EC Treaty which conferred upon the Community the task of developing and pursuing actions leading to a strengthening of its economic and social cohesion. To this end the EC Treaty (as amended by the Treaty on European Union) provides that the Community is to aim at reducing disparities between the levels of development of the various regions and the backwardness of the least-favoured regions, including rural areas (see **regional policy**). This objective is to be pursued principally by way of three mechanisms: through the co-ordination of national economic policies, through the implementation of Community common policies and the **Internal Market** programme in such a way as to take account of these objectives and to contribute to their achievement, and by way of Community action through the structural funds, the **European Investment Bank**, and other existing financial instruments. Council Regulation (EEC) 1164/94 (OJ L130 25.05.94 p 1) establishes a specific Cohesion Fund, which is to provide financial assistance to Member States whose per capita GDP is less than 90% of the Community average (Greece, Spain, Portugal and Ireland). For the period 1993–99 the fund comprises 15,150 million ECU at 1992 prices and is to contribute to environmental projects facilitating the achievement of the Community's environmental objectives and to transport infrastructure projects of common interest. Additional actions may, in so far as they prove necessary to attain cohesion, be adopted by the **Council** acting unanimously on a proposal from the **Commission**, and after consulting the **European Parliament**, the **Economic and Social Committee** and the **Committee of the Regions**.

JOANNE SCOTT

*Recommended reading*
European Parliament *A New Strategy for Social and Economic Cohesion after 1992* (1991) Office for Official Publications of the European Communities.
European Parliament *The Regional Impact of Community Policies* (1991) Office for Official Publications of the European Communities.

**COLLECTIVE REDUNDANCIES** See **employment protection**.

**COMITOLOGY** A system of procedural mechanisms whereby the Member State governments supervise the **Commission**'s exercise of implementing powers; in certain circumstances, the implementing power reverts to the **Council**.

The comitology system dates from the setting up of the **Common Agricultural Policy** in 1962; while the conferral on the Commission alone of the necessary implementing powers was politically unacceptable, the delegation of legislative discretion to outside agencies was incompatible with the **Court of Justice**'s case law on the institutional balance of the Treaty. The relevant powers were therefore vested in the Commission, subject to supervision by committees of national civil servants chaired by a non-voting Commission representative.

The system was later extended to most areas of Community regulation, though not in accordance with any discernible logical scheme. Introduced by the **Single European Act**, Article 145 EC, third indent, sought to reduce the great variety of types of committee procedure then in existence, by requiring the Council to confer implementing powers on the Commission, and to establish principles and rules governing comitology; the Council may reserve such powers to itself, but only in 'specific cases', supported by an adequate statement of reasons. Under the 1987 'comitology decision' (OJ L197 18.7.87 p 33), committee procedures must now take one of three main forms, of which the latter two have two variants each:

- *advisory committee*, which provides a non-binding opinion on the draft measures;
- *management committee*, whose negative opinion, adopted by a qualified majority with weighting in accordance with Article 148(2) EC, enables the Council to substitute its own measures for those of the Commission;
- *regulatory committee*, whose positive opinion, again adopted by a qualified majority, is required for the Commission to be able to adopt the implementing measures.

The **European Parliament** contests the comitology system as allowing national officials to interfere with the exercise of Community legislative powers.

KIERAN ST C BRADLEY

*Recommended reading*
Bradley 'Comitology and the Law: through a glass, darkly' (1992) 29 CMLRev 693.
House of Lords Select Committee on the European Communities, 1986-87 session, Third Report, 'Delegation of Powers to the Commission (Final Report)' HL38.


**COMMISSION** Following the entry into force of the **Treaty on European Union** on 1 November 1993, the Commission of the European Communities renamed itself the **European Commission**, under which name can be found a full analysis.


**COMMITTEES OF INQUIRY** See **inquiry**.


**COMMITTEE OF THE REGIONS** Article 198a EC provides for the establishment of the Committee of the Regions, which is to consist of 222 representatives of regional and local bodies appointed by the

Council. Membership shall be for a renewable term of four years. The number of members for each Member State is fixed by the Treaty and the Committee shall elect its own chairman and officers. Members are to be independent in the performance of their duties and are to act in the general interest of the Community. The Committee comprises a number of leading local politicians although, strictly, members need not be elected representatives at regional or local level. The Committee shares a common organisational structure with the **Economic and Social Committee** and is divided into subject-based working groups of 'Commissions'. The establishment of the Committee is seen as a concrete manifestation of the principle of substantive **subsidiarity** and also of the concept of 'partnership', which underlies the operation of the Community's **regional policy**.

The Committee enjoys advisory status. The **Treaty on European Union** requires consultation of the Committee by the **Council** in a wide range of areas, including education, culture, public health, **trans-European networks, telecommunications** and energy networks and economic and social **cohesion**. It may also be consulted in other areas at the initiative of either the Council or the **Commission**. The Committee of the Regions is to be informed whenever the Economic and Social Committee is consulted pursuant to Article 198 EC, and it may, where it considers that specific regional interests are involved, issue an opinion. In other areas it may issue an opinion on its own initiative where it considers that such action is appropriate. The Council or the Commission may set a deadline for the submission of the opinion of the Committee of the Regions which shall not be less than one month from the date of the notification of the deadline. Upon the expiry of such a deadline the absence of an opinion shall not prevent further action.

JOANNE SCOTT

*Recommended reading*
George, Bache & Rhodes *The United Kingdom and the Committee of the Regions* (1993) Report to the Staatskanzlei des Landes Nord Rhein-Westfalen.
Hessel & Mortelmans 'Decentralized Government and Community Law: Conflicting Institutional Developments' (1995) 30 CMLRev 905.


**COMMON AGRICULTURAL POLICY** Agricultural policy has a prominent place in European Community law, and not only because it is still the major item in the EC **budget**. It involves a Community-wide system of product or producer support which has an inevitable effect on the external trade policy of the Community.

While in principle the normal Treaty rules apply to trade in agricultural products and cannot be overridden by **Council** legislation (Cases 80 & 81/77 *Ramel v Receveur des Douanes* [1978] ECR 927), Article 42 provides that there is no automatic application of the competition rules to trade in agricultural products, in the absence of

Council legislation to that effect. Council Regulation (EEC) 26/62 (OJ Sp Ed (1959–62) p 129) provides that in principle the rules laid down in Articles 85–90 of the Treaty shall apply to the production of or trade in, agricultural products, but not the substantive state aid rules. The practical result is that the state aid rules can be invoked where they have been introduced under a specific common organisation, but not where the product falls outside the scope of a common organisation.

Article 39 EC sets out five express objectives of the Common Agricultural Policy: to increase agricultural productivity; to ensure a fair standard of living for the agricultural community; to stabilise markets; to assure the availability of supplies; and, lastly, to ensure that supplies reach consumers at reasonable prices.

The **Court of Justice** accepted in Case 5/73 *Balkan v Hauptzollamt Berlin-Packhof* [1973] ECR 1091 that the Community **institutions** may allow any one of these objectives 'temporary priority in order to satisfy the demands of the economic factors or conditions in view of which their decisions are made'. In general, however, the price systems established by common organisations have been taken by the Court to be intended to give guarantees of income to agricultural producers as such, even where a subsidy is actually paid to processors, as in Cases 67–85/75 *Lesieur Cotelle v Commission* [1976] ECR 391.

With regard to the stabilisation of markets, the common organisation of the market in sugar has always included a system of production quotas limiting the volume of sugar subject to Community support, and in Case 250/84 *Eridania* [1986] ECR 117 it was held justifiable to base the quotas on historical production, even where it meant that the quota allocated to producers in a particular Member State was lower than the volume of consumption in that state. Production quotas in the dairy sector were introduced in 1984, coupled to a confiscatory levy if the quota was exceeded, and this has been continued for a further period of seven years from 1 April 1993 by Council Regulation (EEC) 3950/92 (OJ L405 31.12.92 p 1).

Common organisations for most agricultural products which are produced commercially within the Community were in fact introduced by the expiry of the transitional period on 1 January 1970. Even where there was no common organisation, however, the Court of Justice held in Case 48/74 *Charmasson* [1974] ECR 1783 that any special protection of national organisations ended on that date, and that national organisations of the market became subject to the general rules of the Treaty concerning the **free movement of goods**.

The model of a fully developed common organisation is to be found in that governing the market in cereals. At the heart of the system were a 'target price', which it was hoped Community producers would receive, and an 'intervention price', which has traditionally represented the price at which national authorities, such as the United Kingdom Intervention Board for Agricultural Produce, are legally required to purchase products subject to the price system which are offered to them. Under the 1992 reforms, the target and intervention prices were fixed by Council Regulation (EEC) 1766/92 (OJ L181 1.7.92 p 21) so as to be reduced by fixed amounts over a three-year period, starting from a lower level than that previously applied. The reduction in product support has, however, been matched by a move towards producer support, culminating in Council Regulation (EEC) 1765/92 (OJ L181 1.7.92 p 12) which set up a system of compensatory payments for EC producers of arable crops linked to an obligation to 'set aside' an amount initially set at 15% of the relevant area; for 'small' producers, however, (those with an area less than that needed to produce 92 tonnes of cereals) there is no set-aside obligation. It may be observed that under the **Uruguay Round** agreements, domestic support (eg intervention purchasing) is required to be reduced, although payments under production-limiting programmes (eg set-aside) and decoupled income support do not need to be reduced.

In order to ensure that the price structure is not upset by lower-priced imports, the original method of protection was to fix a 'threshold price': if the world price was lower than the threshold price, the difference had to be covered by an 'import levy'. However, under Regulation (EC) 3290/94 (OJ L349 31.12.94 p 105), giving effect to the EC's obligations under the Uruguay Round agreements, import levies are replaced by duties under the common customs tariff with effect from 1 July 1995. As a result of this, the concept of 'target price' for cereals, whose practical utility had been an element in the calculation of the threshold price, was abolished by Council Regulation (EC) 1528/95 (OJ L148 30.6.95 p 3).

In the converse situation, if a Community producer wishes to export into lower-priced world markets, there is power under the Community legislation to pay an 'export refund' to cover the difference. Here again the Uruguay Round agreements require the level of export support to be reduced.

The concept of a common price policy has led to the development of common market organisations based on prices applicable throughout the Community and expressed in units of account rather than national currencies. Originally, the unit of account was based on the gold value of the United States dollar and converted at the IMF parities. However, the collapse of that system in 1971 led to divergent national prices in real terms and the imposition of monetary compensatory amounts (MCAs) in trade between Member States. While the **ECU** was introduced as the agricultural unit of account in 1979, price divergences were such that it had to be converted at an artificial 'green' rate. The disparities were gradually reduced in the 1980s, and the system of MCAs was in principle eliminated by Council Regulation (EEC) 3813/95 (OJ L22 31.1.95 p 1), which, as revised by Regulation 150/95 (OJ L22 31.1.95 p 1), provides for the conversion of ECUs into national currency and vice versa at an agricultural conversion rate based on representative market rates, and recognises that a sum in national currency representing a common price fixed in ECUs may have to be altered even during the course of a marketing year.

JOHN USHER

*Recommended reading*
Ackrill 'The Common Agricultural Policy: its operation and reform' in Healey
  (ed) *The Economics of the New Europe* (1995) Routlege, pp 206–222.
Usher 'The Common Agricultural Policy and Commercial Policy' in Maresceau
  (ed) *The European Community's Commercial Policy after 1992: The Legal
  Dimension* (1993) Kluwer, pp 137–160.


**COMMON COMMERCIAL POLICY (CCP)**  By virtue of Articles 110-115 EC the European Community is vested with comprehensive powers in the area of external trade. These constitute the basis for its Common Commercial Policy. Together with the Common Customs Tariff, the CCP forms the external counterpart of the common market enabling the Community to protect the functioning of its common market and to pursue comprehensive policy aims in external trade relations. The CCP has been of vital importance to economic integration within the Community and to the emergence of the Community as a major actor in international economic relations. In the framework of the CCP the Community has concluded a broad range of trade agreements with third countries and negotiated in the various GATT rounds since the beginning of the 1960s. Although the CCP was formally completed with the end of the transitional period in 1970, technical completion was only achieved in 1993 with the completion of the **Internal Market** programme, which put an end to a large number of quota restrictions and control measures individual Member States had imposed against imports from third countries in a number of sectors such as textiles and consumer electronics.

*Competences*  The nature and the scope of Community competence under the CCP has given rise to a number of controversies between the Commission and the Member States which ended up before the ECJ. As regards the nature of Community competence the **Court of Justice** held in Opinion 1/75 (Understanding on a Local Cost Standard) [1975] ECR 1364 that the exercise of concurrent powers by the Member States in this area is impossible because it would distort the institutional framework and prevent the Community from fulfilling its task of the defence of the common interest. Community competence under the CCP has therefore to be regarded as exclusive, with the effect that the Community replaces the Member States in their role as sovereign trade units. As regards the scope of Community competence in this field, the Court has repeatedly held that the concept of 'commercial policy' has to be understood in a broad sense which takes into account changes in international trade relations requiring the extension of that concept beyond the traditional patterns of trade. In Case 45/86 *Commission v Council* [1987] ECR 1493, for instance, the Court ruled that the link of the Community's generalised preference system with development policy does not cause measures taken under this system to be excluded from the CCP. In Opinion 1/94 (Agreement establishing the World Trade Organization) [1994] ECR I-5267 the Court reaffirmed the open nature of Community competences under the CCP by holding for the first time that trade in services can also be included in Article 113 if it is limited to cross-frontier services rendered by a supplier established in one country to a consumer residing in another. However, in the same case the Court also established certain limits to the scope of Article 113 by declaring that international agreements in the field of transport are excluded from the scope of Article 113 because transport is the subject of a different Title of the Treaty and that the connection between **intellectual property** rights and trade in goods is not sufficient to bring them within the scope of the CCP. (On the question of 'mixed' competences see **mixed agreements**.)

*Autonomous commercial policy* The CCP comprises both autonomous and conventional commercial policy. The autonomous commercial policy comprises all unilateral measures adopted by the Community in order to protect its interests. Most of these have been revised following to the 1994 WTO Agreement. Four major categories can be distinguished:

(a) *Anti-dumping measures* may be imposed if a dumping practice of a third country causes or threatens to cause material injury to the domestic market (Council Regulation (EEC) 384/96, OJ L349 31.12.94 p 1).

(b) *Anti-subsidy* or *countervailing measures* may be imposed to off-set any subsidy bestowed directly or indirectly in the country of origin or export upon the manufacture, production, export or transport of any product whose release for free circulation in the Community causes injury (Council Regulation (EEC) 3284/94, OJ L349 31.12.94 p 22).

(c) *Protective measures* may be imposed if Community producers are facing serious injury because of a considerable increase of certain imports from third countries (Council Regulation (EEC) 518/94, OJ L67 10.3.94 p 77). They can consist of either surveillance measures (destined to establish clearly the volume of imports or serious injury to Community producers) or of safeguard measures such as quantitative restrictions (quotas).

(d) Measures taken under the *New Commercial Policy Instrument* in order to protect Community producers against illicit trade practices of third countries (Council Regulation (EEC) 2641/84, OJ L252 1.11.84 p 1). These measures may comprise the suspension of trade concessions, the raising of existing customs duties, the introduction of other charges on imports or the introduction of quantitative restrictions.

*Conventional commercial policy* The Community's conventional commercial policy comprises all agreements with third countries based partly or exclusively on Article 113 EC. Major categories of bilateral trade agreements are the framework agreements for commercial and economic co-operation concluded with Canada, India, Thailand and other countries and the sectoral trade agreements concluded with a large number of countries on such products as cane sugar, handicrafts, wine, cheese and manioc. Major categories of multilateral trade agreements are the international commodity agreements concluded within the framework of UNCTAD on coffee, natural rubber, cocoa, tin, jute and other commodities; the co-operation agreements concluded with groups of third countries such as the Andean Pact and the ASEAN countries; and agreements concluded in the framework of the GATT such as the Multilateral Agreements on Trade in Goods and the General Agreement on Trade in Services which form part of the results of the **Uruguay Round**. Since all external agreements of the Community are an integral part of Community law (Opinion 1/78 (International Agreement on Natural Rubber) [1979] ECR 2871) they are a source of legal obligations not only for the Community but also for the Member States and individuals. The Treaty-making procedure regulated by Articles 113 and 228 EC is cumbersome. It is the task of the **Commission** to make recommendations to the **Council** as regards the opening of negotiations with third countries and to act as the Community's negotiator once these are opened. Yet it has to conduct these negotiations within the framework of usually very detailed negotiating Directives issued by the Council and under close supervision by the Council's 'Article 113 Committee', which means that it has to negotiate for most of the time with both the third countries and the Member States within the Council. The agreements are concluded by the Council, acting by a qualified majority on a proposal from the Commission. The **European Parliament** is kept informed on the results of the negotiations by the so-called 'Westerterp procedure', but its consultation before conclusion of an agreement is only facultative. Since the Parliament has also no say in respect to autonomous commercial measures, the CCP is one of the Community policy areas most affected by the **democratic deficit**.

JÖRG MONAR

*Recommended reading*
Emiliou & O'Keeffe (eds) *The European Union and World Trade Law* (1996) Wiley.
Maresceau (ed) *The European Community's Commercial Policy After 1992: The Legal Dimension* (1993) Martinus Nijhoff.

**COMMON CUSTOMS TARIFF** Article 9 EC requires the establishment of a Common Customs Tariff. This is the legal instrument providing the rate and/or amount of customs duty for each product identified in a customs nomenclature. The same customs duty applies wherever the product is customs cleared in the Community.

The Common Customs Tariff is published every year in the Official Journal of the European Communities, generally in September or October. This publication contains the customs nomenclature and the duty rate for each product identified in the nomenclature.

The customs nomenclature, which is generally referred to as the 'Combined Nomenclature' is based on the 'Harmonized Commodity Description and Coding System' which was adopted by the Customs Cooperation Council (ie the international customs organisation in charge of customs matters under the GATT, which has now developed into the World Customs Organisation). The Combined Nomenclature identifies goods on the basis of the six-digit tariff headings referred to in the Harmonized System but adds thereto two additional digits which allow for greater precision in the identification of goods.

The Common Customs Tariff contains conventional and autonomous customs duty rates. Conventional duties are the customs duty rates agreed upon by the Community under the auspices of the GATT. Thus, the Common Customs Tariff which entered into force on 1 January 1995 implements the first reduction of the five-year term reduction of customs duties agreed upon by the Community in the **Uruguay Round**. Autonomous duties theoretically apply to goods for which no conventional duties were agreed upon or when the autonomous duties are lower than the conventional duties. In practice, these autonomous duties rarely apply.

The customs duties provided for in the Common Customs Tariff are either ad valorem duties (stipulated by way of percentage), specific duties (a fixed amount) or a combination of the two.

PAULETTE VANDER SCHUEREN

*Recommended reading*
Kelley & Onkelinx *EEC Customs Law* (1991) ESC Publishing Ltd.
Vaulont *The Customs Union of the European Economic Community* (1986) The European Perspectives Series.

**COMMON EXTERNAL TARIFF** See **customs union.**

**COMMON FOREIGN AND SECURITY POLICY (CFSP)** The Common Foreign and Security Policy was established by Title V of the Treaty on European Union. It constitutes the 'Second Pillar' of the European Union, replacing the former European Political Cooperation (EPC), set up in 1970 to co-ordinate the foreign policies of the Member States. Although part of the TEU, the CFSP remains outside the traditional Community system: in particular, the **Court of Justice** has practically no jurisdiction over this area.

The CFSP is therefore not a common policy in the sense of the **Common Commercial Policy**. It does, however, go further than the simple co-ordination of national policies. The positions and policies which result from it contribute over time to the forging of an international personality for the **European Union**, recognised as such by foreign countries. This effect is achieved through a range of instruments proper to the CFSP (declarations, *démarches*, common positions and joint actions) and by making use of EC instruments (sanctions, economic assistance, contractual relationships).

The position of the Union with regard to world events is defined in a large number of declarations issued practically on a daily basis (more than 100 in 1994). While not designed to be operational, these declarations nevertheless build up a corporate image of the Union, while the process of drafting and securing agreement on a final text assists in harmonising the views of the participants. The Union's positions can be drawn to the attention of other countries by diplomatic *démarches*. These two instruments were already available to EPC. The instruments of common positions and joint actions were established by the TEU (Articles J.2 and J.3); in the absence of a legal definition in the text, their characteristics must be deduced from practice. Common positions resemble declarations, but usually give a policy orientation on an important question (eg Rwanda, Ukraine). Joint actions allow the Union to engage in external activities either collectively or by delegation. Examples are the supervision of the elections in Russia and the administration of the town of Mostar.

The CFSP may also have recourse to EC economic instruments in order to give effect to political objectives it has defined. This practice developed on an informal basis under EPC (the imposition of economic sanctions against the Soviet Union, Argentina and Iraq; the deployment of additional economic assistance to Central America and for the victims of apartheid), and was given further encouragement by the 'consistency' provisions of the **Single European Act** and the TEU. The process accelerated under the impact of the fall of communism in Eastern Europe, leading to the conclusion of **Europe Agreements** with the East and Central European countries. However, with the exception of Article 288a, which provides for a CFSP decision before economic sanctions can be imposed, the TEU fails to regulate the relationship between the First and Second Pillars. The 'grey area' thus created has given rise to a number of 'joint action' decisions under the CFSP, which require action in the EC to follow. According to some, this deprives the Community of its full decision-making capacity. The decisions regarding the Middle East peace process and South Africa are examples.

The decision-making procedures of CFSP remain largely intergovernmental. Decisions are taken by consensus, and the role of supranational institutions is strictly limited. However, the consensus rule is not equivalent to a veto. There is strong peer pressure to reach a positive conclusion, and not to block a position held by a majority. Provision for voting by qualified majority for joint actions is introduced in Article J.3, but it is hedged about with such stringent conditions that many observers believe it can never be used.

CFSP decisions are taken by the **Council** of the European Union, whose agenda does not distinguish between CFSP and EC items. This reform was introduced by the TEU. Previously, EPC items had been dealt with by the Foreign Ministers meeting in a separate foreign policy formation; if, as happened with increasing frequency, these items were dealt with during Council meetings, they were clearly distinguished from EC items. Although **COREPER** formally prepares all items on the Council agenda, the substantive preparation of CFSP items is in practice left to the Political Committee, made up of the Political Directors of the Foreign Ministries of the Member States. Working to the Political Committee is a large number of Working Groups, with either horizontal (United Nations, non-proliferation) or vertical (Latin America, Asia) responsibilities. These Working Groups are manned by officials from Foreign Ministries in the capitals. Following the entry into force of the TEU, an attempt was made to merge these groups with the Groups of the Council, manned by officials from the **Permanent Representations** in Brussels, so far with mixed results.

The Member States, the **Commission** and the Council Secretariat are linked by a confidential telex system called the 'Coreu network'.

Member States' Embassies and the Delegations of the Commission in third countries hold frequent CFSP meetings among themselves and with the authorities of the host countries.

The CFSP is managed by the Presidency with the assistance of the Council Secretariat, which has taken over the responsibilities of the former EPC Secretariat. The CFSP section of the Secretariat remains organisationally separate from its external relations colleagues, however, only coming together at the level of Director General for external relations, and half its staff are seconded diplomats. It provides the normal services of the Council Secretariat, having no autonomous right of initiative.

The TEU awards to the Presidency the role of external representation of the Union. It may exercise that role alone, for example in issuing declarations on behalf of the Union and in receiving representatives of foreign countries, but is frequently assisted by the Troika, composed of the current Presidency and the immediately preceding and succeeding Presidencies, together with a representative of the Commission.

The Commission is fully associated with the CFSP, and acquired through the TEU a non-exclusive right of initiative, on the same footing as the Member States.

SIMON NUTTALL

*Recommended reading*
Forster & Wallace 'Common Foreign and Security Policy: a new policy or just a new name?' in Wallace & Wallace (eds) *Policy-Making in the European Union* (1996) Oxford University Press, pp 411–435.
Ryba 'La politique étrangère et de sécurité commune (PESC)' (1995) 14 Revue du Marché commun et de l'Union européenne 384.

**COMMON TRANSPORT POLICY** The Community's transport regime is set out in Articles 74–84 EC. These Articles contain a variety of provisions which recognise the distinctive features of transport within the **Internal Market**. They provide, in essence, for a common transport policy (Article 74); the laying down of common rules applicable to international transport; the conditions of operation of transport services by non-resident carriers; measures to improve transport safety and ancillary measures (Article 75(1)); a standstill provision on Member State action which treats non-nationals less favourably (Article 76); additional state aid rules (Article 77); the prohibition of discrimination on the grounds of country or origin or destination (Article 79); the prohibition, subject to Commission approval, of Member State support or protection by means of rates and conditions (Article 80); and the progressive reduction of charges or dues on the crossing of internal frontiers (Article 81). These provisions apply to rail, road and inland waterway transport, and to a varying degree to sea and air transport.

Accordingly, the transport sector is regulated, rather than constituting a free market. This takes into account the distinguishing features of the sector, including the dominance of **state monopolies**, public service obligations and the use of transport policy as a corollary to **industrial** and security policies. Furthermore, the transport sector has historically been, and remains to an appreciable degree, one in which international practices have been solved by bilateral or multilateral agreements (for example, the Chicago Convention 1944, providing that each state shall have exclusive sovereignty over its own airspace).

Partly due to these exceptional features of the transport sector, legislative progress at the Community level has been slow and piecemeal, and developments have taken place separately in each of the road, rail, inland waterway, air and maritime sectors. The increasing recognition of the interchangeability of modes of transport on certain routes (for example, that of air and rail for business travellers on the London to Paris route, Commission Decision (CE) 94/663 (OJ L259 7.10.94 p 20)) has led to recent initiatives to globalise the Common Transport Policy, including two recent Commission policy documents. First, the White Paper on the future development of the Common Transport Policy of December 1992 set out its objectives, in general terms, to achieve an integrated, safe, efficient, competitive and environmentally-friendly transport system, which takes into account the needs of users and workers in this sector. This should be based upon advanced technological development, should seek to achieve an improved functioning of the Internal Market and should include broadening of the external dimension. It further called for the integration of all transport networks relating to the various modes of transport into a single **trans-European network**. Second, the Common Transport Policy Action Programme 1995–2000 was published on

12 July 1995 and set out the Commission's legislative programme to meet these objectives (but see the Economic and Social Committee's reservations (OJ C39 12.2.96 p 43)). These policies interrelate with the developments for a 'Citizen's Network' (Green Paper, COM (95) 601 final) and guidelines, currently under negotiation, in respect of transport trans-European networks (COM (94) 106 final).

The Council did not initially establish a Common Transport Policy. Such action was only taken after the European Parliament successfully challenged this omission in Case 13/83 *European Parliament v Council* [1985] ECR 1513. The Court of Justice held that the Council (which, at that time, was able to act by unanimity on its own initiative) was required by Articles 3(e) and 74 EC to establish a framework of the Common Transport Policy, whether in a single decision or a series of decisions, regarding the common rules applicable to international transport and the conditions under which non-resident carriers may operate transport services within a Member State. The legislative progress has, however, remained piecemeal, and covers areas as disparate as tacographs, licences for inland waterway vessels, noise emissions from subsonic aircraft and maritime environmental standards.

In the absence of an all-inclusive legislative programme, transport issues have arisen most significantly in respect of the Community's **competition policy** (the sector's initial exclusion from the scope of Council Regulation (EEC) 17/62 (OJ Sp Ed 1959–62 p 87) having been replaced by various specific regulations, and see Case 66/86 *Ahmed Saeed* [1989] ECR 803), **merger control** regulation, **state aids**, **taxation** policy and the **free movement of goods**, **services**, **establishment** and **persons**. One recent example concerns the mutual recognition of driving licences (see Council Directives 80/1263 (OJ L375 31.12.80 p 12) 91/439 (OJ L237 24.8.91 p 1) and 94/72 (OJ L337 24.12.94 p 86)). The Court of Justice held in Case C-193/94 *Skanavi* [1996] 2 CMLR 372 that in view of the importance of individual means of transport, the possession of a driving licence duly recognised by a host state may affect the exercise of the freedom of movement. Therefore, whilst the provisions on the freedom of establishment entitled Member States to require the exchange of driving licences by persons who exercise their Community right to reside permanently in that state, the failure to comply with that administrative formality can neither extinguish the existence of a right to drive a motor vehicle nor subject the defaulter to criminal penalties. The Court therefore recognised the rights of individuals on the basis of freedom of establishment, prior to the entry into force on 1 July 1996 of Article 1(2) of Directive 91/439, which provides for such mutual recognition without any formality.

WILLIAM ROBINSON

*Recommended reading*
Greaves *Transport Law of the European Community* (1991) Athlone.
House of Lords Select Committee on the European Communities *Common Transport Policy*, Session 1993-94, 8th Report, HMSO.

**COMMUNITY CHARTER OF FUNDAMENTAL SOCIAL RIGHTS OF WORKERS** The Community Charter of Fundamental Social Rights of Workers was adopted at the meeting of the European Council under the Presidency of France, then celebrating the 200th anniversary of the Declaration of the Rights of Man and of the Citizen, by 11 Member States (except the United Kingdom) on 9 December 1989.

Initially formulated to cover all **citizens**, the final version was limited to the rights of workers. This highlights the ambiguity of whether it projects merely the social dimension of the Single European Market, or something more: the welfare state orientation of the emerging European polity.

The Charter's 30 Articles should be seen in the historical context of those fundamental social and economic rights which were particularly prominent in the new constitutions of Greece, Portugal and Spain, Member States who joined the Community in the period leading up to 1989. The Charter covers:

- freedom of movement (Articles 1–3), including access to employment and social protection, conditions of residence and recognition of qualifications;
- employment and remuneration (Articles 4–6) including a fair and equitable wage;
- improvement of living and working conditions (Articles 7–9), including different forms of employment (such as part-time and temporary working), rest periods and annual paid leave, and clearly stipulated working conditions;
- social protection (Article 10), including social security benefits and social assistance;
- freedom of association and collective bargaining (Articles 11–14), including the right to strike;
- vocational training (Article 15), including both initial and continuing training;
- **equal treatment** for men and women (Article 16), including measures to reconcile occupational and family obligations;
- information, consultation and participation for workers (Articles 17–18), especially in transnational operations;
- **health and safety at work** (Article 19);
- protection of children and adolescents (Articles 20–23), including training, remuneration, and working time;
- elderly persons (Articles 24–25), including medical and social assistance;
- disabled persons (Article 26).

Lacking unanimous approval of the Member States in the **European Council**, the Charter is not a legally binding instrument. None the less, the political momentum behind it is illustrated by the **Commission**'s Action Programme, containing a large number of proposals for its implementation. Some measures have been approved: Directives on fixed-term and temporary workers (Council Directive

(EEC) 91/383 (OJ L206 19.7.91 p 19)), information on working conditions (Council Directive (EEC) 91/533 (OJ L288 18.10.91 p 32)), pregnancy and maternity (Council Directive (EEC) 92/85 (OJ L348 28.11.92 p 1)), working time (Council Directive (EEC) 93/104 (OJ L307 13.12.93 p 18)), young workers (Council Directive (EEC) 94/33 (OJ L216 20.8.94 p 12)), European Works Councils (Council Directive (EEC) 94/45 (OJ L254 30.9.94 p 64)).

The role of the social partners, labour and management (Article 118b EC) was given significant recognition by the Charter. Article 27 formally embodied the jurisprudence of the **Court of Justice**, recognising collective agreements as valid instruments for the implementation of Community law measures. In a harbinger of debates to come, the preamble stated that 'the respective roles of Community rules, national legislation and collective agreements must be clearly established'.

Two years later, the **Social Policy Protocol** of the Treaty on European Union began by 'noting that 11 Member States . . . wish to continue along the path laid down in the 1989 Social Charter; that they have adopted among themselves an Agreement to this end'. The new social competences of the EU provided by the Agreement reflect the rights outlined in the Social Charter. The Agreement formally enshrines in EU law the role of the social partners in the formulation through social dialogue and implementation through agreements of EU social law.

The Community Charter remains a vital part of the EU social constitution in waiting. It is the substantive part; the Maastricht Protocol and Agreement are the procedural part. If and when a United Kingdom government opts in to EU social policy, it will be time to achieve a definitive synthesis.

BRIAN BERCUSSON

*Recommended reading*
Bercusson 'The European Community's Charter of Fundamental Rights' (1990) 5 MLR 624.
Liebfried & Pierson (eds) *European Social Policy: Beboreen Fragmentation and Integration* (1995) Brookings Institution.


**COMMUNITY PREFERENCE** This principle, which is sometimes regarded as a specific expression of the principle of solidarity between Member States laid down in Article 5 EC, is mentioned in Article 44(2) EC, which speaks of 'the development of a natural preference between Member States' in the agricultural context.

However, in Case C-353/92 *Greece v Council* [1994] ECR I-3411 at 3433, **Advocate General** Jacobs said that he considered it questionable whether Article 44(2) provided a foundation for a **general principle** of Community preference. In that case, Greece sought to rely, inter alia, on such a principle in challenging the validity of two regulations which, it said, placed Community producers of soya beans at a competitive disadvantage *vis-à-vis* producers of soya beans from third countries. Advocate General Jacobs took the view that 'that Community preference, although sometimes regarded as a legal principle, is rather a matter of policy' (at 3432). He added: 'While the Court has recognized the legitimacy of Community preference as an element in agricultural policy, it has not treated Community preference as a legal requirement the violation of which would result in the invalidity of the legislation. It has merely recognized that in certain circumstances it is not unlawful to give preference to Community production' (at 3433). The Advocate General concluded that Community law did not contain a general requirement that preference should be given to Community producers. Any such requirement would, he thought, be difficult to reconcile with the Treaty's aim, mentioned in its preamble and in Article 110 EC, of contributing to the progressive abolition of restrictions on international trade. Moreover, he pointed out that the Community's international obligations might in some circumstances render Community preference unlawful.

The views of Advocate General Jacobs were expressly endorsed by the Court, which observed that 'Community preference is not . . . a legal requirement the violation of which would result in the invalidity of the measure concerned' (para 50).

ANTHONY ARNULL

*Recommended reading*
Eeckhout *The European Internal Market and International Trade: A Legal Analysis* (1994) Oxford University Press, pp 342–344, 352–354.
Toth *The Oxford Encyclopaedia of European Community Law* (1990) Oxford University Press, vol I, pp 102-103.


**COMPANY LAW** The EC company law harmonisation programme has had considerable impact on the laws of the Member States, but has not yet succeeded in establishing a common profit-motivated business organisation in Europe. The following are the major instruments and proposals affecting company law.

*The Regulation to establish the European Economic Interest Grouping (EEIG)* (OJ L199 31.7.85 p 1) came into effect on 1 July 1989. It provides for the introduction of a new form of undertaking which will have some of the advantages of a company including separate legal personality. However, profit making must not be its primary motive and its members will have unlimited liability. The founder members must come from at least two Member States. The idea is to encourage business to co-operate across national frontiers within the EC.

*The First Directive of 1968* (OJ Sp Ed 1968 p 41) provided a system of publicity for all companies. Member countries must ensure disclosure of the memorandum and articles, officers of the company, paid up capital, balance sheet and profit and loss account, winding up and appointment of liquidators.

*The Second Directive of 1976* (OJ L26 30.1.77 p 1) lays down minimum requirements for the formation of public companies and the maintenance, increase and reduction of capital. Companies must disclose their corporate form, name, objects, registered office, share capital, classes of shares and the composition and powers of the various organs of the company. The minimum subscribed capital of a public limited company must exceed 25,000 ECU.

*The Third Directive of 1978* (OJ L295 20.10.78 p 26) regulates mergers between public companies where the assets and liabilities of the acquired company are transferred to the acquiring company. The shareholders of both companies receive a stake in the acquiring company equivalent to their previous holdings. The rights of employees are covered by Directive 77/197 (OJ L61 5.3.77).

*The Fourth Directive of 1978* (OJ L222 14.8.78 p 11) contains detailed rules regarding the drawing up of the accounts of individual companies.

*The Sixth Directive of 1982* (OJ L378 31.12.82 p 47) covers the division of an existing company into smaller units. The allocation of assets and liabilities among the new units requires provisions to protect creditors.

*The Seventh Directive of 1983* (OJ L193 18.7.83 p 1) specifies how and in what circumstances consolidated accounts are to be prepared and published by companies with subsidiaries.

*The Eighth Directive on the Qualification of Auditors* (OJ L126 12.5.84 p 20) requires Member States to ensure that auditors are independent and properly qualified. It lays down minimum requirements for the education and training of auditors.

*The Eleventh Directive on the disclosure requirements of branches of certain types of company* (OJ L395 30.12.89 p 36) deals with information to be published in one Member State by branches of companies which are registered in another Member State or a non-EC country. A branch does not have a legal personality of its own. The Directive therefore requires disclosure of information concerning the company of which the branch is part, including its accounts, drawn up in accordance with the Fourth and Seventh Directives or in a manner 'equivalent thereto'.

*The Twelfth Directive of 1989* (OJ L395 30.12.89 p 40) requires Member States to allow private limited companies with a single member. All the shares would have to show the name of the person owning them. The member would have to: exercise the powers of the general meeting; record in minutes the decisions taken under those powers; and draw up in writing any agreement between the sole member and the company. Otherwise the company would be subject to the restraints of company law in the usual way.

*The Major Shareholdings Directive* (OJ L348 17.12.88 p 62) requires a buyer of shares to reveal his identity when he acquires a major block of shares in a company listed on the Stock Exchange. The purpose of the Directive is to prevent takeovers by stealth.

*The Insider Dealing Directive* (OJ L334 18.11.89 p 30) was adopted in November 1989 and implemented in the United Kingdom by the Criminal Justice Act 1993.

*A Proposal for a Regulation for a **European Company Statute*** (OJ C176 8.7.91 p 1 and COM (91)174) would provide, if adopted, for a corporate structure with limited liability, available as an alternative structure for businesses across the Member States.

The present proposal contains a 'core' of company law provisions in a Regulation with a Directive said to be 'indissolubly associated' with the Regulation, containing worker participation proposals similar to those in the Fifth Directive. The laws of the Member States are to be used to fill in the 'gaps' left by the statute.

*The Proposed Fifth Directive* (OJ C240 9.9.83 p 2 and COM (83)185) will require all public companies to adopt a corporate structure which conforms with its provisions. Two major aspects of the Directive are the provisions concerning the management structure of the company and those concerning the involvement of employees.

It sets out two basic models for company management, a two-tier system with a supervisory board and an executive board and a single-tier system where executive and non-executive directors sit together. Within those two models various alternatives are available.

*Worker participation schemes* Where companies employ on average over 1,000 people, the proposal is that Member States must make the adoption of one of the schemes compulsory. The schemes are:
(a) Employee participation in the appointment of the members of the supervisory organ. In this scheme between one-third and one-half of the supervisory board are to be appointed by the employees of the company.
(b) Employee participation through a body representing company employees. In this case a body representing the employees will have a right to regular information and consultation on the administration, situation, progress and prospects of the company, together with its competitive position, credit situation and investment plans.
(c) Employee participation through collectively agreed systems. By this alternative, employee participation is to be regulated in accordance with collective agreements concluded between the company and organisations representing employees. The minimum contents of such agreements are specified.

*The Proposed Thirteenth Directive on Takeovers* (OJ C240 26.9.90 p 8) would require Member States to introduce rules similar to those operated by the City Panel on Takeovers. The rules would regulate takeovers. The proposal encountered opposition and is not likely to be adopted in the immediate future.

JANET DINE

*Recommended reading*
Dine *EC Company Law* (1991) Wiley Chancery Law.
Hopt & Wymeersch *European Company and Financial Law* (1994) Walter de Gruyter.

**COMPETENCES** The EC is based on the principle of limited powers *(competénces d'attribution)*. At least in theory, it has only the powers which are specifically attributed to it by the Treaties, and these powers are limited in scope. The principle of limited powers is implicit in Article 4(1) EC, which provides that, in carrying out its tasks, each EC **institution** must act within the limits of the powers conferred upon it by the Treaty. In addition, Article 3b EC (**subsidiarity**) states that the EC shall act within the limits of the powers conferred upon it by this Treaty and of the objectives assigned to it therein. The principle is enforced in the last instance by actions under Article 173 EC for the annulment of Community acts on grounds of lack of competence or of infringement of an essential procedural requirement, particularly the duty imposed on Community institutions by Article 190 EC to state the reasons on which their acts are based, including not only substantive reasons but also the Treaty Article conferring on the Community the power to act in respect of the matter in question.

The history of the EC and the expansion of its competences have tended, however, to undermine any strict theory of attributed powers, and to some extent the related concept of the EC as a special purpose association *(zweckverband)*. This has occurred partly through the use by the EC of its 'residual powers' under Article 235 EC. In addition, starting with Case 22/70 *Commission v Council* (ERTA) [1971] ECR 263, the **Court of Justice** has developed the concept of the Community's **implied powers**, especially in the field of external economic relations. Furthermore, amendments to the founding Treaties have expanded EC express competence; powers concerning **environmental policy**, social and economic **cohesion** and **research and development**, for example, were expressly conferred on the EC by the **Single European Act**. Though nominally consistent with the theory of attributed powers, such amendments have extended the EC powers in areas previously reserved to the Member States and to an extent impossible to foresee when the EC was founded.

This trend was halted to some extent by the Treaty on European Union. The TEU reiterated the principle of powers of attribution: cf Article 3b. It specifically attributed to the EC new powers concerning **industrial policy**; the development of **trans-European networks**;

**public health; education** and **cultural policy; consumer** protection; **energy;** civil protection; tourism; and **economic and monetary union.** However, these new powers are in most cases concurrent with those of the Member States (eg consumer protection) or limited to the encouragement of co-operation or co-ordination rather than involving the autonomous enactment of legally binding acts (eg public health).

FRANCIS SNYDER

*Recommended reading*
Curtin 'The Constitutional Structure of the Union: A Europe of Bits and Pieces' (1993) 30 CMLRev 17.
Lane 'New Community Competences under the Maastricht Treaty' (1993) 30 CMLRev 939.

**COMPETITION POLICY** Article 3(g) of the EC Treaty provides that one of the activities of the Community shall be 'the institution of a system ensuring that competition in the Internal Market is not distorted'. The specific rules on competition are found in Articles 85–94. Article 85(1) prohibits agreements or informal arrangements ('**concerted practices**') that restrict competition and which might affect trade between the Member States of the Community (see **cartels**). This prohibition applies both to 'horizontal' agreements (that is, agreements between competitors operating at the same level of the market) and to 'vertical' agreements (that is, between firms operating at different levels of the market, for example between a producer and a distributor). The Treaty recognises, however, that some agreements that restrict competition nevertheless may have beneficial features: for example, they may lead to an improvement in the production or distribution of goods or in technical or economic progress. Because of this, Article 85(3) provides that, in some circumstances, an exemption may be given from the prohibition contained in Article 85(1). Such exemptions may be given on an individual basis to an agreement that has been notified on Form A/B to the **Commission**; they may also be conferred 'en bloc' to specific types of agreement, normally by a Commission (but occasionally by a Council) Regulation (see **competition procedure**). Many agreements, for example licences of **intellectual property** rights, joint ventures for research and development, franchises and distribution agreements, fall within Article 85(1) but benefit from an individual or bloc exemption under Article 85(3).

Article 86 prohibits the abuse of a dominant position on the market in so far as trade between Member States might be affected (see **monopolies**). Examples of abusive behaviour are the imposition of unfair purchase or selling prices, limiting or controlling markets, discriminatory practices, 'tie-in' transactions and certain refusals to supply. Attempts by dominant firms to exclude smaller competitors from the market are particularly seriously punished.

Article 90(1) deals with the obligations of Member States in respect of public undertakings or undertakings to which they have granted 'special or exclusive rights' (see **State monopolies**). In such circumstances, a Member State must not enact nor maintain in force any measure which would infringe the Treaty, in particular Article 6 EC (which prohibits discrimination on grounds of nationality) and the competition rules contained in Articles 85–94. Article 90(2) provides that the competition rules apply to such undertakings, except in so far as this would obstruct them from performing the tasks entrusted to them. The Commission is able to adopt Directives and decisions under Article 90(3) in order to ensure the application of Article 90(1) and (2). Most notably it has taken action under Article 90(3) in respect of telecommunications terminal equipment and, subsequently, **telecommunications** themselves. Much of the Commission's current programme is concerned with the possibility of introducing competition into sectors that have traditionally been regarded as natural monopolies or that have been characterised by the existence of special or exclusive rights.

Articles 92–94 prohibit **State aids** given by Member States that could have a distortive effect on competition in the common market in so far as they could affect trade between Member States. These provisions are vigorously applied by the Commission, and it is possible for the **Court of Justice** to order that illegal state aids should be repaid by the recipient thereof.

The competition rules apply to all sectors of the economy, subject to the following exceptions: Article 85 does not apply to agricultural products as they are subject to the **common agricultural policy**; coal and steel may fall to be dealt with under the special rules in the **European Coal and Steel Community** Treaty. The competition rules apply both to goods and services; arguments that particular sectors such as the liberal professions, banking, **insurance** and other **financial services** should enjoy some immunity from Articles 85 and 86 have been flatly rejected by the Commission and Court. Air, maritime and inland transport are also covered, although they are subject to specific procedural regimes.

The competition rules are enforced by the Commission, under powers delegated to it by the **Council of Ministers** in Council Regulation (EEC) 17/62 (OJ Sp Ed (1959-62) p 87) or in the specific Regulations in the transport sector; the Commission is subject to **judicial review** by the **Court of First Instance**, from which there is an appeal on a point of law to the Court of Justice. Among the Commission's powers, it may request information from undertakings, carry out on-the-spot investigations, require the discontinuance of prohibited practices and impose fines. The current policy of the Commission is to impose very substantial fines for blatant infringements of the competition rules; the maximum fine that can be imposed is 10% of a firm's turnover (including all group turnover) in the preceding financial year. The risks of infringing the competition rules are so great that all firms should instate a compliance policy to ensure that employees are fully aware of those rules and that infringements are avoided. Quite apart from the Commission's powers of enforcement, the competition rules, and in particular Articles 85 and 86, have direct effect, which means that they may be invoked, both as a shield and a sword, in proceedings in domestic courts. The Commission's current policy is to encourage complainants who claim that they have been or are being harmed by an infringement of the competition rules to go to their national courts to seek redress rather than bringing the matter to it. This would mean that the Commission would be able to expend its resources on other matters, such as the formulation of policy, the drafting of legislation and the development of links with other competition authorities and international organisations; the Commission would take enforcement action only in cases having a 'Community interest', for example that have legal, economic or political significance (see **complaints to the Commission**).

A dominant feature of the Commission's approach to the competition rules has been its determination to ensure that firms do not, by their commercial behaviour, contribute to the geographical partitioning of the **Internal Market**. Many provisions in the Treaty are concerned with the elimination of obstacles to the **free movement of capital, goods, persons** and **services** erected or maintained by Member States; these provisions would be undermined if, for example, firms were able to enter into agreements not to poach on each others' territories or if a dominant undertaking were to deter or block new entrants to its geographical market. The Commission will impose substantial fines in serious cases of market compartmentalisation. Some commentators argue that the Commission is too ready to conclude that agreements conferring exclusivity on, for example, distributors or licensees infringe Article 85(1): the argument runs that many such agreements are in fact pro-competitive and therefore should fall outside Article 85(1) altogether. However, given the overriding requirement, embodied in the Treaty itself, that there should be full integration of national markets, it seems likely that the Commission will continue in such cases, unless directed to do otherwise by the Court, to apply Article 85(1) strictly, albeit subject to the possibility of individual or block exemption being available under Article 85(3).

RICHARD WHISH

*Recommended reading*
Bellamy & Child *Common Market Law of Competition* (4th edn, 1993) Sweet & Maxwell.
Whish *Competition Law* (3rd edn, 1993) Butterworths.

## COMPETITION PROCEDURE

*Notification* Notification is not mandatory under the EU's competition rules. However, the parties may seek a ruling of the Commission in relation to their own particular agreement or conduct only by means of formal notification pursuant to Council Regulation (EEC) 17/62 (OJ Sp Ed 1959-62 p 87) ('the Regulation'). Furthermore, only the **Commission** has the power to grant exemption under Article 85(3).

Notification must be made in the prescribed form (Form A/B) in order to seek either a so-called 'negative clearance' (that the agreement does not come within the terms of Article 85(1) at all) or a decision that the agreement is caught by Article 85(1) but merits the exemption under Article 85(3).

Form A/B was substantially revised in 1994 and is now set out in Commission Regulation 3385/94 (OJ L377 31.12.94 p 28). A substantial amount of market and other information is required in order to complete the form and considerable care must be taken in replying to each question. The supply of incorrect or misleading information may give rise to a fine under Article 15(1)(a) of the Regulation, together with the refusal of exemption and the loss of immunity from fines in respect of any infringements of the substantive rules.

The revised form A/B contains two separate sets of questions, one for use in standard notifications and another for use in notifying structural joint ventures for which 'accelerated treatment' is requested (ie a first response from the Commission within two months). The purpose of this is to enable the Commission to extend to structural co-operative joint ventures benefits akin to the fast track clearance procedure applicable to concentrative joint ventures notified under the Merger Regulation (see below).

Notification does not of itself render an agreement enforceable or provisionally valid in the period prior to the grant of exemption. Until the grant or refusal of exemption, the parties are, however, protected from the imposition of fines for infringements of Article 85(1) or 86 in respect of acts taking place after notification, provided they fall within the limits of the activity described in the notification.

Following notification there is likely to be the opportunity for informal discussions with the Commission. The Commission may seek amendments to the agreement and/or undertakings from the parties. In practice, the Commission takes few formal decisions in response to notifications and by far the greater number of cases are settled informally, often by means of a 'comfort letter'. A comfort letter is a letter signed by a senior official of DG IV indicating that the Commission is closing its file and intends to take no further action. The letter may state a reason, for example that the notified agreement falls outside Article 85(1) or that it merits an exemption under Article 85(3) or falls within a block exemption regulation. In some cases the Commission indicates that the agreement is caught by Article 85(1) and is not suitable for exemption but that no further action is proposed to be taken. This kind of comfort letter is sometimes referred to as a 'discomfort letter'.

The legal effect of comfort letters has been considered in a number of cases, most notably in Joined Cases 253/78, 1–3, 37 & 99/79 *Perfumes* [1980] ECR 2327. In the view of the **Court of Justice**, such letters do not prevent national courts coming to a different view, on the basis of the information before them, as to the applicability of Article 85(1), although the Court has directed the national courts at least to have regard to such a letter before coming to any decision.

The question has also been raised whether a comfort letter can have any binding effect on the Commission. In Case 31/80 *L'Oréal v De Nieuwe AMCK* [1980] ECR 3775 the view was expressed that ' . . . having regard to the principle that legitimate expectation must be upheld, the Commission may depart from the judgment arrived at by its officers only if the factual circumstances change or its finding was reached on the basis of incorrect information'.

The revised Form A/B places additional weight on these comfort letters. Where previously the parties were asked to state whether a comfort letter would be acceptable, the new form restates Commission policy that cases 'will normally be dealt with by means of comfort letter'.

*Commission's powers of investigation*  Under Article 11 of the Regulation the Commission has wide powers to compel undertakings and associations of undertakings to provide 'all necessary information'. The Commission must first make a formal request to the undertaking, sending a copy to the competent authority of the relevant Member State. In addition to those undertakings whose conduct is under investigation, the Commission may address such requests to undertakings who are not themselves suspected of infringement. The Commission may therefore use Article 11 to make inquiries of competitors or customers of undertakings suspected of infringing Article 85 or 86. The appropriate representatives of the undertaking in receipt of such a request are under an obligation to furnish the information requested. If the information is not supplied within the time-limit fixed by the Commission, the Commission may then take a formal decision under Article 11(5) requiring the information to be provided. If the undertaking further defaults in the supply of information, then the Commission may by decision impose penalties.

As to whether the information is 'necessary', the Commission appears to have substantial discretion. In Case 374/87 *Orkem v Commission* [1989] ECR 3238 the Court of Justice held that it is for the Commission to decide whether particular information is necessary to define the scope of the infringement or to determine its duration or to identify the undertakings concerned. There must be some connection or relationship between the information requested and the infringement being investigated.

Under Article 12 of the Regulation the Commission has the power to conduct a general inquiry into any economic sector in which it has cause to believe competition is being restricted or distorted within the common market. Thus far, this power has been little used by the Commission.

Article 14 of the Regulation empowers the Commission in carrying out its duties to undertake all necessary investigations into undertakings and associations of undertakings. These investigations may be carried out either under an authorisation from the Commission or under a formal decision, either with or without prior notice to the undertakings involved. Sometimes the Commission officials will arrive at the undertaking's premises without warning (so-called 'dawn raids'). Officials of the competition authorities of the Member State concerned may be called upon to assist the Commission officials in the investigation. Under Article 13 of the Regulation the Commission may require the competent authorities of the Member State to undertake an investigation on the Commission's behalf.

In the case of an investigation under authorisation, the officials of the Commission are required to produce the form of authorisation or 'mandate', which must indicate the subject matter and purpose of the investigation. The undertaking is entitled to refuse to submit to this kind of investigation, although in that event the Commission is likely to pursue an investigation by decision.

A decision to investigate can only be made by the Commission following consultation with the competent authorities in the Member State concerned. Once a decision has been taken, the Commission can take steps to compel submission to the investigation, either with the assistance of the courts in the Member State concerned or by the imposition of periodic penalty payments.

The Commission's investigatory powers cannot be used simply to conduct 'fishing expeditions'. The subject of the investigation will be described in the authorisation or decision and it is for the Commission official to determine what documents are relevant to be examined. Article 14(1) specifies that Commission officials are empowered to examine books and other business records (and to take copies of or extracts therefrom), to ask for oral explanations on the spot and to enter any premises, land or means of transportation.

*Merger Regulation* Council Regulation (EEC) 4064/89 (see the consolidated text OJ L257 21.9.90 p 14) ('the Merger Regulation') confers on the Commission exclusive jurisdiction over concentrations which have a 'Community dimension'.

The concept of the 'concentration' is widely defined, but will include mergers or acquisitions, certain joint ventures, and other transactions involving an undertaking jointly controlled by two or more others.

The size of the parties' worldwide and Community-wide turnovers determines whether a concentration has a 'Community dimension'.

Concentrations with a Community dimension must be notified to the Commission and certain waiting periods must be observed before they can be put into effect. Notification is in Form CO, which underwent revision in 1994 and is now set out in Commission Regulation 3384/94.

Concentrations with a Community dimension must be appraised for their compatibility or otherwise with the common market. Under Article 2 of the Merger Regulation this will turn on whether or not the concentration creates or strengthens a dominant position as a result of which effective competition will be significantly impeded in the common market or in a substantial part of it. A Merger Task Force was set up within DG IV with responsibility for the examination of notifications and the preparation of decisions under the Merger Regulation.

GARTH LINDRUP

*Recommended reading*
Brown 'Notification of Agreements to the EC Commission: whether to submit to a flawed system' (1992) 17 ELRev 323.
Kerse *EC Antitrust Procedure* (3rd edn, 1994) Sweet & Maxwell.

**COMPLAINTS TO THE COMMISSION CONCERNING INFRINGEMENTS OF EC COMPETITION LAW** According to Council Regulation (EEC) 17/62 (OJ Sp Ed 1959-62 p 87) Article 3(2)(b), natural or legal persons who claim a 'legitimate interest' may complain to the **Commission** of an alleged infringement of Article 85 or 86 EC (see **concerted practice** and **monopolies**). 'Form C' is available for persons wishing to lodge a formal complaint, although a simple letter is sufficient, provided it is signed, and includes a name and address.

The Commission is obliged to consider the complaint (Case 210/81 *Demo-Studio Schmidt* [1983] ECR 3045), and failure to do so may be the subject of Article 175 EC proceedings (**action for failure to act**) (Case T-28/90 *Asia Motor France* [1992] ECR II-2285). However, the Commission is not obliged to conduct an investigation on the strength of the complaint, but need only give reasons for not pursuing it (Case 125/78 *GEMA* [1979] ECR 3173; Case T-24/90 *Automec II* [1992] ECR II-2223). Legitimate reasons may include the Commission's priorities in **competition policy**, and in particular the 'Community interest' (*Automec II*, paras 81, 84–86; Commission Notice (OJ C39 13.2.93 p 6, paras 13–16)). The complainant is entitled to an 'Article 6 letter' (Council Regulation (EEC) 99/63 (OJ Sp Ed 1953–4 p 47), Article 6) informing the complainant of the Commission's reasons, and giving time for a response. Although the Article 6 letter is a definition of position for the purposes of Article 175(2) EC (*GEMA*; *Asia Motor*), the letter, as a provisional position reached by the Commission in the course of an ongoing procedure, is not a decision of the Commission reviewable in accordance with Article 173 EC (**action of annulment**) (Case T-64/89 *Automec I* [1990] ECR II-367). Although the **Court of Justice** has not yet ruled on this matter, it is likely that the complainant is entitled to a final, reviewable decision on the matter of its complaint (implied by *Automec II*, para 47; see also Case 26/76 *Metro I* [1977] ECR 1875 and *Demo-Schmidt Studio*, and the principle of reviewability of acts of the Commission where the person seeking review is **directly and individually concerned**). In fact, it is Commission practice to give a definitive decision on rejection or acceptance of the complaint; the complainant has **locus standi** to seek review of that decision under Article 173 EC (*Metro I*).

TAMARA K HERVEY

*Recommended reading*
Shaw 'Competition complainants: a comprehensive system of remedies?' (1993) 18 ELRev 427–441.
Vesterdorf 'Complaints concerning Infringements of Competition Law within the context of European Community Law' (1994) 31 CMLRev 77–104.

**CONCERTED PRACTICE** A form of concerted behaviour between undertakings falling short of an agreement that is prohibited, subject to the possibility of exemption, by Article 85 EC where it prevents, restricts or distorts competition and is capable of affecting trade between Member States. A concerted practice has been defined by the **Court of Justice** as a form of co-ordination between undertakings which, without having reached the stage of an agreement properly so called, knowingly substitutes practical co-operation between them for the risks of competition. It may arise out of co-ordination that is apparent from market behaviour; although parallel behaviour is not the same thing as concerted behaviour, it may be inferred that undertakings have acted in concert where their behaviour differs from that to be expected in competitive conditions (see Case 48/69 *ICI v Commission (Dyestuffs)* [1972] ECR 619, paras 64–68). The Court has added (see Cases 40–48, 50, 54–56, 111, 113–114/73 *Suiker Unie v Commission (Sugar)* [1975] ECR 1663, paras 172–174) that the criteria of co-ordination and co-operation required for a concerted practice to exist do not require an actual plan; they must be understood in the light of the concept inherent in the competition provisions of the EC Treaty, namely that each trader must determine independently the policy that he intends to adopt on the common market and the conditions that he intends to offer to his customers. This requirement of independence does not deprive traders of the right to adapt themselves intelligently to the existing or anticipated conduct of their competitors, but it does strictly preclude any direct or indirect contact between them, the object or effect of which is to create conditions of competition that do not correspond to the normal conditions of the market in question.

It is a feature of most of the reported cases that the concept of a concerted practice has been considered from an 'external' standpoint, ie the observation of conduct on the market that is explicable only by the conclusion that undertakings have acted in concert; judgments such as that in Cases 89, 104, 114, 115, 117, 125–129/85 *Ahlström v Commission (Wood Pulp)* [1993] ECR I-1307 have emphasised that that inference cannot properly be drawn unless it is the *only* plausible explanation of the observed behaviour. As a result, discussion of the concept in the cases has tended – unlike, for example, discussion of the concept of an 'arrangement' for the purposes of the Restrictive Trade Practices Act 1976 – to focus more upon the observed behaviour on the market, for the purpose of examining whether it must have been concerted, than upon the precise mechanism by which the concertation has been brought about. Evidence of the contacts between the parties (if available) is, however, taken into account; for an example of an inquiry focusing on the nature of such contacts (see Case T-1/89 *Rhône-Poulenc v Commission* [1991] ECR II-867 and related cases).

The concept of a concerted practice raises issues of particular interest. It is clear that a concerted practice can be either horizontal or vertical, though the circumstances will be very different in the two situations; vertical concerted practices typically arise out of threats by a supplier acquiesced in by customers (as to which see below). For purposes of analysis, it is necessary to distinguish a concerted practice both from an agreement properly so called and, more importantly in practice, from forms of parallel behaviour not falling within Article 85 EC.

The distinction between an agreement and a concerted practice is of little practical relevance (both falling equally within Article 85 EC) and has received little attention in the cases, the Commission being content on occasions to describe observed behaviour as the result of 'at least a concerted practice'; some cases have been dealt with as cases of concerted practices when, had the full evidence been available, it might well have established an agreement. In *Rhône-Poulenc* the **Court of First Instance**, while stressing that the concepts are distinct, held that the Commission was entitled to describe a sustained process of collusion, some of which amounted to an agreement and some to a concerted practice, as 'an agreement and a concerted practice' without separately classifying the elements of each. It is submitted that the distinction lies in the presence or absence of a promise or mutual promises (however communicated and whether or not intended to create legal relations) as to future conduct. In *Sugar* the Court rejected a submission that a concerted practice presupposes a plan, and the **Advocate General** in *Wood Pulp* (at 1483–1484) referred to this as illuminating the difference between the two concepts; however, it is not clear that the term 'plan' means more than is inherent in an exchange of promises.

The more difficult and important question is what elements, falling short of a promise or mutual promises, are either necessary or, in combination, sufficient to give rise to a concerted practice. It appears now to be established, as a result of the *Wood Pulp* decision, that a series of public announcements will not in itself do so; in its judgment in that case the Court described a system of quarterly price announcements to the market as 'market behaviour which does not lessen each undertaking's uncertainty as to the future attitude of its competitors' and held that it did not amount in itself to a concerted practice. The Court appears thereby to have rejected the thesis that the use, without more, of public announcements in order to influence the conduct of competitors ('price signalling') can constitute prohibited behaviour under Article 85 EC; it seems that a concerted practice must involve private communications going beyond what the communicator discloses to the world at large.

Such reciprocal communication of parties' intentions thus amounts to a concerted practice where their market behaviour will foreseeably be affected, even though the communications fall short of *promises* to behave in the manner indicated. A comparison may be drawn with English decisions on the meaning of the term 'agreement' in the Restrictive Trade Practices Act 1976, a term which is statutorily defined as 'an agreement *or arrangement*'. It has been held that the concept of an arrangement includes a situation in which parties communicate with one another so as to give rise to mutual expectations that each will act in a certain way and to create a sense of mutual obligation so to behave.

It is less clear to what extent a concerted practice must involve *reciprocal* communications. The Advocate General in *Wood Pulp* concluded, in the context of an alleged concerted practice between producers, that it must; but that view may be too narrow. Earlier decisions have recognised at least one form of concerted practice (action in response to a 'complaint') that does not necessarily involve reciprocal communications. It is submitted that, as a matter of principle, a communication of intention can give rise to a concerted practice even in the absence of a reciprocal communication; one English judge, while emphasising the requirement of mutuality in an arrangement within the meaning of the 1976 Act, considered that it was sufficient that one party communicated his intentions to another, with the aim of influencing the behaviour of the other if the other knew that this was the aim and his behaviour was in fact influenced (see *British Basic Slag* [1963] 1 WLR 727, per Diplock LJ). Though that view has been criticised as overlooking the necessity for there to be a sense of mutual obligation in order for there to be an arrangement under the Act, it is submitted that the situation which it describes probably would be held to amount to a concerted practice within the meaning of Article 85 EC.

That conclusion is supported by decisions of the ECJ to the effect that a concerted practice is established where one party alters his behaviour in response to a 'complaint' from another (see eg *Sugar*, paras 279-283 and Case 86/82 *Hasselblad v Commission* [1984] ECR 883, paras 24–29). It was not a necessary element in the concerted practices there in issue that the addressee should have intimated his preparedness to comply; it was sufficient that he did comply. It is hard to see why a greater measure of reciprocity should be required in a case where the communication takes the form of a statement of the future intentions of the communicator rather than a complaint about the conduct of the addressee. While it is likely that an element of reciprocity will arise from repeated communications (whether 'complaints' or statements of intention) since the addressee's observed behaviour will signal that he is likely to react to such communications, it is submitted that that additional element is not essential.

Another situation that can give rise to a concerted practice is that of communications of *information* as to existing or past fact (such as prices, terms of supply or sales volumes). Both forms of supply of information have been condemned in Commission decisions. The exchange of information can be the subject of an agreement properly so called, the mere agreement to exchange the information being sufficient to fall within Article 85(1) EC. But it seems that the communication of such information can also give rise to a concerted practice either where a pattern of reciprocal communication develops or where information is communicated by one party to another with the intention and effect of influencing the market behaviour of the addressee. It is submitted that the crucial consideration in distinguishing concerted practices of this sort from lawful behaviour is the character of the information that is communicated – in particular, whether it is information that is or (perhaps) will shortly be publicly available – and the circumstances in which it is communicated. The private communication of information not easily available by observation of the market is likely to be regarded as amounting to a concerted practice.

JEREMY LEVER QC
NICHOLAS PAINES

*Recommended reading*
Bellamy & Child *Common Market Law of Competition* (4th edn, 1993) Sweet & Maxwell.
Hawk *United States, Common Market and International Antitrust: A Comparative Guide* (2nd edn, 1987) Prentice Hall.

**CONSTITUTIONAL REFORM** As the European Community has developed federalist characteristics, it has become more constitutional (see **federalism**). The goal of the original Treaty of Rome of 'ever closer union among the peoples of Europe' implied the continual political integration of the Member States according to the rule of law. Despite various setbacks, notably during the terms of President Charles de Gaulle of France (1958–69) and Prime Minister Margaret Thatcher of Britain (1979–90), the integration of Western Europe has continued along constitutional lines.

The corpus of EC law based on the terms of the various Treaties is now broad in its application and deep in its effect. No domestic constitution of any Member State has remained unaffected by **accession** to the Community. The character and procedure of most representative institutions, both governmental and non-governmental, have had to adapt to cater for the new European dimension. Ideally, within a federal system, each level of government should be as fit and capable as the next: this means that every revision of the Treaty should require a fresh process of institutional reform at home. This occurred most obviously in Denmark, France and Ireland after the **Treaty on European Union**, where referenda were needed to sanction the new phase of European integration, and in Germany, where formal constitutional amendments were made to allow for 'European Union'. The process of constitutional reform happens least obviously in Britain, where governments have been as opposed to the devolution of powers within the United Kingdom as they are to the evolution of powers to the EC.

Constitutional reform of the Union has always been subject to the unanimity – in other words, **amendment of the Treaties** can only be made by their ratification in all Member States, according to domestic constitutional requirements, of Treaties negotiated and signed by intergovernmental agreement. The **institutions** of the Community are almost wholly excluded from the constituent process. There must be doubt, especially in a Union which seems set for further **enlargement**, whether this system can last.

Circumstances will not allow the **Intergovernmental Conference** convened in 1996 to complete the constitutional settlement of the European Union, but it may revise the constituent process (Article N) in a number of ways so that a successor conference could achieve more substantial constitutional reform. First, the **European Commission** and **Parliament** could be allowed to play a full part in constitutional negotiations. Second, Treaty amendment might be permitted by a super-qualified majority vote of states (perhaps representing a large majority of the Union's population). Third, the new constitution could come into force once ratified by, say, three-quarters of the Member States. Fourth, the ratification process should certainly include a vote of assent by an absolute majority of the European Parliament and, possibly, by an EU-wide referendum. Fifth, the right of voluntary secession from the Union may have to be built into the Treaty.

A good constitution for the European Union would let people know how they are governed, by whom and from where. There have been several proposals – notably the European Parliament's Draft Treaty on European Union, drawn up by the Italian federalist Altiero Spinelli in 1984. It would contain a Bill of Rights based on the **European Convention on Human Rights and Fundamental Freedoms** in order to enhance **citizenship** and entrench **subsidiarity**. Its other purposes might be to keep the peace, to ensure economic and social **cohesion** and to deepen parliamentary democracy.

ANDREW DUFF

*Recommended reading*
Duff, Pinder & Pryce (eds) *Maastricht and Beyond: building the European Union* (1994) Routledge, for the Federal Trust.
Duff *Reforming the European Union* (1997) Federal Trust, London.


**CONSTITUTIONALISATION** The European Union and its corepiece, the European Community, originate in international Treaties between the Member States, negotiated in diplomatic conferences of an intergovernmental nature (see **Intergovernmental Conferences**). Yet Community law has its own distinctive elements which make it transcend traditional mutual obligations under international Treaties concluded by sovereign states. In the framework of the progressive strengthening of the economic, political and social links between the EU countries, these elements have been more and more developed, gradually forming a system of fundamental legal principles which are very similar to constitutional principles of states. The main agent of this process of the 'constitutionalisation' of the Community legal order has been the **Court of Justice** with its interpretation of the Treaties. Yet the development of the role of the **European Parliament** and recent Treaty amendments have also brought further progress in constitutionalisation. The Court established the basis of this process, by formally affirming that the Community constitutes a 'new legal order' for the benefit of which the Member States have 'limited their sovereign rights', and by establishing the **direct effect** of Community law, ie the possibility for individuals of invoking Community law before a national court in order to safeguard their rights under the Treaties (Case 26/62 *Van Gend en Loos* [1963] ECR 1). This was followed by the establishment by the Court of the **supremacy** of Community law, ie the prevailing of Community law in the event of conflict with national law (Case 6/64 *Costa v ENEL* [1964] ECR 585), by the Court's identification of an unwritten catalogue of fundamental **human rights** in the Treaty (Case 29/69 *Stauder v Ulm* [1969] ECR 419, Case 4/73 *Nold v Commission* [1974] ECR 491) and by the gradual creation of a number of **general principles of Community law** within the Community legal order, such as **equality, legal certainty** and **proportionality.** The Court also ruled that (unlike under classic international law) Member States can amend the Treaty only according to the procedure of Article 236 EC (now Article N TEU), thereby affirming the existence of binding internal constitutional rules of the Community (Case 43/75 *Defrenne v Sabena* [1976] ECR 455). The combination of all these distinctive characteristics led the Court in December 1991 to declare that the EC Treaty constitutes the 'constitutional charter of a Community based on law' (Opinion 1/91

(EEA Agreement) [1991] ECR I-6079). The increasing role of the European Parliament, fostered, in particular, by its powers in the EC **budgetary procedure** and its direct election, can be regarded as well as a major feature of the constitutionalisation process. The Union Treaty has introduced two further constitutional elements: the principle of **subsidiarity** (Article 3b EC) as a fundamental principle governing the division of powers between the Community and the Member States and the **citizenship** of the Union (Article 8 EC), which establishes for the first time a direct constitutional relationship between the Union/Community and its citizens.

The process of constitutionalisation does not mean, however, that in the end there will be a real constitution of the European Union. Essential elements of a constitution such as, for example, a formal constitutional document approved by the peoples of Europe or the European Parliament and a comprehensive bill of rights are still lacking, and there are also a number of major obstacles, such as the fact that the constituent power is still exercised by the Member States, who remain the ultimate holders of this power, and the absence of a European people as such (see **constitutional reform**). The process is also hampered by the complexity of the present structure of the Treaties with their three 'Pillars' and 920 Articles, which have been amended again and again without having ever been rationalised. Opinions on further constitutionalisation remain deeply divided, not only on the desirability of any further progress, but also on the final aim of further progress. Possible models range from an intergovernmental model preserving Member States' sovereignty over a co-operative model of federalism which would aim at a balance between a European level of government legitimised through democratic participation of European citizens and the legitimacy of Member States' governments, to a fully fledged federal constitution similar to those of Switzerland or Germany with some sort of Union government. Although the 1996 Intergovernmental Conference on the revision of the Union Treaty did not receive a mandate to elaborate a constitution of the European Union, it offers a chance for defining more clearly the constitutional identity of the Union which is an essential condition for public acceptance of the whole political and legal system.

JÖRG MONAR

*Recommended reading*
Curtin 'The Constitutional Structure of The Union: A Europe of Bits and Pieces' (1993) 30 CMLRev 17.
Mancini 'The Making of a Constitution for Europe' (1989) 26 CMLRev 595.

**CONSULTATION PROCEDURE** See **decision making**.

**CONSUMER POLICY** Protection of the economic interests and health and safety concerns of consumers was not envisaged by the founders of the Rome Treaty as a specific competence or responsibility of the Community. The absence of a specific Treaty provision, however, has not prevented the Community from adopting measures protecting consumer interests. First, the need to act in this field has resulted from Articles 30 and 36 EC on the **free movement of goods** and the Court's case law on these Articles. Whereas Article 30 EC prohibits Member States from imposing quantitative restrictions on imports or measures of equivalent effect, Article 36 EC justifies such restrictive measures on grounds of, inter alia, the protection of health and life of persons. Under the 'rule of reason' in the celebrated *Cassis de Dijon* case (Case 120/78 [1979] ECR 649), the Court accepted consumer protection as an additional exception to Article 30 EC. Because many national measures fell within these exceptions, the Community was forced to institute a wide range of harmonising measures to eliminate resulting barriers to the attainment of the Internal Market. These measures vary from misleading advertising, consumer credit, package travel, timesharing and unfair contract terms to product liability and product safety. Further, in conformity with the Court's agility in detecting protectionist measures, it has on occasion directed that consumer interests can be sufficiently protected by means of product labelling (eg Case 178/84 *German Beer* [1987] ECR 1227). This has led to the adoption of various Community Directives on labelling criteria for diverse products. In addition, more Community involvement in consumer protection has appeared necessary where the principle of mutual recognition has demonstrated drawbacks as a regulatory instrument (see Case 188/84 *Commission v France* [1986] ECR 419).

Second, the 1970s saw the rise of national consumer movements, which did not leave Community policy unaffected. Having received the political green light by the Paris Summit of 1972, the Community officially tabled its first consumer protection policy programme in 1975. Subsequently, the Community has developed an active policy on consumer protection, the growing importance of which (see Case C-362/88 *GB-INNO-BM* [1990] ECR I-667) recently led to the creation of a separate Commission Directorate General on Consumer Affairs. Consumer protection measures by the Community have gradually evolved on the dual basis of Internal Market policy and consumer protection policy, whilst they also touch upon the Community's competition, industrial and agricultural policy.

Over the years, the pervasiveness of the Community action relating to the protection of the health and safety and the economic interests of consumers has raised ardent debate as to the Community's competence in this area. With the introduction of Article 100A EC, which imposes qualified majority voting, the Single European Act recognised the necessity of basing proposals concerning health and safety, environmental and consumer protection on a high level of protection (para 3). The frequent resort to this Article, depriving the Member States of their right of veto under unanimity voting required by Articles 100 and 235 EC, reignited the competence issue (see Case C-359/92 *Germany v Council* [1994] ECR I-3681). The Treaty on European Union finally included consumer protection among the activities of the Community (Article 3(s) EC), and introduced a specific provision on consumer policy, Article 129A EC. This Article confirms Community competence on consumer protection through Article 100A EC measures in the Internal Market context, and empowers the Community to support and supplement national consumer protection policies, thereby giving expression to the subsidiarity principle.

ELLEN VOS

*Recommended reading*
Askham & Stoneham *EC Consumer Safety* (1994) Butterworths.
Reich & Woodroffe (eds) *European Consumer Policy after Maastricht* (1994) Kluwer.

**CONSULTATION PROCEDURE** See **decision making**.

**CONTRACTUAL LIABILITY OF THE COMMUNITY** Article 215(1) EC provides that 'The contractual liability of the Community shall be governed by the law applicable to the contract in question'. The applicable law will be determined by the proper law of the contract.

Disputes arising under contracts to which the Community is a party will fall within the jurisdiction of the relevant national court. The national court's jurisdiction is exclusive. This must be so because in the absence of a Treaty Article conferring jurisdiction over such disputes (as exists as regards the non-contractual liability of the Community (Article 178 EC)), the **Court of Justice** has no inherent or general **jurisdiction** to hear such cases.

The Court of Justice may hear disputes regarding the contractual liability of the Community if an arbitration clause has been included in the contract expressly conferring such jurisdiction (Article 181 EC). Article 181 provides that jurisdiction may be conferred upon the Court of Justice irrespective of whether the contract is governed by public or private law. Similarly, Article 35(4) of the Statute of the **European System of Central Banks** and the **European Central Bank** and Article 19(4) of the Statute of the European Monetary Institute provide for the jurisdiction of the Court of Justice pursuant to arbitration clauses included in the contracts entered into by these bodies.

The Court of Justice is required to decide cases brought under Article 181 EC according to the relevant national law of the contract. Whilst the number of cases brought by this procedure is small, it is

Contractual liability of the Community

noteworthy that the Court of Justice has, since it has been possible, allocated every Article 181 case to a chamber of three judges.

A further form of contractual dispute for which the Court of Justice has jurisdiction is staff cases. Article 179 EC provides that any dispute between the Community and its servants may be brought before the Court of Justice, or, more accurately, before the **Court of First Instance**, within the limits and under the conditions laid down in the Staff Regulations or the Conditions of Employment.

WILLIAM ROBINSON

*Recommended reading*
Brown & Kennedy *The Court of Justice of the European Communities* (4th edn, 1994) Sweet & Maxwell.
Wyatt & Dashwood *European Community Law* (3rd edn, 1993) Sweet & Maxwell.

**CO-OPERATION IN THE FIELDS OF JUSTICE AND HOME AFFAIRS** Co-operation in the Fields of Justice and Home Affairs (CJHA) constitutes the so-called 'Third Pillar' of the European Union, as created by the 1992 Treaty on European Union (TEU). The CJHA was agreed by all Member States of the Union, and placed next to the three European Communities and the **Common Foreign and Security Policy (CFSP)**. The CJHA shares the single institutional framework of the Union (Article C (1) TEU) with the other two Pillars. However, from a legal point of view, the CJHA forms a special type of co-operation on an intergovernmental level.

In contrast to the European Communities and the European Political Co-operation which preceded the CFSP, a coherent and institutionalised form of co-operation dealing with justice and home affairs was lacking prior to the coming into force of the TEU. Previously, only some scattered co-operation took place outside the institutional structure of the European Communities on a minor scale in the framework of working groups and international Treaties, although problems arising in the context of the **Internal Market** in particular made cross-border co-operation inevitable in order to ensure the successful implementation of the goals set out in the Treaty of Rome. Intergovernmental co-operation between all or only some of the Member States had always been confined to individual problems. Cases in point are the TREVI group and the Rhodes group, the **Brussels Convention** on Jurisdiction and the Enforcement of Judgments in Civil and Commercial Matters, and the Treaties of **Schengen** and Dublin.

The basic structure of the CJHA is laid out in Articles K–K.9 TEU. The provisions set up an institutionalised and comprehensive form and forum of co-operation between the Member States. Apart from laying down procedures, they also list the subject matters to which the new procedures may be applied. In Article K.1 TEU the following, partially overlapping, 'matters of common interest' are identified:

**asylum** policy; rules governing the crossing by persons of the external borders of the Member States and the exercise of controls thereon; immigration policy and policy regarding nationals of third countries; combating drug addiction; combating fraud on an international scale; judicial co-operation in civil matters; judicial co-operation in criminal matters; customs co-operation; police co-operation for the purposes of preventing and combating terrorism, unlawful drug trafficking and other serious forms of international crime, including if necessary certain aspects of customs co-operation, in connection with the organisation of a Union-wide system for exchanging information within a European Police Office (Europol). According to Article K.1 TEU, these areas shall be regarded by the Member States as matters of common interest for the purposes of achieving the objectives of the Union, in particular the free movement of persons, and without prejudice to the powers of the European Community.

The legal and political concept of CJHA continues to follow essentially the pattern of intergovernmental co-operation, rather than that of supranationalism, although the Union's single institutional framework is used to translate the goals of the CJHA into action. For the time being, the responsibility in these areas rests with the Member States. This fundamental distribution of powers is reflected in the fact that in principle all decisions of the Council have to be taken unanimously, notwithstanding some exceptions laid down in the TEU (Article K.4(3)). Moreover, the roles of those institutions that feature strong supranational characteristics are narrowly confined: both the **European Commission** and the **European Parliament** are limited to rights of participation lacking any binding legal force (Articles K.4(2); K.6 TEU). However, the influence of the Commission is slightly enhanced by a right to initiative (Article K.3(2) TEU) with regard to six of the mentioned areas, as well as by the participation of the President of the Commission in the **European Council**. The current lack of any mandatory jurisdiction of the **Court of Justice** within the ambit of the Third Pillar is yet another feature mirroring the absence of supranationalism in the CJHA. It remains to be seen whether the Member States are willing to submit their action in this field to an authoritative interpretation and to an effective enforcement of the rule of law.

Consequently, when acting under the CJHA heading, the **Council** is barred from using the well-established forms of **legislative acts** laid down in the EC Treaty. Instead, for the Third Pillar a new category of actions was introduced, the concept and precise meaning of which is still awaiting clarification. According to Article K.3(2) TEU, the Council may adopt joint positions, promote any co-operation contributing to the pursuit of the objectives of the Union, adopt joint action and the corresponding implementing measures, draw up Conventions and recommend them to the Member States for adoption.

Matters falling under the Third Pillar and those falling into the competence of the EC *may overlap* to some extent, in particular when considering the requirements and the effects of establishing the Internal Market. Consequently Article K.1 TEU explicitly precludes the CJHA from having any prejudice to the powers of the EC. In addition, Article K.9 TEU expressly opens the door for the Member States to attach a stronger degree of supranationalism to six of the nine areas mentioned by Article K.1 TEU (only the judicial co-operation in criminal matters, together with customs co-operation and **police co-operation** are exempt from this option). This would include a voting system more flexible than unanimity, as well as the Court of Justice obtaining full jurisdiction to rule on these subjects. Such decisions might also have the welcome effect of streamlining the currently rather complex constitutional structure of the Union as the need for several Pillars diminishes.

PETER-CHRISTIAN MÜLLER-GRAFF

*Recommended reading*
Monar & Morgan (eds) *The Third Pillar of the European Union* (1994) European Interuniversity Press.
Müller-Graff 'The legal bases of the third Pillar and its position in the framework of the Union Treaty' (1994) 31 CMLRev 493–510.

## CO-OPERATION PROCEDURE See **decision making**.

## COREPER

COREPER (from the French acronym for the Committee of Permanent Representatives) was initially set up on an informal basis to provide continuity of the **Council**'s work and was officially recognised by Article 4 of the Merger Treaty 1965 (now in Article 151 EC and Article 121 Euratom). COREPER consists of the **Permanent Representatives** (Ambassadors) of the Member States to the European Union. It has as its main responsibility the preparation of the work of the Council and carries out tasks assigned to it by the Council, in co-operation with the Secretariat General of the Council. There are two parallel committees: COREPER I and II. The former is made up of Deputy Permanent Representatives and the latter, the Permanent Representatives themselves, who deal mainly with major political matters of an institutional nature. The chairmanship of COREPER rotates in the same way as that of the Presidency of the Council.

COREPER has no formal jurisdiction but its work is critical in decision making. Each COREPER meeting may consist of 50 or more members, including civil servants and experts. Issues are forwarded to COREPER which may create specialist or ad hoc committees or working parties staffed by national officials (there may be more than 100 at any one time) to deal with matters in detail. The issues then return to COREPER where they will be further discussed, with a Commission representative present. If there is unanimous agreement they are put in Part A of the Council agenda and will be adopted without further discussion, unless the Council objects when the matter is returned to COREPER. If there is no agreement in COREPER the matter is put in Part B of the Council agenda for discussion. COREPER has been criticised by members of the **European Parliament** as a non-democratic institution.

There is a growing tendency for sectoral committees to bypass COREPER by reporting directly to particular technical Councils (see, for example, the Special Agricultural Committee (SCA), the Monetary Committee working for ECOFIN, and the Political Committee which deals with **Common Foreign and Security Policy**). Members of these committees are appointed by their respective Ministers, and may have wider powers than the experts in the COREPER working groups.

PHILIP BASTOS MARTIN

*Recommended reading*
Hartley *The Foundations of European Community Law* (3rd edn, 1994) Oxford University Press.
Weatherill & Beaumont *EC Law* (1993) Penguin.

**COUNCIL OF EUROPE** The Council of Europe ('the Council') was founded by Treaty signed in London on 5 May 1949 in response to post-war calls for the unification of Europe. Originally comprising ten Member States, its current membership is 39, Russia being the most recent accession. It cites its aims and objectives as being 'to work for greater European Unity, to improve living conditions and develop human values, and to uphold the principles of parliamentary democracy and human rights'. The Council is best known for its work in the last of these fields.

The Council comprises two organs: the Committee of Ministers ('the Committee') and the Parliamentary Assembly ('the Assembly'). Both are served by the Secretariat. The Committee is comprised of the Foreign Ministers of each of the Member States of the Council and has two functions: to provide a forum for the discussion of political issues of European interest, and to decide what action should be taken on recommendations from the Assembly or experts, or on governmental proposals.

Committee decisions may take the form of non-binding recommendations to Member States, or the Committee may adopt international Treaties which become binding on those states which choose to ratify them.

The Assembly is comprised of representatives nominated by the national parliaments of their home states. The number of representatives per state is proportional to the state's population, and each country's delegation reflects the political strength of the various parties in the home state. The Assembly is a consultative and deliberative body with no legislative powers. Its role is to make recommendations to the Committee. The Assembly also elects the judges of the European Court of Human Rights.

The Council sees one of its chief roles as meeting social challenges which need to be addressed at a European level. To this end, its various activities have led to the adoption of the European Convention on Human Rights, the Social Charter, the Water Charter, the European Cultural Convention, Conventions on the conservation of wildlife and natural habitats, the prevention of torture and the suppression of terrorism. Most recently, the Committee has taken up work which was initiated by the Assembly on bioethics, the protection of the rights of minorities and the impact of the information superhighway on representative democracy.

However, despite this breadth of activity, the Council is best known for its human rights activities and its most famous initiative in that arena is the **European Convention for the Protection of Human Rights and Fundamental Freedoms** (ECHR). The ECHR was drawn up by the Council in 1950. As at January 1996, there were 30 states party to the Convention. Recently, the Council has made it a condition that any state seeking to become a member of the Council must undertake to become a party to the ECHR within a year of membership.

Supervision of the application of the ECHR is currently shared between the European Commission ('the Commission'), the Court of Human Rights ('the Court') and the Committee. The Commission is made up of lawyers elected by the Committee from those put forward by national delegations in the Assembly. The Court is comprised of one judge from each Member State, elected by the Assembly. Currently, both the Commission and the Court work part-time. However, the two bodies will be replaced by a single permanent court when Protocol 11, which opened for signature on 11 May 1994, has been ratified by all states party to the EHCR. At present, about half the participating states have ratified the Protocol.

In the case of an alleged breach of the ECHR by a state party, other state parties or individuals affected may, subject to exhausting local remedies, bring a complaint to the Commission. However, for individuals to be able to complain, the state allegedly in breach must have accepted the right of individual petition under Article 25 ECHR. In practice, all participating states have given such authorisation. The entry into force of Protocol 11 will abolish this requirement altogether.

Once the Commission has decided that a complaint is admissible, it draws up a report and tries to negotiate a friendly settlement. Its final, confidential, report is sent to the Committee. Both the state concerned and the Commission may send the case on to the Court. However, for the individual affected to be able to bring his or her case to the Court, the respondent state must be a party to Protocol 9 of the ECHR. About half the participating states are party to this Protocol.

If the case is not brought before the Court within three months of the Committee receiving the report of the Commission, the Committee rules on whether or not the Convention has been breached. Like the

Court, it has authority to afford a remedy, which includes an award of damages, to the victim. The Council of Europe is not a European Community **institution** and should not be confused with the **Council of the European Union**, an EC institution, or the **European Council**.

SUNDHYA PAHUJA

*Recommended reading*
Council of Europe *The Council of Europe: A Concise Guide* (1982) Strasbourg.
Council of Europe *Activities of the Council of Europe: 1994 Report* (1995) Council of Europe Publishing.

**COUNCIL OF MINISTERS** The Council of Ministers renamed itself the **Council of the European Union** following the entry into force of the **Treaty on European Union** on 1 November 1993.

**COUNCIL OF THE EUROPEAN UNION** The Council of the European Union is the principal **decision-making** body of the **European Union** (see **legislative acts**). The term 'Council of the EU' was adopted with the implementation of the **Treaty on European Union** on 1 November 1993 and replaced the term 'Council of Ministers'. The new term not only recognised the establishment of the EU but also provided a single term for ministerial meetings in all three of the so-called Pillars of joint activity set out in the TEU.

Ministerial meetings have been a feature of European integration since the **European Coal and Steel Community**. As the breadth of supranational activity grew from the 1950s, so did the number of meetings of the Council of Ministers. The 1965 Merger Treaty created one Council of Ministers, but this formal situation was somewhat misleading. In reality there were numerous Councils: each formation reflecting the subject matter under consideration. There are currently some 20 formations of the Council of the EU. The three which meet most frequently are the General Affairs Council (Foreign Ministers), the Council of Agriculture Ministers and ECOFIN (the Council of Economics and Finance Ministers).

Meetings of the Council of the EU bring together Ministers from all Member States. Each Minister is accompanied by civil servants as part of a negotiating team. The **Commission** also has a delegation at the meetings, although its influence varies according to the subject matter under discussion in line with varying Treaty provision.

The Council of the EU has a rotating Presidency: each member government is responsible for chairing meetings over a six-month period, following a pre-determined rota system. Apart from chairing all meetings – whether the **European Council**, the Council of the EU, or meetings of national diplomats and civil servants – the Presidency has some limited power to shape the EU's priorities. It also has an important role in seeking to build a consensus between member governments in order that the EU's work may be successful. The government holding the Presidency is also responsible for handling the increasingly important relationship with the **European Parliament**. The General Secretariat of the Council offers the continuity which the rotating Presidency lacks. It provides the Council with legal advice as well as servicing its meetings.

Meetings of the Council of the EU tend to have two purposes. They either ratify agreements prepared by civil servants or they seek to resolve policy differences between the member governments. In both cases the desired end-result is decision making. The Council was considered for many years to be the Community's legislature. Since the **Single European Act** and the TEU, however, this role has come to be shared with the European Parliament. As a quantitative indicator of its decision making, in 1993 the Council adopted 63 Directives and 319 Regulations in the EC Pillar. In the other **Pillars**, decisions are normally made by political declarations rather than through EC law.

Decisions are taken in the Council of Ministers by one of three means: by simple majority, by qualified majority, or by unanimity. Simple majority voting is used principally for procedural matters. Qualified majority voting (QMV) was supposed to have been introduced to a wide range of policy areas from 1966. However, a clash between the French government and the others in 1965 led to a crisis which could only be resolved by all the member governments agreeing, in January 1966, to reach decisions by consensus. The **Luxembourg Compromise**, as it was termed, created a 'veto culture' in that a member government could block agreement where its vital national interests were at stake. With the revival of integration, especially with the Single European Act, the provision for, and practice of, qualified majority voting has increased significantly. A further increase has followed changes in the TEU. QMV now applies to most areas of policy making in the EC Pillar.

Where voting is by QMV, the Member States have weighted votes to reflect their differing size. France, Germany, Italy and the United Kingdom have ten votes; Spain has eight; Belgium, Greece, The Netherlands and Portugal have five; Austria and Sweden have four; Denmark, Finland and Ireland have three; and Luxembourg has two votes. A qualified majority now necessitates 62 of the total of 87 votes.

Unanimous voting is now much more limited than before in the EC Pillar, but it still applies to Treaty reform and to enlargement of the EU. However, in the **Common Foreign and Security Policy**, and **Co-operation in the Fields of Justice and Home Affairs**, unanimity is the predominant mode of decision making.

The laborious preparatory work for meetings of the Council of the EU is undertaken by civil servants, some of whom are based in the national permanent representations to the EU in Brussels while others travel to Brussels as needed. These officials convene in a variety of committees which are ultimately responsible to the Council, the most well-known one being the Committee of Permanent Representatives (**COREPER**).

SIMON BULMER

*Recommended reading*
Kirchner *Decision-making in the European Community: the Council Presidency and European Integration* (1992) Manchester University Press.
Nugent *The Government and Politics of the European Union* (3rd edn, 1994) Macmillan, ch 5.

**COURT OF AUDITORS** The Court of Auditors was established in 1975, constituted in 1977 and elevated to the status of an **institution** of the Community in Article 4 EC, following that provision's amendment by the Treaty on European Union. It has its seat in Luxembourg. The provisions regarding the Court of Auditors are found in Articles 188a–188c EC.

The Court of Auditors consists of 15 members, each of whom must either have belonged to a national external audit body or be 'especially qualified' to be a member of the Court of Auditors. Each member is appointed for six years by the Council, acting unanimously after consulting the European Parliament. Although there is no formal requirement, one member is appointed from each Member State.

The Court of Auditors is charged with the duty of carrying out the audit, being the examination of the accounts of all revenue and expenditure of the Community and, as far as applicable, bodies set up by the Community. Accordingly, it produces annual accounts which, together with the replies of the institutions, are published in the Official Journal. In addition to the annual accounts, the Court of Auditors may produce, at the request of the institutions, special reports and opinions. Through its reports, the Court of Auditors has emphasised not only the lawfulness and regularity of revenue and expenditure, but has also embraced the delicate question of value for money, which it considered to be a necessary ancillary to 'sound financial management' referred to in Article 188c(2) EC.

The Court of Auditors may bring an action before the Court of Justice under Article 175 EC on account of its status as an institution to seek the sanction of a failure to act of the European Parliament, the Council or the Commission. Such an action is possible if an institution should refuse to produce documents for the inspection of the Court of Auditors. However, no specific reference is made to the Court of Auditors as either a plaintiff or as a potential defendant regarding actions for annulment (Article 173 EC). The Court of Auditors has not, to date, brought or defended any substantive action.

WILLIAM ROBINSON

*Recommended reading*
Harden, White & Donnelly 'The Court of Auditors and Financial Control and Accountability in the European Community' (1995) European Public Law 599.

O'Keeffe 'The Court of Auditors' in Curtin & Heukels *Institutional Dynamics of European Integration* (1994) Martinus Nijhoff.

**COURT OF FIRST INSTANCE** The Court of First Instance is the administrative tribunal of the European Community. It has the power of **judicial review** over the acts or the failure to act of the Community institutions at the request of natural or legal persons and can award damages to them.

The Court of First Instance was established by Council Decision (ECSC, EEC, Euratom) 88/591 (OJ L319 25.11.88 p 1) of 24 October 1988 based on Article 168a EC in order to maintain the effectiveness and the quality of judicial review in the Community legal order, and to enable the **Court of Justice** to concentrate on its fundamental task of ensuring uniform interpretation of Community law. The establishment of the Court of First Instance has contributed to these objectives in three ways.

First, the transfer of jurisdiction to the Court of First Instance has substantially alleviated the case load of the Court of Justice. This not only enhanced the effectiveness of judicial review, by making it possible for judgments to be delivered within a reasonable period of time, but also enabled the Court of Justice to focus on its fundamental task of ensuring the uniform interpretation of Community law within the Community legal order by way of preliminary rulings and judgments given on appeal. At first, the jurisdiction of the Court of First Instance was restricted to staff cases (Article 179 EC; Article 152 EAEC), to direct actions (Articles 173(4), 175, 178 EC) in competition cases and, within the realm of the ECSC Treaty, to direct actions (Articles 33(2), 35, 40(1),(2) ECSC) in matters concerning levies, production, prices, restrictive agreements, decisions or practices and concentrations. Gradually, its jurisdiction has been extended to include all classes of action brought by natural or legal persons against a Community institution. It is possible to extend still further the Court's jurisdiction as, on the basis of the present wording of Article 168a EC, only requests for a preliminary ruling cannot be transferred. Thus, during the years to come, certain classes of action brought by Member States or Community institutions may also be transferred to the Court of First Instance.

Second, the establishment of the Court of First Instance enhanced the quality of judicial review by creating a two-tier jurisdiction based on a right of **appeal** before the Court of Justice, on points of law only, from final decisions of the Court of First Instance.

Finally, the Court's establishment also increased the quality of judicial review in cases involving complex facts, as it opened the way to a close examination of those facts. The Court's approach to the scrutiny of the evidence presented in a case is thorough and is reflected by Article 64 of its Rules of Procedure (OJ L136 30.5.91 p 1), a provision which does not figure in the Rules of Procedure of the Court of Justice. On the basis of Article 64 the Court can order a variety of measures of organisation of the procedure, enabling it to take a more active part in the conduct of the proceedings and the assessment of the facts of the case.

The jurisdictional relationship between the Court of Justice and the Court of First Instance is further specified in Article 47 EC. The purpose of this provision is to avoid contradictions in cases with the same subject matter which, on the one hand, are brought by a Member State or a Community institution before the Court of Justice and, on the other hand, by a private party before the Court of First Instance.

The Court of First Instance consists of 15 judges. There is no nationality requirement for a judge to be appointed, but in practice there is one judge of each Member State. Judges are appointed for a renewable term of six years. They are chosen from the persons whose independence is beyond doubt and who possess the ability required for appointment to judicial office. The members of the Court elect a President for a renewable term of three years. In general, the Court sits in chambers of three or five judges. Only occasionally, where the legal difficulty, or the importance of the case, or special circumstances so justify, may the Court hear a case in plenary session. There are no **Advocates General** appointed to the Court but in some cases the judges may be called upon to perform the task of an Advocate General. A Registrar, who is responsible for the judicial and practical organisation of the Court, is appointed by the judges. The Court of First Instance, which is attached to the Court of Justice has, just as the latter, its **seat** in Luxembourg. Its judgments are published in Part II of the European Court Reports, except for those concerning staff cases, which are published in the Reports of European Community Staff Cases.

KOEN LENAERTS

*Recommended reading*
Lenaerts 'The Development of the Judicial Process in the European Community after the Establishment of the Court of First Instance' in *Collected Courses of the Academy of European Law* (1991) Martinus Nijhoff, pp 53–113.
Millet *The Court of First Instance of the European Communities* (1990) Butterworths.

**COURT OF JUSTICE** The Court of Justice is the institution created by the **ECSC, EC** and **EAEC** Treaties which is entrusted with the function of ensuring that in the interpretation and application of the Treaties the law is observed. The Court exercises its powers under the conditions and for the purposes provided for in those Treaties, any subsequent Treaties and Acts modifying or supplementing them (including the **Single European Act**) and the **Treaty on European Union**. The latter recognises the Court as part of the institutional framework serving the **European Union**. Originally, each of the ECSC, EC and EAEC Treaties created its own Court. By the Convention on Certain Institutions Common to the European Communities (1957), the Member States agreed that the jurisdiction of each Court would be exercised by a single Court of Justice. In 1988 the **Council of Ministers**, acting under the Single European Act, established the **Court of First Instance**, which was entrusted with exercising at first instance the jurisdiction of the Court of Justice in certain matters. The basic rules governing the constitution and jurisdiction of the Court are in Articles 31–45 ECSE, Articles 164–188 EC and Articles 136–160 EAEC. Important limitations are placed on the jurisdiction of the Court by Article 31 of the Single European Act and Article L of TEU. Certain international agreements, apart from the Treaties, and other instruments have conferred jurisdiction on the Court, in particular the **Brussels Convention** on Jurisdiction and the Enforcement of Judgments in Civil and Commercial Matters, the **Rome Convention** on the Law applicable to Contractual Obligations, the Agreement on the **European Economic Area**, the Agreement relating to Community Patents and Council Regulation (EEC) 40/94 (OJ L11 14.1.94 p 1) on the Community trademark. The Court's procedure is laid down in a Protocol (the Protocol on the Statute of the Court) attached to each of the ECSC, EC and EAEC Treaties and in the Rules of Procedure adopted by the Court, subject to the approval of the Council (OJ L176 4.7.91 p 7, OJ L383 29.12.92 p 117, OJ L44 28.2.95 p 61).

The Court has its seat in Luxembourg and is permanently in session (save that hearings are not usually fixed during the judicial vacations). It consists of a specified number of judges, assisted by a specified number of **Advocates General**. One Advocate General delivers an opinion in each case (save in relation to certain procedures in which all the Advocates General are consulted). The judges and Advocates General are chosen by the common accord of the governments of the Member States from persons whose independence is beyond doubt and who possess the qualifications required for appointment to the highest judicial office in their respective countries or who are jurisconsults of recognised competence. They rank equally in precedence according to their seniority in office. Their term of office is a renewable term of six years. Every three years there is a partial replacement of the judges and Advocates General but retiring members are eligible for reappointment. The number of judges and Advocates General is determined by the Member States and may be increased by the Council if the Court so requests. The number has changed over the years. In general terms, the practice of the Member States is that there should be as many judges as there are Member States; and that the larger Member States should be entitled to nominate for appointment one Advocate General each. Decisions of the Court are valid only when an uneven number of judges sits in the deliberations (subject to a quorum of nine for plenary sessions). Accordingly, the one Member

State, one judge practice causes difficulties where there is an even number of Member States. During such periods, the Member States may agree (and at different times have agreed) that one Member State should be entitled to nominate two judges or that the right to nominate a second judge shall be held by each Member State or by some of the Member States in rotation. In order to balance the entitlements of the Member States, it may be agreed that other Member States may be entitled to nominate an additional Advocate General. Additional Advocates General have also been appointed due to the requirements of the Court's workload. At the time of writing, it had been agreed that there should be 15 judges in practice, one from each Member State, and eight Advocates General (save that, until 6 October 2000, there should also be a ninth); each of Germany, France, Italy, Spain and the United Kingdom have one Advocate General, while the remaining Member States participate in a system involving the rotation between them of the remaining three Advocates General. The judges and Advocates General are immune from legal proceedings while they hold office and thereafter benefit from partial immunity in respect of acts performed by them in an official capacity. Immunity may be waived by the Court.

Every three years the judges elect one of their number as President of the Court for a renewable term of three years. The President directs the judicial business and administration of the Court and presides at hearings and deliberations. He normally hears and determines applications for interim relief. The Court sits either in plenary session or in Chambers (see further below). The Court appoints the Presidents of each Chamber (who must be a judge attached to that Chamber). They hold that office for one year. The President of a Chamber performs for that Chamber the same functions as those performed by the President of the Court for the Court as a whole. When proceedings are initiated before the Court, the President of the Court appoints one of the judges to act as Judge Rapporteur. The function of the Judge Rapporteur is to report to the Court on the progress of the case and make recommendations as to how best it ought to be dealt with (such as whether or not witnesses ought to be heard or questions put to the parties). The Judge Rapporteur is usually (but not invariably) responsible for drafting the judgment. Apart from delivering an opinion in each of the cases assigned to him or her, the Advocate General is consulted before the Court (or the President) makes certain procedural decisions relating to a case. The Advocate General does not participate in the discussions between the judges (known as the 'deliberations') leading up to the elaboration of the judgment. The judges and Advocates General are each assisted by a small personal staff or **cabinet**. The Court as a whole is assisted by its Registrar (appointed by the Court for a renewable term of six years), who is responsible, under the authority of the President of the Court, for the Court's administration, financial management and accounts, and for the Court's Registry and the acceptance, transmission and custody of documents. The Registrar is present in person or by a substitute at all hearings of the Court or a Chamber and at all meetings of the Court (with the exception of those held to consider whether a member of the Court should be deprived of office and the deliberations of the Court on matters which do not concern its own administration). The Court has its own translation and interpretation services, a library, research and documentation service, and an information office.

Apart from sitting in plenary sessions (for which the quorum is nine), the Court also sits in Chambers, which may be formed of three, five or seven judges. The quorum of Chambers of three or five judges is three; that of Chambers of seven judges is five. At the time of writing, there are four Chambers of three judges and two Chambers of five judges. In practice, having regard to the existing number of judges, two of the smaller Chambers with four judges each and the two larger Chambers have seven each. In the case of the smaller Chambers with four judges, the additional judge does not participate in the deliberations of the Chamber (because its decisions would be invalid if he or she did). The same applies to the two additional judges attached to the larger Chambers but for different reasons. The membership of the Chambers is determined at the commencement of the judicial year. Cases may be allocated to a Chamber either for the purpose of undertaking preparatory inquiries (see below) or for the purpose of adjudication. The Court is obliged to sit in plenary session when a Member State or Community institution, being a party to the proceedings, so requests. Otherwise, the Court has a discretion in the matter. Accordingly, under the Rules of Procedure, any case can be assigned to a Chamber for adjudication in so far as the difficulty or importance of the case or particular circumstances are not such as to require it to be heard in plenary session; however, a case must be heard in plenary session if so requested by a Member State, unless the case is a staff dispute between the Community and one of its servants. The parties to a case are expressly precluded from requesting the composition of the Court or a Chamber to be altered on grounds of nationality. A judge or Advocate General may not take part in any case in which he or she has previously taken part as an agent or adviser or has acted for one of the parties or on which he or she has been called upon to pronounce as a member of a court, tribunal or commission of inquiry or in any other capacity.

The proceedings which can be brought before the Court fall into two broad categories: contentious and non-contentious proceedings. The main contentious proceedings are the following: **actions for annulment** of an act having legal effect adopted by the Council, the Commission, the European Parliament, the Court of Auditors or the European Central Bank; actions for a declaration that the Council, Commission, European Parliament or the European Central Bank has, in breach of the Treaty, failed to act; actions brought by the Commission or a Member State for a declaration that a Member State has failed to fulfil a Treaty obligation (see **action for failure to fulfil an obligation**); actions for compensation for loss caused by the Community otherwise than in the context of a contractual relationship ('**non-contractual liability**'); disputes between the Community and its servants; **appeals** from decisions of the Court of First Instance. In general terms, the jurisdiction to hear and determine at first instance those classes of action (save, obviously, the last) has been transferred to the Court of First Instance in cases where the proceedings are commenced by a person other than a Member State or Community institution. In the context of most contentious proceedings commenced before the Court (including appeals), application may be made to the President of the Court for interim relief pending the outcome of the proceedings, where appropriate. The main non-contentious proceedings are the following: references made by national courts for a **preliminary ruling** concerning the interpretation of the Treaty or other provision of Community law or the validity of acts of the Community institutions (including the European Central Bank); references made by national courts for a preliminary ruling, and other requests for interpretative rulings, concerning the meaning of certain Conventions and other agreements; review of the discharge by the Community institutions of the duty of sincere co-operation owed to national courts and tribunals; and certain special procedures in which the Court is called upon to consider proposed amendments to a Treaty or the compatibility with the Treaty of a proposed agreement between the Community and a third country or international organisation.

Contentious proceedings begin with the lodgement at the Court of a written application. A written defence must be lodged within one month thereafter (a time-limit that can be extended on application by the defendant). The applicant is then given an opportunity to lodge one further written pleading (the reply). If he does not do so, the written part of the procedure ends. If he does do so, the defendant is given an opportunity to lodge a rejoinder. After the close of the written procedure, the judge appointed as judge rapporteur in the case presents a report to the Court containing recommendations as to the next steps to take in the procedure. Those steps may include the ordering of a preparatory inquiry, that is, the assembly of the evidence necessary to decide any issues of fact. The Court may order the following: the parties to appear before it in person; information and documents to be produced; witnesses to be examined; experts' reports; inspection of a place or thing. The next stage of the procedure is the oral part. Unless the Court with the consent of the parties otherwise orders, the procedure always includes an oral part. The oral part comprises the hearing of the parties, through their representatives, and the delivery of the Advocate General's opinion. After the delivery of the opinion (usually some time after the parties have been heard), it remains possible for the Court to reopen the oral procedure but normally the Court proceeds to deliberate on the case. The decision of the Court is reached by majority vote, but the judgment setting out the decision and the reasons for it is signed by all the judges taking part in the deliberations. The judgment is delivered in open court and is binding from the date of delivery. In addition to disposing of the issues in the case, the judgment determines which party (normally the losing party) shall pay the costs (the costs in question are those of the parties to the proceedings; the Court does not charge the parties for its services save, for example, in the case of copying or translation costs incurred at the instance of a party). The procedure in appeals from the Court of First Instance follows the same pattern, broadly speaking, with certain variants that reflect the fact that the proceedings are appeals (such as the possibility that the judgment on the appeal may result in the remission of the case back to the Court of First Instance for decision in cases where the Court of Justice cannot decide the matter finally itself).

In the course of the proceedings, a party (invariably the applicant) may apply to the President of the Court for interim relief if that is necessary in order to prevent the occurrence of serious and irreparable damage prior to the point at which judgment can be delivered. Interested persons may intervene in the proceedings (with some exceptions). The Court may grant legal aid to an impecunious party. The Court may dismiss the action without considering the merits if it has no jurisdiction or the case is manifestly inadmissible. The Court may also decide to consider admissibility separately from the merits of the case. If no defence is lodged, judgment can be given in default of defence, leaving the defendant with the task of applying to set judgment aside, if the defendant thinks fit. After the delivery of judgment, the Court is in principle *functus officio*, but various exceptional procedures exist by which a judgment can be varied on application by an interested third party, revised in the light of a new fact not known when judgment was delivered or interpreted on the application of a party if its meaning or scope is in doubt.

The procedures in non-contentious proceedings are much more varied. Comment will be limited to the main non-contentious procedure: references for a preliminary ruling. The proceedings start with the lodgement at the Court of the order for reference made by the referring national court. The order for reference should set out the questions referred to the Court for a ruling and an account of the facts giving rise to the making of the reference and the arguments of the parties. Those matters enable the Court to satisfy itself that it has jurisdiction over the questions referred. If it is plain on the face of the order for reference that the Court does not have jurisdiction, the order for reference can be dismissed as inadmissible immediately. Otherwise, the parties to the proceedings before the referring court, the Member States, the Commission and, if need be, the Council, are sent a copy of the order for reference and invited to submit written observations within two months. Each party invited to submit written observations is sent a copy of the other parties' observations, but there is no right to reply in writing. The procedure includes an oral part but the Court has power to dispense with it, after informing the parties and consulting the Advocate General, unless one of the parties has asked to present oral argument. As in the case of contentious proceedings, the oral part consists of the hearing of the parties and the Advocate General's opinion. The judgment is made and delivered in the same way as in contentious proceedings; and a copy is sent to the referring court. The exceptional procedures for varying, revising or interpreting a judgment delivered in contentious proceedings do not apply to judgments in references for a preliminary ruling; but the referring court may make a second reference to the Court in respect of any issue of Community law arising from the judgment on the first reference.

K P E LASOK

*Recommended reading*
Butterworths *European Court Practice* (1993).
Lasok *The European Court of Justicwi Practice and Procedure* (2nd edn, 1994) Butterworths.

**CULTURAL POLICY** Article 128 EC inserted by the **Treaty on European Union**, allows the Community to adopt 'incentive measures' (ie financial support schemes) for a number of cultural objectives. The aim of the drafters of the Treaty was to regularise the existing practice whereby the Community funded some cultural activities (architectural heritage, translations, training of artists, support for minority languages) on the basis of annual appropriations in the Community **budget** but without any explicit mandate in the Treaty.

Article 128 EC insists on the fact that the primary responsibility for cultural policy should remain, as before, with the Member States. A procedural guarantee for this division of powers is the rule that Community incentive measures must be adopted by a unanimous vote of the **Council**. Furthermore, the Community is expressly denied the power to **harmonise** national laws and regulations in the field covered by Article 128.

Yet, despite the fact that the Treaty does not allow the Community to regulate cultural matters as such, the EC **institutions** have adopted in recent years some Directives and Regulations which, although adopted within the framework of the **Internal Market** or external trade, have an important side-impact on national cultural policies. Well-known examples are the Directive 'Television without Frontiers' of 1989, and a Regulation and Directive on the trade of works of art adopted in 1992 and 1993 respectively. The fact that the economic and cultural policy spheres cannot be neatly separated is also brought out by a number of judgments of the **Court of Justice** in which national rules of cultural policy were examined as to their compatibility with the EC Treaty rules on free movement or competition.

BRUNO DE WITTE

*Recommended reading*
Loman, Mortelmans, Post & Watson *Culture and Community Law – Before and After Maastricht* (1992) Kluwer.
Niedobitek *Kultur und Europaisches Gemeinschaftsrecht* (1992) Duncker & Humblot .

**CUSTOMARY LAW** Whereas customary law plays a role in national constitutional systems and in international law (and therefore arguably in the Treaty on European Union), its role in Community law, which establishes a separate legal order, is not obvious.

It is likely that national customary law may be relevant for establishing the existence of a general principle of law. Furthermore, in Case C-286/90 *Poulsen/Diva* [1992] ECR I-619 the European **Court of Justice** has used rules of customary international law as an aid in the interpretation of a Regulation. Whether a customary rule can be used to override secondary Community law is, however, uncertain. Arguably, a rule of international *ius cogens* would override even the Community Treaties.

**Amendment of the Treaties** by the Member States through any other means than those specified in Article N TEU is highly controversial. Whereas institutional practice does not seem to be capable of amending the EC Treaty (because the institutions have enumerated tasks and procedures), there is evidence that the Court would accept a 'legislation conform' interpretation of the Treaty, in the sense that the Court, when interpreting the Treaty, seeks to avoid conflicts between that Treaty and measures taken by the institutions for their implementation (eg the interpretation of Article 48 EC as applying only to Community nationals to the exclusion of nationals of third states).

NANETTE NEUWAHL

*Recommended reading:*
Bieber *Das Verfahrensrecht von Verdassungsorganen. Ein Beitrag zur Theorie der Inner und Interorganischen Rechtsetzung in der EG, in Staatsrecht und im Völkerrecht* (1992) Nomos.
Paasivirta & Rissanen (eds) *Principles of Justice and the Law of the European Union. Proceedings of the COST A7 Seminar, Hanasaari, Helsinki, Finland October 17-19, 1994* Publications of the Helsinki University Institute of International Economic Law (1995).

**CUSTOMS UNION** Pursuant to Article XXIV(8)(a) of the General Agreement on Tariffs and Trade which applies also in the Community, a customs union is: 'the substitution of a single customs territory for two or more customs territories, so that (i) duties and other restrictive regulations of commerce . . . are eliminated with respect to substantially all the trade between the constituent territories of the union or at least with respect to substantially all the trade in products originating in such territories, and (ii) . . . substantially, the same duties and other regulations of commerce are applied by each of the members of the union to the trade of territories not included in the union.' Accordingly, a customs union has an internal aspect governing trade among members of the customs union and an external aspect governing the trade of the members of the customs union with third countries. The same is true in the Community, which has worked out these aspects in great detail so as to build a customs union without which there would be neither an **Internal Market**, nor a **Common Commercial Policy**. However, although it is far advanced, the establishment of the customs union is not complete and provisions are still adopted to further the uniform implementation in the Community of the rules relating to the functioning of the customs union.

The internal aspect of the Community's customs union is regulated by Articles 9–17 EC. The main provision is Article 9 EC which prohibits the imposition of customs duties and other duties or charges having equivalent effect in the internal trade among Member States. This prohibition not only covers products originating in the Community but extends also to products originating in third countries which were customs cleared in the Community (Article 10 EC). Thus, goods manufactured in the Community from Community and/or third country products can circulate freely within the Community without becoming subject to customs or other duties. Equally, products originating in a country outside the Community but for which customs duties have been paid in any Community Member State and for which all customs formalities have been performed can circulate freely within the Community without any additional customs or other duties being imposed.

The external aspect of the customs union is regulated by Articles 9 and 18–32 EC. Article 9 EC provides for the establishment of a so-called '**Common Customs Tariff**'. This is the instrument which specifies for each of the products identified in a special nomenclature, the customs duty rate which applies uniformly upon customs clearance in the Community. Accordingly, a product can be imported into the Community subject to the same customs duty rate and the same customs clearance formalities irrespective of the Member States in which it is customs cleared.

In the interests of uniformity and the Internal Market, the provisions for the operation of the Community's customs union have been codified into one single legal instrument which is generally referred to as the 'Customs Code' (Council Regulation (EEC) 2913/92 (OJ L302 19.10.92 p 1) as implemented by Commission Regulation (EEC) 2454/93 (OJ L253 11.10.93 p 1)). Of the provisions contained in the Customs Code, three sections most directly and significantly affect economic operators. These are the provisions regarding the tariff classification, the origin determination (see **rules on origin**) and the valuation of goods, all of which have been subject in the past to differences in implementation by the Member States.

Tariff classification determines the tariff heading of goods in the nomenclature and the customs duty rate applicable upon their customs clearance into the Community. Articles 11 et seq of the Customs Code provide that, following an application by an importer, the Member State customs authorities are compelled to issue a 'Binding Tariff Information' (ie a ruling generally referred to as a 'BTI'), identifying the tariff heading of a product. A BTI is binding in all Member States. As a result, the holder of a BTI issued by, for example, the Finnish customs authorities can present it to the customs authorities in Greece which will be compelled to recognise the tariff heading set forth in the Finnish BTI and to apply to the product the customs duty rate corresponding to that heading.

Customs valuation determines the value of the product at the Community frontier. Since most of the customs duty rates are specified ad valorem (ie as a percentage of the value of the goods to be customs cleared in the Community), the customs value rules are essential to determine the amount to which such customs duty rates must be applied. With the growing internationalisation of trade, many goods are the subject of successive sales transactions before being customs cleared in the Community. The determination of the customs value in case of these chain sales has been the subject of differences in application among the Member States. Therefore, the Community has provided that the last sale in the transaction which led to the introduction of the goods into the Community customs territory constitutes the customs value for the calculation of the amount of the customs duty.

Rules on origin are among the most controversial customs rules, since they are directly linked to the application of commercial policy measures such as the application of **anti-dumping** duties or quantitative restrictions. In addition to co-operating with the international harmonisation of the origin rules under the auspices of the World Customs Organisation, the Community currently plans to establish a framework for the issuance of origin information which will be binding throughout the Community similarly to the BTI.

PAULETTE VANDER SCHUEREN

*Recommended reading*
Kelley & Onkelinx *EEC Customs Law* (1991) ESC Publishing.
Vaulont *The Customs Union of the European Economic Community* (1986) The European Perspectives Series.

**DAMAGES** Damages may be sought through various forms of action. First, **causes of action for damages for breach of Community law** exist in national law and may include **damages against a Member State (*Francovich* liability)**. Second, as regards contractual liability,

Article 181 EC provides that the Court of Justice has jurisdiction to hear disputes regarding contracts entered into by the Community and which contain an arbitration clause expressly conferring on it such jurisdiction. Third, Article 215(2) EC provides for the **non-contractual liability of the Community**.

**DAMAGES AGAINST MEMBER STATES** In Joined Cases C-6/90 & C-9/90 *Francovich* [1991] ECR I-5357 the **Court of Justice** enunciated the **general principle** that Member States are obliged to make good loss and damage caused to individuals by breaches of Community law for which they can be held responsible. Such liability, said the Court, is inherent in the general system of the Treaty and its fundamental principles. The conditions under which that liability gives rise to a right to reparation depend on the nature of the breach of Community law giving rise to the loss and damage. In that case, which concerned loss arising from the failure by Italy to implement Council Directive (EEC) 80/987 on the protection of employees of insolvent companies (OJ L283 20.10.80 p 23), the Court held that there were three conditions: the rule of law infringed must be intended to confer rights on individuals; the content of those rights should be identifiable from the Directive; and the existence of a causal link between the breach of the state's obligation and the loss and damage suffered by the injured party.

The recognition by the Court of Justice of the principle of the liability of Member States in damages for breaches of Community law was a bold step in the judicial protection of the individual and the *effet utile* of Community law. It provides individual litigants with the ability to enforce Community law directly against a defaulting Member State. However, the formulation of the conditions of liability in *Francovich* was terse, and left many facets of liability undiscussed. Several of these lacunae have been resolved in the follow-up cases of Joined Cases C-46/93 & C-48/93 *Brasserie du Pêcheur and Factortame III* [1996] ECR I-1029, Case C-392/93 *R v HM Treasury, ex p British Telecommunications plc* [1996] ECR I-1631, Case C-5/94 *R v Minister of Agriculture, Fisheries and Food, ex p Hedley Lomas (Ireland) Ltd* [1996] ECR I-2553 and Cases C-178 & 179, 188-190/94 *Dillenkofer*, judgment of 8 October 1996.

First, as a matter of principle, the Court of Justice held in *Brasserie du Pêcheur and Factortame III* that the **non-contractual liability** of the Communities, which is found in Article 215(2) EC, and *Francovich* liability derive from the same overarching general principle of Community law. There exists a parallelism of liability between the two actions in which the conditions of liability have become intertwined.

Second, in *Brasserie du Pêcheur and Factortame III* the Court of Justice clarified the conditions of liability. It adopted a two-stage analysis of the unlawful act or omission: did the Community rule intend to confer rights on individuals; and if so, was the breach 'sufficiently serious' (*violation suffisamment caractérisée*)? By applying these criteria in the cases of *Brasserie du Pêcheur, BT, Dillenkofer* and *Hedley Lomas*, the Court has confirmed that these conditions are to apply to all breaches of Community law by a Member State, whether legislative, executive or administrative. However, in assessing whether a breach of Community law will be 'sufficiently serious', the Court of Justice recognised that there may be an element of discretion in the adoption of normative acts. Where this element of discretion exists, Member States may be liable if they have 'manifestly and gravely' disregarded the limits on the exercise of their powers or there has been a sufficiently serious breach of a superior rule of Community law for the protection of individuals. In contrast, in the case of administrative acts which do not involve normative choices, the margin of discretion is considerably reduced, if not eliminated. In such cases, the simple breach of Community law is sufficient to establish that the breach is sufficiently serious (see *Hedley Lomas*).

Third, the Court of Justice refused to consider the Member States' internal constitutional arrangements for the division of powers in the application of the principle of *Francovich* liability. The Member State must be considered as a single entity. It may be liable in damages whatever be the organ of the state whose act or omission was responsible for the breach (*Brasserie du Pêcheur and Factortame III*, para 32). This interpretation not only conforms with public international law theory, but also assures the protection of the rights of the individual. It may, nevertheless, raise difficult national law questions as to the nature and division of liability between various national authorities, particularly regarding nationalised industries and quasi-autonomous non-governmental organisations.

Fourth, the Court of Justice rejected the argument made by the German, Irish and The Netherlands governments in *Brasserie du Pêcheur and Factortame III* that *Francovich* liability only bit where the provisions breached were not directly effective. It held that the full effectiveness of Community law would be impaired if this argument was accepted. Indeed, **direct effect** constitutes only a minimum guarantee of the rights of individuals and that *Francovich* liability was a necessary corollary of the direct effect of Community provisions (paras 20 and 22). The application of *Francovich* liability to directly effective provisions of Community law significantly strengthens the protection of the individual.

Lastly, the Court of Justice has clarified to some degree the **causes of action** in national law through which litigants may seek damages against the Member State. The first aspect of this clarification concerns the factors which the national court may take into account in establishing whether a breach of Community law is 'sufficiently serious'. This test avoids the notion of 'fault', which differs in the various legal systems of the Member States. However, the Court of

Justice recognised that the notions may overlap. It therefore said, in *Brasserie du Pêcheur and Factortame III*, that national courts may take into account a basket of objective and subjective factors, such as whether the infringement was caused intentionally or involuntarily, and whether any error of law was excusable or inexcusable (para 56). This approach effectively gives the national courts a wide margin of discretion to consider a range of objective and subjective fault criteria.

The second aspect of this clarification in *Brasserie du Pêcheur and Factortame III* was to consider the causes of action in issue in the light of the well-established line of case law, according to which national procedural and substantive rules must not apply less favourably to those seeking to enforce Community rights than to those making similar national claims based on domestic law and must not be such as in practice to make it impossible or excessively difficult to obtain reparation (see Case 33/76 *Rewe* [1976] ECR 1989 and Case 45/76 *Comet* [1976] ECR 2043). The conditions imposed by the English law of misfeasance in public office and the German law requirement of a breach of a higher ranking national law did not satisfy this test (paras 72 and 73).

WILLIAM ROBINSON

*Recommended reading*
Heukels & McDonnell *The Action for Damages against the European Communities* (forthcoming) Kluwer.
Van Gerven 'Non-contractual Liability of Member States, Community Institutions and Individuals for breaches of Community Law with a view to a Common Law for Europe' (1994) Maastricht Journal for European and Comparative Law 6.

**DASSONVILLE** Case 8/74 *Procureur du Roi v Dassonville* [1974] ECR 837 is considered under the **free movement of goods**.

**DECISION MAKING** There is not one single decision-making process in the EU, but several different ways of taking decisions or **legislative acts** depending on the area of policy concerned.

The different decision-making processes are laid down in the **Treaty on European Union** and the earlier Treaties.

The Treaty on European Union established three 'Pillars': the European Community Pillar, covering mainly traditional economic policy areas, the so-called Second Pillar, dealing with the **Common Foreign and Security Policy** and the Third Pillar, dealing with **Co-operation in the Fields of Justice and Home Affairs**. Most legislative decision making takes place in the EC Pillar. It is the more supranational Pillar. The Council usually acts by majority, with exceptions in especially sensitive areas; the **European Parliament** must, as a minimum, be consulted or exercise some powers in the legislative process. Legislation is directly binding; its implementation is monitored by the **Commission** and it is justiciable before the **Court of Justice**. Decision making in the Second and Third Pillars is more intergovernmental. The Commission does not have a monopoly of initiating proposals and on some Third Pillar subjects cannot initiate proposals. Parliament is little involved; decisions are mostly taken by unanimity. Second and Third Pillar decisions are not justiciable before the Court of Justice. There is a special decision-making process for the annual **budget**, involving Parliament and Council as the two branches of the budgetary authority. Parliament can amend or reject the draft budget proposed by Council based on a preliminary draft prepared by the Commission.

In the legislative field, decisions are taken through the interinstitutional triangle, involving the EU's three political institutions: Commission, Council and Parliament. Here there are at least four main types of decision-making process. There are variants within each type. The basic differences relate to the majority by which the Council decides (qualified majority or unanimity) and the degree of involvement of the European Parliament.

The simplest and oldest (indeed initially the only method) involves simple consultation of Parliament. Here, the Commission makes a proposal, which it can amend at any time until the Council has reached a final decision and which Council can only amend unanimously. Parliament must be asked for its opinion. Though the opinion must be sought, Parliament cannot delay giving its opinion indefinitely. The content of Parliament's opinion, such as proposed amendments, is not binding on the Commission or Council. Council then reaches a decision either (as the Treaty stipulates) by qualified majority or unanimously. This procedure still applies to **Common Agricultural Policy** legislation.

Under the co-operation procedure introduced by the **Single European Act** in 1987 and applied to almost all **Internal Market** legislation, the role of Parliament was strengthened and the area of majority voting was extended considerably. The first phase is identical, except that Council adopts a common position by majority in almost all cases rather than in a final decision. Parliament can hold a second reading and vote amendments to the common position by a majority of its members (now 314/626). If those amendments are accepted by the Commission, then the Council can accept them by a qualified majority, otherwise only unanimously. Parliament can also reject the common position, in which case Council can only approve it unanimously.

The co-decision procedure introduced by the Treaty on European Union in 1993 applies to all Internal Market legislation and some other areas, such as the Research Framework Programme. Here, Parliament's powers have been further strengthened. Under co-decision, again the first phase is identical. Parliament may either move to reject the common position. If it does so, the legislation falls. Alternatively, it may vote amendments. If those are not accepted by the Council, a conciliation committee meets to try and reach a compromise between Council and Parliament. Should this fail, the Council can once again adopt its common position, possibly with some of Parliament's amendments. This then becomes law unless Parliament rejects it. Legislation under co-decision can not be adopted against Parliament. In a very few cases, such as the common electoral system, the legislative assent procedure applies. Here, the Commission makes a proposal; once it is agreed by Council it becomes operative if Parliament assents. Where the Union negotiates **international agreements** (except **accession** agreements) such as the **GATT** or **association agreements**, the Commission negotiates on behalf of the Union, on the basis of a Directive given by the Council. Accession agreements, association agreements and other important agreements also require the assent of Parliament.

JOHN FITZMAURICE

*Recommended reading*
Nugent *The Government and Politics of the European Union* (3rd edn, 1994) Macmillan.
Wallace & Wallace *Policy-Making in the European Union* (1996) Oxford University Press.


**DECISIONS** See **legislative acts**.


**DECLARATION (TO TREATIES)** A Declaration is an act usually adopted or made at the time of signing a Treaty and annexed thereto. Thus, a number of Declarations have been annexed to the EEC and **Euratom** Treaties, the Accession Treaties, the **Single European Act** and the **Treaty on European Union**. Some of these have been adopted by the Conference which negotiated the Treaty, some made by the Member States individually or jointly, and some by the Community **institutions**. The precise legal nature of these Declarations is not clear. Some lay down instructions to the institutions; some express the Member States' or the institutions' intentions, while others contain political statements or clarifications or interpretations of Treaty provisions. From the point of view of international law, they cannot be characterised as reservations as they do not meet the relevant criteria of the Vienna Convention on the Law of Treaties. From the point of view of Community law, they cannot be classified as Community acts as they have not been adopted in accordance with the Community legislative process. They are 'hybrid' measures lying between international and Community law. However, they possess binding force under neither. This is because, unlike the Annexes and Protocols which also accompany the Community Treaties, they have not been incorporated in the Treaties by express provisions and therefore do not form an integral part thereof. They are, strictly speaking, not annexed directly to the Treaties but to the Final Acts of the Conferences adopting them and, unlike the Treaties, Annexes and Protocols, are not subject to ratification which alone could endow them with binding force. Moreover, Declarations relating to the SEA and TEU are expressly excluded from the jurisdiction of the **Court of Justice** (Article 31 SEA; Article L TEU). The Court therefore has no power to interpret or apply them. They can in no way restrict, exclude or modify the legal effects of the Treaties.

AKOS G TOTH

*Recommended reading*
Schermers 'The Effect of the Date 31 December 1992' (1991) 28 CMLRev 275.
Toth 'The Legal Status of the Declarations Annexed to the Single European Act' (1986) 23 CMLRev 803.

**DEMOCRATIC DEFICIT** In democratic systems representatives are elected to parliament with powers to propose, amend, reject or adopt draft legislation which would affect their electorate.

The EC Treaty together with amending treaties, the **Single European Act** the **Treaty on European Union** and case law of the **Court of Justice** transferred certain legislative powers from Member States to the European Community without either a corresponding transfer of power to a democratically elected body, the **European Parliament** (EP) or with national parliaments retaining adequate powers of control over EC legislation.

Despite measures to extend the powers of the EP since its first election in 1979, there still remain defects in the democratic system (see **decision making**). For example, when the **Council** consults the EP, it must receive the EP's opinion before adopting the proposed legislation (Case 138/79 *Roquette Frères v EC Council* [1980] ECR 3333) but no account need be taken of its contents. Also, the co-operation procedure granted the EP limited powers in matters concerning the **Internal Market**, within certain procedural restrictions, resulting in amendments adopted by the EP being accepted by the Council, and the possibility of rejecting the proposed legislation. Furthermore, co-decision, introduced in Article 189b TEU, and available in a limited number of sectors, involves a conciliation procedure between the EP and Council. The EP may reject the proposal subject to an overall majority of the Members.

The right to propose EC legislation is reserved to the non-elected Commission. The EP has been accorded the right under Article 138b TEU to request the Commission to submit an appropriate proposal for a Community act required to implement the Treaty.

The EP cannot raise taxes, but it does have the power to amend non-obligatory expenditure and to reject the EC **budget**.

The EP, unlike many national parliaments, may give or withhold assent to certain types of agreement, including international agreements under Article 228(3) TEU.

The Council of Ministers, in whom lies the ultimate power to adopt legislation, maintains that Ministers are individually accountable to their national parliaments and are consequently subject to democratic control. The SEA, however, contains a number of provisions allowing for a qualified majority vote. It is therefore possible for a Member State government to be outvoted with ministerial accountability and democratic control by a national parliament consequently weakened. The Council usually meets in camera and there is limited access to Council documents, so official information as to the stand taken by each Member State is lacking. A practice has recently been introduced in which the results of votes in the Council's press statement are published, subject to unanimous agreement.

The Commission acquired increased powers under Article 145 SEA so that most of the EC secondary legislation is now subject to consideration only by national civil servants, following Council Decision 87/373/EEC (OJ L197 18.07.87 p 33) on **'comitology'** concerning advisory, management and regulatory committees. Recognition of lack of parliamentary scrutiny of EC secondary legislation has led to an **interinstitutional agreement** (EP, Council and Commission) to establish procedures whereby draft regulations would be subject to EP scrutiny.

Following entry into the EC, the Danish Parliament set up a committee, now the European Affairs Committee, with the objective of having control over the government's negotiating mandate. Both Houses of the United Kingdom Parliament set up scrutiny committees and, while **House of Lords Select Committee** reports have gained a high reputation and influence, they do not have direct effect on legislative proposals.

Today, all the Member States' national parliaments have established committees to scrutinise draft EC legislation more closely and to arrange closer co-operation with the EP in order to overcome the serious lacunae in democratic control of the EC legislative decision-making process.

BARONESS ELLES

*Recommended reading*
Boyce *The Democratic Deficit of the European Community Parliamentary Affairs* (1993).
Lodge 'Transparency and Democratic Legitimacy' (1994) 32 Journal of Common Market Studies 343.


**DEVELOPMENT POLICY** Community development co-operation policy can be taken to mean the whole range of instruments and measures adopted by the Community in order to promote economic and social progress in poor countries. It has been built up over time through the development of normative rules, which have generally been backed up by practical intervention by the Community, using all means at its disposal. However, it was only with the entry into force of the Treaty on European Union that Community development co-operation policy came to be formally recognised as an area of Community law-making competence. Its legal basis and framework rules are found in Articles 130u–130y EC. Article 130u lays out the objectives of the Union in the field of development. Its aim is to foster 'the sustainable economic and social development of the developing countries, and more particularly the most disadvantaged among them; the smooth and gradual integration of the developing countries into the world economy; the campaign against poverty in the developing countries'.

Prior to the TEU, several provisions of the Treaty of Rome allowed the development, de facto, of an ambitious development co-operation policy. They included Article 113 (**Common Commercial Policy**), Article 238 (competence of the Community to conclude **association agreements**), Articles 229–231 (Community relations with the United Nations and other International Organisations), and Article 235 (**implied powers**). The recognition of Community authority with respect to Community development co-operation policy was necessary to facilitate transition from de facto to de jure status.

Under Article 130u EC, Community development co-operation policy is to be *complementary to the policies pursued by the Member States.* Article 130x provides that the policies of the Community and those of the Member States shall be co-ordinated, which includes an obligation on the Member States to consult each other with respect to aid policy. Further, the Community itself, under Article 130v EC, is bound to take account of the objectives of Community development co-operation policy in implementing other Community policies that are likely to affect developing countries. Sectors of EC regulation that are likely to be subject to this duty include agricultural policy, commercial policy and environmental policy.

Community development co-operation policy can be activated in two ways. First, contractual agreements grant preferences and privileges to certain regions outside the Community. A second mechanism governs worldwide action. The regional agreements that have been struck include the **Lomè Convention,** agreements concluded with Maghreb countries (Algeria, Tunisia, Morocco) and agreements entered into with Mashrek countries (Egypt, Lebanon, Jordan, Syria and Israel). The legal basis of these accords is Article 238 EC. Worldwide action includes commercial agreements concluded with Asian and Latin American developing countries, that are based on Articles 113 and 235 EC. Worldwide action also encompasses measures taken within the framework of the Community Generalized System of Preferences (legal basis Article 113 EC), financial and technical aid to Asian and Latin American developing countries (legal basis Article 235 EC), humanitarian aid distributed in food aid, emergency aid, aid to refugees (legal basis Articles 43, 113, 114 and 228 EC). It also provides special funds for the fight against hunger in the world.

Individual arrangements entered into with regions are contractual in nature. They are characterised by their continuity, their institutional sophistication and their tendency toward supporting long-term financing arrangements. They cover a diverse range of activities (commercial, technical, financial and cultural) and are enshrined in international Treaties that are ratified by the various parliaments of the Member States. In contrast, worldwide action is characterised by its fragmentary nature and the lack of continuity in the measures taken. For example, it sometimes merely involves intervening in other fields of Community activity, such as the Generalised Preferences System or food aid policy. Worldwide action can also funnel into measures taken by the Community on a unilateral basis, such as financial and technical aid to non-associate countries, emergency aid, and co-financing of projects with NGOs.

ANNA LIXI

*Recommended reading*
Baragiola *North-South: The EC Development Policy* (1991) Club de Bruxelles.
Cosgrove & Jamar (eds) *The European Community's Development Policy: the strategies ahead* (1986) De Tempel.


**DIRECT AND INDIVIDUAL CONCERN** Direct and individual concern are two tests necessary to enable a natural or legal person to raise an **action of annulment**, in other words to seek **judicial review** before the **Court of First Instance**, of an act of a Community **institution** of which he is not the addressee (see **locus standi**). Such a person is required to show that the act in question affects his interests both directly and individually (Article 173(4) EC).

A person is affected directly by the act of an institution when that act requires and admits no further intervening act by Community or national authorities, or leaves no room for discretion, or no real likelihood of its exercise, in its application to him (Case 62/70 *Bock v Commission* [1971] ECR 897; Case 11/82 *Piraiki-Patraiki v Commission* [1985] ECR 207). He is individually affected when the act 'individualises' him in the same way as its actual addressee(s) (or putative addressee(s) in the case of a Regulation), either because of characteristics peculiar to him or because of factual circumstances which distinguish his situation, as a function of membership of a small group, the identity of which is fixed and ascertainable, from that of virtually everyone else (Case 25/62 *Plaumann v EEC Commission* [1963] ECR 95; Cases 106 & 107/63 *Toepfer v EEC Commission* [1965] ECR 405; Case 100/74 *CAM v Commission* [1975] ECR 1393; Case 11/82 *Piraiki-Patraiki* [1985] ECR 207; Case 26/86 *Deutz & Geldermann v Council* [1987] ECR 541; Case C-309/89 *Codorniu v Council* [1994] ECR I-1853).

Direct and individual concern are cumulative tests, and an action of annulment raised where either is absent is inadmissible. The latter test, recognised early on by the **Court of Justice** to be 'clearly restrictive' (Case

95

40/64 *Sgarlata v EEC Commission* [1965] ECR 215), is especially difficult to meet. However, the Court has been relatively and increasingly lenient in recognising that the interests of third parties are individually affected in three particular areas: those of **anti-dumping** legislation (Cases 239 & 275/82 *Allied Corporation v Commission* [1984] ECR 1005; Case 264/82 *Timex v Council and Commission* [1985] ECR 849; Case C-358/89 *Extramet Industrie v Council* [1992] ECR I-3813); **competition** (Case 26/76 *Metro v Commission* (No 1) [1977] ECR 1875; Case 75/84 *Metro v Commission* (No 2) [1986] ECR 3021); and **state aids** (Case 730/79 *Philip Morris v Commission* [1980] ECR 2671; Case 169/84 *COFAZ v Commission* [1986] ECR 391; Case C-188/92 *TWD Textilwerke Deggendorf v Germany* [1994] ECR I-833; Case T-435/93 *ASPEC v Commission* [1995] ECR II-1281). All three areas address aspects of competition, and in each a Community act is adopted following some form of investigation which provides for procedural guarantees. In each a complainant, a party participating or playing a significant role in the investigation, and sometimes other competitors, so long as appreciably affected by it, have sufficient interest in and so are usually individually concerned by the act in question. A producer or exporter/importer of goods subject to anti-dumping duties is similarly affected by the duties, and the recipient or intended recipient of a state aid as well as its competitors, and even a relevant trade association (Case C-313/90 *CIRFS v Commission* [1993] ECR I-1125; Case T-435/93 *ASPEC*), are individually affected by a decision to approve or prohibit an aid or not to proceed with an investigation. A natural or legal person seeking the annulment of a Community act has until recently been required to show not only direct and individual concern but also that the act was not one of general application, but this test seems now to have been relaxed (see **locus standi**).

ROBERT LANE

*Recommended reading*
Albors-Llorens *Private Parties in European Community Law: Challenging Community Measures* (1996) Clarendon Press.
Arnull 'Private Applicants and the Action for Annulment under Article 173 of the EC Treaty' (1995) 32 CMLRev 7.

**DIRECT EFFECT** According to the doctrine of 'direct effect', provisions of Community law may, in certain circumstances, confer rights on individuals which they can enforce before national courts. These rights flow directly from Community law and are entirely independent of national law. Indeed, the doctrine of direct effect is usually relied upon precisely where national rules somehow preclude enforcement of the Community law.

Although the EC Treaty makes no express provision for direct effect, the **Court of Justice** deduced from the Treaty's nature and objectives that the Community constitutes a 'new legal order', whose laws can confer rights on individuals which national courts must protect (Case 26/62 *Van Gend en Loos* [1963] ECR 1).

The importance of this doctrine cannot be underestimated. Direct effect transforms Community law from an instrument of international law, reliant upon state implementation, into a system which is as accessible to the individual as national law. Furthermore, while the Treaty provides for no system of enforcement, direct effect garners to Community law the considerable enforcement machinery at the disposal of a national judge. Individual action also complements the supervision machinery of the Treaty (see **action for failure to fulfil an obligation**), since the individual has a particular interest to ensure his rights are respected.

The essence of direct effect is that the provision at issue is capable of judicial application without any need for further legislative or executive intervention. In other words, the norm is complete or 'self-executing' and derives force directly from the Community legal order. To be directly effective the norm must be clear, precise and unconditional. Thus, its application must not be dependent upon the adoption of further implementing measures, either at national or Community level (see *Van Gend en Loos*).

In *Van Gend en Loos* Article 12 EC was held to have direct effect since it imposed a clear and unconditional prohibition and its application was not conditional upon the adoption of further measures. Conversely, Article 90(2) EC does not have direct effect (see Case 10/71 *Muller* [1971] ECR 723) since its application is conditional upon an appraisal of economic policy which is entrusted to the Commission. In other words, it is not capable of judicial application in the absence of this appraisal.

The provisions of Regulations may also produce direct effects if the norm in question satisfies the requirements of being unconditional and sufficiently clear and precise.

More problematic has been the direct effect of Directives. Unlike Regulations, they do not form part of the national legal order, since they are not 'directly applicable', and implementation at national level is therefore required (Article 189 EC). Arguably, they are conditional on this implementation. However, Directives are binding upon the Member States to whom they are addressed 'as to the result to be achieved', and this result may well be perfectly clear and precise.

Focusing on this latter element the Court has held that it would be incompatible with the binding nature of Directives to deny individuals the right to enforce them against Member States once the period for implementation has expired (see Case 148/78 *Ratti* [1979] ECR 1629). Such a denial would allow a Member State to take advantage of its own failure to implement a Directive and would undermine the *effet utile* of the Directive. The provisions of a Directive can therefore have direct effect, but, crucially, only as against the Member States bound by them (so-called 'vertical' direct effect) (see Case C-91/92 *Faccini Dori* [1994]

ECR I-3325). Directives have no direct effect as against individuals ('horizontal' direct effect), since they are never bound by them.

The conditions which apply to the direct effect of Directives are once again that the obligation imposed on the Member State be unconditional and sufficiently clear and precise. In the context of Directives, these conditions can, however, only be fulfilled where a Member State has failed to implement correctly the Directive within the time-limit set for this. Before that date the 'result' to be achieved is not binding on the Member State.

The distinction between horizontal and vertical direct effect gives rise to anomalous results. For instance, a Directive conferring rights on employees can only be enforced against state employers or against 'emanations of the state', that is to say bodies under state control or bodies with special powers conferred on them (see Case C-188/89 *Foster* [1990] ECR I-3313). Those in the private sector cannot rely on Directives directly and must use alternative remedies (see **indirect effect** and **damages against Member States**).

Several Advocates General have therefore proposed that the horizontal direct effect of Directives be recognised (Advocate General Van Gerven in Case C-271/91 *Marshall* [1993] ECR I-4367; Advocate General Jacobs in Case C-316/93 *Vaneetveld* [1994] ECR I-763; Advocate General Lenz in *Faccini Dori*). The Court has so far refused this invitation, emphasising that Directives are only binding upon the Member States.

Since Decisions are also binding on the addressee (see Article 189 EC), the reasoning which applies to Directives extends to them (Case 9/70 *Grad* [1970] ECR 825). Although not yet clear, it would seem logical that the Court likewise limits their direct effect to enforcement against the addressee(s), which can include either individuals or Member States.

Provisions of international agreements can also have direct effect provided that, regard being had to the overall nature and objective of the agreement, the provision in issue is unconditional and is clear and precise (see Case C-192/89 *Sevince* [1990] ECR I-3461). However, the nature of many international agreements does not lend itself to unconditional obligations. Such agreements are often founded on reciprocity and a flexibility of approach that is very different to the unconditional character of the Community Treaties. For these reasons such agreements are often denied direct effect (see Case 24/72 *International Fruit Company* [1972] ECR 1219, where the Court held that the **GATT** did not have direct effect).

NICOLAS LOCKHART

*Recommended reading*
Edward 'Judicial Activism – Myth or Reality? *Van Gend en Loos, Costa v. ENEL* and the *Van Duyn* family revisited' in Cambell & Voyatzi (eds) *Legal Reasoning and Judicial Interpretation of European Law, Essays in honour of Lord Mackenzie-Stuart* (1996) Trenton.
Weatherill & Beaumont *EC Law* (2nd edn, 1995) Penguin.

**DIRECT ELECTIONS** Members of the **European Parliament** are elected in elections held approximately simultaneously throughout the territory of the **European Union**. Prior to the first elections in 1979, Parliament was composed of delegates from the national parliaments. The European Parliament is the world's first transnational parliamentary assembly to be so elected, and direct elections are considered to add an element of democratic legitimacy to the Union's constitution.

Article 138(3) EC fixes direct elections in accordance with a uniform electoral procedure as a Treaty objective; this objective has been partly achieved by the 1976 Direct Elections Act (OJ L278 8.10.76 p 5), supplemented by Article 8b(2) EC and by Council Directive (EC) 93/109 (OJ L329 30.12.93 p 34). These establish the following principles:
- members are elected by direct universal suffrage for a five-year term commencing at the opening of Parliament's constituent session (new Member States are allowed a transitional derogation);
- seats are distributed amongst the Member States in accordance with a degressive proportionality rule which favours the smaller Member States;
- elections are held in each Member State over a four-day period (Thursday–Sunday), with the counting of votes commencing after polling closes in the last Member State;
- membership of Parliament is compatible with membership of a national parliament, and incompatible with membership of a government of a Member State, and membership of, or active service with, a Community institution or body;
- Union **citizens** resident abroad may vote and stand as a candidate under the same conditions as nationals of their Member State of residence, though no one may vote more than once in each election.

The power to regulate other aspects of electoral procedure, such as the voting system used, is currently reserved to the Member States. Further Community provisions on electoral procedure require the assent of an absolute majority of the European Parliament and the approval of the Council acting unanimously, and are subject to national ratification procedures.

KIERAN ST C BRADLEY

*Recommended reading*
Bradley & Feeney 'Legal Developments in the European Parliament' (1994) 13 Yearbook of European Law 383, 391-393, 395-397.
Bradley 'The European Parliament' in *Common Market Reporter* (1996) CCH.

**DIRECTIVES** See **legislative acts**.

**DISCRIMINATION** The importance of the notion of discrimination, or rather non-discrimination, is underlined by the fact that it appears in Part One of the EC Treaty, entitled 'Principles' (see also **equality**).

Article 7 EEC / Article 6 EC states that: 'Within the scope of application of this Treaty, and without prejudice to any special provisions contained therein, any discrimination on the grounds of nationality shall be prohibited.'

In the context of free movement of persons that principle has been implemented by Articles 48, 52 and 59. However, in Case C-193/94 *Skanavi* [1996] ECR I-929 the Court said that Article 6 EC applied independently only to situations governed by Community law in respect of which the Treaty lays down no specific prohibition on discrimination. As the Court observed in Case C-43/95 *Data Delecta*, judgment of 26 November 1996, Article 6 EC requires perfect equality of treatment in Member States of persons in a situation governed by Community law and nationals of the Member State in question. However, the principle of non-discrimination extends beyond nationality. As the **Court of Justice** observed in Case C-132/92 *Roberts v Birds Eye Walls* [1993] ECR I-557 Article 119 EC on **equal pay** for men and women embodies in a specific form the general principle of non-discrimination. Similarly, Article 40(3) EC excludes any discrimination between producers or consumers in the Community. On the strength of these constitutional precedents the Court has ruled that there is a **general principle** of non-discrimination in Community law (Case 1/72 *Frilli v Belgium* [1972] ECR 457, para 19; Case 152/73 *Sotgiu v Deutsche Bundespost* [1974] ECR 153, para 11; Case 168/82 *ECSC v Ferrier Sant'Anna* [1983] ECR 1681).

Community law recognises, and in principle outlaws, both direct and indirect discrimination. Article 119 EC, for example, requires equal pay without either direct or indirect discrimination based on sex. Direct or 'overt' discrimination involves one sex being treated differently and usually less favourably than the other: in the context of equal pay it may mean that the woman is receiving less pay than the man. In principle, the only defences to direct discrimination are those expressly provided. While Article 48(3) and (4) EC provide defences on the grounds of **public policy, public security, public health** and employment in the public service (and Articles 56(1), 55 and 66 EC provide equivalent defences in respect of establishment and services) Article 119 EC does not expressly provide for any defences. This prompted the **Commission** and the **Advocate General** in *Roberts v Birds Eye Walls* to suggest that direct discrimination can be justified. The Court has not yet expressly ruled on this point.

In the context of Article 119 EC, indirect discrimination arises when the application of a gender-neutral criteria or practice (Case 170/84 *Bilka Kaufhaus* [1986] ECR 1607; Case C-127/92 *Enderby* [1993] ECR I-5535) in fact disadvantages a much higher percentage of women than men. Unless that difference can be justified by objective factors unrelated to any discrimination on the grounds of sex, the measure breaches Article 119 (Case 170/84 *Bilka Kaufhaus*; Case 171/88 *Rinner-Kühn* [1989] ECR 2743).

The Court is moving in the direction of recognising indirect discrimination in the field of **free movement of persons**. For example, in Case C-272/92 *Maria Chiara Spotti v Freistaat Bayern* [1993] ECR I-5185 the Court ruled that since the great majority of language assistants were foreign nationals, a German law which required contracts with foreign language assistants to be for a limited duration placed them at a disadvantage in respect of German nationals. Consequently, the Court ruled that the German law was indirectly discriminatory contrary to Article 48(2) EC, unless it was justified 'for objective reasons' unrelated to nationality (see also Case C-237/94 *O'Flynn*, judgment of 23 May 1996, paras 18–19; Case C-300/90 *Commission v Belgium* [1992] ECR I-305 and Case C-204/90 *Bachmann v Belgium* [1992] ECR I-249, where the European Court talked of justification in order 'to safeguard the cohesion of the tax system'; cf Case C-175/88 *Biehl* [1990] ECR I-1779).

While many of the earlier cases concerned measures which directly or indirectly discriminated against non-nationals, more recent cases have concerned measures which do not discriminate directly or indirectly against foreigners but do hinder free movement in some way. As the Court put it in Case C-415/93 *Bosman* [1995] ECR I-4921, 'the transfer rules constitute *an obstacle to the freedom of movement of workers* prohibited in principle by Article 48 of the Treaty' (emphasis added). In Case C-76/90 *Säger* [1991] ECR I-4221, for example, the Court said Article 59 EC requires not only the elimination of all discrimination against a person providing services on the ground of his nationality, but also 'the abolition of any restriction, even if it applies without distinction to national providers of services and to those of other Member States, when it is liable to prohibit or otherwise impede the activities of a provider of services established in another Member State where he lawfully provides similar services'.

The Court recognised that such a measure breached Article 59 EC unless 'justified by overriding reasons in the public interest' (C-288/89 *Gouda* [1991] ECR I-4007) or 'justified by imperative reasons relating to the public interest' (Case C-76/90 *Säger* above). These requirements borrow heavily, in their turn, from the mandatory requirements laid down by the Court in Case 120/78 **Cassis de Dijon** [1979] ECR 649, preventing measures which would otherwise be restrictive of the **free movement of goods** from breaching Article 30 EC. In the context of free movement of persons the Court no longer seems to be adopting a discrimination-based approach. This contrasts with the situation in Article 30, where, post-Cases C-267 & 268/91 *Keck* [1993] ECR I-6097, the Court seems to focus on issues of discrimination, where indirectly discriminatory measures breach Article 30 unless objectively justified while non-discriminatory measures fall right outside the scope of the Treaty provision.

CATHERINE BARNARD

*Recommended reading*
Ellis 'The Definition of Discrimination in European Community Sex Equality
Law' (1994) 19 ELRev 563.
Bleckmann 'Considerations sur l'interpretation de l'article 7 du Traite CEE'
(1976) Revue Trimestrielle de Droit Européen 469.

**DIVISION OF POWER**   The European Communities are a type of
divided-power system, in which power is divided between two or more
levels of government.   The most important levels so far are the
Communities and the Member States. For several reasons, however, the
division of power in the EC is especially complex. First, the EC consists
of three legally distinct Communities: the **EC**, the **ECSC** and the **EAEC**.
Each distinct Community is based on a separate international Treaty, and
each Treaty establishes a slightly different division of power between the
Community and the Member States.   Second, the division of power
between the EC and the Member States as provided by the Treaties is not
always clear. For example, the Treaty provisions are frequently expressed
in general terms; and for this reason, among others, the division of power
has often been subject to controversy.   Third, this division of power has
been modified in practice as a result of judicial interpretation of the
Treaties and secondary legislation by the **Court of Justice.**   Fourth, the
**Treaty on European Union** extended the **competences** of the EC, and as
a result of this Treaty the European Communities now form one of the
three **Pillars** of the **European Union.** In contrast to the EC, the other two
Pillars (Title V **Common Foreign and Security Policy**; Title VI
**Co-operation in the Fields of Justice and Home Affairs**) are mainly
intergovernmental arrangements, with a different division of power
between the EC and the Member States; and the result of the combination
of the EC and these other Pillars is an extremely complex division of
powers between the two levels.

   The EC is based on the principle of limited powers (*compétences
d'attribution*), according to which the EC enjoys those powers attributed
specifically to it, while other powers remain to be exercised by the
Member States.  In theory, the powers of the EC under the ECSC and the
EAEC Treaties are strictly limited: cf especially Articles 2, 3, 5, 8, 26, 37,
46, 47, 49–51 ECSC; Articles 1, 2, 3, 52–76, Annex I EAEC. Under the more
general EC Treaty the EC has the power to undertake the tasks specified
in Article 2 by using the means described in Article 2 and, for this
purpose, by engaging in the activities listed in Article 3. This principle
of limited powers has, however, been substantially attenuated in practice
until recently, in particular by the use by the EC of its 'residual powers'
and also by the doctrine of implied powers.

   Each Treaty also provides for the exercise by the EC of 'residual
powers', subject to specific conditions: cf Articles 95 ECSC, 203 EAEC,
235 EC.  For example, Article 235 EC provides that if action by the
Community should be necessary to attain, in the course of the operation
of the **Internal Market**, one of the objectives of the Community and this

Treaty has not provided the necessary powers, the **Council** shall, acting unanimously on a proposal from the **Commission** and after consulting the **European Parliament**, take the appropriate measures. The use of Article 235 EC as the legal basis of legislation is justified only, however, when (a) in the course of the operation of the Internal Market (b) EC action is necessary to attain one of the objectives of the Community and (c) no other provision of the Treaty gives the Community institutions the necessary power to adopt the measure in question (Case 45/86 *Commission v Council* [1987] ECR 1493).

To continue the EC example, in carrying out its tasks, each EC institution must act within the limits of the powers conferred upon it by the Treaty (Article 4(1) EC). This limitation is usually taken in practice to refer, not simply to a principle of institutional balance concerning relations among EC institutions per se, but also to the principle of attributed powers. This principle is enforced in the last instance by actions under Article 173 EC for the annulment of Community acts on grounds of lack of competence or of infringement of an essential procedural requirement, particularly the duty imposed on Community institutions by Article 190 EC to state the reasons on which their acts are based, including not only substantive reasons but also the Treaty Article conferring on the Community the power to act in respect of the matter in question.

The **Treaty on European Union** rendered even more complex the division of power between the EC and the Member States. It established a European Union, based on the EC but also including other policies and forms of co-operation. With regard to the EC, it reiterated the principle of limited powers (cf Article 3b). However, it also attributed to the EC various new competences, usually shared with the Member States. In addition, with regard to economic policy, the broad guidelines of the Member States' economic policies are subject to EC controls (cf Articles 3a, 102a-104). In matters of monetary policy, Member States are subject to stricter discipline, including eventually the irrevocable fixing of exchange rates leading to the introduction of a single currency and the definition of a single monetary policy and exchange rate policy.

The TEU also elaborates the principle of **subsidiarity** into a **general principle** of EC constitutional law; previously as a result of the **SEA**, this principle applied, in a different form, in environmental matters. It is now defined in Article 3b to provide that, in areas which do not fall within the EC's exclusive competence, the EC shall take action only if and in so far as the objectives of the proposed action cannot be sufficiently achieved by the Member States and can therefore, by reason of the scale or effects of the proposed action, be better achieved by the Community. It thus does not confer any new powers on the EC; instead it refers to the exercise of those powers which fall within the competence of both the EC and the Member States. It is an expression of the Member States' intention to limit the expansion of EC powers, to share as much as possible the exercise of power in matters for which both the EC and the Member States have competence, and to ensure that such powers are exercised in a decentralised way as much as possible.

In addition, the TEU establishes other forms of co-operation, in particular concerning a common foreign and security policy (CFSP) and co-operation in the fields of justice and home affairs. Both matters are within the powers of the Union but outside those of the EC, *stricto sensu*. With regard to the former, the Union and the Member States are required to define and implement a CFSP. With regard to the latter, and without prejudice to the powers of the EC (concerning the free movement of persons in particular), the TEU requires Member States to regard as matters of common interest the areas of **asylum** policy, **border controls**, immigration policy and policy regarding third-country nationals, combating drug addiction, international fraud, judicial co-operation in civil and criminal matters, customs co-operation, and **police co-operation** for specified purposes. According to Article F of the Common Provisions of the TEU, the Union shall provide itself with the means necessary to attain its objectives and carry through its powers. This provision may presage a subsequent extension of the powers of the EC, together perhaps with the decentralisation of the exercise of certain powers, and hence a new division of powers between the EC and the Member States.

FRANCIS SNYDER

*Recommended reading*
Bleckmann et al *Division of Powers between the European Communities and the Member States in the Field of External Relations* (1981) Kluwer.
Weiler 'The Transformation of Europe' (1991) 100 Yale Law Journal 2403.

**DOMINANT POSITION** See **monopolies**.

**DUBLIN CONVENTION** See **border controls**.

**DUMPING** See **anti-dumping**.

**ECONOMIC AND MONETARY UNION** See **economic union** and **monetary union**.

**ECONOMIC AND SOCIAL COHESION** See **cohesion**.

**ECONOMIC AND SOCIAL COMMITTEE** This Committee is an advisory body, established by the Treaty of Rome, whose 189 members represent the main economic and social groups of the EU's population. The Committee's task is to express the views of these groups, during the preparation of European legislation, to the **Council** and **Commission**. The latter must consult the Committee when preparing legislation in a number of specific areas, including the **Common Agricultural Policy**, mobility of labour, the right of establishment, transport, **approximation** of laws, **social policy**, the **European Social Fund** and vocational training.

In addition to the opinions it gives when consulted, the Committee is entitled to issue opinions on its own initiative. Its opinions on such issues as the Citizens' Europe (1992) and Growth, Competitiveness and Employment (1993) have exercised a certain influence on the EC's policy orientations.

The representative character of the Committee derives from the fact that its members are not only proportionate to the Member States (24 from each of the larger states and 12 or fewer from the smaller ones) but are also chosen for their affiliation with one or other of the Committee's three constituent groups. These are: Group I (Employers); Group II (Workers); and Group III ('Various Interests', meaning the professions, small businesses, transport, environmental and consumer groups and craftsmen).

In the work of the Committee, the representatives of these three groups are spread over nine working sections, each responsible for a functional policy area. The viewpoints of all the interests represented in the Committee are thus brought together in the preparation of the Committee's formal opinions, which are debated in the appropriate section before being voted on in a plenary session.

Some of the 180 or so opinions issued annually by the Committee have little influence, but in general its role has been acknowledged as an important and constructive one.

ROGER MORGAN

*Recommended reading*
Brüske *Der Wirtschafts- und Sozialausschuss der Europäischen Gemeinschaft* (1979) Schäuble-Verlag.
Morgan *The Consultative Function of the Economic and Social Committee of the EC* (1991) European University Institute.

**ECONOMIC UNION** The orthodox theory of international integration distinguishes five stages of economic integration: a free trade area, defined as an area within which there are no obstacles to trade in goods and services; a customs union, being a free trade area in which Member States adopt a uniform **common commercial policy** towards non-member countries; a common market, which goes beyond the customs union by providing for the free movement of factors of production (labour and capital); an economic union in which measures of national economic policy (eg taxation) are harmonised to the extent necessary for the effective functioning of the common market; and total economic integration whereby national economies are totally integrated and a single, common currency is in circulation (see **monetary union**).

The economic benefits from integration derive from three sources, each of which originates in the removal of barriers to trade and factor flows. First, the elimination of import restrictions provide consumers with access to the lowest cost supplier and results in *trade creation*; second, the resultant increase in the effective market size allows firms to exploit economies of scale and thereby increase their competitiveness; third, intensified competition will produce efficiency gains to be passed on to consumers through lower prices. Together, these benefits can be expected to produce dynamic benefits in the form of an increase in the general rates of economic growth for the participating countries, although the process of economic integration is likely to be accompanied by sectoral adjustment difficulties in particular Member States.

The founding Treaty of Rome provides explicitly for the creation of a common market (Article 2 EC). Initially, the process involved a staged transition to a customs union over 12 years from the entry into force of the Treaty. In the event this was achieved by July 1968 – some 18 months ahead of schedule. However, the establishment of a fully-fledged common market took much longer and was not completed until December 1992 (see the **Internal Market**). This was because the elimination of non-tariff barriers to trade in goods and services, along with the removal of restrictions to the movement of labour and capital, required harmonisation between national economic policies and this proved difficult. Despite provision being made for this in the EEC Treaty (Article 100), the economic circumstances of the 1970s – characterised by currency turbulence and global recession – were such that intra-EC obstacles to trade were raised rather than lowered.

It was with the publication of the Commission's White Paper 'Completing the Internal Market' in June 1985 that the project to create a truly common market in the EC was relaunched. The White Paper called for the elimination of all remaining physical, technical and fiscal barriers by 31 December 1992. That timetable (and much else) was given legal force with the ratification of the **Single European Act** in 1987.

Behind the White Paper lay a perception that the fragmentation of the internal EC market was obstructing recovery in the EC economies. The White Paper set out some 300 measures that, when implemented and in conjunction with the principle of mutual recognition, would create an Internal Market free from all obstacles to the **free movement of capital, goods, persons, services** and labour. The principle of **mutual recognition** as a mechanism for securing market access within the EC Internal Market was established by the European Court of Justice in its landmark decision in Case 120/78 *Cassis de Dijon* [1979] ECR 649. Its significance lay in the fact that it made **harmonisation** of national standards unnecessary for the vast range of goods moving within the Internal Market. Instead, products lawfully marketed in one Member State could not be excluded from access to the market of another Member State (other than under Article 36 procedures). Harmonisation of standards was required only in a comparatively few instances. In addition, the successful implementation of the Internal Market programme reflected also the adoption of **qualified**

**majority voting** in the **Council of Ministers** on matters pertaining to the completion of the Internal Markets except proposals relating to the free movement of persons, fiscal provisions, and the rights and interests of employed persons (Article 100a EC).

Although there remained some outstanding issues involving the harmonisation of fiscal policy, by the end of 1992 the European Community approximated an economic union. The 'four freedoms' had, for the major part, been established and the hitherto national economies were, increasingly, operating as a single, Community, economy.

ANDREW SCOTT

*Recommended reading*
Emerson et al *The Economics of 1992* (1988) Oxford University Press.
Tsoukalis *The New European Economy* (1993) Oxford University Press, ch 3, pp 46–76.

**ECU/EURO** From 1975 until 1979 the European Unit of Account preceded the European Currency Unit (ECU) as a composite currency for inter-bank settlements. The renaming took place when the **European Monetary System** (EMS) was created.

To this day the ECU is based upon a basket of national currencies. Each currency is given a weighting according to its importance and stability. Thus, the weight of the German mark is around 30%, while that of less important currencies, such as the Greek drachma, may be less than 1%. The weightings are reviewed periodically, normally every five years. However, they also vary in accordance with exchange rate fluctuations. The exchange rate of the national currencies to the ECU is computed every day on the basis of the weightings and the aggregate bilateral exchange rates, the so-called currency grid, and published in the Official Journal (see **publications of the EU**).

Even though individuals and undertakings can make inter-bank payments in the **Internal Market** in ECU, and ECU-bonds totalled some 1,700 million ECU at the end of 1995, neither bills nor coins are in circulation and central banks have always continued to use national currencies when intervening in financial markets. Thus, the ECU has never gained real importance as a currency.

The provisions on the creation of a **monetary union** introduced by the **Treaty on European Union** are also referring to the ECU as the future common currency (see Article 1091(4), (5) EC). However, this ECU will neither replace nor resemble the above-mentioned composite currency. Appropriately, it was decided at the **European Council** in Madrid in December 1995 to name the future common currency 'Euro', rather than ECU.

On the first day of the third stage of monetary union, the Council will fix once and for all the exchange rates between the currencies of those Member States that participate from the beginning (the 'ins') and the new common currency Euro, see Article 1091 (4). Subsequently, the national currencies of the 'ins' will be replaced gradually, as Euro bills and coins become available, probably in the year 2002, and banks change their accounting systems. Until then a number of technical problems have to be solved, such as the production of sufficient numbers of coins and bills, and the adjustment of computer software, vending machines and cash dispensers, price tags, etc. Otherwise, however, the replacement of national currencies will merely be an exchange, comparable to the exchange of sterling for francs, and will not affect the value of property and other assets and claims. Thus, legal problems should in principle not arise.

Even after the beginning of monetary union, the composite ECU will continue to exist for inter-bank transfers between the new currency area and those Member States not participating (yet) – the 'outs' – and amongst the latter. Besides the problem that a sufficient number of Member States qualify for monetary union by fulfilling the convergence criteria, rules for the future relations between ins and outs are the chief problem yet to be solved.

FRANK EMMERT

**EDUCATION POLICY** Initially, education as such was not mentioned in the EEC Treaty. When it was finally introduced by the TEU (Article 126 EC) the **competence** attributed to the EC was narrowly drawn and explicitly excludes 'any **harmonisation** of the laws and regulations of the Member States' (Article 126(4)). The Community's activities in the educational sphere are thus secondary. It can encourage, support and supplement Member State action 'if necessary ... while fully respecting the responsibility of the Member States for the content of teaching and the organization of education systems and their cultural and linguistic diversity' (Article 126(1)). Article 127 EC allows the EC a limited role in the sphere of vocational training. Since 1995 the Commission has had a Directorate General for Education (DG XXII).

Despite the initial lack of explicit competence, the activities of the Community of the sphere of education preceded the TEU for two prime reasons. First, 'vocational training' was mentioned in Article 128 EEC and was given a very broad scope by the **Court of Justice** in Case 293/83 *Gravier* [1985] ECR 593; Case 309/85 *Barra* [1988] ECR 355; Case 24/86 *Blaizot* [1988] ECR 379; and Case 263/86 *Humbel* [1988] ECR 5365 (see **Students**), thus allowing Community competence in this area via Article 128 EEC. The Court of Justice's distinction between education and vocational training was not beyond question.

Second, the Community action of funding educational initiatives was supported by the Court of Justice in the *Erasmus* case (Case 242/87 *Commission v Council* [1989] ECR 1425), this despite the research element (cf Joined Cases C-51/89, C-90/89 & C-94/89 *UK v Council* [1991] ECR I-2757). The funding of (non-mandatory) activities was a permissible use of the EC **budget** and there was a mushrooming of EC-funded activities with an education component. The main EC programmes in the educational area have recently been renewed and are mainly included in the *SOCRATES* (Council Decision 819/95/EC (OJ L87 20.4.95 p 10)) and *Leonardo da Vinci* programmes (Council Decision 94/819/EC establishing an action programme for the implementation of a EC vocational Training Policy (OJ L340 29.12.94 p 8)) (see **research and development policy**). These programmes illustrate the broad aims of EC educational and vocational training policy and exemplify the scope of action under Articles 126 and 127. Many familiar acronyms (eg ERASMUS, COMMETT, LINGUA, etc) are included within these broad programmes. The Community is also likely to expand its encouragement of academic recognition of diplomas and awards, which was kick-started by the European Credit Transfer System (ECTS: Action 3 of the ERASMUS programme), as explained in the policy Communication issued in December 1994 (COM(94)656) (see **mutual recognition of diplomas**). An example of direct impact of the EC in the sphere of education through a funding initiative is provided by the Jean Monnet initiative. This scheme, which is voluntary, binds recipients of funds to teach EC matters or maintain EC-related posts and to maintain such provision for at least three years after the European co-funding expires.

Education also features as a component of the EC's other policies (eg environment or public health) and individuals in the educational sector have all the right of **free movement, freedom of establishment** and the right to provide or receive services (see **free movement of services**).

JULIAN LONBAY

*Recommended reading*
Lonbay 'Education and the Law: the Community context' (1989) 14 ELRev 363.
McMahon *Education and Culture in European Community Law* (1995) Athlone
   Press.

**EEA** See **European Economic Area**.

**EFFET UTILE** *Effet utile* is a principle of law that has been developed by the **Court of Justice** in order to foster effective enforcement of EC rules within the legal systems of the Member States. As a normative principle, it has largely evolved in case law concerning the remedies and procedures available in Member States to enforce Community rules.

The Court of Justice has held that, in the absence of Community legislation, it is for the legal systems of the Member States to designate remedies and procedures to enforce EC measures, provided that: (a) such rules are not less favourable than those governing analogous domestic actions (principle of non-discrimination); and (b) they do not make it impossible in practice or excessively difficult to enforce the rights claimed (principle of *effet utile*). These obligations are derived from the Article 5 EC duty of Member States to 'take all appropriate measures, whether general or particular' to ensure fulfilment of EC measures, and are often cited in tandem with the notion that Community law, in some circumstances, vests individuals with rights which national law has a duty to protect. They could also be viewed as a necessary corollary to the fundamental right in EC law to effective judicial review (eg Case 222/84 *Johnston v Chief Constable of the Royal Ulster Constabulary* [1986] ECR 1651).

The Court of Justice has increasingly been willing to rule that national measures are incompatible with Community law due to infraction of *effet utile*. For example, it has been held that the principle of *effet utile* will be violated by national rules on unjust enrichment which prevent payments being made which are due under the terms of a Directive (Case C-377/89 *Cotter and McDermott* [1991] ECR I-1155). The same conclusion was reached by the Court of Justice with respect to domestic rules that limit the authority of judicial bodies to grant interim relief (Case C-213/89 *Factortame* [1990] ECR I-2433). Other Member State rules that have been held to precipitate breach of the requirement for *effet utile* include:

(a) fetters on actions for damages against national legislatures for breach of Community law (see Joined Cases C-46/93 & C-48/93 *Brasserie du Pêcheur and Factortame III*, judgment of 5 March 1996);

(b) domestic limitation periods for bringing proceedings, at least in so far as they apply to enforcement of Directives (Case C-208/90 *Emmott v Minister for Social Welfare and Attorney General* [1993] ECR I-4637; but cf Case C-338/91 *Steenhorst Neerings* [1993] ECR I-5475 and Case C-410/92 *Johnson* [1994] ECR I 5483);

(c) onerous obligations pertaining to the standard of proof (eg Case 199/82 *San Gorgio* [1983] ECR 3595); and

(d) rules preventing litigants from raising points of Community law due to an expiry of time-limits for the raising of new arguments (Case C-312/93 *SCS Peterbroeck* [1995] ECR I-4599; but cf Joined Cases C-430/93 & C-431/93 *van Schijndel and van Veen* [1995] ECR I-4705).

The principles of *effet utile* and non-discrimination have been most commonly applied by the Court of Justice in cases referred to it under Article 177 EC, in which private parties have sought enforcement of *individual rights* that arise from Community law. However, *effet utile* and non-discrimination have also been enforced in Article 169 actions brought by the Commission, in which Member State were ordered to secure adequate enforcement of *obligations* imposed by Community law on private parties. For example, it has been held that infringements of Community law must be penalised by Member State authorities under conditions, both procedural and substantive, which are analogous to those applicable to infringements of domestic law of a similar nature, and that in any event the penalty provided must be effective, proportionate and dissuasive (Case 68/88 *Commission v Greece* [1989] ECR 2965, para 24).

It is not yet entirely clear whether the principles of *effet utile* and non-discrimination will apply to principles of Community law that lack the preconditions for direct effect. On two occasions the Court of Justice has ruled in favour of applicants who have sought to obtain damages for breach of Community obligations due to the imperatives of *effet utile*, even though the doctrine of direct effect was of no relevance to the resolution of substantive issues (Joined Cases C-6/90 & C-9/90 *Francovich v Italian Republic* [1991] ECR I-5357; Case C-177/88 *Dekker v VJV* [1990] ECR 3941; see also the opinion of Advocate General Tesauro of 28 November 1995 in Joined Cases C-178/94, C-179/74, C-188/94 & C-190/94 *Dillenkofer* judgment of 8 October 1996 (not yet reported)). However, at this stage the vast majority of cases in which national remedies and procedures have been held to be incompatible with Community law have concerned disputes in which individuals have sought to enforce directly effective Community norms. No decision has been issued thus far by the Court of Justice to indicate that improvement of domestic remedies and procedures might be required, for example, when a claim concerns the duty of national judges to interpret Community law in conformity with EC rules.

ANGELA WARD

*Recommended reading*
Steiner *Enforcing EC Law* (1995) Blackstone Press.
Ward 'National Sanctions in EC Law: A Moving Boundary in the Division of Competence' (1995) 1 European Law Journal 205.

**ELECTIONS** See **direct elections**.

**EMPLOYMENT PROTECTION (INDIVIDUAL AND COLLECTIVE)**
Employment protection is provided in specific circumstances by four EC Directives: Council Directive (EEC) 75/129 on the approximation of the laws of the Member States relating to collective redundancies (OJ L48 22.2.75 p 29), subsequently amended by Council Directive (EEC) 92/56 (OJ L245 26.8.1992 p 3) ('the Collective Redundancies Directive'); Council Directive (EEC) 77/187 on the approximation of the laws of the Member States relating to the safeguarding of employees' rights in the event of transfers of undertakings (OJ L61 5.3.77 p 27) ('the Acquired Rights Directive'); Council Directive (EEC) 80/987 on the approximation of the laws of the Member States relating to the protection of employees in the event of the insolvency of their employer (OJ L283 28.10.80 p 23) ('the Insolvency Directive'); and Council Directive (EEC) 533/91 on an employer's obligation to inform employees of the conditions applicable to the contract or employment relationship (OJ L288 18.10.91 p 91). All four Directives are based on Article 100 EC, suggesting that their aim is to **harmonise** conditions of competition in the Member States as regards the employment-related

costs of undertakings. However, the origins of both the Collective Redundancies Directive and the Acquired Rights Directive in the Social Action Programme 1974 (Bull EC, Supp 2/74) and of the Directive on information about conditions applicable to the employment relationship in the 1989 **Community Charter of Fundamental Social Rights of Workers** indicate that these Directives were also designed to pursue social aims.

The Collective Redundancies Directive lays down procedural standards which must be followed by employers in the handling of redundancies: its core requirements are that 'workers' representatives' should be informed and consulted about redundancies as soon as the employer is 'contemplating' them (Article 2) and that the competent public authority be notified in writing of the projected redundancies (Article 3). Article 4 provides that the projected redundancies are to take effect only after a particular period has elapsed. The aim of these procedures, as stated in Article 2(2) of the Directive, is to avoid the redundancies, or at least reduce the numbers involved. The Directive was amended in 1992 to ensure that such information and consultation procedures should also apply in the case of transnational undertakings, namely, where a decision to effect redundancies is taken by an undertaking in a Member State other than the one where the workers are employed. In Case C-383/92 *Commission v United Kingdom* [1994] ECR I-2479 the **Court of Justice** held that the United Kingdom had failed to implement correctly the Directive as it failed to designate a system of worker representation for the purposes of the Directive. In the same decision, the ECJ underlined at para 40 that the Directive obliged the Member States to impose 'effective, proportionate and dissuasive' sanctions for failure to observe its procedures.

The aim of the Acquired Rights Directive is to prevent the transfer of an undertaking from adversely affecting the rights and conditions of employment of the employees. Like the Collective Redundancies Directive, it requires that employees' representatives be informed and consulted about the implications of the transfer for the employees (Article 6(1)). Therefore, on the same grounds as in Case 383/92 above, the ECJ held in Case C-382/92 *Commission v United Kingdom* [1994] ECR I-2435 that the United Kingdom had failed correctly to implement this Directive. Consultations must take place 'in good time' and with 'a view to seeking agreement' (Article 6(2)). The Directive requires, where there is a 'transfer of undertaking' within the meaning of Article 1(1) of the Directive, that employees continue to be employed on the same terms and conditions as prior to the transfer (Article 3(1)). Article 3(2) requires the transferee to observe the terms and conditions agreed in any collective agreement with the transferor, although Member States may limit the period for observing such terms and conditions, provided that it is not less than one year. Article 4(1) of the Directive provides that the transfer in itself shall not be a ground for dismissal. Dismissal will, however, be permitted if the employer can prove that the dismissals take place for 'economic, technical or organisational reasons entailing changes in the workforce'. The ECJ has interpreted broadly the scope of application of the Directive: it can apply in the absence of a contract between the transferor and transferee, such as in the case of the re-assignment of a lease of a business (Case 324/86 *Daddy's Dance Hall* [1988] ECR 739), the change of recipient of a subsidy paid by a local authority (Case C-29/91 *Redmond Stichting* [1992] ECR I-3189) and the contracting out of a service (Case C-209/91 *Rask* [1992] ECR I-5755). It applies even where the transfer of a single employee is involved (Case C-392/92 *Schmidt* [1994] ECR 1311). For the Directive to apply to a particular transfer, it must be shown that, despite the transfer, 'the business in question retains its identity' (Case 24/85 *Spijkers* [1986] ECR 1119, para 11). This is a question of fact to be decided by national courts.

The Commission has put forward a proposal to revise the Acquired Rights Directive in a number of important respects (COM(94) 300 final).

The Insolvency Directive aims to protect employees in the event of their employer becoming bankrupt or otherwise insolvent. The Directive requires the Member States to take the necessary measures to establish guarantee institutions which guarantee payment of employees' outstanding claims resulting from their contract of employment (Article 3(1)). The Directive leaves the Member State discretion to choose between a number of options concerning the details of the content of the guarantee and the liability of the guarantee institutions. Despite the provisions of the Directive not being capable of direct effect in national law, the ECJ held in Cases C-6 & 9/90 *Francovich* [1991] ECR I-5357 that a Member State could be liable in damages to individuals suffering loss as a result of its failure to implement the Directive (see **damages against Member States**).

The Directive on information about conditions applicable to the employment relationship obliges employers to provide employees with documents notifying them of the 'essential aspects' of their contract or employment relationship (Article 2(1)). The Directive stipulates what information should be provided (Article 2) and requires that it be given to the employee within two months of the commencement of the contract by means of a written contract of employment or a letter of engagement or some other form of written document which contains the required information (Article 3). The Directive leaves, however, a discretion to the Member States to exclude application of the Directive in the case of contracts of a less than a month's duration, or with a working week not exceeding eight hours, or where non-application is justified by 'objective considerations' (Article 1(2)). The Directive has thus far not required any interpretation by the ECJ.

GILLIAN MORE

*Recommended reading*
House of Lords Select Committee on the European Communities, 'Transfer of Undertakings: Acquired Rights' Session 1995–96, 5th Report (1995) HMSO.

Nielsen & Szyszczak *The Social Dimension of the European Community* (2nd edn, 1994) Handelshøjskolens Forlag.

**ENERGY POLICY** The **ECSC** and **Euratom** Treaties specifically addressed the coal and nuclear energy industries. However, in 1957, the EEC Treaty contained no express provision for either the energy sector or energy policy. Indeed, the EC Treaty as amended now only contains fleeting references to energy: namely, Article 3t ('measures in the sphere of energy' as an objective of the Treaty); Article 129b ('energy infrastructures' within the ambit of **trans-European networks**); and Articles 130r ('the prudent and rational utilisation of natural resources') and 130s (the adoption of 'measures significantly affecting a Member State's choice between different energy sources and the general structure of its energy supply'), both within the remit of Community **environmental policy**. In the continuing absence of specific provisions regarding the energy sector as a whole, a lacuna which the **European Parliament** has recommended is filled by a new and separate Chapter of the EC Treaty, the Community's energy policy competence must be found in the achievement of the **Internal Market**, the four freedoms and competition provisions.

Although the **Court of Justice** has consistently considered cases in the energy sector, it was only within the context of the commitment to achieve the Internal Market that the **Commission** for the first time initiated a legislative policy in the sector (COM (88) 238 Final). The goals, for the energy market within the Community, include the elimination of exclusive production, transportation and distribution rights, the 'unbundling' (in accounting terms) of the various components of vertically integrated undertakings and the creation of limited third party access to networks for large energy consumers or distributors. The Commission has adopted a three-stage approach to achieve these goals.

The first phase of achieving these goals was the adoption of three Council Directives: Council Directive (EEC) 90/377 on price transparency for electricity and gas (OJ L185 29.7.90 p 16) and Council Directives (EEC) 90/547 and 91/296 on the transit of electricity (OJ L313 13.11.90 p 30) and gas (OJ L147 12.6.91 p 37) respectively. These Directives sought to free the relevant markets by increasing, first, the consumer's access to charges throughout the Community and, second, the long-distance mobility of the goods.

The second phase of legislation concerned far-reaching proposals for the liberalisation of the structure of the electricity and gas sectors. As a corollary to this phase, the Council adopted two general Council Directives, known as the 'Procurement Directive' (Council Directive (EEC) 92/13 (OJ L76 23.3.92 p 14)) and the 'Utilities Directive' (Council Regulation (EEC) 93/38 (OJ L307 9.8.93 p 84)) on **public procurement** procedures of entities operating in, inter alia, the energy sector. These

Directives, which form part of wider public procurement policy, aim to free competition in the energy market through open and non-discriminatory procurement procedures and to facilitate the national review of procurement decisions.

As to specific second phase energy legislation, the Commission twice proposed legislation to the Council, in February 1992 and February 1994, on 'common rules' in the electricity and gas sectors. However, the proposals met solid resistance from certain Member States. Issues such as the strategic importance of energy supply, security of supply, sovereignty over natural resources, the economic and political strength of existing undertakings, the variations between Member States' regimes and the 'special status' of energy have dogged progress within the Energy Council. The Commission, frustrated at the lack of progress and spurred on by the case law of the Court of Justice in analogous fields, lodged five actions before the Court of Justice in 1994 seeking declarations under Article 169 EC that the import and export regimes of the electricity and gas markets of The Netherlands, Italy, France and Spain fail to fulfil the free movement of goods requirements of the EC Treaty (Cases C-157-160/94, pending, OJ C202 23.7.94 p 9).

On 20 June 1996, subsequent to the hearing of these cases by the Court of Justice but prior to judgment, the Energy Council announced that it had unanimously agreed a compromise common position on the draft Directive on common rules for the Internal Market in electricity (Proposal OJ C123 4.5.94 p 1; Agreement, *Agence Europe Documents*, No 1993, 10 July 1996). The Council's 'common position' has now returned to the European Parliament in accordance with the co-decision procedure (see **decision making**). The agreement covers the main facets of the Commission's objectives, including the organisation of the sector and public service obligations, the elimination of exclusive generation, transmission and distribution systems, increased transparency, market opening, wider access and greater competition on a Community-wide basis. The agreement, which is limited to the electricity market, is a major breakthrough in the liberalisation of energy sector, and, if successfully adopted, may pave the way for similar agreements in the neighbouring market of natural gas.

The third phase of the Commission's policy is the consolidation, completion and extension of the liberalisation achieved in the second phase. The particulars of this phase will be evaluated in the light of the operation of the common rules for the Internal Market in electricity and gas, once adopted.

WILLIAM ROBINSON

*Recommended reading*
Hancher *EC Electricity Law* (1992) Chancery Law Publishing.
MacDougall & Wälde *European Community Energy Law* (1994) Graham & Trotman/Martinus Nijhoff.

**ENLARGEMENT**  Enlargement has been a central issue of the European integration from its early beginnings. Far from being an issue of geographical extension alone, it raises fundamental questions about the scope, identity and final aims of the integration process. So far, the European Community/Union has been enlarged four times: to Denmark, Ireland and the United Kingdom in 1973, to Greece in 1981, to Portugal and Spain in 1986 and to Austria, Finland and Sweden in 1995. Each of these had its particular challenges and problems. The first was delayed for more than a decade mainly because of De Gaulle's doubts about British willingness to accept the political principles of integration but was then welcomed for the democratic traditions of the new members and the economic and political benefits of their **accession**. The enlargement first to Greece and then to Portugal and Spain raised concerns about the relative economic weakness of the applicants, but was accepted as a means of stabilising the young democracies in these countries. The 1995 enlargement finally posed problems of increased diversity with the EU's borders stretching further both to the North and East and of the applicants' tradition of military neutrality, but was nevertheless rather non-controversial due to the strength of the applicants' economies and the new political context in Europe after the revolution in Central and Eastern Europe.

Due to these successive enlargements from six to 15 Member States, the Union has become more heterogeneous, both economically and politically. Yet although the **decision-making** system (originally designed for only six Member States) and financial solidarity between richer and poorer Member States have come under increasing strain, the Union has absorbed these enlargements rather well, benefiting both from increased trade and added international weight.

The next round of enlargement, however, constitutes a challenge of a different size: first, because of the sheer number of applicant countries which has at present already reached 13 (Turkey, Malta, Cyprus, Poland, the Czech Republic, Slovakia, Hungary, Slovenia, Romania, Bulgaria, Estonia, Latvia, Lithuania); second, because of the economic level of the applicants, most of which have a GDP per capita well below half the average of the EU; and third, because of the political problems some of these countries would bring into the Union (eg minority problems in some of the Central and Eastern European countries, the Cyprus conflict, human rights problems in Turkey, tensions between the applicant Baltic States and Russia). These points cast some doubt on the desirability of further enlargement at all, but there are also strong political and economic reasons for the Union to accept at least some of the applicants as new members. This is particularly true for most of the Central and Eastern European countries (CEECs), whose accession could make a substantial contribution to the stability and security of the region, remove the last remnants of the former division of Europe and increase trading opportunities within the **Internal Market**, thereby consolidating the Union's position in international relations and as the world's biggest trading power. The Copenhagen **European Council** of June 1993 agreed on conditional eventual membership of the CEECs, provided that these would have stable institutions (guaranteeing democracy, the rule of law, human rights and respect of minority rights), a functioning market economy, the capacity to cope with competitive pressure within the Internal Market and the ability to take on the obligations of membership including adherence to the aims of political, economic and monetary union. In order to help the CEECs to meet these tough requirements, the Essen European Council of December 1994 adopted a 'pre-accession' strategy providing for a structured political relationship of the CEECs with the Union institutions which goes beyond the existing **Europe Agreements** and a number of measures for the progressive integration of the CEECs into the Internal Market. Yet there are still wide differences in levels of economic, political and social development between the core Central CEECs and the more Eastern ones, so that a phased Eastern enlargement appears the most likely outcome.

As regards the other applicants, the Union has already committed itself to start accession negotiations with Cyprus and Malta shortly after the end of the 1996 Intergovernmental Conference (although as a result of its 1996 elections, Malta's application is 'frozen'), this in spite of the unresolved Cyprus conflict and of the difficult question of the representation of small states in the Union institutions. An early enlargement to the Baltic countries and Turkey seems unlikely, in the first case because of formidable economic problems and the tense relations with Russia, in the second case mainly because of concerns about Turkey's human rights record and fears about the economic consequences of Turkish accession, especially on the EU labour market.

Yet enlargement is not only a question of whether applicant countries are able to fulfil the requirements of membership but also of the Union's capacity to absorb new members without putting at risk the momentum of the integration process. At present serious doubts may be raised about this capacity, both from an institutional and a financial point of view: on the institutional side, any further enlargement will alter the existing balance between larger and smaller Member States and put additional strain on the functioning of decision-making procedures and institutions. The Council's voting rules, the rotation of the Presidency, the size of the Commission and representation in the European Parliament will all need to be reconsidered if the process of policy making is not going to be blocked. On the financial side, additional demands on the EU budget are at least initially likely to be heavy: in case of an Eastern enlargement, according to Commission estimates, expenditure for the **Common Agricultural Policy** will raise by 9 to 12 billion ECU under present rules and structural funds will need to double in size. Yet with all the budgetary difficulties Member States are facing at home they are unlikely to agree on a substantial increase of the Community budget, and the alternative, a radical reform of the Common Agricultural Policy and of structural policies, remains highly controversial. One way to reduce the pressure on existing Union policies would be to devise forms of partial membership under which applicants would join the EU but would remain temporarily excluded from sensitive policies. Yet such a multi-tier solution is likely to meet considerable opposition from the applicant countries and would not resolve the institutional problems of further enlargement. The Union seems therefore to have no choice but to engage in a process of fundamental reform if further enlargement is not going to lead to its paralysis or even break-up.

JÖRG MONAR

*Recommended reading*
Baldwin *Towards an Integrated Europe* (1994) Centre for Economic Policy Research.
Lintner 'The Economic Implications of Enlarging the European Union' in Healey (ed) *The Economics of the New Europe* (1995) Routledge.

**ENVIRONMENTAL POLICY** In response to the call for action at the 1972 United Nations Stockholm Conference on the Human Environment, the Heads of Government of the Member States of the Community declared the establishment of a European Community environmental policy in 1972. The Declaration stated that 'economic expansion is not an end in itself . . . rather its aim is to reduce disparities in living conditions and to improve the quality and standard of living'. Following this Declaration, the **European Commission** drew up the First Environmental Action Programme in 1973 (OJ C112 20.12.73 p 1), a declaration which provided the policy framework for Community action over the next four years as well as specific suggestions for legislation. The First Action Programme which ran from 1973 to 1976, and the Second, from 1977 to 1981, were primarily concerned with pollution control. The Third, from 1982 to 1986, and the Fourth, from 1987 to 1992, have extended these to take a more preventative strategy and long-term approach and to develop a concern with the conservation of resources. The Fourth Action Programme was aimed at improving the enforcement and implementation of existing legislation and to integrate environmental considerations into all other policy areas so that policy for the environment would no longer be marginal in decision making. The Fifth Environmental Action Programme, *Towards Sustainability: A European Community Programme of Policy and Action in Relation to the Environment and Sustainable Development* (OJ C138 17.5.93 p 1), departs from the previous programmes by focusing on activities – **industry, energy, transport,** agriculture and tourism – rather than environmental media in and its concern with sources rather than receptors of pollution. The programme stresses the need for integration of environmental protection requirements into other policy areas, for example transport.

In drawing up the First Environmental Action Programme, the Commission relied upon a dynamic interpretation of the Treaty of Rome which mentions 'the constant improvement of the living and working conditions of their peoples' as one of the Community's essential objectives. The Commission also relied upon Article 2 EEC, which broadly declares the Community's tasks as promoting 'harmonious development', 'increased stability', 'raising the standard of living through the establishment of a common market and a programme of approximating Member States' economic policies'.

The EC's environmental policy also has an economic base. A **Council** declaration on the adoption of the First Environmental Action Programme (1973) stated that the establishment of the Common Market could not be realised without an effective campaign against pollution and nuisance and an improvement in the quality of life and protection of the environment. For example, competition might be inhibited by Member States' differing product regulations set for 'environmental' reasons and differing regulation of industrial processes. Indeed, the **Court of Justice** in Case 91/79 *Commission v Italy* [1980] ECR 1099 at 1106 confirmed that conditions relating to environmental protection 'may be a burden upon the undertakings to which they apply, and if there is no harmonisation of national provisions on the matter, competition may be appreciably distorted'.

In the absence of an explicit legal base for legislation relating to the environment, Article 100 EC and Article 235 EEC were relied upon. Articles 130r–130t EC, inserted by the **Single European Act**, provided an explicit legal base for European Community environmental law and policy and confirmed the Community's de facto **competence** in environmental matters. The Single European Act concerned itself with environmental protection because of the distorting effects of differing national environmental laws on competition and intra-Community trade. A further influence was the likelihood of environmental harm caused by increased transportation, industrial restructuring and enhanced economic growth accompanying fulfilment of the Internal Market.

The **Treaty on European Union** confirms this constitutional base for the Community's legal action on the environment. Article 130s EC provides that in some cases environmental measures may be adopted under the procedure referred to in Article 189c EC, though measures of a fiscal nature, town and country planning, land use, the management of water resources and certain measures affecting a Member State's choice between different energy sources still require unanimity.

The objectives of the Community's environmental policy, listed under Article 130r(1) EC are wide ranging: preserving, protecting and improving the quality of the environment; protecting human health; the prudent and rational utilisation of natural resources; and promoting measures at international level to deal with regional or worldwide environmental problems. Article 2 EC introduces the objectives of promoting 'harmonious and balanced development of economic activities and sustainable and non-inflationary growth respecting the environment'. This redraft of Article 2 places environmental concerns at the centre of the Community's goals.

There are a number of guiding principles of European Community environmental policy set out in Article 130r(2) EC: the principle of preventing pollution rather than remedying its effects (see the **precautionary principle**); the principle that environmental damage should as a priority be rectified at source, together with the '**polluter pays principle**', ie that the cost of preventing and eliminating nuisances must be borne by the polluter, and the principle that environmental protection requirements must be integral part of the definition and implementation of other Community policies. Also, the principle of **subsidiarity** (Article 3b EC) determines the 'appropriate level' of action in each category of pollution.

The European Community has adopted three main approaches in its environmental policy: sectoral protection of the environment by way of controlling pollution; the regulation of land use; and preventative and integrated measures. These approaches broadly represent the chronological development of EC environmental policy.

The sectoral approach is represented by laws which have as their objective the protection of a single environmental medium such as water or air. The main techniques adopted in this approach are administratively enforced emission standards and the establishment of environmental quality standards. In terms of preventing water pollution, the primary legal instrument is Directive 76/464 on Pollution Caused by Certain Dangerous Substances Discharged into the Aquatic Environment of the Communities (OJ L129 18.5.1976 p 23). This combines the use of emission standards and environmental quality standards. Water quality standards are also used, for example, in Directive 80/778 on the Quality of Water Intended for Human Consumption (OJ L299 30.8.80 p 11) and Directive 76/160 on the Quality of Bathing Water (OJ L31 5.2.78 p 1). Air pollution is regulated on an entirely sectoral basis. The most widely adopted technique is to establish air quality standards. Directives currently set standards for sulphur (Directive 80/779 on Sulphur Dioxide and Suspended Particulates, OJ L229 30.8.80 p 30); lead (Directive 82/884 on Limit Values for Lead in the Air (OJ L884 3.12.82 p 15)); and nitrogen dioxide (Directive 85/203 on Air Quality Standards for Nitrogen Dioxide (OJ L87, 27.3.85 p 1)). In addition, several Directives are aimed at particular activities or installations. The first of these was Directive 84/360 on Combating Air Pollution from Industrial Plants (OJ L188 16.7.84 p 20).

A second approach is the regulation of land use by designating land for special uses and protection, for example, Directive 79/409 on the

Conservation of Wild Birds (OJ L103 27.4.79 p 1) and Directive 92/43 on the Conservation of Natural Habitats and of Wild Flora and Fauna (OJ L206 22.7.92 p 7), and by the establishment of procedural mechanisms as seen in Directive 85/337 on the Assessment of the Effects of Certain Public and Private Projects on the Environment, the 'environmental impact assessment' Directive' (OJ L175 27.6.85 p 40).

A third approach of the European Community's environmental policy is the regulation of sources of pollution by using preventative and integrated methods. The common technique is the generation of information on industrial activities, in the expectation that environmental groups and others will use this information in demanding from industry and enforcement agencies more effective application of EC environmental law. Such an approach is adopted in Directive 90/313 on Access of Information on the Environment (OJ L158 23.6.90 p 56); Regulation 92/880 on a Community Eco-Labelling Scheme (OJ L99 11.4.92 p 1); and Regulation 93/1836 on the establishment of an Eco-Management and Auditing Scheme (OJ L168 10.7.93 p 1).

JANE HOLDER

*Recommended reading*
Kiss & Shelton *Manual of European Environmental Law* (1994) Cambridge University Press.
Haigh *Manual of EC Environmental Policy: The EC and Britain* (1992) Longman.

**EQUAL PAY** Article 119 EC requires Member States to ensure that men and women receive 'equal pay for equal work'. It has been directly enforceable in the courts of the Member States since 8 April 1976: Case 43/75 *Defrenne (No 2)* [1976] ECR 455. The **Court of Justice** explained that Article 119 serves both an economic purpose (the prevention of commercial disadvantage to those who pay men and women equally) and a social purpose (the improvement of living and working conditions) and that the principle of equal pay forms part of the foundations of the Community.

'Pay' is defined by Article 119 as 'the ordinary basic or minimum wage or salary or any other consideration, whether in cash or in kind, which the worker receives, directly or indirectly, in respect of his employment from his employer'. This has been interpreted broadly by the ECJ; it covers all payments arising out of employment, those made in the absence of contractual obligation, and those which are notional only (Case 69/80 *Worringham* [1981] ECR 767). It extends to payments made after a contract of employment has ended (Case 12/81 *Garland* [1982] ECR 359), including **pensions**, whether paid under a scheme supplementing a state scheme (Case 170/84 *Bilka Kaufhaus* [1986] ECR 1607) or one substituting part of a state scheme (such as 'contracted-out' schemes in the United Kingdom (Case C-262/88 *Barber* [1990] I-ECR 1889). But note that such claims can only be made in relation to benefits payable in respect of periods of service after 17 May 1990 (Case C-200/91 *Coloroll* [1994] ECR I-4389). It does not extend to state pensions (Case 80/70 *Defrenne (No 1)* [1971] ECR 445), as to which the principle of equality is applied separately (see **social security**). 'Pay' also includes certain statutorily regulated payments, in particular redundancy payments (*Barber*) and sick pay (Case 171/88 *Rinner-Kuhn* [1989] ECR 2743).

Men and women perform 'equal work' where the nature of the services which they provide is the same (*Defrenne (No 2)* and Case 129/79 *Macarthys* [1980] ECR 1275), even where they do not work contemporaneously with one another (*Macarthys*). Work is also 'equal' where, though not identical in nature, it is equal in value; this is spelled out in Article 1(1) of the Equal Pay Directive (Council Directive (EEC) 75/117 (OJ L45 19.2.75 p 19)), but is also inherent in Article 119 (Case 96/80 *Jenkins* [1981] ECR 911). Article 119 can be enforced to demand equal pay even where the claimant, though paid less than the comparator, does work of greater value (Case 157/86 *Murphy* [1988] ECR 673). There must, however, be an actual, not merely a theoretical, worker of the opposite sex with whom a comparison can be made (*Macarthys*).

Article 119 forbids both direct and indirect **discrimination** (as to which, see also **equal treatment**). After a period of doubt as to the meaning of these terms in this context, the ECJ has established that direct discrimination occurs where a pay differential is referable, expressly or impliedly, to sex and that indirect discrimination encompasses the situation where an employer's pay practices produce an adverse impact for one sex and cannot be justified by reference to objective, non-discriminatory criteria (*Jenkins* and *Bilka Kaufhaus*). The mere existence of separate wage bargaining arrangements for claimant and comparator does not constitute such objective justification (Case C-127/92 *Enderby* [1993] ECR I-5535).

Where an employer operates a 'non-transparent' pay system, such that employees cannot know how their final pay has been computed, and there is a statistical pay imbalance between the sexes, the employer bears the burden of proving that Article 119 has not been breached (Case 109/88 *Danfoss* [1989] ECR 3199).

Discriminatory pay must be 'levelled up' to that of the comparator (*Defrenne (No 2)*), but in amending for the future the rules of formerly discriminatory pension schemes it is permissible to 'level down' (*Coloroll*).

EVELYN ELLIS

*Recommended reading*
Ellis *European Community Sex Equality Law* (1991) Clarendon Press.
Burrows & Mair *European Social Law* (1996) Wiley.


**EQUAL TREATMENT** The equal treatment of men and women is both a general principle of law recognised by the **Court of Justice** and the subject matter of an important Directive (Council Directive (EEC) 76/207 (OJ L39 14.2.76 p 40)). The latter regulates access to employment, promotion, vocational training, and working conditions (Article 1(1)). Equal treatment means that there must be 'no **discrimination** whatsoever on grounds of sex either directly or indirectly by reference in particular to marital or family status' (Article 2(1)). Direct discrimination occurs where an employment decision is grounded, expressly or impliedly, on sex; where the most important reason for a detrimental employment decision can only apply to one sex, such as where the reason is pregnancy, that decision is directly discriminatory (Case C-177/88 *Dekker* [1990] ECR I-3941). It is unnecessary for this purpose to compare the woman's treatment with that receivable by a hypothetical male comparator (Case C-32/93 *Webb* [1994] ECR I-3567). Indirect discrimination occurs where an employer's practices produce an adverse impact for one sex and they cannot be justified by reference to objective, non-discriminatory criteria (see, for example, Case C-360/90 *Bötel* [1992] ECR I- 3589).

The Directive's main provisions have been held by the ECJ to be directly enforceable in the courts of the Member States (see, for example, Case 222/84 *Johnson* [1986] ECR 1651 and Case 152/84 *Marshall (No 1)* [1986] ECR 723). Its effects are not merely to forbid discrimination against individual employees, but also discrimination in laws, regulations, administrative provisions, collective agreements, internal rules of undertakings and rules governing independent occupations and professions (Articles 3, 4 and 5; see also Case C-33/89 *Kowalska* [1990] ECR I-2591 and Case C-184/89 *Nimz* [1991] ECR I-297).

Application of the principle of equal treatment to working conditions includes 'the conditions governing dismissal' (Article 5). 'Dismissal' has been interpreted broadly by the ECJ to include compulsory retirement, even where that is demanded at the same age as a state pension becomes payable (*Marshall (No 1)*); the significance of this ruling lies in the permitted continuance of differential state pensionable ages for men and women under Article 7 of the Social Security Directive (Council Directive (EEC) 79/7 (OJ L6 10.1.79 p 24) (see **social security**). It is widely believed that many instances of sexual harassment in the workplace breach the requirement of equality in working conditions.

Member States must provide redress for the victims of unequal treatment through 'judicial process after possible recourse to other competent authorities' (Article 6). This prohibits national law withdrawing any such cases from the jurisdiction of the courts (*Johnson*). It also requires the provision of sanctions which guarantee 'real and effective judicial protection' and which have a 'real deterrent effect on the employer' (Case 14/83 *Von Colson* [1984] ECR 1891). The particular circumstances of each case must be taken into consideration and, where there has been a discriminatory dismissal, only two

123

possible remedies satisfy the ECJ's criteria: reinstatement and compensation; if a state chooses compensation, it must be adequate to enable the loss sustained to be made good in full, which means that it cannot be subject to a limit and it must encompass the award of interest on the total compensation (Case C-271/91 *Marshall (No 2)* [1993] ECR I-4367).

Member States are permitted to make exclusions from the principle of equality where sex is critical to the nature or context of a job (Article 2(2)). Provisions concerning 'the protection of women, particularly as regards pregnancy and maternity' are also excepted (Article 2(3)); this permits special treatment to protect a mother's biological condition and also her special relationship with her baby (Case 184/83 *Hofmann* [1984] ECR 3047).

Application of the principle of equal treatment to the self-employed is the subject of a further Directive (Council Directive (EEC) 86/613 (OJ L359 19.12.86 p 56)).

EVELYN ELLIS

*Recommended reading*
Ellis *European Community Sex Equality Law* (1991) Clarendon Press.
Burrows & Mair *European Social Law* (1996) Wiley.

**EQUALITY** Various forms of discrimination are expressly prohibited by the EC Treaty. For example, the first paragraph of Article 6 EC (formerly Article 7) prohibits **discrimination** on the grounds of nationality within the scope of the Treaty; Article 40(3) EC requires the common organisation of agricultural markets to 'exclude any discrimination between producers or consumers within the Community'; and Article 119 EC lays down the principle that men and women should receive equal pay for equal work (see **equal treatment**).

The prohibition contained in Article 6 is reiterated, inter alia, in Articles 48(2), 52 and 59 EC. Article 6 'applies independently only to situations governed by Community law in respect of which the Treaty lays down no specific prohibition of discrimination' (Case C-18/93 *Corsica Ferries* [1994] ECR I-1783, para 19). However, breaches of Article 6(1) have been established in a variety of contexts. Where applicable, that provision produces **direct effect** (Joined Cases C-92/92 & C-326/92 *Phil Collins* [1993] ECR I-5145, paras 34-35).

Each specific prohibition of discrimination contained in the Treaty is 'merely a specific enunciation of the general principle of equality which is one of the fundamental principles of Community law. This principle requires that similar situations shall not be treated differently unless differentiation is objectively justified' (Joined Cases 124/76 & 20/77 *Moulins Pont-à-Mousson* [1977] ECR 1795, paras 16 and 17). The principle of equality may also be infringed by treating in the same way two situations which are essentially different (see eg Case 106/83 *Sermide* [1984] ECR 4209, para 28). It is not only overt discrimination which is prohibited, but also covert forms of discrimination which, by the application of other criteria of differentiation, lead in fact to the same result (see eg Case 61/77 *Commission v Ireland* [1978] ECR 417, para 78). In the absence of a specific derogation, it seems that the possibility of objective justification to which the Court of Justice has referred is available only in cases of covert, or indirect, discrimination, although the point is not free from doubt.

ANTHONY ARNULL

*Recommended reading*
Watson 'Equality of Treatment: A Variable Concept?' (1995) 24 ILJ 33.
Toth *The Oxford Encyclopaedia of European Community Law* (1990) Oxford
    University Press, vol I, pp 188–201.

**ESTABLISHMENT** See **freedom of establishment**.

**EURO** See **ECU/Euro**.

**EUROPE AGREEMENTS** The concept of 'Europe Agreements' in European Community law is very much linked with the fundamental political and economic changes taking place in Central and Eastern Europe. The idea was launched by the **Commission** in its Communication of 27 August 1990 on the conclusion of association agreements with countries of Central and Eastern Europe (COM (90) 398 final). Since then, Europe Agreements have been concluded with Hungary and Poland (entry into force: 1 February 1994) and with the Czech Republic, Slovak Republic, Bulgaria and Romania (entry into force: 1 February 1995). Europe Agreements have further been signed with Slovenia and the Baltic States. No Europe Agreements are envisaged with other states of the former USSR. With the latter countries, Partnership and Co-operation Agreements have been signed.

Europe Agreements are **association agreements** and their legal basis is Article 238 EC. They are **mixed agreements** and thus need ratification from all the Member States of the Community before they can enter into force. In order not to postpone the entry into force of the provisions on trade of the Europe Agreements, separate Interim Agreements were signed between the EEC and ECSC on the one hand and the respective associated countries on the other hand.

Originally, Europe Agreements were not conceived as pre-accession Treaties, since their Preambles only referred to '**accession**' as an ultimate goal of the associated country, not as a Community objective. However, at the **European Council** of Copenhagen of 21–22 June 1993 a political reorientation of the relationships with Central and Eastern Europe took place. It was accepted 'that the associated countries in

Central and Eastern Europe that so desire shall become members of the European Union'.

Europe Agreements contain provisions on political dialogue; trade; movement of workers; establishment; supply of services; payments; capital; competition and other economic provisions; approximation of laws; and economic, financial and cultural co-operation. Besides these substantive provisions, Europe Agreements also set up an institutional framework. Only some of the most important political and trade aspects will be further examined here.

The political dialogue (established through the Europe Agreements) has been further implemented and refined through the European Councils of Copenhagen and Essen (1994) and this has led to the organisation of 'structured relations' between institutions of the Union and of the associated countries. The main aim of these 'structured relationships' is to create a pre-accession atmosphere, thereby progressively integrating the associated countries in the activities of the European Union covering areas of common interest. Another aspect of the pre-accession strategy lies in the legal preparation of the associated countries to be integrated into the main parts of the **Internal Market**. This implies a vast programme of **approximation** of laws (see Commission White Paper for the Cannes European Council of 1995, COM (95) 163 final).

As far as trade is concerned, Europe Agreements aim at establishing a free trade zone for all goods (except, for the moment, for agricultural goods), but they do not envisage the establishment of a **customs union**. There is asymmetry in the obligations of the contracting parties in the sense that elimination of trade barriers should be more rapidly completed by the Community than by the associated countries. Notwithstanding this asymmetry, the Community has achieved a trade surplus with the associated Central and Eastern European countries. This also explains why the Copenhagen European Council decided to accelerate the pace of trade liberalisation from the side of the Community (since then implemented by various Community acts).

The implementation of the principle of **free movement of goods** varies according to the nature of the products concerned. A distinction is made between certain categories of industrial products. Liberalisation of trade in industrial products in general is quicker than for textiles and ECSC products. Also, as a result of the implementation of the conclusions of the Essen European Council, there has been alignment in the field of trade liberalisation of imports from Romania and Bulgaria to that of imports from the Visegrad countries. The Europe Agreements provide for immediate elimination by the Community of quantitative restrictions for industrial products. All customs duties on industrial products in general have been eliminated from 1 January 1995 on imports from the associated countries. For steel, the remaining tariffs were eliminated by 1 January 1996. With the entry into force of the Interim Agreements, quotas on imports of steel in the Community were immediately eliminated. However, certain tariff quotas remain for the moment applicable on some sensitive steel products originating in the Czech Republic and the Slovak Republic. For certain coal products (lignite) some Member States may still apply certain quotas for a limited period of time. For textiles the situation is as follows: quantitative restrictions have to be eliminated by 31 December 1997, while tariffs have to be eliminated by 1 January 1997. Free trade in agricultural products is, on the other hand, not a direct objective of the Europe Agreements. For agricultural products additional concessions have been made (quantitative restrictions and levies have been reduced), but the remaining trade barriers are to be further reduced through concessions granted 'on a harmonious and reciprocal basis'. Further concessions will, inter alia, take account of the rules of the **Common Agricultural Policy** and the results of the **GATT** negotiations.

The Europe Agreements allow resort to commercial defence instruments, ie safeguard and **anti-dumping** measures. The Community expects that once the competition rules and **state aid** legislation and practices in the associated countries are **harmonised** with that of the Community the need for such measures will decrease.

All Europe Agreements include a Protocol on **rules on origin**. These Protocols provide for bilateral cumulation of origin between the individual associated countries and the Community. Diagonal cumulation among the Visegrad countries is accepted and diagonal cumulation is also provided for in the EC–Romania Agreement for goods originating in Bulgaria. At the Essen European Council (1994) the EC has accepted the principle to extend diagonal cumulation to all countries with whom Europe Agreements have been concluded, but this implies that the associated countries concerned have taken the necessary legislative measures.

MARC MARESCEAU

*Recommended reading*
Maresceau & Montagatti 'The Relations Between the European Union and Central and Eastern Europe: A Legal Appraisal' (1995) 32 CMLRev 1327.
Maresceau 'Europe Agreements: A New Form of Cooperation Between the European Community and Central and Eastern Europe' in Müller Graff (ed) *East Central European States and the European Communities: Legal Adaptation to the Market Economy* (1993) Nomos Verlag, pp 209–233.


**EUROPEAN ATOMIC ENERGY COMMUNITY (Euratom)** The Euratom Treaty was signed in Rome on 25 March 1957, at the same time as the EEC Treaty, and entered into force on 1 January 1958. It was born of the failure of the draft European Defence Community and the draft European Political Community. In the wake of these failures, the Member States expressed determination at the Messina Conference in 1955 and through the Spaak Report of April 1956 to further the use of atomic energy for peaceful purposes.

The tasks of the Euratom Treaty are, as set out in Article 2 Euratom: the promotion of research and dissemination of technical information; the establishment of uniform safety standards; health and safety; the promotion of investment; the equitable supply of ores and nuclear fuels (the responsibility of the Euratom Supply Agency); the security of nuclear materials; the international pursuit of peaceful uses of nuclear energy; and the creation of a common market in specialised materials and equipment.

To these ends, the Euratom established an autonomous institutional framework similar to that of the European Community. The institutional differences which exist between the ECSC and EC Treaties are therefore not repeated with Euratom.

WILLIAM ROBINSON

*Recommended reading*
Pelzer *New Atomic Energy Law* (1995) Baden-Baden.
'Euratom: the Treaty establishing the European Atomic Energy Community' (1990) 18 International Business Lawyer 227.

**EUROPEAN BANK FOR RECONSTRUCTION AND DEVELOPMENT** The European Bank for Reconstruction and Development, established by Agreement dated 29 May 1990, is an international institution, having an authorised capital of 10 billion **ECU** and entrusted with the task of fostering the transition of the Countries of Eastern and Central Europe (CEEC) towards the principle of open markets and of encouraging private and entrepreneurial initiative in such of those countries as are committed to and are applying the principles of multiparty democracy, pluralism and market economics. Initially, 51% of its capital was owned by the Member States of the **European Union** and by the EC **institutions**. With successive **enlargements** of the European Union that proportion has increased. The balance of the shares are owned by the CEEC, the former CIS States and other leading industrial countries. It is based in London and has unlimited life.

The Bank may make loans, may guarantee debt instruments to be issued on capital markets and may take equity investments. It may provide technical advice and assistance within the sphere of its functions. It may also handle trust funds. No more than 40% of the Bank's loans to any country may be made to the state sector.

The Bank is required to apply sound banking principles to all its operations, and it should make investments on terms reflecting those sought by private investors. Its loans should not be subsidised out of the Bank's own resources. The Bank should follow the political principle of '**subsidiarity**' in that it should not fund an applicant who may obtain sufficient financing elsewhere.

The Bank is managed by a President under the control of a resident Board of Directors and, for broader issues of policy, is subject to the authority of the Board of Governors representing the shareholders. The two Boards have power to interpret the Articles of the Agreement, to increase the capital and by a special majority to amend the Articles.

D R R DUNNETT

*Recommended reading*
Dunnett 'The EBRD: A Legal Survey' (1991) 28 CMLRev 571-597.
Shihata *The EBRD: A Comparative Study of the Constituent Agreement* (1990) Graham & Trotman.

**EUROPEAN CENTRAL BANK** Based on strategic proposals in the 1989 Delors Report, the **Treaty on European Union** foresees the creation of a **monetary union** with a common currency and a **European Central Bank** (ECB) (see Articles 2, 3a(2), and 4a EC).

The first stage toward monetary union, which began on 1 July 1990, saw the liberalisation of capital transfers and the drafting of the convergence criteria. In conformity with Article 109f EC, the European Monetary Institute (EMI) was created at the beginning of the second stage as of January 1994. The EMI has its seat in Frankfurt/Main (Germany). Its President is Alexandre Lamfalussy, a Belgian national and former President of the Bank for International Settlements in Basle. The EMI´s main task is the preparation of monetary union and of the creation of the ECB, see the 4th Protocol annexed to the TEU.

With the beginning of the third stage, presumably in 1999, the EMI will be converted into the ECB. At the same time virtually all national decision-making powers in monetary matters will be transferred to the ECB and the **European System of Central Banks** (ESCB). The importance of the subject matter and the far-reaching transfer of authority explain why the ECB and the ESCB are extensively regulated in Articles 102a-109m EC and several Protocols annexed to the TEU.

The ECB will have legal personality on the European and international level and legal capacity in the Member States. Its decision-making body will be the Governing Council, consisting of the governors of the central banks of all participating states and between four and six independent experts forming the Executive Board. The Council shall meet at least ten times a year and will usually take decisions by a simple majority of its members. The Board shall have a president, a vice-president and between two and four additional members, each appointed 'by common accord of . . . the Heads of State or of government' for full-time service during a term of eight years, not renewable. The Board 'shall be responsible for the current business of the ECB' (see Article 11 of the ESCB and ECB Statute in the 3rd Protocol annexed to the TEU).

Similar to traditional national central banks, the ECB will 'define and implement the monetary policy of the Community'. To that end it 'shall have the exclusive right to authorize the issue of bank notes'. With its subscribed capital of at least 5,000 million ECU it will be able to intervene in financial markets. Furthermore, the ECB shall 'hold and manage the official foreign reserves of the Member States' and – in co-operation with the Council – it shall determine the exchange rate between the Euro and other currencies (see Articles 105, 105a, and 109 EC).

The primary objective of the ESCB and the ECB will be the maintenance of price stability (see Article 105(1)). Only if they do not conflict with this primary objective, other objectives of the EC as laid down in Articles 2 and 3 may be supported. To render credibility to the commitment of the ESCB to low inflation, the ECB itself, its officers, and all national central banks will be independent from Member State governments and Community institutions (see Articles 107 and 108 EC and Article 7 of the Statute). Neither the ECB nor national central banks are allowed to finance public deficits of any Community or national public authority (see Article 104), which might make them subject to political pressure.

The extreme degree of independence has been criticised as making a co-ordination of fiscal policy of the Member States and monetary policy of the ECB difficult, if not impossible. However, a new institution that cannot command the historic acceptance of the German Bundesbank, for example, and that will have to establish its credentials against governments seeking short-term benefits to win elections, needs clear and unambiguous goals and structures in order to be taken seriously.

FRANK EMMERT

*Recommended reading*
Artis 'European Monetary Union' in Artis and Lee (eds) *The Economics of the European Union* (1994) Oxford University Press.
Kenen *Economic and Monetary Union in Europe* (1995) Cambridge University Press.

**EUROPEAN COAL AND STEEL COMMUNITY (ECSC)** The European Coal and Steel Community (ECSC) was established by the Treaty of Paris of 18 April 1951. It was concluded between the 'Benelux' countries, France, Germany and Italy. The United Kingdom, despite having been invited to join, did not do so until its **accession** in 1973. The Treaty was concluded for a period of 50 years and is due to expire in July 2002. It forms, together with the **European Community** and the **European Atomic Energy Community**, the Second Pillar of the **European Union**.

The ECSC adopted the economic aim of creating a common market in coal and steel in an attempt to create real solidarity between its contracting parties in the longer-term pursuit of the political objectives of peace and European unity. The substantive provisions of the common market in coal and steel cover, as described in essence in Article 4 ECSC, import and export duties, discriminatory measures or practices, Member State subsidies or aids, and restrictive practices.

To this effect, the ECSC adopted the innovative approach of removing competencies from the Member States and placing them in the hands of an international body with **legal personality**, the Community, and creating supranational institutions with binding authority. The Special **Council of Ministers** (the Council), the High Authority (the **Commission**), the Common Assembly (the **European Parliament**) and the **Court of Justice** were established, 'to give direction to a destiny henceforward shared' in the ECSC. These institutions formed the model for the institutions of the Euratom and EC Treaties.

Despite the differences which exist between the EC Treaty and the ECSC Treaty, particularly regarding the greater role of the Commission under the ECSC Treaty and the terminology used for **legislative acts**, the Court of Justice has adopted, wherever possible, a unified interpretation of the Treaties as a source of Community law. However, the recent cases of Case C-128/92 *Banks* [1994] ECR I-1209 and Case C-18/94 *Hopkins*, judgment of 2 May 1996, have demonstrated that there remain fundamental differences between the ECSC and EC Treaties. Those cases concerned the powers and duties of the Commission and the lack of direct effect of ECSC provisions, when the analogous EC Treaty provisions have such an effect. The relationship between the Treaties is governed by Article 232 EC. This provides that the provisions of the EC Treaty shall not affect the provisions of the ECSC Treaty (see Case 328/85 *Deutsche Babcock* [1987] ECR 5119).

The future of the ECSC remains undecided. The Maastricht **Intergovernmental Conference** having decided not to consolidate the ECSC provisions into the EC Treaty, it remains to be seen whether the 1996 IGC will take that decision or allow the Treaty to lapse and the coal and steel sectors to be governed by the EC Treaty.

WILLIAM ROBINSON

*Recommended reading*
Merry 'The European Coal and Steel Community: Operations of the High Authority' (1995) VIII Western Political Quarterly 166.
Spierenburg & Poidevin *The History of the High Authority of the European Coal and Steel Community* (1993) Weidenfeld & Nicolson.

**EUROPEAN COMMISSION** The Commission is one of the five Community **institutions** (Article 4 EC) but, under Article E TEU, its role and **competences** are extended to **European Union** policy areas, most notably **Common Foreign and Security Policy** and **Co-operation in the Fields of Justice and Home Affairs**. The Commission is composed of 20 members, comprising at least one and not more than two from each Member State (Article 157 EC). By convention, larger Member States (currently Germany, France, Italy, Spain and the

United Kingdom) have two members. Only Member State nationals can be Commissioners. Members are expected to be independent in the exercise of their duties and take a solemn oath before the **Court of Justice** to this end. The Treaties expressly forbid the acceptance of instructions from governments or other bodies and exhort Commissioners to act in the general interests of the Community. The Commission is headed by a President – currently Jacques Santer (Luxembourg) – and may nominate one or two Vice-Presidents – currently Sir Leon Brittan (United Kingdom) and Manuel Marin (Spain).

The Commission is, and always has been, a collegiate body (the collegiality principle is established in the first Article of its internal rules of procedure). The Commission decides much by written procedure, with the college formally approving measures settled at a lower, preparatory level. It always seeks the broadest consensus among its members, though it may on occasion move to a formal vote (by simple majority of its members – Article 163 EC). However, once a decision is taken it will be accepted and defended by all of its members. Collegiality is one of the most enduring and fundamental characteristics of the Commission.

The Commission typically meets on the Wednesday of each week (held in Strasbourg when the Parliament is in session there, otherwise in Brussels). Each Commissioner is assisted by a small *cabinet* of personal advisers. A weekly meeting of the *chefs de cabinet* prepares the Commission's agenda. The relationship of the *chefs de cabinet* meeting to the college is similar to that of **COREPER** to the **Council**, the object being to boil down to its essentials the Commission's increasingly crowded agenda.

Beneath the political level of the college is an administration (largely based in Brussels, but with some services in Luxembourg) of some 15,000 officials. About 12% of the Commission's administration is involved in translation and interpretation. The administration is headed by a Secretary General and his deputy – currently David Williamson (United Kingdom) and Carlo Trojan (Netherlands), respectively. The administration is divided up into a number of horizontal services (for example, the Secretariat General, the legal service, translation and interpretation, the spokesman's group) and 25 vertical Directorates General (DGs) with specific policy competences (the DGs have been likened to 'mini-ministries'). Thus, the Commission is simultaneously a political organ and an administrative organisation.

The **Treaty on European Union** has revolutionised the Commission's political relationship to the **European Parliament**. Under Article 158 EC, the Commission's mandate was extended to five years (previously four) and synchronised with that of the Parliament (with a six-month lag), thus establishing an explicit link between elections to the Parliament and nominations to the Commission. The current Commission's term of office is from 1995 to 2000. Article 158 provides that the Member State governments should unanimously nominate the person they intend to appoint as Commission President after consulting the Parliament. Then, in consultation with the President-designate, the Member States nominate the other members of the Commission. Lastly, the President-designate and nominated members are subject as a body to a vote of approval by the European Parliament, and the thus-approved college is then unanimously appointed by the Member States.

The procedure was used for the first time in July 1994 and January 1995. The Parliament used its internal autonomy to maximum political effect, including the organisation of parliamentary committee hearings with each nominated member and explicit linkage with the Commission's annual legislative programming exercise. Underlying these arrangements is the Parliament's (so far never used) right to censure – ie dismiss – the Commission (Article 144 EC). The result has been to create new elements of political accountability and responsiveness echoing those of classic executive–legislature relationships.

The Commission is a *sui generis,* multi-purpose organisation, and there is not space here to engage in anything more than a rapid review of its main roles and responsibilities.

The Commission has an exclusive **right of initiative**, legislatively, (Article 155 EC) and its retention of a proprietal right over its legislative proposals is an important element in the balance of the Community's legislative process. The Commission does not legislate in a vacuum. Many proposals result from Council requests (Article 152 EC) and, since Maastricht, the Parliament has had a similar right (Article 138b EC), though the Commission does not accept automaticity in either case. The Commission's legislative intentions are increasingly flagged by consultative Green and White Papers, and the formulation of its proposals is bedded in a consultative network of advisory and expert committees. The Commission is inextricably involved throughout the legislative process (see **decision making**), whether through modification of its proposals, positioning on parliamentary amendments, or mediation between the Parliament and the Council in conciliation committees. Former Commission President Delors recently told the European Parliament that the two unique characteristics of the Commission were its monopoly of the right of initiative in the Community context and its consensus-building function.

The Commission also plays a vital role as political initiator, earning it the epithet of 'motor of integration'. The Exchange Rate Mechanism, the **Internal Market** ('1992'), the Delors Packages on the Community's finances, the Maastricht blueprint for **Economic and Monetary Union** and the 1994 **European Council** initiatives on growth, competitiveness and employment are all examples of major, Commission-driven initiatives.

The Commission exercises important managerial and administrative functions, particularly in relation to the Community's financial responsibilities (for example, the structural funds), and in the European Coal and Steel Community context. The Commission drafts a first version, and implements the final version of the Community **budget**. It enjoys considerable delegated executive powers, particularly in relation to the management of the **Common Agricultural Policy**. The Commission manages and monitors the Internal Market. In particular, the Commission is the Community's entirely independent **competition** authority and increasingly instigates Community-wide **industrial policy** initiatives. The Commission is the Community's external representative and negotiator on trade, as well as its representative in various international organisations and other forums.

The Commission plays a vital role as 'guardian of the Treaties', constantly monitoring the implementation of Community law. It may launch infringement proceedings against Member States (Article 169 EC) (see **action for failure to fulfil an obligation**) and, ultimately, it may urge the Court to impose fines (Article 171 EC). The Commission plays an important role in Community economic policy making and will take on additional duties for the monitoring of Member States' budgetary situations once Economic and Monetary Union has been established.

The Commission plays important informal roles as mediator and conciliator between the Member States, and between the Council and the Parliament. The Commission has also been characterised as the Community's 'conscience', its actions being distinctively coloured by its independence and supranationality and by its collegial identification with the overall Community interest.

MARTIN WESTLAKE

*Recommended reading*
Edwards & Spence (eds) *The European Commission* (1994) Longman.
Philip Morris Institute for Public Policy Research *What Future for the European Commission* (1995) Brussels.


**EUROPEAN COMMUNITIES ACT** The European Communities Act 1972 incorporated Community law into the law of the United Kingdom. The twin principles upon which the Community legal order rests, namely **direct effect** and the **supremacy** of Community law, were specifically implemented into the law of the United Kingdom.

As to direct effect, section 2(1) of the European Communities Act provides: 'All such rights, powers, liabilities, obligations and restrictions from time to time created or arising by or under the Treaties, and all such remedies and procedures arising by or under the Treaties, as in accordance with the Treaties are without further enactment to be given legal effect or used in the United Kingdom shall be recognised and available in law, and be enforced, allowed and followed accordingly; and the expression "enforceable Community right" and similar expressions shall be read as referring to one to which this subsection applies.' Two matters follow from section 2(2). First, Community law having direct effect forms part of the law of the United Kingdom. Those rights which are not reliant upon the direct effect of Community law, in particular the general principles of **'indirect effect'** (the obligation of uniform interpretation of national law with Community law) and **damages against the Member State** (the principle of liability established in Joined Cases C-6/90 & C-9/90 *Francovich* [1991] ECR I-5357), do not, on a narrow construction, fall within section 2(2). Commentators have suggested that this is a possible reason for the divergent case law on the obligation of uniform interpretation by the House of Lords. Second, Community law does not need to be proved (as does foreign law) before the courts of the United Kingdom. A corollary to this is the obligation of the United Kingdom courts to take judicial notice of decisions of the **Court of Justice** (section 3(2)).

As to the supremacy of Community law, section 2(4) of the European Communities Act provides that 'any enactment passed or to be passed ... shall be construed and have effect subject to the foregoing provisions of this section'. Through this device, all legislative Acts enacted subsequent to the European Communities Act are subject to Community law. The judiciary have now clearly accepted that it is the duty of United Kingdom courts to override any rule of national law found to be in conflict with directly effective Community law, and that whatever limitations this might place upon Dicey's model of Parliamentary sovereignty have been accepted by Parliament upon the adoption of the European Communities Act (see *R v Secretary of State for Transport, ex p Factortame* [1991] 1 AC 603, per Lord Bridge).

Section 2(2) of the European Communities Act provides for the implementation of Community secondary legislation, where necessary, by Order in Council. Whilst certain pieces of Community secondary legislation have been enacted by primary legislation, the majority have been implemented through statutory instruments, either under section 2(2) or under other statutory implementing powers in specific fields or under a combination of the two. The Community source of a piece of United Kingdom legislation is therefore not always entirely clear.

The European Communities Act 1972 has been amended by the European Communities (Amendment) Act 1986, which implemented the **Single European Act**, and the European Communities (Amendment) Act 1993, which implemented the **Treaty on European Union** including the reserved positions on the Social Protocol and **economic and monetary union**. The ratification of the Treaty on European Union was the subject of an unsuccessful application for judicial review by Lord Rees-Mogg (*R v Secretary of State for the*

*Foreign and Commonwealth Office, ex p Rees-Mogg* [1993] 3 CMLR 101).

WILLIAM ROBINSON

*Recommended reading:*
Bates 'United Kingdom Implementation of EU Directives' (1996) Statute Law Review 27.
Collins *European Community Law in the United Kingdom* (4th edn, 1990) Butterworths.

**EUROPEAN COMMUNITY (GEOGRAPHICAL SCOPE)** At present, there are 15 Member States of the **European Union,** of which the European Community forms part of one **Pillar:** Austria, Belgium, Denmark, Finland, France, Germany, Greece, Ireland, Italy, Luxembourg, The Netherlands, Portugal, Spain, Sweden and the United Kingdom.

The six founder members of the Communities, the ECSC in 1951 and Euratom and the EEC in 1957, are Belgium, France, Germany, Italy, Luxembourg and The Netherlands. They were followed by Denmark, Ireland and the United Kingdom in 1972, by Greece in 1981, by Spain and Portugal in 1986 and by Austria, Finland and Sweden on 1 January 1995. Norway, whose application to join had been accepted and ratified by the Member States, decided against **accession** to the Community in a referendum and remains a member of the **European Economic Area.**

Annex IV to the EC Treaty contains the names of associated countries and territories, which have special relations with a Member State, to which Part IV of that Treaty applies. (See **association agreements, Lomé Convention** and also **Europe Agreements** and **accession**).

Cyprus and Malta applied in 1990. Their entry is targeted for shortly after the 1996 **Intergovernmental Conference.** A number of Central and Eastern European countries have applied or are expected to apply for membership. Many are at present linked to the Community by the **Europe Agreements.** Hungary, Poland, the Czech and Slovak Republics, as well as Slovenia, are likely to be high on the list, with others such as the Baltic States and some Balkan countries, further behind. The prospects of others, such as the countries which make up the CIS, are in the more distant future. The application of Turkey has been put on hold because of a number of human rights and economic concerns. The remaining EEA counties, Norway, Iceland and Liechtenstein, are closely linked with the Community through the EEA Agreement, but they are not expected to join in the near future. This also applies to Switzerland, which had voted in a referendum in December 1992 not to join the EEA.

MARGOT HORSPOOL

*Recommended reading*
Hartley *The Foundations of European Community Law* (3rd edn, 1994) Oxford University Press, pp 3–10.

Lasok & Bridge *Law and Institutions of the European Union* (6th edn, 1994) Butterworths, pp 17–23.

**EUROPEAN COMMUNITY LAW** EC law is the law of the European Communities as it applies within the **European Union**. It is contained in, or has reference to, the part of the TEU which consists of the amended **EC, ECSC** and **Euratom** Treaties, and its final provisions; the other two intergovernmental 'Pillars' of the **Treaty on European Union** (Title V: **CFSP** and Title VI: **Co-operation in the Fields of Justice and Home Affairs**) do not, strictly speaking, produce 'EC law' and are not under the jurisdiction of the **Court of Justice**.

EC law is contained in the following sources:

(a) The Constitutive Treaties, including Protocols but not **Declarations**; subsidiary Conventions and Acts of **Accession**.

(b) **Legislative acts** adopted under the Treaties, the most important being: Regulations, Directives and Decisions (see Article 189 EC). Regulations are directly applicable in the Member States, whereas Directives are addressed to the Member States and have to be implemented by them. Decisions are addressed to and binding on those to whom they are addressed. International agreements concluded by the Community also form part of EC law as do *sui generis* acts of the institutions, particularly the **Council**. The legal status of the latter acts is not always clear (see the **Luxembourg Compromise**, the **Ioannina Compromise**).

(c) **General principles of Community law** as set out by the ECJ are those which exist in one or more Member States, such as: **legal certainty, proportionality, human rights**.

(d) The case law of the ECJ, although there is no formal doctrine of **precedent**, is nevertheless an important source of EC law. The ECJ has developed important principles of EC law, such as the doctrines of **direct effect** and **supremacy**, and filled gaps in the Treaties by a wide **interpretation** of the texts and by the use of general principles of law (see above).

(e) **'Soft law'** is also considered to be part of EC law, constitution in particular by recommendations, opinions and statements by Commissioners and officials.

MARGOT HORSPOOL

*Recommended reading*
Hartley *The Foundations of European Community Law* (3rd edn, 1994) Oxford University Press, pp 95–189.
Lasok & Bridge *Law and Institutions of the European Union* (6th edn, 1994) Butterworths, pp 81–178.

**EUROPEAN COMPANY STATUTE** If adopted, the proposed European Company Statute (OJ C176 8.7.91 p 1 and COM (91) 174) would provide a corporate structure with limited liability available as an alternative structure for businesses across the Member States.

The present proposal is that of a Regulation governing a 'core' of **company law** provisions, to which a Directive concerning worker participation would be 'indissolubly associated' (see below). The laws of the Member States are to be used to fill in the 'gaps' left by the Statute. The creation of the above supranational body of law is important to the **Commission** as it should help to create a European perspective for businesses.

The fact that the proposed Regulation containing the structural company law is based on Article 100a EC has been criticised, as that Article provides for the **approximation** of laws only. Some (in particular the United Kingdom) argue that approximation does not include the creation of a new supranational instrument. Others feel, however, that approximation extends to the situation where the same laws will in future be found in all Member States. The Directive part of the Statute is based on Article 54(3)(g). It could not be founded on Article 100a, as Article 100a(2) excludes measures involving worker participation provisions. The Statute is still under discussion but has met with so much opposition that its future is uncertain.

*Creation* A European company can be created: (a) through a merger between companies or the creation of a holding company; (b) by creation of a joint subsidiary; or (c) through the creation by an existing European Company of another by merger or the creation of a holding company or a joint subsidiary. There must either be participating companies from more than one Member State or companies in a Single Member state may set up a European Company if they have branches in a Member State other than that of their central administration. The methods are the same as in (a), (b), and (c) above, but the requirement of two legal entities from different Member States is downgraded to a requirement for branches in a Member State other than that of the central administration of the company seeking to convert to European Company form.

*Worker participation* If a business decided to use the European company format, worker participation would be compulsory, however few employees there were. The options for worker participation are very similar to those set out in the Fifth Directive (see **Company law**).
   The schemes are:
(a) Employee participation in the appointment of the members of the supervisory organ. In this scheme between one-third and one-half of the supervisory board are to be appointed by the employees of the company.
(b) Employee participation through a body representing company employees. In this case a body representing the employees will have a right to regular information and consultation on the administration, situation, progress and prospects of the company,

together with its competitive position, credit situation and investment plans.

(c) Employee participation through collectively agreed systems. By this, alternative employee participation is to be regulated in accordance with collective agreements concluded between the company and organisations representing employees. The minimum contents of such agreements are specified.

*Boards* As in the Fifth Directive, there is provision for a single board system and a dual board system.

The two-tier system has a management board appointed, supervised and removed by a supervisory board. The supervisory board must receive quarterly reports on the development of the business and is able to call for information on any company matters at any time. Between a third and a half of the supervisory board may be appointed by employees if the relevant model of worker participation is chosen.

The single-tier system has an administrative board with at least three members unless the company does not have a system of election of employees to the board. In such circumstances the board may have two members or only one member. Earlier drafts required non-executive members to be in the majority and supervise executive members. Article 66 does not require a formal division of functions.

Where a company suffers loss directors are to be jointly and severally liable and a director must prove that he was not in breach of his obligations in order to escape liability.

*Shareholders* A 10% minority can call a general meeting and put items on the agenda. Shareholders' votes must be proportionate to their stake in the company, except in certain circumstances when they can be restricted. The company may not provide for multiple voting rights. A shareholder with a 'legitimate interest' can enforce the articles of association.

*Interface between EC and national law* In accordance with the boundary between EC law and national law, reference is to be had first to the Regulation, supplemented by the rules of the company's constitution as authorised by the Regulation. If that does not provide a solution, the law governing public limited companies in the state of registration will govern the issue, supplemented by the constitution of the company within the limits authorised by the laws governing public limited companies in that Member State. Although this creates a workable hierarchy of rules it will not solve all problems. One major difficulty with the Statute is the extent to which provisions of the Regulation supplant the existing rules of Member States where the Regulation makes no specific provision for a change. Will the existence of supervisory boards and employee directors, for example, change the traditional United Kingdom rule that all directors owe exactly similar fiduciary duties to the company?

The company must be registered in the state where central administration and control are kept and it seems that the European company will be subject to the taxation provisions of the law of the state of registration. Similarly, the insolvency and winding-up provisions of the state of registration will apply.

JANET DINE

*Recommended reading*
Dine *EC Company Law* (1991) Wiley Chancery Law.
House of Lords Select Committee on the European Communities 'European Company Statute' Session 1989-90, 19th Report (1990) HMSO.

**EUROPEAN CONVENTION ON HUMAN RIGHTS AND FUNDAMENTAL FREEDOMS** Signed on 4 November 1950, the European Convention on Human Rights and Fundamental Freedoms (ECHR) is the principal human rights instrument of the Council of Europe. The contracting states undertake to 'secure to everyone within their jurisdiction the rights and freedoms defined in Section I' of the Convention.

Section II established a Commission and Court of Human Rights, which bear primary responsibility for ensuring observance of states' obligations under the Convention. Both institutions are based in Strasbourg (France). Sections III and IV deal with the composition and role of the Commission and Court, respectively. Section V sets out miscellaneous provisions, including those relating to ratification and reservations.

The Convention rights are primarily civil and political in nature, including the right to life, liberty, fair trial, privacy, freedom of religion, expression, assembly and freedom from torture and slavery etc. This list has been expanded by Protocols on property and educational rights, free elections, free movement, rights of aliens, capital punishment, criminal justice etc. Furthermore, the Court of Human Rights interprets the Convention as a 'living instrument' by taking account of current rights standards (*Tyrer v United Kingdom* (1978) 2 EHRR 1).

Most of the rights in the Convention are subject to substantive limitations. For example, the right to privacy may be subject to such limitation as is '. . . in accordance with law and is necessary in a democratic society, in the interests of national security, public safety, or the economic well-being of the country, for the prevention of disorder or crime, for the protection of health or morals, or for the protection of the rights and freedoms of others'. While states are allowed a 'margin of appreciation' in respect of the limitation of rights, this freedom is subject to strict scrutiny by the Commission and Court. In particular, a limitation must be accessible and formulated with precision and be proportionate in that it meets a 'pressing social need' (*Handyside v United Kingdom* (1979/80) 1 EHRR 737).

Exceptionally, the right to bodily integrity and the prohibition of the collective expulsion of aliens are absolute in that they are not qualified by a limitation clause.

Article 15 ECHR permits a state to derogate, to the extent strictly required, from its obligations under the Convention in time of war or public emergency threatening the life of the nation. While states are granted a certain 'margin of appreciation' in such a situation, measures taken remain subject to scrutiny by the Commission and Court. Furthermore, derogation is not permitted in respect of the right to life (apart from death resulting from lawful acts of war), the right to bodily integrity, freedom from slavery and retroactive penal sanction.

Article 24 provides Contracting States with a right of petition where another state party to the Convention is in breach of any provision of the Convention. However, the bulk of the Convention's jurisprudence derives from Article 25, which provides individuals, non-governmental organisations or groups of individuals, who are the alleged victims of a violation of Convention rights, with a right of petition. An application by any such alleged victim must meet several procedural requirements before being deemed admissible by the Commission. Local remedies must first be exhausted, the application must be within a six-month limitation period, it must not be anonymous, substantially the same as one already considered by the Commission, incompatible with the provisions of the Convention, manifestly ill-founded or an abuse of the right to petition.

If the application is deemed admissible, the Commission seeks a friendly settlement between the parties and, failing that, adjudicates upon the merits of the case. Thereafter, the case may be referred (at present by the Commission or a state, but not the individual victim) to the Court of Human Rights for adjudication. The Court, which may sit in Chambers or as a Plenary Court, conducts oral hearings in public and has the power to award 'just satisfaction' where it finds a violation of the Convention. If a case is not referred to the Court, the Committee of Ministers of the Council of Europe may by a two-thirds majority find a violation.

The 11th Protocol to the Convention represents the most significant overhaul of the Convention's mechanism to date. Signed in May 1994, the Protocol will enter into force one year after it has been ratified by all the Convention's Contracting States. The Protocol will replace the existing Sections II, III and IV with a new Section II. One year after its entry into force the functions of the Commission will be conducted by a new permanent Court of Human Rights. Members of this new Court, sitting in Committees of three, will consider the admissibility of all applications and the majority of cases will be heard by Chambers comprising of seven judges. The full Court (Grand Chamber) will hear inter-state cases as well as other cases where a Chamber, with the consent of the parties involved, relinquishes jurisdiction.

PATRICK TWOMEY

141

*Recommended reading*
Harris, Warbrick & O'Boyle *The European Convention on Human Rights* (1995) Butterworths.
Jacobs & White *The European Convention on Human Rights* (2nd edn, 1996) Oxford University Press.

**EUROPEAN COUNCIL** The notion of European Council refers to all or any of the meetings of Heads of State or Government of the Member States of the **European Union**. Over the last two decades these 'summit meetings' have played a key role in the development of the EU.

The creation of the European Council was agreed in 1974; the first meeting was held in March 1975. Even with ratification of the **Treaty on European Union**, the provisions concerning the European Council are minimalist; they are in the Common Provisions of the Treaty (Article D) rather than in the 'supranational' part of the Treaties. This extra-constitutional situation derives from the participants' wishes to retain the European Council's informal, political character and to safeguard its flexibility.

The European Council is composed of the EU Heads of Government (or State) and the President of the **European Commission**. They are assisted by the EU Foreign Ministers and a senior Commissioner. Civil servants are excluded from participation but their advice may be sought from suites adjoining the conference room. The meetings are normally held twice each year in a venue chosen by the Member State holding the Presidency of the **Council of the European Union**. Extra meetings may be called to deal with crisis situations.

Since 1975, the European Council has played a key role in launching initiatives, solving problems deciding on the successive **enlargements** and overseeing the constitutional order and financial framework of the EU. Its main achievement in the 1970s was to launch the **European Monetary System**. In the 1980s it was initially concerned with solving the crisis over British budgetary contributions. Later in the 1980s it opened the way for the Single Market programme and presided over the process leading to the **Single European Act**. In the 1990s the European Council launched the negotiations leading to the TEU, finalising the terms at its Maastricht session in December 1991.

SIMON BULMER

*Recommended reading*
Bulmer & Wessels *The European Council: Decision-Making in European Politics* (1987) Macmillan.
Werts *The European Council* (1992) North-Holland.

**EUROPEAN ECONOMIC AREA (EEA)** The Treaty establishing the European Economic Area was signed on 2 May 1992 in Oporto. Its signatories were the 12, as they were at that time, Member States of the

European Communities, the European Economic Community, the **European Coal and Steel Community** and the seven members of the European Free Trade Area (Austria, Finland, Iceland, Liechtenstein, Norway, Sweden and Switzerland). A Protocol having been signed on 17 March 1993 to make the necessary amendments to the Treaty following the decision by Switzerland, by referendum in December 1992, not to ratify the Treaty, the EEA entered into force on 1 January 1995. The accession of Austria, Finland and Sweden to the European Union has reduced to three (Iceland, Liechtenstein and Norway) the non-Community Member States of the EEA.

The preamble to the Agreement attached importance to the privileged relationship between the parties based on proximity, long-standing common values and European identity. The Agreement therefore aimed to promote trade on equal grounds of competition and according to the same rules. The core obligations of the EEA are the **free movement of capital, goods, persons** and **services** and the horizontal provisions relevant thereto (**social policy, consumer policy, environment**, statistics and **company law**) and **competition policy**. In addition, the parties agreed to strengthen and broaden co-operation in the framework of the Community's activities in the fields such as **research and development**, the environment, **education**, social policy, consumer protection, SMEs and tourism. The parties agreed to be bound by the existing *acquis communautaire*. To this end Annexes I-XXII listed 1,600 legislative acts of the Communities (either directly or by reference) which constituted the *acquis communautaire* in the relevant fields. However, the Agreement notably did not extend the following Community policies to the EEA: the common commercial, agricultural and fisheries policies, to indirect taxation and to economic and monetary policies. The EEA therefore created an extended free trade area but not a customs union.

The EEA established an institutional framework. Six bodies were established: the EEA Council, EEA Joint Committee, EEA Joint Parliamentary Committee, EEA Consultative Committee, EEA Surveillance Authority and the EFTA Court. These institutions differ from those of the Communities. First, the decision-making procedure relies upon consensus between the Community and its Member States, on the one hand, and the EFTA States, on the other. Second, legislative powers have not been transferred to these institutions. The institutions are based upon co-operation, thereby ruling out procedures such as qualified majority voting.

The EEA Council (composed of each Member State's government and the European Commission) and the EEA Joint Committee (composed of representative of the contracting parties) constitute the decision-making bodies. They are advised by the EEA Joint Parliamentary Committee, composed of an equal membership of the European Parliament and EFTA States' parliaments, and the EEA Consultative Committee (the equivalent of the **Economic and Social**

**Committee**), which were established to contribute to a better mutual understanding. Finally, compliance with the Agreement was to be ensured by an EFTA Surveillance Authority and an EFTA Court. The EFTA Surveillance Authority performs a role analogous to the **Commission** for the EFTA Member States. Following the adverse opinion of the **Court of Justice** to the initial proposition for an joint Court (Opinion 1/91 *EEA Agreement* [1991] ECR I-6079), the EFTA Court is composed only of judges from the EFTA Member States and its jurisdiction is so limited. Uniformity of jurisprudence between the EFTA Court and the Court of Justice is maintained by means of exchange of information and, if necessary, the intervention of the EEA Joint Committee.

WILLIAM ROBINSON

*Recommended reading*
Bright & Williams 'Understanding the European Economic Area: context, institutions and legal systems' (1994) Business Law in the European Economic Area 1.
Norberg, Hökberg & Johansson *The European Economic Area: EEA Law: a Commentary on the EEA Agreement* (1993) Fritzes.


**EUROPEAN ENVIRONMENTAL AGENCY**  The objective of this Community organ is to provide information and technical and scientific support to the Community **institutions** and Member States to enable them to take measures to protect the environment assess the results of such measures and ensure that the public, policy makers, business and non-governmental organisations are properly informed about the state of the environment and the pressures on it.

The Agency was created by Council Regulation (EEC) 1210/90 (OJ L120 11.5.90 p 1) and became a legal entity on 30 October 1993. The Agency's headquarters are in Copenhagen. A staff of about 50 are directed by a Management Board, consisting of one representative from each Member State, and headed by an Executive Director. The Management Board is advised by a Scientific Committee comprising of nine individuals designated by the Member States and two representatives from the **European Commission**. In addition, two scientists are designated by the **European Parliament**.

The Agency has a number of key functions. First, developing the Environmental Information and Observation Network (EIONET), which will entail co-ordinating the work and forging links between existing research and policy institutes in the Member States. Second, publishing a report on the state of the European environment every three years and a series of monographs on specific media, regions and environmental problems such as the state of European rivers and lakes, urban air and landscapes. Third, establishing guidelines for assessing and drawing up indicators of the environmental impacts of economic sectors (for example, transport, tourism, and agriculture).

JANE HOLDER

*Recommended reading*
'European Environmental Agency Gets Under Way' (1995) ENDS (Environmental Data Services) No 240, 20–22.


**EUROPEAN FREE TRADE AREA (EFTA)** The European Free Trade Area was established by the Stockholm Convention of 1960. Its original members were Austria, Denmark, Liechtenstein (on account of its customs union with Switzerland), Norway, Portugal, Sweden, Switzerland and the United Kingdom. It established a free trade area. It neither created a customs union nor intended to achieve long-term economic integration. Its membership was increased in 1970 and 1986 with the accession of Iceland and Finland, respectively. However, its membership has decreased on the **accession** of the majority of its members to the Communities: Denmark and the United Kingdom (1973), Portugal (1986) and Austria, Finland and Sweden (1995).

The EFTA States signed the **European Economic Area** Agreement in 1992 in order to strengthen its free trade relationships with the European Communities. Switzerland did not, however, ratify the EEA Agreement following its rejection by referendum by the Swiss in December 1992. Iceland, Liechtenstein and Norway remain as the EFTA States within the EEA Agreement.


**EUROPEAN INTEGRATION (THEORIES OF)** The evolution of integration theory in the last 40 years in part mirrors that of the European Union. Neo-functionalist theories in the late 1950s and early 1960s predicted the gradual transfer of functional responsibilities from the nation state to supranational bodies, an assumption reflected to some extent in the EU's technocratic 'Monnet method'; intergovernmentalist explanations noted the resilience of the nation state and the continued defence of national interests, reflecting the Gaullist vision of a *Europe des patries* and 1970s Euro-sclerosis; the Single Market programme revived both the Union and integration theory, prompting a series of theoretical studies of policy making and EU governance.

Neo-functionalism, whose chief exponents included Ernest Haas and Leon Lindberg, depicted European integration as an incremental process driven by functional necessity and shaped by interest groups who shift their activities to supranational institutions in response to the declining efficacy of the nation state as a utility provider. Functional and political 'spillover' is central to the neo-functionalist account of the integration process, being the sector-by-sector transfer of policies, expectations and loyalties from the national to the European arena.

145

Transnational interest groups and supranational institutions (the **Commission** and **Court of Justice**) become increasingly important as this process gathers momentum.

Federalist ideas have played an important role in the European project, though federalists like Altiero Spinelli have ultimately been disappointed by the incremental and technocratic evolution of the Union. Federal theories portrayed European integration as a political process culminating in the creation of a federal European state whose constitution divides policy responsibility between supranational, national and regional levels of government. But rather than moving towards a federal or functional end-state, the EU has instead developed *sui generis*, a situation reflected in the different interpretations of the nature of the Union offered by international relations theorists and European lawyers (see, for example, the works of John Pinder on neo-federalism and Joseph Weiler on EU constitutionalism).

Intergovernmentalism, pioneered by Stanley Hoffman in the mid-1960s in response to the theoretical and predictive failings of neo-functionalism, accords leading actor status to national governments. National governments are viewed as rational actors, defending their national interests in areas of 'high politics' (such as foreign or macro-economic policy), while accepting the 'Europeanisation' of some areas of 'low politics' as this can (in Alan Milward's phrase) 'rescue the nation state' by increasing the relative autonomy of the executive within the state and allowing it to achieve previously unattainable goals. Andrew Moravcsik's 'liberal intergovernmentalist' perspective uses the concept of a 'two-level game': national governments link the international and domestic levels, defending their interests in the EU but bargaining with interest groups when formulating their European policy in the domestic arena. The focus on domestic politics thus helps overcome the tendency of early intergovernmentalist accounts to treat nation states as unitary actors.

The relaunch of the EU in the mid-1980s in turn revived the study of European integration. Differing accounts of the origins and significance of the Single Market programme emerged: some resurrected neo-functionalist notions of 'spillover' and supranational politics; others, like Moravcsik, focused on inter-state bargaining and domestic factors. More significantly, there has also been a trend away from the competing international relations assumptions which inform neo-functionalist and intergovernmentalist models (which draw on pluralist and realist paradigms respectively), towards the application of political science and comparative politics methods to the study of the EU (by, for example, Simon Bulmer). Empirical studies of policy networks (structures of interest mediation and policy making), multi-level governance (horizontal and vertical links between EU, state and regional actors) and 'new institutionalism' (the role of EU institutions and norms) have added to the understanding of EU governance.

Studies of the Single Market project and the EMU have highlighted a range of explanatory factors – political economy, domestic politics, inter-state bargaining, and multi-level EU policy making – rather than offering one over-arching theoretical or prescriptive framework.

PHILIP LYNCH

*Recommended reading*
Nelsen & Stubb *The European Union, Readings on the Theory and Practice of European Integration* (1994) Rienner.
Sinnott *Understanding the European Union* (forthcoming) Macmillan.


**EUROPEAN INVESTMENT BANK** The European Investment Bank is an international organisation established by Article 198d EC. The Statute of the Bank is appended to the Treaty. Its members are the Member States of the **European Union**. The Bank's issued capital is 57 billion ECU. With annual lending of 20 billion ECU it is the development bank with the largest volume of business in the world. The aim of the Bank is to further the balanced and steady development of the economics of the Member States of the EU in the common interest of all.

It acts by making loans and granting guarantees in support of investment projects and programmes that principally advance regional development, that exploit advanced technology or that involve co-operation between nationals of different Member States. Some 10% of its present lending activity is directed to countries formally associated with the EU in Eastern Europe, Africa, America, Asia and the Pacific. These loans are made under the guarantee of the EC or the Member States. Its loans are not subsidised; their terms reflect interest rates prevailing on the international bond markets. The Bank, which is non-profit making, seeks in its lending policy to promote free public tendering of goods and services and the highest environmental standards practised within the EU.

The Bank must obtain as security for its loans the guarantee of a Member State or other 'adequate security'. Its loans, where not made to government, should be made in the 'productive' sector of the economy.

The current business of the Bank is conducted by a Management Committee under the President of the Bank. Credit and current policy decisions are made by the Board of Directors comprising representatives of the Member States and the **Commission**. General policy guidelines are laid down by the Board of Governors comprising ministers of the governments of the Member States.

The chief present-day issues concerning the Bank include the application of the principle of **subsidiarity** and the pressure to adapt to the prevailing economic trend towards privatisation of state services and infrastructure. Liquidity and liberalisation of the capital markets also pose a challenge, and shortage of capital *per se* is no longer part of the Bank's *raison d'être*. The Bank finds a role in the relative adaptability of its loan conditions to project needs and in its capability for economic and technical analysis of investment projects.

D R R DUNNETT

*Recommended reading*
Dunnett 'European Investment Bank: autonomous instrument of common policy?' 31 CMLR Rev. 721–763.
EIB *The European Investment Bank: the European Community's financial institution* (1992) Office for Official Publications.

**EUROPEAN INVESTMENT FUND** The European Investment Fund was brought into existence in June 1994 by a decision of the Finance Ministers of the Member States of the **European Union** in their capacities as Governors of the **European Investment Bank**. This decision was taken under powers expressly accorded to them by virtue of a Treaty of 25 March 1993 amending the Protocol to the EC Treaty on the Statute of the European Investment Bank. The object of the creation of the Fund was to provide through a Community body the means to assist and improve the effectiveness of the **Internal Market** and the competitiveness of Community industry. The Fund does this by guaranteeing finance for **trans-European networks** (TENs) in the fields of **transport**, **energy** and **telecommunications** and by providing temporary equity funding for small and medium enterprises (SMES) of the Member States. The Member States took the view that this body was needed to complement the work of the European Investment Bank, since the Bank could not by the terms of its Statute take on all the risks that would be involved in the financing of TENs, and since SMEs were in need less of loans than of equity capital, a means of support that the Bank is unable to provide.

The Fund is to operate so as to earn an appropriate return on it resources. This is provided by its Statute and ensured by the presence of financial institutions of the Member States among its shareholders. These institutions' aggregate participation may reach 30% of the authorised capital of the Fund. Of the balance the shares are split in the proportion 30/40 between the European Union, represented by the EC Commission, and the Bank. The Fund has an initial authorised capital of 2,000 million ECU. The Fund may issue guarantees for up to three times its subscribed capital.

The Fund's sole initial activity is to issue guarantees to support the financing of TENs. Offers of a guarantee of the Fund should considerably increase the volume of loans available to support investment in TENs under private ownership. From June 1996, the Fund is empowered to pursue its second line of activity, namely the taking of equity in SMEs, an activity for which a strong demand is likewise expected. Thus the Fund's sphere will range from very large investment projects to the small.

The Statute of the Fund is a document subject in certain respects to public law and in others to private law. Jurisdiction on internal issues is vested in the **Court of Justice**, while disputes with its contractual partners are within the competence of national courts.

D R R DUNNETT

**EUROPEAN MONETARY INSTITUTE** See **monetary union**.

**EUROPEAN MONETARY SYSTEM (EMS)** Different national currencies can either be left to fluctuate freely according to offer and demand, be managed to fluctuate only in a buffered manner and/or within pre-defined bands, or be fixed permanently at a certain level to each other.

If exchange rates are left to fluctuate freely, they may be subject to rapid and substantial changes as economic conditions in the countries concerned change or as currency speculation generates artificial offer of one currency and demand for another.

In such an environment, business transactions between countries become more expensive. Sellers who are going to receive a foreign currency for their goods or services and resellers who have to pay a foreign currency will adjust their prices if there is a risk that the foreign currency becomes more expensive between the arrangement of the business transaction and the time of payment.

This was basically the situation in the European Communities in the 1970s after the international Bretton-Woods System of managed exchange rates had been abandoned in 1973. Regardless of efforts of the Member States to stabilise exchange rates in the so-called 'snake-in-the-tunnel', exchange rates varied so much that they impaired effective utilisation of the fundamental freedoms in the Common Market. In many cases it was cheaper to buy from a less efficient but domestic supplier than from a more efficient but foreign one. Therefore, the Member States decided in 1979 to move to a European system of managed exchange rates and created the European Monetary System.

The EMS consists of two elements: the European Currency Unit (**ECU**), and the Exchange Rate Mechanism (ERM).

The ECU is an artificial inter-bank currency. Its value is based upon a basket of all national currencies of the Member States and published daily in the Official Journal. The stronger currencies, that is, those least likely to depreciate, are given more weight in the calculation of the ECU, making it a relatively stable unit of account for worldwide trade and banking. However, as the ECU can only be used for inter-bank payments and neither bills nor coins are in circulation, and as the central banks use national currencies for their interventions in financial markets, the ECU has never become an indispensable feature of the EMS.

149

For the ERM official exchange rates were determined between each pair of the participating currencies and a band of +/- 2.25% around the official rates was established within which the exchange rates were allowed to fluctuate. Initially, Belgium, Denmark, France, Germany, Ireland, Luxembourg and The Netherlands participated with their currencies in the narrow band and Italy in a wider band of +/- 6%. Italy moved to the narrow band in 1990. Spain joined the system in 1989, the United Kingdom in 1990. Both newcomers used the wider band of +/- 6%, however.

To restrict currencies from fluctuating beyond the range of the band, the central banks of the relevant countries were committed to intervene by buying depreciating currencies and selling appreciating currencies whenever a currency reached the upper or lower intervention point. This intervention created artificial offer and demand and thus pushed the exchange rate back towards the desired official rate.

If the economic performance of countries participating in a managed exchange rate scheme differs over a longer period or if short-term events affect the countries differently (so-called 'asymmetric shocks'), this affects the international demand for these currencies and makes it hard for the central banks to maintain desired exchange rates. Under the ERM, the Finance Ministers and central bank governors of the participating countries would meet in such cases and agree upon a modification of the official exchange rates, a so-called 'realignment'. This still happened frequently in the first half of the 1980s and always without prior announcement. In the mid-1980s it became the exception rather than the rule.

In light of the stability the system provided, Germany accepted the parallel pursuit of economic and monetary integration at the **European Council** in Hanover in June 1988. Prior to 1988, Germany had insisted that monetary integration with the final goal of monetary union should begin only after the completion of the **Internal Market** and parallel to the creation of a political union. This approach had been based on the belief that the possibility of exchange rate realignments was a necessary transmission mechanism to compensate for diverging economic performance amongst the Member States. The main advantages of monetary union, on the other hand, are the definitive prevention of currency speculation, the elimination of costs related to the exchange of one currency into another (so-called 'transaction costs'), and the facilitation of price calculations for commercial transactions in the Internal Market.

In 1989 **Commission** President Delors presented a strategy paper for monetary union. This Delors Report was adopted by the European Council in Madrid in June 1989 and in December 1990 an **Intergovernmental Conference** was convened with, inter alia, the task of drafting the necessary amendments to the EC Treaty. After lengthy negotiations the **Treaty on European Union** was finally signed in Maastricht in February 1992.

To give credibility to the goal of monetary union and due to the French *franc fort* policy, there had not been a single realignment from 1987 until 1992, although the fall of the iron curtain and German unification had affected Member State economies quite differently. Thus tension had built up between the currencies and this in turn invited international speculation. Additional tensions were caused by the negative result of the first Danish referendum in May 1992, the narrow decision in the French referendum in September 1992, and the lengthy ratification process in Britain, and thus a general uncertainty about perspectives for entry into force of the TEU and its provisions on monetary union. The British pound, the Italian lira, the Portuguese escudo and the Spanish peseta came under excessive pressure and were subsequently forced to leave the EMS at least temporarily. In an effort to save the system as a whole, the Finance Ministers and central bank governors, in a special meeting on 2 August 1993, decided to broaden the band to +/- 15%. Only the Dutch guilder and the German mark remained in the narrow band in their exchange rate to each other.

The crisis of the EMS not only led to the postponement of monetary union from 1 January 1997 to 1 January 1999, it called the entire enterprise into question. It reminded politicians that free movement of capital, fixed exchange rates and autonomous national economic and fiscal policies cannot be had at the same time. This had been Germany's reason until 1988 for insisting on the parallel creation of a political union, a type of federation, where important aspects of economic and fiscal policy – in addition to monetary decisions by a future European central bank – would be decided centrally. By contrast, the present rules in Article 103 EC prescribe only a 'co-ordination' of national economic policies and give the Council only the power to address 'recommendations' to Member States whose policies are inconsistent with the common guidelines of the EC.

FRANK EMMERT

*Recommended reading*
Bladen-Hovell 'The European Monetary System' in Artis and Lee (eds) *The Economics of the European Union* (1994) Oxford University Press.
De Grauwe *The Economics of Monetary Integration* (2nd edn, 1994) Oxford University Press.


**EUROPEAN PARLIAMENT** Since the **Single European Act,** 'European Parliament' (EP) has been the official title of the institution known previously as 'Assembly of the European Communities'. The EP itself had for many years used the name 'Parliament' in the hope of improving its limited status and increasing its influence in the policy-making process of the EC. The agreement by the Member States to adopt the name 'Parliament' is one of a number of improvements in the status of the EP since its members were first directly elected in 1979 (see **direct elections**): until that point, ever since the origins of the EP in the Common Assembly of the **European Coal and Steel Community**, its members had been delegated from the national parliaments of the Member States. Elections are now held every five years: at the last election, in June 1994, 567 MEPs were directly elected by the voters of Europe. The number of parliamentarians from each country is approximately related to its size: Germany, the largest Member State, now elects 99 members, the three next largest states each elect 87 and the others have smaller numbers (eg 25 for Belgium and six for Luxembourg). In January 1995, following the accession to the EU of Austria, Finland and Sweden, the addition of 59 new MPs delegated by the three national parliaments brought the EP's total size to 626.

The Secretariat of the EP is in Luxembourg but its Plenary Sessions (occupying one week of every month of the year except August) are held in Strasbourg, in the building of the Parliamentary Assembly of the **Council of Europe**, and the meetings of the EP's specialist committees and party political groups are held in Brussels. The EP now has a building in Brussels which would allow a number of its Plenary Sessions to be held there instead of in Strasbourg. The supporters of this change argue that it would reduce the cost and inefficiency of the EP's present migrations between its three working sites, and strengthen its role in exercising democratic control over the European **Commission** and the **Council of the European Union**, both in Brussels.

The present powers of the EP, laid down in the **Treaty on European Union**, are nothing like as great as those normally held by parliaments in democracies. It has the power, by a majority vote, to dismiss the entire Commission from office, but this power has never been exercised. The EP also has the right to prevent the annual **budget** of the EP from being adopted (it shares this power with the Council of the European Union, the other branch of the Community's 'budgetary authority'): but the effect of this power is in practice limited by the fact that the Community can operate with a provisional budget, based on that of the previous year, for as long as is necessary to get a new budget approved.

Despite these limitations, the EP exercises considerable influence on the policies of the Community, partly through its role in the legislative process. The Council of Ministers may only enact laws after the proposals of the Commission have been considered by the EP, and its opinion must be taken into account. In the case of certain types of legislation – essentially those on the **Internal Market**, but also certain decisions on research and regional development programmes – the EP's powers go further, thanks to the 'co-operation procedure' introduced by the Single European Act. For this legislation the EP has the right not only to be consulted but also to hold a further ('second reading') debate after the Council has formulated its 'common position', and then either to accept or to reject or amend the Council's proposal. Rejection by the EP means that the proposal falls, unless the Council re-affirms it by a unanimous vote of all the Member States; the amendments proposed by the EP, in turn, provided they have the agreement of the Commission, can only be rejected by a similar unanimous vote of the Council. Many hundreds of legislative amendments proposed by the EP since 1987 have in fact been adopted by the Council.

As well as giving the EP these increased legislative powers, the Single European Act also gave it, through the so-called 'assent procedure', the right to approve or to reject applications to join the EC (through **Accession** Treaties) and also the conclusion or modification of **association agreements** with non-Member States. This right of veto has given the EP a weapon which it can use to get its own way either on the substance of the issue concerned or on other matters.

Despite this, however, the EP remains essentially, unlike most national legislatures in democracies, an organ which has to exercise its influence through powers of persuasion, rather than through votes which determine the fate of governments. Much of the EP's legislative work takes place in its committees, which are designed to correspond to the Directorates General of the Commission: they include committees on agriculture, energy, external relations etc. An important role in the EP's work is played by the party political groups: almost every member of the EP belongs to one or another of these groups according to his or her party affiliation. Since the 1989 election, the Socialist group has been the largest: it had 180 members in 1989 and 221 in 1995. It is followed by the European People's Party group, which had 162 members by the end of the 1989 legislature and 173 in 1995. No other group has had more than 50 members (until the Liberal group reached 52 in 1995), and the two main groups, if they agree, can usually decide the outcome of events.

Since the **Treaty on European Union** came into force in 1993, the powers of the EP have again been somewhat increased, notably (as was seen early in 1995) with regard to its control over the appointment of the President and Members of the Commission. It will clearly try, in the context of the 1996 **Intergovernmental Conference,** to add to its already important role as one of the main **institutions** of the EU.

ROGER MORGAN

*Recommended reading*
Jacobs et al *The European Parliament* (2nd edn, 1992) Longman.
Westlake *A Modern Guide to the European Parliament* (1994) Pinter.

**EUROPEAN PARTY FEDERATIONS** The members of the **European Parliament** are divided into political groups. To this extent a considerable degree of integration is achieved.

Political groups of the European Parliament were established as far back as 1952. The first three groups to be established were the Socialist group, the Christian Democratic group and the Liberal group.

A Federation of political parties is made up of strongly autonomous national political parties.

In 1947 the Christian Democratic parties established the *Nouvelles Equipes Internationales* (NEI), an umbrella organisation, which has since become the European Union of Christian Democrats (EUCD).

In the run-up to the first direct elections of the European Parliament in 1979, the Christian Democratic parties of the Community established a new party, the European People's Party, the Socialist parties formed the Confederation of the Socialist parties of the European Community, while the Liberal parties formed the Federation of European Liberal, Democrat and Reform parties.

The establishment of political parties at European level was further endorsed after the **Treaty on European Union**. According to Article 138a EC political parties at European level are important as a factor for integration within the Union. They contribute to forming a European awareness and to expressing the political will of the **citizens** of the Union.

The major political parties at European level are the Party of European Socialists, established in the Hague in November 1992, the European People's Party and the European Liberals, Democrats and Reformists.

They were created not by Union citizens directly, but by national parties.

However, the prospect is very likely, though within the spirit of the TEU, that these supranational parties could be transformed to real mass parties, in the framework of which individuals could become members, and also that new political parties could be created at supranational level based on individual membership.

EPAMINONDAS A MARIAS

*Recommended reading*
Haas *The Uniting of Europe* (2nd edn, 1968) Stanford University Press.
Marias *European Citizenship* (1994) European Institute of Public Administration.

**EUROPEAN PATENT CONVENTION** The Convention on the Grant of European Patents (EPC) establishes a common system for the grant of patents amongst the Contracting States. Under the EPC, a European patent, valid in as many of the Contracting States as are designated in the application, can be obtained by filing a single application. Contracting States may continue their national patent systems as an alternative means of securing a patent for their territory. The European system is concerned solely with the *grant* of patents. Once granted, the respective national laws of the Contracting States govern matters such as infringement, assignment and licensing.

Contracting States are obliged to ensure that a European patent taking effect in their territory confers the same rights on the proprietor as would have been conferred by a national patent. The EPC establishes the European Patent Organization, which has financial and administrative autonomy. The European Patent Organization comprises the European Patent Office, the executive body responsible for the granting of European patents, and the Administrative Council, which has a supervisory role.

The EPC was negotiated outside the legal framework of the EC and operates independently of it. Although initially it was intended that the membership of the European Patent Organization would be co-extensive with that of the EC, the EPC allows a broader membership. However, the right to accede to the EPC is confined solely to European States. There are now 18 Contracting States, including all the Member States of the European Union together with Switzerland, Liechtenstein and Monaco.

The EPC must be distinguished from the Community Patent Convention (OJ L401 30.12.89 p 1), which differs from the EPC in establishing a system for a unitary Community patent effective throughout the whole territory of the Union. Political problems have prevented this Convention from coming into effect.

D L BOOTON

*Recommended reading*
Singer *The European Patent Convention* (revised English edition, 1995) Sweet & Maxwell.
Vitoria, Jacob, Cornish, Clark & Alexander *Encyclopaedia of United Kingdom and European Patent Law* (1977) Sweet & Maxwell.

**EUROPEAN SOCIAL FUND** The European Social Fund is the oldest of the Community Structural Funds administered by the Commission, having been established in 1957 'to improve employment opportunities for workers in the Internal Market and to contribute thereby to raising the standard of living'. Its objectives are to promote the employment prospects and mobility of workers within the Community and to facilitate their adaptation to change by way in particular of vocational training and retraining (see Articles 123 et seq and Title XIV EC and Protocol 15).

The Structural Funds were reformed in 1988 and 1994 into a single co-ordinated instrument of programmed economic and social development. See Council Regulations (EEC) 2081/93 (OJ L193 31.7.93 p 5), 2082/93 (OJ L193 31.7.93 p 20) and 2084/93 (OJ L193 31.7.93 p 39). The Community's structural action has been focused on five priority Objectives, amongst which the ESF is responsible for Objective 3 (actions taken to combat long-term unemployment (over 12 months) and to facilitate the occupational integration of young people (under 25) and those threatened with exclusion from the labour market), and for Objective 4 (actions taken to facilitate workers' adaptation to industrial changes and to changes in production systems). The ESF also contributes to the regional and rural Objectives 1, 2 and 5b.

The ESF part-finances vocational training, start-up aid and innovative measures, together with certain training and education schemes and research and development. The budget of the ESF for 1995 amounted to just under 6.5 billion ECU. ESF funding is additional to, rather than a replacement for, funding for programmes developed at national level. 9% of structural financing has been devoted to Community initiatives, including support for the position on the labour market of women, the handicapped or seriously disadvantaged, and unqualified young people under the age of 20.

CHRISTOPHER DOCKSEY

*Recommended reading*
Commission of the European Communities *Community Structural Funds 1994-
    1999, Revised Regulations and Comments* (1993) Office for Official Publications
    of the European Communities.
European Commission *Seventh Annual Report, The Implementation of the Reform
    of the Structural Funds, 1995* COM(96)502 (30 October 1996) Office for
    Official Publications of the EC.


**EUROPEAN SYSTEM OF CENTRAL BANKS** The **European Central Bank** (ECB) and the European System of Central Banks (ESCB) will be created at the beginning of the third stage of monetary union, presumably in 1999. Their legal framework is already laid down in Articles 102a-109m EC and several Protocols annexed to the **Treaty on European Union**.

According to Article 106 EC the ESCB shall be composed of the ECB and the national central banks of those Member States that participate in monetary union. As the governors of those central banks will already be represented in the Governing Council of the ECB, the main purpose of the institutional framework provided by the ESCB will be to demonstrate the close co-operation between the European and the national central banks necessitated by monetary union. De facto, national central banks will lose most of their competences in monetary matters to the ESCB, or – to be precise – to the ECB, as the ESCB shall not have legal personality or legal capacity. It will be represented and managed by the decision-making organs of the ECB, namely the Governing Council and the Executive Board.

The objectives and tasks of the ESCB – and therefore the ECB – are laid down in Article 105 EC and in Articles 2 and 3 of the ESCB and ECB Statute. The Statute was adopted as the 3rd Protocol annexed to the TEU. It is therefore part of Community primary law and can only be changed in the procedure laid down by Article N TEU. However, a simplified amendment procedure is provided for some Articles of the Statute in its Article 41.

The primary objective of the ESCB (and the ECB) will be the maintenance of price stability. It shall support other economic policies of the Community in particular those listed in Article 2 EC only if this does not conflict with the pursuit of price stability. To fulfil its task, the ESCB, acting through the ECB, will 'define and implement the monetary policy of the Community', 'conduct foreign exchange operations', 'hold and manage the official foreign reserves of the Member States', and 'promote the smooth operation of payments systems' (see Article 3(1) of the Statute).

On the one hand, the lack of legal personality of the ESCB avoids potentially conflicting decisions and vests all monetary competences in the ECB. On the other hand, Article 105(5) reserves prudential supervision of credit institutions largely for the national central banks. The latter thus retain this and other important functions beyond their governors' involvement in the ECB.

In an effort to insulate the ESCB from political pressure which might be exerted on behalf of Member State governments or of Community institutions, the ECB and all national central banks must be fully independent and may neither seek nor take instructions from anybody (see Article 7 of the Statute). This rigorous provision, commonly attributed to German insistence at the 1990 Intergovernmental Conference, is justified by empirical analysis showing a direct correlation between central bank independence and price stability. It requires substantial changes in the formal structures but also in the perception of central banks in most Member States, including Britain and France.

FRANK EMMERT

*Recommended reading*
Artis 'European Monetary Union' in Artis and Lee (eds) *The Economics of the European Union* (1994) Oxford University Press.
Kenen *Economic and Monetary Union in Europe* (1995) Cambridge University Press.

**EUROPEAN UNION** The establishment of the European Union is the latest step in the constitutional development of the European integration process which was started with the Schuman Plan in 1950. The decision to establish the Union was taken at the end of the two **Intergovernmental Conferences** on Political and on Economic and Monetary Union at the Maastricht **European Council** of December 1991. The Union is based on the **Treaty on European Union** signed in Maastricht on 7 February 1992 which entered into force on 1 November 1993. The Treaty is the result of various compromises which had to be struck during the intergovernmental negotiations of 1991 between the diverging interests of the Member States. The main line of compromise which runs through the Treaty is the one between the Community model of **decision making** with its supranational elements of decision making and enforcement and the intergovernmental model which is based on decision making by consensus among the Member States without any transfer of sovereignty to the **institutions** set up by the Treaty. This line of compromise reflects the struggle between the two different political concepts, federal unity on one hand and confederation of sovereign states on the other, which has accompanied the integration process from its very beginnings. As a result, the European Union is a hybrid construction whose institutional set-up and policy areas are in varying degrees subject to one or the other of these two rather different policy-making systems. Linked with the establishment of the Union are a number of ambitious political aims such as the realisation of Economic and Monetary Union (Articles 102a-109m EC), the introduction of a **Common Foreign and Security Policy** (CFSP, Title V TEU) and the establishment of a comprehensive **Co-operation in the Fields of Justice and Home Affairs** (CJHA, Title VI TEU).

*Nature and structure of the Union*  Contrary to what the term 'Union' might suggest, the Member States have not, by establishing the European Union, created a new entity under public international law. In contrast with the European Communities, the Union has not been vested with a **legal personality** by the Member States and it has also not been the object of any transfer of sovereign powers from the Member States. Instead it is explicitly 'founded' on the existing European Communities which are 'supplemented' by the policies and forms of co-operation established by the Union Treaty (Article A TEU). The Union therefore appears as a superstructure of the European Communities. This superstructure has a number of objectives such as the promotion of economic and social progress and the assertion of its identity on the international scene (Article B TEU) and it is also served by a single institutional framework (see **institutions**), destined to ensure the consistency and continuity of the Union's activities (Article C TEU). However, the Union as such does not have any real powers or competences. Only within the framework of the three Community Treaties the institutions of the Union continue to be vested with real powers. These Treaties have been amended by the Union Treaty but persist as distinct legal systems within that Treaty. The distinctness and independence of the Communities' legal order is underlined by the fact that it is one of the objectives of the Union to maintain in full the **'acquis communautaire'** (Article B and M TEU) and that the powers of the Court of Justice are not extended to the other policy areas of the Union outside of the framework of the Community Treaties (Article L TEU). These policy areas comprise the CFSP and CJHA. Although both CFSP and CJHA are linked to the Community system by the single institutional framework and a number of 'bridge' provisions, both policy areas are governed by essentially different rules of decision making and by legal instruments characteristic of intergovernmental co-operation. As a result, the Union consists essentially of three distinct policy-making systems: the Community system, which comprises the three original Communities – **ECSC**, **EAEC** and the **EC** – as amended by the Union Treaty, the CFSP and CJHA. These three constructions are now commonly referred to as the three 'Pillars' of the European Union, with the Communities forming the 'First', CFSP the 'Second' and CJHA the 'Third' Pillar. The unity of the three Pillar structure is underlined by the fact that third countries can accede only to the Union as a whole and not only to one or two of the Pillars (Article O TEU). Taking into account, however, that the Community Pillar is by far the most comprehensive of the three and that all other areas of Union policy making are based on the intergovernmental model, the Union may best be described as an institutionalised framework for intergovernmental co-operation between the Member States of the Union established on and around the original three European Communities.

*The institutional set-up* The supreme decision-making body of the Union is the European Council consisting of the Heads of State and Government of the Member States and the President of the **European Commission**. The Treaty on European Union defines its tasks as to provide the Union with 'the necessary impetus for its development' and to 'define the general political guidelines thereof' (Article D). In practice, all major political decisions on issues affecting one or all of the three Pillars of the Union are taken by the European Council, whose guidelines are then implemented by the European Commission and / or the **Council of Ministers** within the Pillars. The special role of the European Council as the only Union institution outside and above the three Pillars is underlined by the fact that it is subject neither to democratic control by the **European Parliament** nor to judicial control by the Court of Justice. The institutional set-up of the Community Pillar has also been adopted for CFSP and CJHA, but with different roles for the institutions: within the European Community the Commission retains its traditional policy-initiating and executive functions on the basis of its exclusive **right of initiative** and its powers of implementation. In the two intergovernmental Pillars the Commission has only a non-exclusive right of initiative and implementation is mainly left to the Member States, so that the Commission's role is much more limited. In the Community Pillar the Council, which represents the interests of the Member States, is the central decision-making body, but its predominance is limited by the powers of Commission and European Parliament and the supranational elements of Community decision-making rules. In the intergovernmental Pillars the Council is in every respect the dominant institution. In the Community Pillar the European Parliament enjoys certain powers of co-decision in the budgetary process and a number of other policy areas. In the CFSP and CJHA it only has a very limited consultative function. Yet the most striking difference in roles between the three Pillars is that of the Court of Justice, which acts as the central jurisdiction of the Community Pillar but has no role at all within the other two Pillars, with the exception of a potential one in respect to conventions concluded under the Third Pillar.

*Citizenship of the Union and the principle of subsidiarity* Two constitutional features introduced by the Union Treaty transcend the Pillar structure and are of importance to the Union system as a whole. One is the **citizenship** of the Union, to which every person holding the nationality of a Member State is entitled. Article 8 EC lays down a number of rights, such as the right to move freely and reside within the territory of each Member State (subject to implementation by the Council), which create a direct constitutional relation between the Union and its citizens. The other major constitutional feature is the principle of **subsidiarity**, which provides that in areas which do not fall within exclusive EC competence, the Community shall take action only if and in so far as the objectives of the proposed action cannot be sufficiently achieved by the Member States and can therefore be better achieved by the Community. The principle most specifically regulated in Article 3b EC reflects both the concern of some Member States to prevent any further transfer of powers to the Community system and the general aim enshrined in Article A of the Union Treaty that decisions in the Union should be taken 'as closely as possible to the citizen'. The interpretation of the principle has given rise to a host of different interpretations and its impact on the development of the Union may only become apparent over the years. However, the insertion of the principle in the Union Treaty has already led the institutions to consider and to justify more carefully the need for certain measures at the Community or Union level.

*Problems of the functioning of the Union* Due to the complexity and hybrid structure of the Union system, certain problems of its functioning had been anticipated even before it came into force. The possible need for a revision has been acknowledged by the Treaty itself, which provides in Article N(2) for the convening in 1996 of an Intergovernmental Conference to examine certain Treaty provisions. So far some of the more important problems are the threats posed to the Economic and Monetary Union project by economic developments and the attitudes taken by certain Member States, a less than satisfying performance of the Second and the Third Pillar (which is largely due to the limits in their intergovernmental decision-making systems) and a number of unresolved questions concerning the role of the European Parliament in the intergovernmental Pillars and the interaction between these and the Community Pillar. Whether these problems can be resolved at the Intergovernmental Conference will to a large extent depend on the political will of the Member States to make real progress in accordance with the aim of 'an ever closer union' enshrined in Article A of the Union Treaty.

JÖRG MONAR

*Recommended reading*
Monar, Ungerer & Wessels (eds) *The Maastricht Treaty on European Union* (1993) European Interuniversity Press.
O'Keeffe & Twomey (eds) *Legal Issues of the Maastricht Treaty* (1994) Wiley Chancery.

**EXTERNAL FRONTIERS CONVENTION** See **border controls**.

**EXTERNAL RELATIONS** Aspects relating to the external relations of the European Communities may be divided into: first, the nature and scope of external relations (**legal personality, international agreements** and **mixed agreements**); second, the Communities' relationship with neighbouring countries (**accession, association agreements, Europe Agreements, Mediterranean policy** and **enlargement**); third, international trade (**common commercial policy, anti-dumping, GATT** and **World Trade Organization**); and, finally, the **Common Foreign and Security Policy**.

*FACTORTAME* There have been three *Factortame* cases before the Court of Justice: C-213/89 *R v Secretary of State for Transport, ex p Factortame (No 1)* [1990] ECR I-2433; C-221/89 *(No 2)* [1991] ECR I-3905; and C-48/93 *(No 3)* [1996] ECR I-1029. *Factortame (No 1)* concerned the power of national courts to grant interim relief where rights claimed under Community law are at issue, and was considered in the landmark judgment of the House of Lords at [1991] 1 AC 603. This case is considered in this volume under **interim measures** and **supremacy**. *Factortame (No 2)* concerned the compatibility of the Merchant Shipping Act 1988 with Community law. *Factortame (No 3)* concerned the conditions of liability for a claim of **damages against a Member State**.

**FEDERALISM** Federalism is the dispersal of power between separate authorities according to the rule of law. It is a constitutional method of enabling liberal democratic states to live peaceably together and to manage their common affairs through a common government. In a full federation the different levels of government – subnational, national and supranational – are co-ordinated but no level is subordinate. Where **sovereignty** is pooled according to the constitution, federal law has **supremacy**.

The European Community is and always has been a federal system. The **Court of Justice** arbitrates in disputes between Member States and between the EC **institutions**. EC law overrides national law in those areas where competence has been transferred under the

161

successive Treaties. The Treaties form a constitutional package (see **constitutionalisation**) and have created a new level of government in which executive and legislative powers are shared among the Commission, Council and Parliament.

Power is exercised according to the federalist principle of **subsidiarity**, which means that decisions should be taken at the most appropriate level, with a bias towards decentralisation. Subsidiarity was made explicit by the Treaty on European Union which, like all Treaties before it, strengthened the federalist elements in the governance of the Community. More power for the **European Parliament** and more majoritarian decision taking in the **Council** are federalist features. The concept of 'European Union **Citizen**' is also a federalist gesture. It postulates a bicameral legislative system whereby popular sovereignty pooled in the Parliament develops a co-equal partnership with Member States' sovereignty pooled in the Council.

For this reason, federalism has always been unpopular with some national governments who, despite their continued membership of the Community, dislike having to give up control. For example, although the Treaty on European Union reinforced the EC, in its Second and Third Pillars, it put **Common Foreign and Security Policy** and **Co-operation in the Fields of Justice and Home Affairs** outside the Community system: the Court of Justice is excluded, the **Commission** and Parliament are marginalised, and the Council has to work almost wholly by unanimity.

Former British colonies (USA, Australia, Canada, India, Nigeria) are federations; seminal British political thinkers have been federalists (John Stuart Mill, Philip Kerr, William Beveridge); and the British were active in supporting new federal republics in post-War Germany and Austria. Yet the Conservative government not only resisted federalist measures both within Europe and the United Kingdom, but sought to stand the meaning of the term on its head. In practice, the British nationalist bogey of a centralised European superstate is unlikely to emerge: the new Europe is more likely to be governed harmoniously by a federal union of its states and peoples.

ANDREW DUFF

*Recommended reading*
Duff, Pinder & Pryce (eds) *Maastricht and Beyond: building the European Union* (1994) Routledge for the Federal Trust.
Bosco (ed) *The Federal Idea* 2 vols (1991 & 1992) Lothian Foundation Press.

**FINANCES OF THE COMMUNITY** The main provisions on the Community finance are Articles 199-209 EC, 78-78i ECSC, and 171-183a Euratom. The general provisions of the Treaties have been supplemented by a number of texts, in particular: Council Decision (EEC) 70/243 of 21 April 1970 (OJ Eng Sp Ed 1970(I) p 224) setting up the own resources system concerning the revenue of the Community, replaced most recently by Council Decision 94/728 of 31 October 1994 (OJ L293 12.11.94 p 9); the two Budgetary Treaties of 22 April 1970 (I) and 22 July 1975 (II) on extension of the powers of the **European Parliament**; the 1975 Joint Declaration (I) of 4 March 1975 (OJ C89 22.4.75 p 1) and the 1982 Joint Declaration (II) of 30 June 1982 (OJ C194 27.8.82 p 1) on improvement of the budgetary procedure; the Financial Regulation of 21 December 1977 (OJ L356 31.12.77 p 1) specifying the procedure for establishing and implementing the budget and for presenting and auditing accounts, last amended by Regulations 95/2333-2335 (OJ L240 7.10.95); the 1988 Interinstitutional Agreement of 29 July 1988 (OJ L185 15.7.88 p 33) on budgetary discipline and improvement of the budgetary procedure (the 1988 Reform); the New **Interinstitutional Agreement** of 29 October 1993, following the 1992 Edinburgh **European Council** on budgetary discipline, adopted in Decision 94/729 of 31 October 1994 (OJ L293 12.11.94 p 14); the financial perspective and framework for expenditure over the period 1993 to 1999; and the final adoption of the 1996 general budget, 96/96 (OJ L22 29.1.96 p 1).

In the early years of the Community, because of the autonomy enjoyed by the institutions set up under the EEC, the **ECSC** and the **Euratom**, as many as five separate budgets had to be drawn up. Since the single Community budget, known as the 'general budget of the European Communities', was created by Article 20 in the Merger Treaty of 8 April 1965, as amended by Article 10 of the 1970 Budgetary Treaty (I), the development of the Community's main financial activities has contributed to a unification of these budgets and there are now only two budgets; the general budget and the ECSC operating budget. The general budget includes the budget of the EC, the administrative budget of the ECSC and the budget of the Euratom. Still excluded from the general budget are mainly, beside the operating budget of the ECSC, borrowing and lending activities and the activities of the **European Investment Bank**. Although the European Development Fund (EDF) since 1993 has been given a subsection in the budget, the financial activities of the Fund are still not entered in the general budget but are financed by contributions from the Member States. However, the 1995 Cannes **European Council** called for a modest contribution from the general budget on the financing of the 8th EDF.

The **Commission** implements the budget in accordance with the Financial Regulation and on its own responsibility, Articles 205 EC, 78c ECSC and 179 Euratom. At the end of the financial year, the European Parliament, acting on a recommendation from the **Council** (which itself acts by a qualified majority), gives a discharge to the Commission after considering the accounts and financial statements submitted by the Commission and the annual report of the **Court of Auditors**, Articles 205a and 206 EC, 78g ECSC and 180b Euratom.

In order to avoid power conflicts the Commission, the European Parliament and the Council have agreed on the above-mentioned joint declarations of 1975 and 1982 and interinstitutional agreements of 1988 and 1993 on budgetary discipline and improvement of the budgetary procedure which now are adopted in the EC Treaty (Article 201a EC (budgetary discipline), Article 202(3) (classification of all expenditure) and Article 203 (budgetary procedure)).

The main principles of the Community **budget** are adopted by Articles 199–209 EC and are to be found in the Financial Regulation. The principle of unity means that all Community expenditure and revenue must be brought together and shown in a single document. With regard to the principle of universality, no revenue must be allocated to particular expenditure and all items must be entered in full in the budget without any adjustment. The budget covers in accordance with the principle of annuality one financial year equal to the calendar year. The principle of 'specification' means that all expenditure must have a special purpose and be assigned to a special objective in order to prevent any confusion between appropriations. The budget shall be in balance, which requires that the estimated revenue for a financial year have to be equal to the expenditure of that year (the principle of 'equilibrium') and, as a final principle, the estimates of the expenditure and revenue in the budget are drawn up in **ECU**.

The general budget consists of statements of the expenditure and of the revenue of all the institutions. The expenditure for each institution shall be set out in separate parts of the budget (Article 202(4)) (see **budget (structure)**). The Community revenue was previously based solely on contributions from the Member States but was replaced by a system of own resources by the decision of 21 April 1970. Following the recent decision on own resources of 31 October 1994, the main sources of Community revenue are agricultural duties, customs duties, a part of the value added tax (VAT) imposed by the Member States and revenue based on the GNP of the Member States (the 'Fourth Resource') introduced by the 1988 revision of the 1970 decision, Council Decision (EEC) 88/376 of 24 June 1988 (OJ L185 15.7.88 p 29). This additional resource is a variable, budget-balancing resource which is calculated during the budgetary procedure in such a way as to cover the amounts not yielded by the other budget revenue. The 1988 decision on own resources raised the ceiling of the total of own resources to 1.21% of the total Community GNP in 1995 and, in stage, up to 1.27% in 1999. The uniform VAT rate will be gradually reduced from 1.4% to 1% in 1999 and the VAT base will be restricted, in stage, to 50% of the GNP instead of the 1995 level of 55%. The new own resources decision entered into force with effect from 1 January 1995.

The 1988 Interinstitutional Agreement introduced the first Financial Perspective (1988 to 1992, Delors I Package) which is followed by the present Financial Perspective for the period 1993 to 1999 adopted by the 1992 Edinburgh European Council (Delors II Package). The

Financial Perspective, which is an agreement and therefore only a supplement to the annual budget, contains the main budgetary priorities for the following period and establishes a framework showing the maximum amount and the composition of foreseeable expenditure to be compared with the ceiling on own resources.

Finally, the majority of the Reflection Group preparing the 1996 **Intergovernmental Conference** does not recommend the IGC to deal with the question of resources and suggests that any examination hereof should wait the expiration of the recent Financial Agreement in 1999 (Reflection Group's Report, Final Version, Messina, 2 June 1995, Bruxelles, 5 December 1995, para 135). However, in accordance with Article 209a EC a majority of the Group is in favour of a strengthening of the fight against fraud by increasing the role of the Court of Auditors and establishing closer networks with national bodies (para 139).

RASMUS DILLING

*Recommended reading*
Strasser *The Finances of Europe* (7th edn, 1992) Office for Public Publications.
Walder *The Budgetary Procedure of the European Economic Community* (1992) Böhlau.

**FINANCIAL SERVICES** The provisions of the Treaty of Rome creating **freedom of establishment,** freedom to provide services, and the **free movement of capital** throughout Member States have required several Directives to be adopted in the field of financial services. The most significant of these are the Second Banking Directive (Council Directive 85/345/EEC (OJ L183 16.7.85 p 19)) and the Investment Services Directive (Council Directive 93/22/EEC (OJ L141 11.6.93 p 27)) which introduce the principle of home state recognition with respect to credit institutions and investment services firms. Home state regulatory authorities are now responsible for the prudential supervision of undertakings registered with them in respect of the business of those undertakings throughout the **European Economic Area**. Member States retain the right to regulate conduct within their jurisdiction and so to legislate, for instance, on the marketing of investments. The effect of home state recognition is to allow undertakings the freedom to provide investment or banking services throughout the European Economic Area under a single 'passport' provided by the regulatory authorities of their home state (although certain requirements concerning notification to host state authorities remain). The two Directives also introduced enhanced rights of establishment in other Member States, whether operating through branches or subsidiaries. Undertakings must notify their intention to take advantage of these. In order to ensure that the new regime may not be used to avoid proper supervision of their business by undertakings, the Directives permit the regulatory authorities of each Member State to pass on information between themselves more freely. There is also a specific anti-avoidance provision designed to prevent 'regulatory arbitrage'.

With the introduction of the single passport, the Commission has sought to harmonise consumer protections and also regulatory costs for credit institutions and investment services firms throughout Member States and has initiated a number of Directives aimed at this. The most important of these have been Directives addressing capital adequacy requirements, in particular the Own Funds Directive (Council Directive (EEC) 89/299 (OJ L124 5.5.89 p 16)), the Solvency Ratio Directive (Council Directive (EEC) 89/647 (OJ L386 30.12.89 p 14)) and the Capital Adequacy Directive (Council Directive (EEC) 93/6 (OJ L141 11.6.93 p 1)). These three Directives set out the tiers of capital on which a credit institution or investment services firm may rely to support its assets, and the minimum ratio between the two. The Directives apply similar criteria to both credit institutions and investment services firms, although credit institutions require higher initial capital. The Council has also adopted a Directive on Deposit Guarantees (Council Directive (EEC) 94/19 (OJ L135 31.5.94 p 5)). Deposit-taking institutions which operate cross-border under the single passport need only comply with the deposit guarantee legislation of their home state which will extend protection to all their customers wherever it is situated. However, should any institution feel inclined to subscribe to the more generous (*vis-à-vis* the consumer) deposit guarantee legislation of another Member State in which that institution provides financial services, it should be free to do so.

The Council has also adopted a Directive on Money Laundering (Council Directive (EEC) 91/308 (OJ L166 28.6.91 p 77)). This requires financial and other relevant undertakings to make a positive identification of new customers. This obligation extends in certain circumstances to an obligation to go behind any agent, nominee or trustee and establish the identify of any beneficial owner. The Directive then imposes a proactive role on the undertaking to report suspicions of money laundering to the relevant authorities.

ROBERT STRIVENS

*Recommended reading*
Antenas & Kenyon-Slade *EC Financial Market Regulation and Company Law* (1993) Sweet & Maxwell.
Moreiro Gonzalez *Banking in Europe after 1992* (1993) Dartmouth.

**FISHERIES POLICY** The EC Treaty includes within its definition of 'agricultural products' the 'products of . . . fisheries'. This means that the provisions of the Treaty dealing with agriculture authorise and require the adoption of a Common Fisheries Policy (CFP). The first steps to implement a CFP were taken in 1970. Thereafter, little further was done until the late 1970s. The main catalyst for developing the CFP was the extension of fishing limits from 12 miles to 200 miles in the North Atlantic in 1977 and the finding by the **Court of Justice** in Case 804/79 *Commission v United Kingdom* [1981] ECR 1045 that the conservation and management of the fisheries resources found in EC

Member States' waters are within the exclusive competence of the Community. Since 1983 the CFP has had four principal elements.

The first of these is a Community system for the conservation and management of fish stocks found within Member States' fishing limits. Originally contained in Council Regulation (EEC) 170/83 (OJ L24 27.1.83 p 1), the basic framework legislation providing for this system is now found in Council Regulation (EEC) 3760/92 (OJ L389 31.12.92 p 1), which is scheduled to last until 2002. Like its predecessor, Regulation 3760/92 authorises the Council to adopt a variety of conservation and management measures. In practice, the main such measures have been a series of annual regulations setting total allowable catches for most fish stocks and dividing these catches into quotas allocated to individual Member States, supplemented by technical conservation measures which regulate fishing gear and prohibit fishing at certain times and in certain areas. As a result of the principle of equal access adopted in 1970, any EC vessel can fish anywhere in any area where the Member State in which it is registered has a quota, the main exception being the 12-mile limit off other Member States' coasts. There is a team of EC fisheries inspectors to oversee the enforcement by Member States of the above measures.

The second element of the CFP is the conclusion of agreements with third states. The negotiation and conclusion of such agreements is a matter within the exclusive competence of the Community (see Joined Cases 3, 4 & 6/76 *Kramer* [1976] ECR 1279). So far, the EC has concluded agreements with over 30 third states, mainly providing for EC vessels to fish in third states' waters. In addition, the EC has become a member of a number of international fisheries organisations concerned with fisheries conservation and management beyond 200-mile limits.

Structural matters form the CFP's third element. This has a number of features, the principal one being the provision of Community financial aid for modernising fishing fleets with the aim of adapting each Member State's fleet to the catch potential available to it. Aid is also available for developing aquaculture and improving onshore facilities such as fish-processing plants. The basic regulation in this area is Council Regulation (EEC) 4028/86 (OJ L376 31.12.86 p 7).

The final element of the CFP is the common organisation of the market in fishery products. There has been a succession of basic regulations on this matter, the latest of which is Council Regulation (EEC) 3759/92 (OJ L388 31.12.92 p 1). The main features of the common organisation of the market are a common pricing system (which seeks to maintain prices by withdrawing fish from the market when prices start to fall), encouraging the formation of producers' organisations (through which the pricing system is largely operated), establishing common marketing standards to improve the quality of fish, and various measures to prevent EC prices being undermined by cheap imports.

R R CHURCHILL

*Recommended reading*
Churchill *EEC Fisheries Law* (1987) Martinus Nijhoff.
Holden *The Common Fisheries Policy* (1994) Fishing News Books.


**FOSTER** Case C-188/89 *Foster v British Gas Corporation* [1990] ECR I-3313 concerned the definition of the entities or emanations of the Member State against which an individual could claim the **direct effect** of a Directive.


**FRANCOVICH** Joined Cases C-6/90 & C-9/90 *Francovich & Bonifaci* [1991] ECR I-5357 are discussed under **damages against Member States** and **employment protection**.


**FREE MOVEMENT OF CAPITAL** The free movement of capital is the only one of the basic freedoms established by the EC Treaty in its original form which was not held to be **directly effective** by the **Court of Justice**, and it is also the only one of those basic Treaty freedoms to have been reformulated under the **Treaty on European Union**.

Complete liberalisation from 1 July 1990 for most Member States resulted from Council Directive (EEC) 88/361 (OJ L178 8.7.88 p 5), Article 1 of which was held to be directly effective in Cases C-358 & C-416/93 *Bordessa and Mellado* [1995] ECR I-361.

The capital movement provisions operative from 1 January 1994 (the start of the second stage of **Economic and Monetary Union**) are drafted in a style more like that of the other Treaty freedoms. Article 73b EC sets out a basic principle of prohibition of restrictions on both the movement of capital and payments between Member States, subject to a safeguard clause in Article 73d EC. This permits Member States to differentiate between taxpayers who are not in the same situation with regard to their place of residence or with regard to the place where their capital is invested. It also allows Member States to take other measures in the field of taxation and the prudential supervision of financial institutions, or to require the declaration of capital movements, or to take measures which are justified on grounds of **public policy** or public security. It would appear that the public policy considerations may relate to the purpose for which the monetary movement is made as much as to the movement itself (Case C-148/91 *Veronica v Commissariaat voor de Media* [1993] ECR I-487).

Furthermore, until a Member State participates in the third stage of economic and monetary union, restrictions may continue to be authorised by the Commission under Article 109h EC to protect its balance of payments.

More positively, in principle the new capital movement provisions apply not only to movements between Member States but also to movements between Member States and third countries, subject to special safeguard measures in Articles 73c and 73f EC. The external aspect of Article 73b has nevertheless been held to be directly effective with regard to monetary movements to Turkey and Switzerland in Cases C-163/94, 165/94 & 250/94 *Sanz de Lera* [1995] ECR I-4821.

JOHN USHER

*Recommended reading*
Brealey & Quigley *Completing the Internal Market . . . Financial Services and Capital Movements* (1994) Kluwer.
Usher 'Capital Movements and Maastricht: Evolution or Revolution?' (1992) 12 Yearbook of European Law 35.

**FREE MOVEMENT OF GOODS** The Treaty rules on Free Movement of Goods call, first, for the establishment of a **customs union** (Articles 9–29 EC) and, second, for the elimination of all 'quantitative restrictions' between Member States (Articles 30–37 EC). These rules seek to create a 'common market' in which the movement of goods between Member States is not hindered by their crossing national or regional frontiers. To that end, the first set of rules prohibit any pecuniary charges being imposed on goods crossing such a frontier (tariff barriers), while the second set precludes all other national rules which limit cross-frontier trade (non-tariff or physical barriers).

The starting point for consideration of the rules on non-tariff barriers must be Article 30 EC, which prohibits 'quantitative restrictions' on imports between Member States as well as all 'measures having equivalent effect' (MEEs) thereto. It should be noted that these prohibitions are tempered by Article 36 EC, which enables a Member State, in limited circumstances, to justify rules contrary to Article 30.

As for Article 30, it is clear that the prohibition against 'quantitative restrictions' aims at classical quotas, which limit importation of a particular product to a quantifiable amount, and at complete bans.

The Treaty does not, however, make clear what 'measures' can be regarded as 'equivalent' thereto and the Court has frequently been called upon to interpret the expression. The *locus classicus* is that Article 30 prohibits 'All trading rules enacted by Member States which are capable of hindering, directly or indirectly, actually or potentially, intra-Community trade' (Case 8/74 *Dassonville* [1974] ECR 837, para 5).

The breadth of this definition is immediately obvious. It is not restricted to rules of a particular form but to all rules which have a restrictive effect, however small. Furthermore, there is no need to prove what that effect actually is, since the rule must simply be 'capable' of 'potentially' hindering trade. Indeed, a Member State cannot seek to disprove this potential by reference to statistics showing that, despite the adoption of a 'measure', sales of imports increased (Case 249/81 *Commission v Ireland* [1982] ECR 4005).

It would also be misleading to assume that an MEE must come in the form of a traditional 'rule'. The Court has held that a practice or conduct, such as a publicity campaign for the promotion of domestic products, can constitute an MEE (Case 222/82 *Apple and Pear Development Council* [1983] ECR 4083).

Although Article 30 only applies to measures adopted by the Member State, it none the less extends to all manifestations of the state and not simply to the most obvious examples of government activity. Thus, the Apple and Pear Development Council, although a non-governmental organisation, was covered by Article 30 since it was set up under law and financed by a compulsory charge on the industry.

MEEs are generally divided into two categories, those that are 'distinctly applicable' and those that are 'indistinctly applicable'.

As the name suggests, distinctly applicable measures apply different rules to imports and domestic products in such a way that trade is hindered. The most common examples in the case law are customs formalities, such as licensing requirements, which impose additional costs and delays on imports but do not apply to domestic products (see, for example, Case 41/76 *Donckerwolcke* [1976] ECR 1921).

Of a more subtle nature are indistinctly applicable measures, which – at least on their wording – treat imports and domestic products in the same way but which, in practice, operate so as to hinder trade. Seemingly innocuous requirements, such as that margarine be marketed in cube-shaped boxes or that beer have a maximum acidity, have been found to be MEEs, since they force importers to produce goods adapted specially for the destination market (see Case 261/81 *Rau* [1982] ECR 3961 and Case 94/82 *De Kikvorsch* [1982] ECR 947). Such rules entail additional costs for the importer and therefore hinder trade.

The seminal judgment which underpins these cases is *Cassis de Dijon* (Case 120/78 *REWE-Zentral AG* [1979] ECR 649), where the Court ruled that, in principle, goods lawfully produced and marketed in one Member State can be introduced into any other Member State. Significantly, the Court added that, in the absence of common rules, obstacles to free movement must be accepted in so far as they are necessary to secure overriding objectives of general interest (so-called 'mandatory requirements').

So far, the indistinctly applicable measures considered have concerned rules laying down requirements to be met by goods – product specification rules on matters such as designation, form, weight, composition and packaging. Besides these, the Court has also been asked to consider rules relating to the marketing of products. These rules regulate matters such as where and when goods can be sold, by whom they can be sold and subject to what controls, conditions and publicity.

On this ground the Court has, for instance, ruled that national rules prohibiting the sale of educational material by way of canvassing, restricting certain forms of advertising and fixing a minimum retail sale price are all capable of hindering trade (see, for example, Case 286/81 *Oosthoek* [1982] ECR 4575 and Case 82/77 *Van Tiggele* [1978] ECR 25). Such rules were capable of restricting the volume of imports and therefore hindered trade.

Clearly, many – if not all – regulatory rules could conceivably reduce the volume of imports and be prima facie contrary to Article 30. Indeed, by this reasoning the Court was persuaded that national regulation of Sunday shop-opening might hinder trade (Case 145/88 *Torfaen BC* [1989] ECR 3851). Applying this test of 'hindrance', the scope of Article 30 seemed limitless and it had become a charter for deregulation.

However, the early Sunday trading cases marked the high-water point for the scope of Article 30. In a dramatic about-turn the Court stated that 'contrary to what has been previously decided', rules affecting 'selling arrangements' did not fall within the *Dassonville* formula provided they were indistinctly applicable and, more importantly, affected in the same manner, in law and in fact, the marketing of imports and domestic products (Cases C-267 & 268/91 *Keck and Mithouard* [1993] ECR I-6097, para 16). The judgment expressly distinguished – and left intact – the *Cassis de Dijon* case law on rules relating to product specification.

While a clear definition of 'selling arrangements' has yet to emerge, the case law since *Keck* indicates that it will now be very difficult to bring such a rule within Article 30. For a selling arrangement to hinder intra-Community trade it seems that one must demonstrate that the rule operates so as to give domestic products protection against similar or competing imports or that the rule results in unequal treatment of the two categories of product as regards access to the market (see Case C-391/92 *Commission v Greece* [1995] ECR I-1621, para 18; see also Case C-418/93 *Semararo Casa Uno Srl*, judgment of 20 June 1996, para 24).

The Treaty also prohibits quantitative restrictions on exports and measures having equivalent effect (Article 34). Although it is worded similarly to Article 30, the Court has ruled that Article 34 is only infringed where national rules treat domestic and export trade differently such that the latter is disadvantaged (Case 15/79 *Groenveld* [1979] ECR 3409).

A national rule infringing either Article 30 or 34 may, as indicated above, be justified on the grounds provided in Article 36, which include public morality, public security, and the protection of health and life of humans. Furthermore, as noted above, the Court stated in *Cassis de Dijon* that mandatory requirements, such as the fairness of consumer transactions, encouragement of national culture, and protection of the environment, can also justify obstacles to trade.

Since they permit restrictions on free movement, these rules are interpreted strictly. Thus, not only must the national rule pursue a legitimate objective but it must be necessary and proportionate for the attainment of that objective. The rule must therefore be indispensable to the objective and must be the least restrictive means of securing it. For instance, a rule prohibiting absolutely the sale of beer containing non-traditional ingredients would not be justifiable on the grounds of consumer protection since clear labelling of the ingredients will suffice.

Article 36 also states that the obstacle cannot be a 'means of arbitrary discrimination or a disguised restriction on trade'. Essentially, Member States cannot employ double standards by simultaneously banning importation of a product and allowing a domestic trade in it. Similarly, mandatory requirements can only be invoked if the offending rule is indistinctly applicable.

Finally, if the Community legislator harmonises rules in a particular field then that legislation displaces the primary Treaty rules, although it must still be interpreted in light of those rules (Case C-315/92 *Clinique* [1994] ECR I-317). Article 36 cannot therefore justify obstacles to trade which are contrary to harmonising legislation (Case C-5/94 *Hedley-Lomas*, judgment of 23 May 1996).

NICOLAS LOCKHART

*Recommended reading*
Due 'Dassonville Revisited or No Cause For Alarm?' in Cambell & Voyatzi (eds) *Legal Reasoning and Judicial Interpretation of European Law, Essays in honour of Lord Mackenzie-Stuart* (1996) Trenton.
Weatherill 'After *Keck*: some thoughts on how to clarify the clarification' (1996) 33 CMLRev 885.


**FREE MOVEMENT OF PERSONS** The activities of the Community include an **Internal Market** characterised by the abolition, as between Member States, of obstacles to the free movement of goods, persons, services and capital (Article 3(c) EC). Free movement of persons is generally regarded as encompassing workers, establishment, and services under Articles 48–66 EC. Directives grant rights of free movement for students and retired persons, provided they are not a burden on the social assistance schemes of the Member State of residence, and for persons of independent means. Article 8a EC recognises these rights as incidents of European **citizenship**.

Beneficiaries of the rules are nationals of the Member States. Companies or firms must meet both a nationality and 'residence' test; they must, under Article 58 EC be formed under the law of a Member State and have their registered office, central administration or principal place of business within the Community. To claim the rights accorded by Community law, there must generally be some activity which engages the Community rules (Case 175/78 *Saunders* [1979] ECR 1129; Case C-41/90 *Höfner v Macrotron* [1991] ECR I-1979). So-called **reverse discrimination** is permitted (Cases C-332/90 & C-132/93 *Volker Steen* [1992] ECR I-341 and [1994] ECR I-2715), but the rights deriving from Community law can be pleaded against the state of which the person is a national if there is some connecting factor to the situations contemplated by Community law (Case C-370/90 *Surinder Singh* [1992] ECR I-4265).

Community law defines a worker as someone obliged to provide services for another, in return for reward, and subject to the direction and control of that other person (Case 66/85 *Lawrie-Blum* [1986] ECR 2121). Those in low-paid, part-time work are included, provided that their work is effective and genuine and not on such a small scale as to be regarded as purely marginal and ancillary (Case 53/81 *Levin* [1982] ECR 1035), though in applying this test account need only be taken of the pattern of work in the Member State of residence (Case C-357/89 *Raulin* [1992] ECR I-1027).

Establishment includes self-employment, the setting up of agencies, branches and subsidiaries, and activities by companies or firms. A modest continuing presence will constitute establishment (Case 205/84 *Commission v Germany* [1986] ECR 3755). Freedom of movement exists for both providers and recipients of services (Case 186/87 *Cowan* [1989] ECR 195). Services are activities provided for remuneration. Education principally financed by public funds is not a service (Case C-109/92 *Wirth* [1993] ECR I-6447).

Where Community law applies, there is a prohibition on any form of **discrimination** based on nationality. A breach of Community law could flow from a non-discriminatory provision which has the effect of hindering free movement (Case C-415/93 *Bosman*, judgment of 15 December 1995, [1996] 1 CMLR 645).

Those within the Community provisions have a right of entry and residence in the Member State, and are entitled to a residence permit under Council Directives (EEC) 68/360 (OJ Sp Ed 1968-69 p 485) and 73/148 (OJ L172 1973 p 14). There are rights for both the economic actor and his or her spouse and members of their families. Non-national spouses are treated as if they were nationals of a Member State (Case 131/85 *Gül* [1986] ECR 1573). Council Regulation (EEC)1612/68 (OJ Sp Ed 1968-69 p 475) spells out the rights of workers and their families. There is a right to remain after a period of economic activity in a Member State.

Work seekers enjoy a limited right of entry and residence, but not other social rights accorded to those who have found work (Case 316/85 *Lebon* [1987] ECR 2811).

Failure to recognise qualifications, and regulation of the activity by the host state have generated much case law in relation to establishment and services. Equality of treatment with nationals is required, but where there are **harmonising** Directives, those prevail. Among the most important are the Mutual Recognition Directives 89/48 and 92/51 (OJ L19 24.1.89 p 16 and OJ L209 24.7.92 p 25). But even in the absence of harmonising Directives, the equal treatment provisions of the Treaty give rise to an obligation to consider the equivalence of qualifications and schemes of regulation. In all cases there is an obligation to give reasons for any refusal to recognise qualifications, which must be susceptible of challenge in the Member State to test the compatibility of the decision with the requirements of Community law (Case 222/86 *Heylens* [1987] ECR 4097).

National rules regulating economic activity can only be applied where they can be justified by imperative reasons relating to the public interest, where they apply equally to all persons engaged in that activity in the Member State, where there are no applicable safeguards applied in the home state, where the controls are objectively necessary, and where the measures imposed are the least restrictive to secure the legitimate objective (Case C-106/91 *Ramrath* [1992] ECR I-3351).

The rights are subject to exceptions and limitations. Limitations may be imposed on grounds of **public policy, public security and public health** under Articles 48(3), 56(1) and 66 EC, spelled out in Council Directive (EEC) 64/221 (OJ Sp Ed 1963-64 p 117). The public policy ground requires the presence of a genuine and sufficiently serious threat to the requirements of public policy affecting one of the fundamental interests of society (Case 30/77 *Bouchereau* [1977] ECR 1999). The genuineness of the limitation is tested by looking at the regulation of the objectionable conduct within the state (Joined Cases 115 & 116/81 *Adoui and Cornuaille* [1982] ECR 1665).

Article 48(4) EC excludes employment in the public service. A functional test has been adopted for identifying such employment: it must involve the exercise of powers conferred by public law, and responsibility for safeguarding the interests of either central and local government (Case 149/79 *Commission v Belgium* [1980] ECR 3881 and [1982] ECR 1845). Articles 55 and 66 EC exclude from the rights of establishment and services activities connected with the exercise of official authority. Again, a functional approach is adopted (Case 2/74 *Reyners* [1974] ECR 631).

Whenever adverse decisions are taken in respect of entry and residence, there are due process guarantees in Articles 5–9 of Directive 64/221.

ROBIN C A WHITE

*Recommended reading*
Handoll *Free Movement of Persons in the EU* (1995) Wiley.
Schermers et al *Free Movement of Persons in Europe* (1993) Martinus Nijhoff.

**FREE MOVEMENT OF SERVICES** The provisions on the freedom to provide services are contained in Articles 59–66 EC. These provisions apply where the provider and the recipient of the services (being **citizens** of the Union or companies or firms formed in accordance with the law of a Member State) are established in different Member States. The right to free movement may be enjoyed by those travelling to another Member State not only to provide services but also to receive services (Joined Cases 286/82 & 26/83 *Luisi and Carbone* [1984] ECR 377). 'Services' are defined in Article 60 EC as those which are normally provided for remuneration. The **Court of Justice** has interpreted 'services' widely to include tourism, medical services and vocational training (see **students**). This definition of services has led to the application of Community law in corollary areas (eg Case 186/87 *Cowan v Trésor Public* [1989] ECR 195, in which a tourist in Paris could not be discriminated against on the grounds of nationality before the French criminal injuries compensation board for injuries he suffered whilst a tourist).

The Chapter on the free movement of services is an adjunct to the freedom of establishment, and the two Chapters should be read together. However, the Court of Justice has held that the Chapter on services is subordinate to that on establishment (Case C-55/94 *Gebhard* [1995] ECR I-4165). Services are provided on a temporary basis, which may be assessed by having regard to their duration, regularity, periodicity or continuity. The temporary nature of services does not, however, preclude the provider from equipping himself with the necessary infrastructure in the host state. However, a person may not use the provisions on services in order to circumvent the rules of establishment of the host state (Case 33/74 *Van Binsbergen* [1974] ECR 1299)

Article 59, which has **direct effect**, requires not only the elimination of all **discrimination** on grounds of nationality against providers of services who are established in another Member State but also the abolition of any restriction, even if it is applied without distinction to national providers of services and to those of other Member States, which is liable to prohibit, impede or render less advantageous the activities of a provider of services established in another Member State where he provides similar services. The Court has held that certain restrictions may be justified 'by an imperative reason of public interest' (Case C-384/93 *Alpine Investments* [1995] ECR I-1141). Restrictions must fulfil four conditions in order to be justified: they must be applied in a non-discriminatory manner; they must be justified by imperative requirements in the general interest; they must be suitable for securing the attainment of the objective which they pursue; and they must not go beyond what is necessary in order to attain it. This jurisprudence has clear parallels with the *Cassis de Dijon* jurisprudence with regard to the **free movement of goods**. However, the Court has explicitly refused to adopt a *Keck* limitation (Cases C-267 & 268/91 *Keck and Mithouard* [1993] ECR I-6097) to the freedom to provide services (see *Alpine Investments*).

A key tool used by the Court has been the principle of **mutual recognition**. The host Member State may not impose restriction, which may otherwise be justified, if adequate protection of the public interest is provided in the home Member State (eg Case 272/94 *Guiot, Climatec*, judgment of 28 March 1996). The Treaty recognises that certain sectors, in particular medical and allied professions, pharmaceuticals and the banking and **insurance** markets, are regulated (see **financial services**). The liberalisation of these sectors is to be undertaken through co-ordination between Member States and in step with the **free movement of capital**, respectively. Specific Directives have been adopted in these sectors to liberalise restrictions and mutually recognise qualifications. Notably, however, the Court of Justice held recently (Case C-101/94 *Commission v Italy*, judgment of 6 June 1996) that professional rules requiring stockbroking firms to have a permanent presence in specified legal form in Italy, for security of the market and regulatory purposes, was contrary to the Treaty's provisions on the freedom of establishment and free movement of services. Despite the existence of harmonising Directives (although not exhaustive) and the regulated nature of these sectors, their restrictions remain subject to the strict tests laid down by the Court of Justice.

Article 66 EC, by reference to the relevant Articles in the Chapter on the freedom of establishment, disapplies the provisions on services to activities which are connected, even occasionally, with the exercise of official authority. The Article provides that Member States may apply by law, regulation or administrative action special treatment for foreign nationals on the grounds of **public policy, public security or public health**. These grounds are the only method of justification for discriminatory restrictions to the freedom to provide services.

WILLIAM ROBINSON

*Recommended reading*

Art 'Legislative lacunae, the Court of Justice and freedom to provide services' in Curtin & O'Keeffe (eds) *Constitutional Adjudication in European Community and National Law* (1992) Butterworths, p 121.

Marenco 'The notion of restriction on the freedom of establishment and the freedom of services in the caselaw of the Court' (1991) Yearbook of European Law 111.

**FREEDOM OF ESTABLISHMENT** The provisions on the freedom of establishment are contained in Articles 52–58 EC. The right of establishment is granted both to legal persons (companies or firms created in accordance with the law of a Member State) and to natural persons who are nationals of a Member State. 'Establishment' means the participation, on a stable and continuous basis, in the economic life of a Member State other than the state of origin. Subject to the exceptions and conditions laid down, it allows all types of self-employed activity to be taken up and pursued on the territory of any other Member State, undertakings to be formed and operated, and agencies, branches or subsidiaries to be set up. Accordingly, persons may be established in more than one Member State.

Article 52(1) provides that restrictions on the freedom of establishment of nationals of a Member State and on the setting-up of agencies, branches or subsidiaries shall be abolished by the end of the transitional period. The **Court of Justice** has held that the prohibition has **direct effect**. Although, as a specific implementation of the prohibition contained in Article 6 EC, the basis of the restriction is non-**discrimination** on the grounds of nationality, the Court has frequently held that the prohibition applies, prima facie, to national measures liable to hinder or make less attractive the exercise of the right of establishment (Case C-19/92 *Kraus* [1993] ECR I-1663). When considering restrictions, the Court has focused upon the actual activity to be undertaken in the host Member State, rather than the national title or profession.

Article 52(2) provides that freedom of establishment is to be exercised under the conditions laid down for its own nationals by the law of the country where such establishment is effected. A person seeking to pursue an activity in another Member State must comply in principle with the rules (to the extent that they exist) relating to organisation, qualifications, professional ethics, membership of professional bodies, supervision and liability. However, as these may constitute restrictions which are liable to hinder or make less attractive the exercise of fundamental freedoms guaranteed by the Treaty, they must fulfil four conditions in order to be justified: they must be applied in a non-discriminatory manner; they must be justified by imperative requirements in the general interest; they must be suitable for securing the attainment of the objective which they pursue; and they must not go beyond what is necessary in order to attain it (see Case C-55/94 *Gebhard* [1995] I-4165).

In order to make it easier for persons to take up and pursue activities as self-employed persons, the **Council** has legislative authority to enact Directives for the **mutual recognition** of diplomas, certificates and other evidence of formal qualifications (Article 57 EC). There have been three stages of development in the mutual recognition of diplomas. First, the Council attempted a sectoral **harmonisation** of qualifications, which resulted in a series of Directives covering, amongst others, doctors, vets, midwives and architects. This approach was only partially successful due to the often marked divergences between the professions and the resultant inordinate delay in adopting Community legislation. Second, the Court of Justice recognised the principle of mutual recognition or equivalence. Whilst Member States remained competent to regulate professions in accordance with Article 52(2), Article 52(1) required them to recognise foreign qualifications as equivalent unless there are reasonable grounds for not so doing (Case 71/76 *Thieffry* [1977] ECR 765). Third, this development prompted the Council to adopt Council Directive (EEC) 89/48 (OJ L19 24.1.89 p 16), which creates a general system for the recognition of higher education diplomas. In those areas not harmonised by specific Directives adopted under the first stage, Member States are required mutually to recognise university (or equivalent) qualifications awarded in another Member State.

Articles 55 and 56 EC contain exceptions to the right of establishment. These may be applied to discriminatory national restrictions. Article

55 provides that the Chapter on the freedom of establishment shall not apply to activities which are connected, even occasionally, with the exercise of official authority. In keeping with the general principle that derogations to fundamental freedoms should be construed restrictively and in accordance with the Court's preference to consider the activity being undertaken rather than the characterisation of the employment, the Court has held that there must be a direct and specific connection with the exercise of official authority to justify the use of Article 55 (Case C-42/92 *Thijssen* [1993] ECR I-4047). Article 56 provides that Member States may apply by law, regulation or administrative action special treatment for foreign nationals on the grounds of **public policy, public security or public health**. Such restrictions on economic activities remain subject to the requirement that they are proportional and necessary to the achievement of the justifying objective.

WILLIAM ROBINSON

*Recommended reading*

Marenco 'The notion of restriction on the freedom of establishment and the freedom of services in the caselaw of the Court' (1991) Yearbook of European Law 111.

Weatherill & Beaumont *EC Law* (2nd edn, 1995) Penguin.


**FULL EFFECTIVENESS OF COMMUNITY LAW** See *effet utile*.


**GATT** The original objectives of the General Agreement on Tariffs and Trade (GATT), signed in 1947, were to increase economic well-being worldwide and to promote trade liberalisation in the international economy.

The General Agreement was signed during the course of broader negotiations aimed at establishing the International Trade Organisation (ITO). Its aim was to implement and protect the tariff reductions agreed upon during the ITO negotiations. There was general expectation that the General Agreement would fall under the mantle of the ITO once it came into existence. This eventuality never occurred and the GATT continued alone, becoming the main international instrument regulating trade between nations.

The GATT sought to achieve its twin goals of international economic prosperity and increased trade in two ways. First, it sought to eliminate discriminatory treatment in international trade through two main provisions: the Most-Favoured-Nation (MFN) clause in Article I which prohibited discrimination among countries in certain trade matters, and the national treatment clause in Article III, which prohibited discrimination between national and foreign products in certain trade areas.

Second, the GATT tried to reduce tariff and other trade barriers by creating a procedure for establishing maximum tariff rates and generally prohibiting quotas and other non-tariff barriers. To achieve tariff reductions, the GATT sponsored eight 'rounds' of Multilateral Trade Negotiations (MTNs), the last one being the **Uruguay Round** (1986–94), during which each contracting party offered tariff reductions so that a mutually acceptable balance was achieved.

As average levels of global tariffs gradually decreased under the GATT-sponsored MTNs, increasingly non-tariff barriers to trade became more obvious impediments to the free flow of goods. In these circumstance, the GATT increasingly attempted to tackle the myriad forms of non-tariff barriers including subsidies, anti-dumping mechanisms, technical standards, customs procedures and government procurement. These subjects were placed on the agenda of the Tokyo Round MTNs and have progressively become the focus of the trade negotiations held under the auspices of the GATT.

The GATT eventually had more than 100 members, termed 'Contracting Parties', including the European Community. In fact the **Court of Justice** confirmed in Opinion 1/94 (Competence of the Community to Conclude International Agreements Concerning Services and the Protection of Intellectual Property [1994] ECR I-5267) that the Community has exclusive competence to conclude multilateral trade agreements in goods, including GATT. Individual Member States are no longer able to negotiate individual trade agreements; negotiations on such matters should be conducted by the Commission.

On the entry into force of the Uruguay Round agreements on 1 January 1995, the **World Trade Organization** (WTO), took over GATT's role as the principal international forum for trade negotiations and dispute settlement.

The GATT formally ceased to exist as an organisation on 31 December 1995, and in that month a 'final session' of the contracting parties, the organisation's general council, was held to mark its passing. However, the text of the General Agreement itself, as amended, was adopted into the WTO Agreement as the GATT 1994.

FIONA MURRAY

*Recommended reading*
Jackson *The World Trading System* (1989) Massachusetts Institute of Technology.
Pescatore et al *Handbook of WTO/GATT Dispute Settlement* (1995) Transnational Juris Publications Inc.

**GENERAL PRINCIPLES OF COMMUNITY LAW** These constitute a body of unwritten principles to which the Community judicature has recourse in order to supplement the Treaties and acts made thereunder. The development of general principles as a source of Community law represents one of the **Court of Justice**'s boldest and most inspired initiatives. The only express reference to general principles in the EC Treaty is to be found in Article 215(2), according to which the **non-contractual liability of the Community** is to be determined in accordance with 'the general principles common to the laws of the Member States'. None the less, there is some authority elsewhere in the EC Treaty for the use of general principles of law to fill gaps in the written law of the Community. Article 164 EC, for example, requires the Court of Justice to 'ensure that in the interpretation and application of this Treaty the law [French: *le respect du droit*] is observed'. That provision would be redundant if it was referring simply to the law expressly laid down by or under the Treaty itself. Similarly, Article 173 EC mentions as one of the grounds on which Community acts may be declared void by the Community judicature 'infringement of this Treaty *or of any rule of law relating to its application*' (emphasis added).

General principles of law may be invoked not only as a ground for annulment under Article 173 EC and in actions for damages under Article 215(2) EC, but also in interpreting written rules of Community law. Such principles are binding on both the Community **institutions** and on the Member States when they act within the scope of Community law (see Case C-260/89 *ERT* [1991] ECR I-2925, paras 41–45). Indeed, it is sometimes suggested that breach of a general principle by a Member State is actionable under Article 169 EC at the suit of the **Commission**. The question may be academic, however, since it is difficult to conceive of a situation in which such a breach would not also involve an infringement of an express provision of Community law.

In formulating general principles, the Community judicature draws inspiration from the constitutional traditions common to the Member States and from international Treaties on which the Member States have collaborated or of which they are signatories. An example of such a Treaty which has special significance in the Community legal order is the **European Convention on Human Rights**, which supplies guidelines on the fundamental rights protected by the Community judicature as an integral part of the general principles of law (see *ERT* para 41).

A valuable insight into the approach taken by the Court when it has recourse to the national laws of the Member States is provided by H Kutscher, a former judge: 'There is complete agreement that when the Court interprets or supplements Community law on a comparative law basis it is not obliged to take the minimum which the national solutions have in common, or their arithmetic mean or the solution produced by a majority of the legal systems as the basis of its decision. The Court has to weigh up and evaluate the particular problem and search for the "best" and "most appropriate" solution. The best possible solution is the one which meets the specific objectives and basic principles of the Community . . . in the most satisfactory way' ('Methods of Interpretation as Seen by a Judge at the Court of Justice', p I-29, Judicial and Academic Conference, Luxembourg 1976).

That passage was cited by **Advocate General** Slynn in Case 155/79 *AM & S v Commission* [1982] ECR 1575 at 1649, where he went on to explain that 'Such a course is followed not to import national laws as such into Community law, but to use it as a means of discovering an *unwritten* principle of Community law' (emphasis in the original). This means that, once a principle derived from national law is incorporated into Community law, it acquires a life of its own independent of its domestic forebears. In *AM & S*, the Court held that Council Regulation (EEC) 17/62 on the application of the Treaty competition rules (OJ Sp Ed 1959-62 p 87) was to be interpreted as protecting, subject to certain conditions, the confidentiality of written communications between lawyer and client (see **competition procedure**). The principle of such protection was generally recognised in the legal systems of the Member States, although its scope and the criteria for applying it varied and it was not expressly recognised by Regulation 17/62.

The national laws of the Member States have been the source of a number of other principles which have come to play a central role in the functioning of the Community legal order. A prominent example is the principle of **legal certainty**, which seems to have been modelled principally on German law. That principle has a number of offshoots, such as the protection of **legitimate expectations, non-retroactivity** and vested rights. At the risk of over-simplification, it may be said that the essence of legal certainty is that the rules applicable in particular circumstances should be reasonably clear and that their effect should be predictable. Another principle derived from German law which has assumed great importance is the principle of **proportionality**, which essentially requires measures adopted by public authorities to be in proportion to their ultimate objectives. Mention may also be made of the right to a hearing, established as a general principle of law in Case 17/74 *Transocean Marine Paint v Commission* [1974] ECR 1063.

A third source of general principles is the Treaties themselves. The Court may treat a specific provision as embodying a general principle which applies outside the scope of the provision concerned. An example is Article 40(3) EC, according to which the common organisation of agricultural markets 'shall exclude any discrimination between producers or consumers within the Community'. The Court has held that the prohibition of **discrimination** laid down in that provision 'is merely a specific enunciation of the general principle of **equality** which is one of the fundamental principles of Community law' (Joined Cases 124/76 & 20/77 *Moulins Pont-à-Mousson* [1977] ECR 1795, para 16).

ANTHONY ARNULL

*Recommended reading*
Akehurst 'The Application of General Principles of Law by the Court of Justice of the European Communities' (1981) 52 BYIL 29.
Arnull *The General Principles of EEC Law and the Individual* (1990) Leicester University Press.

**GENEVA CONVENTION** For the UN Convention on the status of Refugees 1951 and the 1967 Protocol, see **asylum**.

**GOOD ADMINISTRATION** This principle is sometimes invoked (often as a last resort) in an attempt to show that a Community act is vitiated by some defect in the manner in which the adopting **institution** conducted itself before the contested act was adopted. Neglect of the rules of good administration was cited by the Court in Case 179/82 *Lucchini v Commission* [1983] ECR 3083, where a fine imposed by the **Commission** on a steel producer for exceeding its production quota was reduced because the Commission failed to answer a telex from the applicant offering in advance to offset the excess in one quarter during the following quarters. However, in Case 64/82 *Tradax v Commission* [1984] ECR 1359 at 1385–1386, **Advocate General** Slynn said that he did not consider 'that there is any generalized principle of law that what is required by good administration will necessarily amount to a legally enforceable rule'. Thus, in Joined Cases 96 to 102, 104, 105, 108 & 110/82 *IAZ v Commission* [1983] ECR 3369, a competition case in which a Commission decision was challenged, the Court accepted that the failure of the Commission to react to a document which had been sent to it by the applicants was 'regrettable and inconsistent with the requirements of good administration' (para 15). However, the Court declined to treat that failure as 'a procedural defect vitiating the legality of the Decision' (ibid).

The 'interests of good administration' are reflected in the rules of procedure of the Community institutions (see Case C-69/89 *Nakajima v Council* [1991] ECR I-2069, para 49). An infringement of such a rule may constitute a breach of an essential procedural requirement where the rule in question is not concerned solely with the institution's internal working arrangements but creates rights and contributes to **legal certainty** for natural and legal persons (Joined Cases T-79, 84–86, 89, 91–92, 94, 96, 98, 102, 104/89 *BASF and Others v Commission* [1992] ECR II-315, para 78; Case C-137/92 P *Commission v BASF and Others* [1994] ECR I-2555).

ANTHONY ARNULL

*Recommended reading*
Schermers & Waelbroeck *Judicial Protection in the European Communities* (5th edn, 1992) Kluwer, p 88.
Usher 'The "Good Administration" of European Community Law' (1985) 38 Current Legal Problems 269.

**HARMONISATION** The terms 'harmonisation' and '**approximation**' are sometimes used interchangeably. Article 100a(4) EC refers to the 'adoption of a harmonisation measure by the Council acting by a qualified majority' but leaves the term 'harmonisation' undefined.

The relevant measures appear to relate to the **Council**'s powers in Article 100a(1) EC to 'adopt the measures for the approximation of the provisions laid down by law, regulation or administrative action in Member States which have as their object the establishment and functioning of the **Internal Market**'.

Harmonisation is frequently referred to as either a method or a policy for achieving the dismantling of barriers to trade between Member States and replacing them with a common, unified Community system. It is therefore a powerful means of creating an Internal Market and requires legislative intervention by the Community with the result of superseding national law. One of the major achievements of the **Single European Act** was the insertion into the EEC Treaty of Article 100a(1) which enabled Community harmonisation legislation intended to complete the Internal Market to be passed by **qualified majority vote**, rather than requiring unanimity. This greatly speeded up the range and number of laws, particularly in the form of Directives, which were subsequently enacted for this purpose. For instance, each of the 'four freedoms' have been complemented by harmonisation legislation. A substantial harmonisation programme has also been undertaken in the field of **company law** and VAT (see **taxation**).

ROSE D'SA

*Recommended reading*
Kapteyn & Verloren Van Themaat in Gormley (ed) *Introduction to the Law of the European Communities* (2nd edn, 1989) pp 467–484.
Shaw *European Community Law* (1993) Macmillan, pp 306–312.


**HEALTH AND SAFETY AT WORK** The EEC Treaty contained no explicit reference to a role for the Community in regulating health and safety at work in the Member States. Article 118 merely gives the **Commission** the role of promoting co-operation between the Member States in this and other **social policy** fields. However, from 1970 onwards, attention turned towards what is a vital aspect not only of social policy, but also of overall economic efficiency. A number of Directives were adopted by the **Council**, mainly using Article 235 EEC as a legal basis. The **Single European Act** brought a new era, with the introduction of Article 118a as a specific legal basis. The Council of Ministers may adopt Directives, using the co-operation procedure, aimed at 'encouraging improvements, especially in the working environment, as regards the health and safety of workers'. The aim is to achieve the '**harmonisation** of conditions in this area, while maintaining the improvements made'.

Nearly 20 Directives have now been adopted on the basis of Article 118a, of which the most significant is the Framework Directive (Council Directive (EEC) 89/391 (OJ L183 29.6.89 p 1)), which imposes a generally increased level of responsibility on employers in respect of the health and safety of the workforce. It requires them to evaluate

183

risks at all stages of the production process, to inform workers, to provide them with adequate training and to monitor constantly their health. Article 16 of the Directive provides for so-called 'daughter' Directives to be adopted regarding specific risks, and so far 13 such Directives have been adopted, covering matters relating from the use of machines and equipment (Council Directive (EEC) 89/655 (OJ L393 30.12.89 p 13)) to the protection of pregnant workers, and workers who have recently given birth or are breastfeeding (Council Directive (EEC) 92/85 (OJ L348 28.11.92 p 1)).

In recent years the Council of Ministers has adopted a number of particularly controversial Directives based on Article 118a: Council Directive (EC) 93/104 on working time (OJ L307 13.12.93 p 18) and Council Directive (EC) 94/33 on young people at work (OJ L216 20.8.94 p 12). The key to the limits of Article 118a as a legal basis lies in the concept of the 'working environment'. In Case C-84/94 *UK v Council*, judgment of 12 November 1996 (not yet reported) the United Kingdom challenged the use of Article 118a as the basis for the Working Time Directive. The Court emphasised that the term 'working environment' was to be interpreted broadly, and as justifying measures to cover 'all factors, physical or otherwise, capable of affecting the health and safety of the worker in his working environment, including in particular certain aspects of the organisation of working time'. The Court re-emphasised that the effect of Article 118a is to confer internal legislative **competence** on the Community in respect of social policy.

Article 100a EC also contains a reference to the need for the Commission to have regard to high standards of protection for the health and safety of workers in the proposals which it makes for measures aimed at the completion of the Internal Market. Article 100a has been the legal basis for a number of important measures in this field including the Machinery Directive (Council Directive (EEC) 89/392 (OJ L183 29.6.89 p 9)) and the Product Safety Directive (Council Directive (EEC) 92/59 (OJ L228 11.8.92 p 24)). The Commission's work has generally been structured by action programmes drawn up in advance. A fourth programme of action was issued in 1993 (Com (93) 560) and foresees both legislative and non-legislative (eg educational, promotional, training etc) activities continuing. 1994 saw the establishment of the European Agency for Health and Safety, located in Bilbao, Spain (Council Regulation (EC) 2062/94 (OJ L216 20.8.94 p 1)), which will supplement the work of the Commission, particularly in the field of research.

JO SHAW

*Recommended reading*
Neal & Wright *1992 European Communities Health and Safety Legislation* (1992) Chapman & Hall.
Nielsen & Szyszczak *The Social Dimension of the European Community* (2nd edn, 1993) Handelshojskolens Forlag, pp 207–212, 231–264.

**HOUSE OF COMMONS SELECT COMMITTEE ON EUROPEAN LEGISLATION (UK)** The Select Committee on European Legislation, with a membership of 16, scrutinises European Community documents, which include all proposals for legislation by the **Council** and other documents published for submission to the Council or the **European Council** (HC Standing Order 127). These documents are deposited in the House as soon as they are available. The government provides an Explanatory Memorandum summarising the subject matter of each document, identifying any legal, procedural or **subsidiarity** issues and explaining the government's policy, the financial implications and timetable. As soon as possible thereafter, the Committee (which normally meets weekly while the House is sitting) examines the document. If the Committee decides that a document raises questions of legal or political importance, it reports on it to the House and may recommend further consideration. If it does so recommend, the document stands referred to one of the two European Standing Committees in which the responsible Minister may be questioned and which debates the document on a Government motion (HC Standing Order 102). Debates on some of the more important documents are held on the floor of the House.

The House has resolved (resolution of the House of 24 October 1990, CJA 1989-90, para 646) that, subject to certain exceptions, no Minister should give agreement in the Council to any proposal for Community legislation which is still subject to scrutiny by the Committee or to a recommendation for further consideration. If, however, the Minister concerned decides that, for special reasons, agreement should be given to a proposal which is still subject to scrutiny or further consideration, he may do so, but in that event he must explain his reasons to the Committee at the first opportunity after reaching his decision and, in the case of a proposal awaiting further consideration by the House, to the House at the first opportunity after giving agreement.

TIMOTHY J G PRATT

*Recommended reading*
Fourth Report from the Select Committee on Procedure, HC 622 I & II of Session 1989-90: *The Scrutiny of European Legislation.*
First Report from the Select Committee on Procedure, HC 31 of Session 1991-92: *Review of European Standing Committees.*

**HOUSE OF LORDS SELECT COMMITTEE ON THE EUROPEAN COMMUNITIES (UK)** The House of Lords Select Committee on the European Communities was set up in 1974, following the Maybray-King Report. Its terms of reference are: 'To consider Community proposals whether in draft or otherwise, to obtain all necessary information about them, and to make reports on those which, in the opinion of the Committee, raise important questions of policy or principle, and on other questions to which the Committee considers that the special attention of the House should be drawn.'

All **Commission** proposals and certain other documents are deposited in Parliament on arrival in London. An Explanatory Memorandum gives the government a view of policy, legal and financial implications and likely timing. The Chairman of the Committee sifts the significant documents to one of the specialist Sub-Committees:

– Economic and Financial Affairs, Trade and External Relations (A);
– Energy, Industry and Transport (B);
– Environment, Public Health and Consumer Affairs (C);
– Agriculture, Fisheries and Consumer Protection (D);
– Law and Institutions (E); and
– Social Affairs, Education and Home Affairs (F).

Sub-Committee E has special terms of reference covering significant changes to UK law, developments in Community law and legal base questions. Additional Sub-Committees may be set up ad hoc: for example, on the 1996 **Intergovernmental Conference**.

A Sub-Committee may write to the Minister or undertake a full inquiry, inviting written and oral evidence from Community **institutions**, government departments and other interested bodies and individuals. Reports agreed by the Sub-Committee, and then by the Committee are published with the evidence as a report to the House. Over half are debated and the reports go to those involved in the legislation, witnesses and the press. The government must reply within two months, and has undertaken not to agree to any proposal in the **Council** while it remains under scrutiny by the Committee. The Committee seeks to influence, but cannot mandate Ministers. Since 1994, the Committee has extended its scrutiny procedures to the intergovernmental **Pillars** of the European Union.

EILEEN DENZA

*Recommended reading*
European Parliament *The European Parliament and the Parliaments of the Member States: Parliamentary scrutiny and arrangements for cooperation* (July 1994).
Denza *La Chambre des Lords: Vingt Années d'Enquêtes Communautaires, Revue du Marché commun et de l'Union Européenne* (1993), p 740.

**HUMAN RIGHTS PROTECTION** Given the primarily economic nature of the European Communities and the existence of the **European Convention on Human Rights**, human rights protection was not originally perceived as being central to the legal order of the Communities. Nevertheless, an approach to the protection of fundamental rights has developed tentatively within the jurisprudence of the **Court of Justice**.

It was in the context of the **supremacy** of Community law over national law, that the human rights lacuna in the Community legal order first arose. In Case 1/58 *Stork v High Authority* [1959] ECR 17 the ECJ declined to allow the examination of Community law for compliance with the human rights provisions of Member States' constitutional law. To permit this, according to the Court, would be to allow the doctrine of the supremacy of Community law to be overridden. Subsequently, following adverse reaction from the German Constitutional Court, the ECJ altered its stance in an obiter statement, in Case 29/69 *Stauder v City of Ulm* [1969] ECR 419, where it accepted that fundamental human rights were enshrined in the **general principles** of Community law and protected by the Court. This was elaborated upon in Case 11/70 *Internationale Handelsgesellschaft* [1970] ECR 1125, where the ECJ noted that the fundamental rights contained within the general principles of Community law were inspired by the 'common constitutional traditions of the Member States'. Nevertheless, the requirement of the supremacy of Community law entails that such rights be protected in accordance with the structure and objectives of the Community.

Further elaboration as to the source of these rights was provided in Case 4/73 *Nold v Commission* [1974] ECR 491, where the Court observed that '. . . international Treaties for the protection of human rights on which the Member States have collaborated or of which they are signatories, can supply guidelines which should be followed within the framework of Community law'. Principal among these treaties is the ECHR, which the EC **institutions** committed themselves to respecting in a Joint Declaration in 1977. In Case 36/75 *Rutili* [1975] ECR 1219 the ECJ referred specifically to the ECHR for the first time and, subsequently, in Case 44/79 *Hauer v Land Rheinland-Pfalz* [1979] ECR 3727 engaged in a detailed analysis of substantive rights guaranteed by the ECHR.

A gradual expansion of human rights protection in the Community legal order is evident from case law such as Case 5/88 *Wachauf* [1989] ECR 2609, to the effect that Member States in their application of Community law must ensure 'as far as possible' that human rights are protected, and Case C-260/89 *ERT* [1991] ECR I-2925, whereby derogations permitted under Community law must also comply with human rights norms. Nevertheless, the role of the ECJ in the context of human rights protection is curtailed by the objectives of the EC and a certain reluctance, as was evident in Case C-159/90 *SPUC v Grogan* [1991] ECR I-4685, to enter into particularly sensitive rights issues.

The ECJ's jurisprudential basis for protecting rights is echoed in the **European Union**'s commitment to human rights. Article F.2 TEU, states that 'the Union shall respect fundamental rights, as guaranteed by the European Convention on Human Rights and Fundamental Freedoms signed in Rome on 4 November 1950 and as they result from the constitutional traditions of the Member States, as general principles of Community Law'. However, its location within Title I of the TEU means that this Article, by contrast with the **citizens**' rights set out in Title II, is not enforceable before the ECJ. Also at the Union level,

Article K.2 provides that matters of common interest in **Co-operation in the Fields of Justice and Home Affairs** shall be dealt with in accordance with the requirements of the ECHR and the 1951 Refugee Convention. The real strength of this commitment to rights protection is dependent upon the extent to which Conventions on matters of common interest are made subject to **judicial review**.

In any event, dissatisfaction with the piecemeal development of human rights protection to date has fuelled an ongoing debate on the merits, or otherwise, of a detailed Bill of Rights and/or accession to the ECHR. The latter issue was resolved for the time being by Opinion 2/94 [1996] ECR I-1759 in which the Court held that, in the absence of a Treaty amendment, the EC does not have the required competence to accede. The external aspect of human rights policy is manifest in Articles J.1(2) TEU and Article 130u(2) EC, which identify human rights promotion as objectives in the context of Common Foreign and Security Policy and development co-operation, respectively.

PATRICK TWOMEY

*Recommended reading*
Weiler, Cassese & Clapham (eds) *Human Rights and the European Community* (1991) Nomos Verlag, vol II.
Neuwahl & Ross (eds) *The European Union and Human Rights* (1995) Nijhoff.

**IGC** See **Intergovernmental Conference**.

**IMMIGRATION POLICY** Immigration policy development results primarily from the free movement provisions of Article 7a EC, which provides for creation of an area without internal frontiers within which people, services, goods and capital can move freely. It also implies that entry, residence and movement by people from third countries become matters of common concern. Consequently, the liberalisation of free movement engenders a paradox: EU citizens can benefit from freedoms bestowed by the Treaty, but so-called 'third country nationals' cannot, unless covered by reciprocal agreements between their country of origin and the EU.

Between 1986 and ratification of the Treaty on European Union in November 1993, co-operation on immigration was characterised by 'informal intergovernmentalism'. In 1986 the British government was instrumental in establishing the Ad Hoc Group on Immigration. In 1988 the Rhodes Group of Free Movement Co-ordinators was created and brought forward the Palma Programme – a series of measures deemed essential if free movement of people within the Internal Market was to be realised. Informal intergovernmentalism sought to promote co-operation in two main ways. First, to develop common procedures for **asylum**-seekers (the Dublin Convention 1991). Second, to draft an external frontiers convention (1991), which remains unsigned because of a dispute between the British and Spanish over Gibraltar. Informal intergovernmentalism was criticised for a number of reasons, one of which being that it exacerbated the democratic deficit by extracting immigration co-operation from the effective purview of democratic and judicial institutions at national and supranational level.

The Maastricht meeting of the **European Council** reached agreement on a revision to the EC Treaty which saw replacement of informal intergovernmentalism by the **Co-operation in the Fields of Justice and Home Affairs** Pillar, Title VI of the Treaty on European Union. The CJHA Pillar recognised immigration as a common interest and introduced a Treaty obligation to co-operate within a single institutional structure. Article K.1 TEU outlines nine areas of common interest, three of which relate to immigration policy: Article K.1.1 on asylum; Article K.1.2 on rules governing the crossing of external borders of Member States; and Article K.1.3 on immigration policy and policy regarding nationals of third countries.

The Council acts by unanimity when deciding on conventions, joint actions and joint positions (Article K.3). Supranational institutions have limited involvement. The **Commission** has watered-down powers of initiative which it shares with Member States. The Commission does have powers under Article 100c EC (added by the Treaty on European Union) to determine a list of countries whose nationals require visas to enter the EU. In October 1995 a Council Regulation, based on a Commission proposal under Article 100c, listed 101 countries whose nationals must be in possession of a visa when crossing the external borders of Member States (Council Regulation (EC) 2317/95 (OJ L234 3.10.95 pp 1-3)). A complication is that other aspects of visa policy, such as conditions for issue, are determined under Title VI of the Treaty. The European Parliament only has the right to be informed about discussions covered by CJHA provisions (Article K.6). The Court of Justice is given authority to review decisions and adjudicate in disputes only if the CJHA Council decides by unanimity to extend such powers (Article K.3.2). There is a potential bridge from the CJHA Pillar to the Community Pillar as Article K.9 provides for a *passerelle*, whereby Article 100c of the Treaty could be extended to cover other immigration issues, provided all Member States agree. Article K.4 establishes a co-ordinating committee of senior officials (known as the K4 Committee) to service the CJHA Council.

The Schengen countries (see **Schengen Agreements**) have pressed ahead to attain free movement objectives more quickly and Schengen has served as a testing ground for immigration spin-offs from free movement provisions. This is reflected in recent EU measures and proposals which echo Schengen arrangements, such as the visa regulation and the establishment of a computerised information system to monitor migrants, which is based on the Schengen Information System.

In its 1994 Communication on Immigration and Asylum Policy, the Commission outlined an approach to policy development based on three interrelated elements. First, action on migration pressure to deal with root causes. Second, controlling immigration flows by formulating basic principles on such items as admissions policy. Third, strengthening integration policies and introducing measures to tackle racism and xenophobia. So far, little effective action has been taken to address conditions in sending countries, problems of racism and xenophobia or better integration of immigrants and their families. Recent developments may go some way to correct this imbalance, although it is too early to judge. In March 1996 the CJHA Council adopted a Joint Action concerning measures to combat racism and xenophobia. Each Member State undertook to ensure effective judicial co-operation to punish racist and xenophobic behaviour such as: holocaust denial; public dissemination of racist or xenophobic tracts; and participation in groups which involve violence, discrimination or racial, ethnic or religious hatred.

Nevertheless, whether the EU can be said to have an immigration 'policy' is a moot point. Member States have recognised immigration as a matter of common interest and rule-based **approximation** – rather than **harmonisation** – has tended to occur. Development of a fully-fledged supranational immigration policy would imply a much greater role for the Commission, Parliament and Court of Justice than is currently the case. However, *communitarisation* of immigration policy is likely to continue in the coming years because of the close links between free movement objectives and immigration policy. A restrictionist emphasis is detectable which contributes to an under-nourished conceptualisation of the immigration issue as a problem of numbers of immigrants. Meanwhile, other important issues remain unresolved. One of the most pressing is the legal, social and political position of the 15 million third country nationals resident in Member States, many of whom are permanently resident, but are excluded from the rights and freedoms extended by the Treaty framework.

ANDREW GEDDES

*Recommended reading*
Ford *Fascist Europe: The Rise of Racism and Xenophobia* (1992) Pluto Press.
Handoll *Free Movement of Persons in the European Union* (1995) John Wiley & Sons.

**IMPLEMENTING POWERS** These are the powers to adopt and apply the detailed rules which are required to give effect to Community legislation based directly on the Treaty. Such implementing provisions may be adopted by a different **institution** from that which adopts the primary legislation, or by the same institution but under a different procedure.

The **Court of Justice** has held on various occasions that discretionary decisional powers may not be delegated by the institutions to outside bodies, such as private law agencies. Implementing powers can therefore only be conferred on a Community institution, and their exercise is subject to the jurisdiction of the Court. The basic elements of a matter to be regulated must be laid down in the primary legislation, which must clearly specify the bounds of the power conferred. Unless the contrary is provided, implementing provisions cannot derogate from the basic measure; authorised derogations may not jeopardise the essential elements of the primary legislation.

The concept of implementing powers is extensively interpreted, and the **Council** may validly confer wide powers of discretion and action on the **Commission**. Where the exercise of such powers requires the evaluation of a complex economic situation, the Court will only annul implementing provisions for a manifest error, a misuse of powers or lack of competence (see **action of annulment**). Conversely, implementing provisions which impede the achievement of a Treaty objective will be strictly interpreted, and they may not impinge on an area exhaustively regulated by primary legislation.

The Council is obliged to confer implementing powers on the Commission, but may subject their exercise to supervisory mechanism known as '**comitology**'; in specific cases, the Council may reserve the implementing powers to itself (Article 145 EC, third indent). The Commission may delegate management responsibilities and the power of signature to individual Commissioners or to its officials, but it may not confer discretionary powers on them.

KIERAN ST C BRADLEY

*Recommended reading*
Lenaerts 'Regulating the regulatory process "delegation of powers" in the European Community' (1993) 18 ELRev 23.
Toth *Oxford Encyclopaedia of Community Law* (1990) Clarendon Press, vol I, entry on the Commission, pp 73-75.

**IMPLIED POWERS** The EC has two types of powers: those granted expressly by the Treaties, and implied powers recognised by the **Court of Justice**. The latter are based on the principle that the law must be interpreted as providing all the powers necessary to achieve its objectives. The role of implied powers in the EC is limited, however, because the Treaties provide for most of the necessary powers expressly and also contain a general authorisation to legislate (see, for example, Article 235 EC).

Implied powers with regard to the internal sphere concern the role of specific **institutions** and thus the institutional balance and relations between the EC and Member States. For example, the Court of Justice has held that where an Article of the EEC Treaty conferred a specific task on the Commission, it also conferred on the Commission necessarily and per se the powers which are indispensable in order to carry out that task (Joined Cases 281, 283-285 & 287/85 *Germany v Commission* [1987] ECR 3203).

Implied powers with regard to the external sphere usually refer to the EC's Treaty-making capacity, and hence the relation between the EC and the Member States. They are based on the doctrine of parallelism: implied powers in external relations potentially extend to any topic within the scope of the Community's express powers in internal matters. They may flow from Treaty provisions and from measures adopted, within the framework of these provisions, by the EC institutions (Case 22/70 *Commission v Council (ERTA)* [1971] ECR 263). They are not limited to areas in which there is a common policy and previously it was considered that they may follow even from measures adopted under Article 235 EC (Opinion 2/91 (Re ILO Convention 170) [1993] ECR I-1061). Nor were they limited to areas in which the internal powers of the Community have already been exercised (Opinion 1/76 (Laying-Up Fund) [1977] ECR 741). An implied power does not become exclusive, however, until the express power on which it is dependent is exercised either internally or externally and Article 235 cannot in itself vest in the Community an exclusive external competence (Opinion 1/94 *World Trade Organisation* [1994] ECR I-5267). In the meantime, the Member States must act within the respect of the Community obligations, in particular Article 5 EC (Joined Cases 3, 4 & 6/76 *Kramer* [1976] ECR 1279) and the obligation to co-operate which flows from the requirement of unity in external affairs (Opinion 1/94, *supra*) (see also **division of power**).

FRANCIS SNYDER

*Recommended reading*
Demaret (ed) *Relations extérieures de la Communauté européenne et marché intérieur: aspects juridiques et fonctionnels* (1988) Story Scientia.
Groux & Manin *Les Communautés européennes dans l'ordre international* (1984) Office for the Official Publications of the EC.

**INDIRECT EFFECT** The **Court of Justice** recognised the **direct effect** of Directives in Case 41/74 *Van Duyn* [1974] ECR 1337 and then limited to individuals the possibility of invoking such direct effect against the state or emanations of the state in Case 152/84 *Marshall I* [1986] ECR 723 (the so-called 'vertical direct effect of Directives'). In the absence of 'horizontal direct effect of Directives', an individual may not rely directly upon the terms of a Directive against another individual, as a Directive cannot impose obligations on the latter (confirmed in Case 91/94 *Faccini Dori* [1994] ECR I-3325). The inability for litigants to rely upon the direct effect of unimplemented Directives against private parties clearly causes inequality.

The Court of Justice stepped back from the principle of direct effect in order to assist those seeking to claim Community rights enshrined in Directives against a private party. In Case 14/83 *Von Colson and Kamann* [1984] ECR 1891 the Court combined two principles: first, the Member States' obligation arising from Article 189 EC to achieve the result envisaged by a Directive; and, second, the Member States' duty under Article 5 EC to take all appropriate measures, whether general or particular, to ensure fulfilment of their Treaty obligations extends to all authorities of Member States, including, for matters falling within their jurisdiction, the courts. In these circumstances, the Court held, as a general principle, that national courts are required to interpret their national law in the light of the wording and the purpose of the Directive in order to achieve the result referred to in Article 189. National courts are therefore under an obligation of uniform interpretation of national law in conformity with Community law in order that they, as part of the state, do not assist in a breach of Community law.

The extent of this indirect effect of Directives was clarified in Case C-106/89 *Marleasing* [1990] ECR I-4135. In that case, the Court made it clear that the national court is under a duty to interpret national law, whether adopted before or after the Directive, in the light of the wording and purpose of the Directive. The national courts are not under an absolute duty, so as to interpret national law *contra legem*, but only 'as far as possible'. Accordingly, national courts must consider all national law in the relevant field, whenever adopted, and establish whether that legislation can bear an interpretation in conformity with the wording and purpose of the Directive. This principle is general, and will apply whether or not a Directive has been implemented into national law.

The principle of uniform interpretation has given rise to two distinct lines of jurisprudence in the House of Lords. In one line, exemplified by *Litster v Forth Dry Dock Ltd* [1990] 1 AC 546, the House of Lords was prepared to read words into national Regulations adopted in order to implement a Directive. Lord Templeman considered this a purposive interpretation of national law which did not amount to a distortion of the meaning of the Regulations. However, in the second line, typified by *Duke v GEC Reliance Ltd* [1988] AC 618, the House of Lords has not been prepared to distort the meaning of national legislation where that legislation was not enacted to implement the relevant Community Directive. The line between purposive interpretation and distortion of the meaning appears very fine indeed. To the extent that the House of Lords has relied upon the sequence of adoption of the relevant Acts and the intention of Parliament, it may not be complying fully with its obligations as set out by the Court of Justice in *Marleasing*.

The Court of Justice clarified in *Faccini Dori* that an individual who cannot derive a directly effective right from a Directive should seek to obtain a remedy in the national courts, first, through the principle of uniform interpretation and, second, through the liability of the Member States in damages (Joined Cases C-6/90 & 9/90 *Francovich* [1991] ECR I-5357). The latter action remains possible as the national court is not required to interpret national law *contra legem* in order to achieve the purpose of an unimplemented Directive.

WILLIAM ROBINSON

*Recommended reading*
Maltby 'Marleasing: What is all the fuss about?' (1993) 109 LQR 301.
Steiner 'From direct effect to Francovich: shifting means of enforcement of
    Community law' (1993) 18 ELRev 3.

**INDUSTRIAL POLICY** Prior to the **Treaty on European Union** the EC
had no specific powers in the area of industrial policy, although the
powers it had in a number of areas, in particular state aids, competition,
the **Internal Market** and **research and development**, enabled it to take
action relating to industrial policy.

The Treaty on European Union added to the list of activities of the EC
set out in Article 3 'the strengthening of the competitiveness of Community
industry'. It also inserted into the EC Treaty a new Title headed 'Industry',
comprising one Article, Article 130. That Article provides that the
Community and the Member States are to ensure that the conditions
necessary for the competitiveness of the Community's industry exist.
The action they take is to be in accordance with a system of open and
competitive markets and is to be aimed at speeding up the adjustment of
industry to structural change, encouraging an environment favourable
to change and to the development of undertakings, particularly small
and medium-sized undertakings, encouraging an environment favourable
to co-operation between undertakings, and fostering better exploitation
of the industrial potential of policies of innovation, research and
technological development.

The **Council** is given power, acting unanimously, to decide on specific
measures in support of action taken in Member States to achieve these
objectives. Article 130 EC expressly recognises that other provisions of
the Treaty are important in achieving them as well. It also provides that
it is not to be a basis for the introduction by the Community of any
measure which could lead to a distortion of competition.

In 1993 the Commission published its White Paper on 'Growth,
competitiveness and employment – the challenges and ways forward
into the 21st century'. It set out a medium-term strategy for the Community
and the Member States. On the basis of the White Paper the Brussels
**European Council** of December 1993 decided to implement an action
plan based on measures at the levels of the Union and the Member States.

The Commission has produced a number of reports and
communications setting out its priorities for action to be taken by the
Community and the Member States. Based on these, the Council has
adopted resolutions setting out the principles to guide industrial policy
initiatives and proposals.

STEPHEN HYETT

*Recommended reading*
Bangemann *Meeting the Global Challenge* (1992) Kogan Page.
Commission White Paper on 'Growth, competitiveness and employment' Bulletin
    of the EC Supplement 6/93.

**INFRINGEMENT PROCEEDINGS** See **action for failure to fulfil an obligation**.

**INQUIRY** The **European Parliament**'s right of inquiry was introduced by the **Treaty on European Union**. Article 138c EC provides that in the course of its duties, the European Parliament may, at the request of a quarter of its members, set up a temporary Committee of Inquiry to investigate, alleged contraventions or maladministration in the implementation of Community law.

Accordingly, the temporary Committee of Inquiry is competent to examine alleged contraventions or maladministration occurring in the framework of an **institution** or a body of the European Communities, or a public administrative body of a Member State or of persons empowered by Community law to implement that law.

The European Parliament's right of inquiry is exercised without prejudice to the powers conferred by the Treaty on other institutions or bodies.

A temporary Committee of Inquiry has no right to investigate matters at issue before a national or Community court until such time as the legal proceedings have been completed.

The detailed provisions governing the exercise of the right of inquiry is determined by common accord of the European Parliament, the **Council** and the **Commission**.

The composition and rules of procedure of temporary Committees of Inquiry are determined by the European Parliament. Hearings and testimony take place in public. Witnesses and experts have the right to make a statement or provide testimony *in camera*. When it completes its work, the temporary Committee of Inquiry is obliged to submit to the European Parliament a report on the results of its work, containing minority opinions if appropriate. On the basis of this report the European Parliament adopts recommendations which may forward it to the institutions or bodies of the European Communities or to the Member States.

The temporary Committee of Inquiry ceases to exist on the submission of its report within the time-limit laid down when it was set up.

EPAMINONDAS A MARIAS

*Recommended reading*
Bourlanges & de Giovani *Report on the European Parliament's right of inquiry* EP Session Documents, A4-0003/95.
European Parliament DG for Research, Parliamentary Committees of Inquiry in the Community Member States (1993).

**INSTITUTIONS OF THE EUROPEAN UNION** Article 4(1) EC states that the tasks entrusted to the Community shall be carried out by a **European Parliament**, a **Council**, a **Commission**, a **Court of**

**Justice** and a **Court of Auditors**. These bodies constitute the institutions of the Community wherever such a reference is made in the Treaty. They are required to act within the limits of the powers conferred upon them. This forms the single institutional framework of the Communities. The Treaties also provide for the establishment of several additional bodies: Article 4(2) EC refers to an **Economic and Social Committee** and a **Committee of the Regions**; Article 4a EC establishes a **European System of Central Banks** and, in the future, a **European Central Bank**; Article 4b EC establishes the **European Investment Bank**; and Article 168a EC provides for a **Court of First Instance** to be 'attached' to the Court of Justice.

Initially, however, each of the European Economic Community, the **European Coal and Steel Community** and the **European Atomic Energy Community** instituted an autonomous institutional framework. For budgetary reasons, and anxious to limit the number of institutions responsible for carrying out similar tasks, the Member States signed the Convention on certain institutions common to the European Communities on 25 March 1957, at the same time as the Treaties of Rome. This Convention merged from their inception the Assemblies (European Parliaments), the Courts of Justice and the Economic and Social Committees of the three Treaties. In contrast, the Member States delayed until 1965 to sign a Treaty establishing a Single Council and a Single Commission of the European Communities (the Merger Treaty, OJ 152 13.7.67). The Merger Treaty completed the single institutional framework by establishing a common Council, Commission and Court of Auditors.

In addition to the institutions which have been established by the Treaties, two further categories of body exist. First, Article D TEU provides for the **European Council** 'to provide the Union with the necessary impetus for its development and [to] define the general political guidelines thereof'. The European Council is made up of the Heads of State or Government of the Member States and the President of the Commission, and meets at least twice a year. It was first recognised in the Single European Act.

Second, within the scope of the Treaties, the Council and the Commission have established a number of agencies, offices and centres to assist in the operation of the Communities. These bodies are staffed by Community officials and national experts and may only act within the scope of the legislative acts by which they are established. They include the European Environmental Agency, the European Training Foundation, the Office for Veterinary and Plant Health Inspection and Control, the European Monitoring Centre for Drugs and Drug Addiction, the European Agency for the Evaluation of Medicinal Products, the Agency for Health and Safety at Work, the Office for Harmonization in the Internal Market (Trade Marks, Designs and Models) and the European Centre for the Development of Vocational Training.

The Member States have only recently agreed the **seat of the institutions** and bodies set up under the Treaties.

MARGOT HORSPOOL

*Recommended reading*
Lasok & Bridge *Law and Institutions of the European Union* (6th edn, 1994)
 Butterworths.
Noel *Working Together – The Institutions of the European Communities* (1991)
 Office for Official Publications of the European Communities.

**INSURANCE** Insurance has traditionally been regulated to a high degree in most EU Member States. Most states other than The Netherlands and the United Kingdom evolved protectionist legislation requiring not only the licensing of insurance companies but also strict controls over premium rates and policy conditions. In addition, most Member States prohibited policyholders from insuring themselves with companies that were not locally licensed or imposed penalties on those who did.

EU legislation has developed through several generations of Directives deriving from the general wording of Articles 52 and 59 EC providing for the **freedom of establishment** and the **free movement of services** across borders within the Community. The First Non-Life Insurance Directive (Council Directive (EEC) 73/239 (OJ L228 16.8.73 p 3)) and the First Life Assurance Directive (Council Directive (EEC) 79/267 (OJ L63 13.3.79 p 1)) provided a framework for the licensing of insurance companies in each Member State and harmonised the classifications of insurance, in particular distinguishing between long-term business (principally life and permanent health insurance) and general business (including all forms of property, liability and financial loss business, as well as short-term accident and sickness business). The Directives also enshrined the maintenance of a prescribed 'margin of solvency' (the excess of assets over liabilities) as the primary financial tool in the regulation of insurers.

The Second Non-Life and Life Directives (also known as the Services Directives) of 1988 (Council Directive (EEC) 88/357 (OJ L172 4.7.88 p 1)) and 1990 (Council Directive (EEC) 90/619 (OJ L330 29.11.90 p 50)) provided for the freedom of the provision of insurance by a company established in one Member State to those resident in other Member States. Finally, the Third Non-Life and Life Directives (also known as the Framework Directives) of 1992 Council Directive (EEC) 92/49 (OJ L228 11.8.92 p 1) and Council Directive (EEC) 92/96 (OJ L360 9.12.92 p 1) provided for 'home state control', under which insurance companies having their head office in one Member State would have the entirety of their Community-wide operations regulated and monitored only by the regulatory authorities in that Member State. The Third Directives were required to be brought into effect in all Member States by 1 July 1994.

Reinsurance is not affected by the Directives referred to above. A Reinsurance Directive of 1964 (Council Directive (EEC) 64/225 (OJ Sp Ed 1963-64 p 131)) required the removal of restrictions, based merely on nationality, on the freedom of reinsurers based in one Member State to form branches in another and their freedom to supply cross-border reinsurance from one state to another. A number of more specific Directives also exist or are proposed, dealing, inter alia, with motor insurance and export credit insurance, as well as the **harmonisation** of provisions relating to the annual accounts and liquidation of insurance companies. A bilateral agreement approved in 1991 extends certain provisions of the First Non-Life Directives so as to apply between the EU and Switzerland.

JOHN YOUNG

*Recommended reading*
Campbell *International Insurance Law and Regulation* (1994) Longman.
Maitland-Walker *EC Insurance Directives* (1992) Lloyd's of London Press.

**INTELLECTUAL PROPERTY**  Intellectual property rights should be considered in the light of the Community rules on freedom of movement and competition and Community legislation.

*The free movement of goods*  The application of Article 30 EC to intellectual property is subject to exceptions contained in Article 36 EC. Given that Article 36 provides an exception to one of the fundamental principles of the Common Market, the **Court of Justice** has held that it admits exceptions to the free movement of goods only to the extent to which such exceptions are justified for the purposes of safeguarding rights which constitute the 'specific subject matter' of the property (see, for example, Case 119/75 *Terrapin v Terranova* [1976] ECR 1039). The 'specific subject matter' is the fundamental essence of the property and is linked to the essential function of the right claimed (see, for example, Case 15/74 *Centrafarm v Sterling Drug* [1974] ECR 1147, where the Court defines the specific subject matter of a patent).

The exercise of rights provided for under national laws of Member States that go further than those guaranteed by the 'specific subject matter' are subject to the Treaty provisions on free movement of goods. Since, in the opinion of the Court, the 'specific subject matter' only allows for the initial circulation of a product, once a product has been lawfully marketed in a Member State the guarantees afforded to the proprietor are exhausted. Thus the proprietor of a national intellectual property right cannot rely on that law to prevent the importation of a product which, with his consent, has lawfully been marketed in another Member State (see, for example, Case 15/74 *Centrafarm v Sterling Drug*).

*Competition Rules*  Although Article 85(1) EC generally prohibits exclusivity in licensing agreements, not all exclusive licences are so prohibited. In Case 258/78 *Nungesser v Commission* [1982] ECR 2015, the Court of Justice held that so-called 'open licences', whereby the property owner undertakes simply not to grant other licences in respect of the same territory and not to compete himself with the licensee in that territory, were not contrary to Article 85(1). On the other hand, Article 85(1) did prohibit licences which attempted to grant absolute territorial protection, under which the parties sought to eliminate all competition from third parties such as parallel importers.

Licensing agreements can be exempted from the operation of Article 85(1) under Article 85(3). Council Regulation (EEC) 19/65 (OJ Sp Ed 1965-66 p 35) empowers the Commission to apply Article 85(3) by regulation to restrictions imposed in relation to the acquisition or use of industrial property rights and restrictions imposed under 'know-how' licensing agreements. On 1 April 1996, Council Regulation (EC) 240/96 (OJ L31 9.2.96 p 2) came into operation providing for a new technology transfer block exemption. This regulation covers both patent, know-how and mixed patent and know-how licensing agreements. Article 85(1) automatically does not apply to licensing agreements that fall within the limits set out by the block exemption.

It is now well established that mere ownership of an intellectual property right cannot, of itself, amount to a dominant position within the meaning of Article 86 EC. This was recently confirmed by the Court of Justice in Cases C-241/91P & C242/91P *RTE and ITP v Commission* [1995] ECR 1-743 (the so-called *Magill* cases). The Court further held that even where an intellectual property right holder were in a dominant position, the refusal to licence the right, of itself, would not amount to an abuse of that position. However, the Court went on to state that such a refusal might nevertheless amount to an abuse of a dominant position in certain circumstances. If the circumstances of a particular case led to a finding that there had been a violation of Article 86, then a compulsory licence could be granted by way of a remedy.

*Legislation* The Community Patent Convention (OJ L401 31.12.89 p 1) which establishes a system for a unitary Community patent effective throughout the Union, has yet to come into effect. The extent to which the **European Patent Convention** requires Contracting States to harmonise their national patent laws is limited. A significant point of divergence between the laws of the Member States of the Union is the patentability or otherwise of biotechnology. The adoption of a Directive on the legal protection of biotechnological inventions met with moral and ethical objections in the **European Parliament** and although a common position was reached by a Conciliation Committee (OJ C107 9.4.94 p 65), this was rejected by the Parliament (OJ C68 20.3.95 p 26). The Commission has since adopted a new proposal (Com (95) 661 final).

A number of Directives concerning copyright and related rights have been adopted and implemented into the national laws of Member States. These include Directives on the legal protection of computer programs (OJ L122 17.5.91 p 42); rental and lending rights (OJ L346 27.11.92 p 61); satellite broadcasting and cable transmission (OJ L248

26.10.93 p 15); and the duration of protection of copyright (OJ L290 24.11.93 p 9). A Directive on the legal protection of databases was adopted in 1996 (OJ L77 27.3.96 p 20). Most recently, the Commission have proposed a Directive relating to artist resale rights (Com (96) 97 final).

The area of trademark law has seen two significant legislative initiatives by the Community. In December 1988 the Commission adopted a Directive intended to approximate the laws of the Member States relating to trademarks (OJ L40 11.2.89 p 1). In 1993 the Council adopted a regulation establishing a system for a unitary Community trademark (OJ L11 14.1.94 p 1). The regulation permits the filing of a single trademark application to the European Trade Mark Office. A trademark registered under this system receives protection throughout the Union for a renewable period of ten years.

D L BOOTON

*Recommended reading*
Tritton *Intellectual Property in Europe* (1995) Sweet & Maxwell.
Vinje 'Harmonising Intellectual Property Laws in the European Union: Past, Present and Future' [1995] 8 EIPR 361.

**INTERGOVERNMENTAL CONFERENCES** Intergovernmental conferences (IGCs) are the conferences of the Heads of State or Government convened from time to time for the specific purpose of amending the primary law of the European Union, currently in accordance with Article N of the Treaty on European Union. This Article has replaced the former Articles 96 ECSC, 236 EC and 204 EAEC.

The most comprehensive IGCs so far were those leading to the Single European Act, which entered into force 1 July 1987, and to the Treaty on European Union, which entered into force 1 November 1993. The latter among other things introduced the prospective of **monetary union** and the notion of '**Citizenship** of the Union' into the EC Treaty and encapsulated the EC, ECSC and EAEC Treaty in a single Treaty framework while adding 'intergovernmental' titles relating to, respectively, a **Common Foreign and Security Policy**, and Co-operation on Justice and Home Affairs.

The Treaty on European Union was seen as a temporary stage in the process of integration and the need for its amendment was explicitly acknowledged by the inclusion of a provision (Article N.2 TEU) calling for an IGC to be convened in 1996. This Conference, which at that time was sometimes referred to in the corridors as 'Maastricht II', started not in Maastricht but in Turin, in March 1996, and it is to last at least until 1997. A summit meeting of Heads of State or Government will formally conclude the IGC, after which the amendments to the Treaty on European Union, in order to be effective, will still need to be ratified by all the Member States in accordance with their constitutional requirements.

The **European Commission**, the **European Parliament**, the **Court of Justice** and the **Court of First Instance** (none of whom formally take part in an IGC) traditionally feed into the process of amendment of the Treaty by making their views known. The report prepared by the Reflection Group of national experts for the preparation of the 1996 IGC (Council document SN 520/95 (Reflex 21), Brussels, December 1995) has recommended for consideration developments in respect to institutional matters, citizenship of the Union and the Common Foreign and Security Policy.

Given the greatly increased frequency of IGCs, one is tempted to suggest that this intergovernmental procedure has currently taken over from the judicial process in determining the pace of integration.

NANETTE NEUWAHL

*Recommended reading*
European Commission 'Intergovernmental Conference 1996. Commission Report for the Reflection Group; (1995) Office for Official Publications of the European Communities.
Foreign Office 'The British Approach to the European Union Intergovernmental Conference 1996' (1996) HMSO (Internet - http://www.fco.gov.uk/europe/igc/textonly/text)


**INTERGOVERNMENTALISM** See **European integration (theories of).**


**INTERIM MEASURES** Interim measures may be adopted, under specific conditions, by the **Court of Justice**, the **Commission** or national courts for the period between its seizure of a matter and its final decision.

National courts may grant negative (ie suspensory) or positive (ie creating a new legal position) interim relief with regard to Community obligations. This applies irrespective of whether an individual contests the compatibility of national legal provisions with Community law (eg Case C-213/89 *R v Secretary of State for Transport, ex p Factortame* [1990] ECR I-2433) or the validity of secondary Community law. The Court of Justice held in Joined Cases C-143/88 & C-92/89 *Zuckerfabrik* [1991] ECR I-415 that the coherence of interim legal protection of individuals required that a national court should be able to suspend the enforcement of a national administrative rule based on a Community regulation. In Case C-465/93 *Atlanta* [1995] ECR I-3761, the Court held that a national court may grant a positive order disapplying the Community regulation itself. However, the Court of Justice has placed three restrictions on the grant of interim measures by national courts: first, national courts may not declare a Community regulation invalid, that jurisdiction falling solely to the Court of Justice (Case 314/85 *Foto-Frost* [1987] ECR 4199); second, interim relief may only be granted on certain conditions; and third, national courts cannot grant interim measures to mitigate the effects of a purported failure of a Community institution to act (Case C-68/95 *T Port*, judgment of 26 November 1996 (not yet reported).

The Court of Justice restated and clarified the conditions under which national courts may grant interim relief in *Atlanta*. There are six conditions: (1) the national court must have serious doubts as to the validity of the Community act and must refer the question to the Court of Justice (if not already seized of the question); (2) relief must retain the character of an interim measure, applicable only for so long as the Court has not ruled that the Community act is valid; (3) interim measures must be urgent, ie necessary before the decision on the substance can be given, in order to avoid serious and irreparable harm; (4) the national court must take due account of the Community interest in the disapplication of the Community act, including the cumulative effect of similar decisions throughout the Community; (5) if the grant of interim relief represents a financial risk for the Community, the national court must be in a position to require undertakings in damages, or other security, from the applicant; (6) the national court must respect the case law of the Court of Justice in related actions.

On the basis of the Court of Justice's ruling in *Factortame*, the House of Lords granted an interlocutory injunction against the Crown, a remedy which had hitherto been beyond the jurisdiction of the courts (but see now *M v Home Office* [1993] 3 WLR 433). The injunction prevented the Secretary of State for Transport from enforcing the Merchant Shipping Act 1988 which imposed certain nationality requirements on the registration of British fishing vessels. The case is a celebrated example of the **supremacy** of Community law and the binding nature of section 2 of the **European Communities Act** over subsequently enacted primary legislation.

By Articles 185 and 186 EC, the Court of Justice or the **Court of First Instance** may, if it considers that the circumstances so require, order interim relief in the context of an **action of annulment** (Article 173) or an **action for failure to fulfil an obligation** (Article 169). The Court may order that the application of a contested act be suspended or prescribe any necessary measures against a Community institution or a Member State, whether or not they are a party to the proceedings. Orders for interim relief are usually made the President of the Court.

The conditions under which interim relief may be granted by the Court of Justice are clearly set out in Case C-149/95 P(R) *Commission v Atlantic Container Line* [1995] ECR I-2165. The applicant must establish that an order is justified, prima facie, in fact and in law and that it is urgent in so far as it must, in order to avoid serious and irreparable damage to the applicant's interest, be made and produce its effects before the decision is reached in the main action. The Court is also to balance the interests at stake. Applying these conditions, the Court recently dismissed an application by the United Kingdom to suspend the operation of the Commission decision on emergency measures to protect against bovine spongiform encephalopathy (BSE)(Case C-180/96 R *United Kingdom v Commission*, Order of 12 July 1996).

The Commission may, but rarely does, grant interim relief in **competition** cases. The Court of Justice recognised that the Commission has the power to decide, pursuant to Article 3(1) of Regulation 17 and the supervisory tasks conferred upon it by the Treaty, whether it is necessary to take interim measures when it receives a request to that effect (Case 792/79 R *Camera Care v Commission* [1980] ECR 119). Protective measures may be granted only where the practices of certain undertakings are prima facie such as to constitute a breach of the Community rules on competition in respect of which a penalty could be imposed by a decision of the Commission. Accordingly, the Court of First Instance held that the Commission's requirement of 'the probable existence of an infringement' went beyond that of a prima facie case (Case T-44/90 *La Cinq v Commission* [1992] ECR II-1). Furthermore, such interim measures are to be taken only in cases of proven urgency, in order to prevent the occurrence of a situation likely to cause serious and irreparable harm to the party applying for their adoption or intolerable damage to the public interest. Although applicants may be subjected to greater costs liabilities, applications for interim relief in competition matters are more frequently made before national courts due to the direct effect of the relevant competition rules.

WILLIAM ROBINSON

*Recommended reading*
Antunes 'Interim measures under EC competition law: recent developments' (1993) 13 Yearbook of European Law 83.
Sharpston *Interim and Substantive Relief in claims under Community law* (1993) Butterworths.

**INTERINSTITUTIONAL AGREEMENTS** Within the framework established by the Treaties, the **Commission, Council** and **European Parliament** tend to use all political and legal means available to increase their impact on the **decision-making** process or to defend their prerogatives. The resulting interinstitutional dynamic is further enhanced by the framework character of the Community Treaties, which leaves much room for different interpretations of the role to be played by each **institution** and how to apply certain procedures provided for by the Treaties. In order to avoid the resulting danger of conflicts over **competences** and to ensure the smooth application of certain procedures, the EC institutions concluded a broad range of interinstitutional agreements since the beginning of the 1960s. Initially focusing on questions of participation and information of the European Parliament, their scope has been gradually extended to issues of major political importance. The agreements reached by the institutions on budgetary discipline (1988 and 1993), on procedures for implementing the principle of **subsidiarity** (1993), on the regulations governing the **Ombudsman**'s duties (1993) and on the proceedings of the conciliation committee under Article 189b EC (1993) show that such agreements have become an important feature of the evolving constitutional system set up by the Treaties. Interinstitutional agreements can take very different forms, such as exchanges of letters, joint declarations or more formalised 'agreements' published in the Official Journal. A limited number of these agreements are explicitly provided for by the Treaties and consequently fully binding under EC law. Most of them, however, must be situated on a scale between mere political undertakings of the institutions to plain legal obligations.

JÖRG MONAR

*Recommended reading*
Monar 'Interinstitutional agreements: The phenomenon and its new dynamics after Maastricht' (1994) 29 CMLRev 693–719.


**INTERNAL MARKET** The Internal Market, or Single European Market, the first of three stages (together with monetary and political union) towards **European Union,** was achieved on 31 December 1992, following the signing of the **Single European Act** on 17 February 1987. By this Act, the Member States undertook, progressively over a period expiring on 31 December 1992, to unite their 12 national markets into a single economic area without internal borders. The legislative programme completing the Internal Market largely followed the recommendations made in the 1985 Commission 'White Paper on the Completion of the Internal Market'.

The Internal Market has three fundamental aims:

(1) the abolition of the internal borders which divide the 12 national territories of the Community and of the controls which are carried out there;

(2) the complete and definitive realisation of the four fundamental freedoms set out in the Treaty of Rome: the **free movement of capital, goods, persons** and **services**.

(3) the setting up of a series of common rules and policies with the aim, in particular, of promoting a European culture, of safeguarding the **environment**, of protecting the **consumer**, promoting scientific research and technology, encouraging economic and social **cohesion**, organising trade with the outside world, etc.

The abolition of border controls, referred to by the **Commission**'s 'White Paper' as 'physical barriers', was expressly provided for by Article 8a (now 7a) EC, as inserted by the Single European Act. This defines the single market as 'an area without internal frontiers in which the free movement of goods, persons, services and capital is ensured in accordance with the provisions of this Treaty'. The Article imposes a positive obligation upon the Member States to achieve this result.

The four fundamental freedoms consist of the free movement of goods (Articles 9–12 et seq, 30–36, 37 EC), persons (Articles 48–58 EC), services (Articles 59–66 EC) and capital (Articles 67–73 EC).

The free movement of goods, the first of the four freedoms envisaged by the EC Treaty, constitutes one of the foundations of the Community and the most spectacular achievement of the European Single Market. The realisation of this objective has involved initiatives on three fronts:

(1) the abolition of obstacles to trade (customs duties and taxes of equivalent effect, quotas and measures of equivalent effect, and state monopolies);

(2) the prevention of new obstacles to trade by means, first, of Council Directive (EEC) 83/189 of 28.3.83 (OJ L109 26.4.83 p 8), which provides for the notification by Member States of their draft technical regulations to the Commission and other Member States, in order that a prior examination of their conformity with EC law may take place, and second by means of Decision (EC) 3052/95 of the European Parliament and the Council (OJ L321 30.12.95 p 1) which, as of 1.1.97, establishes a procedure for the exchange of information on national measures derogating from the principle of the free movement of goods within the Community;

(3) the harmonisation of national legislation, by means of Articles 100 and 100a EC, which encompasses obstacles to trade which are justified by reasons such as public health, public security or the protection of the environment etc.

The key to an understanding of the principle of the free movement of goods is the Court of Justice's judgment in the case of *Cassis de Dijon* (Case C-120/78 *Rewe-Zentral AG* [1979] ECR 649) and the principle of mutual recognition. According to this, a product lawfully manufactured or marketed in one Member State must, in principle, be allowed to be marketed in another Member State, without having to be adapted to the rules of the latter. Member States are obliged mutually to recognise the rules, procedures and controls applied in any other in so far as they ensure public health, and the protection of the environment and the consumer.

The free movement of people and services involves the freedom for people to go to any Member State of their choosing to carry out an activity, whether employed or self-employed, on the same conditions as those existing for nationals of the host Member State. The free movement for workers involves more particularly the right of exit from their Member State of origin, the right of entry and stay in the host Member State, the right of access to their chosen work, the right to the same social and tax advantages enjoyed by nationals of the host state, and the right to remain in the host state following the completion of the work. The free movement of services involves all non-salaried economic activities which are provided on a non-permanent basis across intra-Community borders. The freedom to provide services also covers the freedom of movement to receive services. The Commission has proposed to modify Council Directive (EEC) 83/189 so as to include within its scope the notification of rules governing the provision of services (OJ C307 16.10.96 p 11).

The freedom of establishment guarantees the right to set oneself up in any Member State and to carry out an independent activity on the same conditions as those reserved for nationals of the host Member State.

Furthermore, it extends to all companies which are set up under the legislation of one Member State, are situated within the Community, and pursue a commercial aim. Finally, the principle of the free movement of people has been extended by Community law to cover generally the non-economically active, persons in retirement and students (respectively Council Directives (EEC) 90/364, 90/365 and 90/366 (OJ L180 13.7.90 pp 26, 28 & 30)).

The above rules confirm two fundamental Community law principles: equality of treatment between nationals and non-nationals and the principle of mutual recognition. Every Member State is obliged to recognise the professional capacity of every worker or self-employed person from another Member State, even if these capacities do not correspond entirely to those required by its own nationals for access to the same work or activity, in so far as they are sufficient to guarantee the proper exercise of such an activity (Cases C-154/89, C-180/89 & C-198/89 *Tourist Guides* [1991] ECR 659, 709, 727 and C-76/90 *Säger* [1991] ECR I-4221).

The Free Movement of Capital has been achieved in two stages. First, restrictions on operations in capital most directly linked to the exercise of the other fundamental freedoms (ie direct investments, guarantees and commercial credits, capital movements of a personal nature as well as securities traded on the stock exchange) were unconditionally removed. Then in 1988 the Community adopted Council Directive (EEC) 88/361 (OJ L178 8.7.88 p 5), which liberates all movements of capital (short-term capital movement, deposit operations, current accounts, loans and credits etc). By virtue of this legislation, all restrictions on capital have been abolished and the access of every Community citizen and economic operator to the financial systems and products of the other Member States has been ensured, notably by the abolition of restrictions on the export and import of capital, purchases and investments of foreign currency, opening of bank accounts in other Member States, and the purchase of foreign shares and bonds etc.

ALFONSO MATTERA AND RHODRI WILLIAMS

*Recommended reading*
Mattera *Le marché unique européen* (2nd edn, 1990) Jupiter.
Mattera (ed) *Revue du Marché Unique Européen* (quarterly) Clément Juglar.

**INTERNATIONAL AGREEMENTS** The European Community can act on the international plane by being party to international agreements with third states and organisations. Express Treaty-making power was originally prescribed only in Articles 113 and 238 EC. However, the **Court of Justice**, relying in particular on Article 210 EC, has held that the Community possesses Treaty-making power across the ambit of the EC Treaty. Community **competence** arises where there is an express power, where such is implied by reason of the adoption of internal legislation, or by virtue of implied competence (see **implied powers**).

The Treaty-making power of the Community is 'exclusive', that is to say, the Member States are not permitted to participate, with the Community, in any international agreement, where the power is express, or where common rules have been adopted (or can only be adopted through the mechanism of an international agreement, see Opinion 1/76 [1977] ECR 741). Originally, the dispute between the Member States and the Community was whether the Community had power to conclude an international agreement. Now the debate has shifted to whether there continues to be a power permitting the Member States to participate in international agreements in conjunction with the Community (eg Opinion 1/94 *World Trade Organization* [1994] ECR I-5267) (ie **mixed agreements**).

The **Commission** negotiates agreements on behalf of the Community, upon authorisation by the **Council**. The **European Parliament** is consulted, prior to conclusion of the agreement by the Council, except in relation to agreements under Article 113(3). The European Parliament has a veto power in limited circumstances (Article 228(3), second paragraph). The Council, the Commission or a Member State may request an opinion from the Court on the compatibility of an agreement with Community law, including the extent of the powers of the institutions to conclude any agreement (Article 228(6)).

International agreements do not require express incorporation into **Community law**, but form an integral part of Community law. Community legislation may be interpreted in the light of international agreements. Further, international agreements may contain provisions which are sufficiently clear and precise to be directly effective (see **direct effect**).

PHILIP MEAD

*Recommended reading*
Cheyne 'International Agreements and the Community legal system' (1994) 19 ELRev 581.
Macleod, Hendy & Hyett *The External Relations of the European Communities* (1996) Oxford University Press.

**INTERPRETATION (METHODS OF)** The European Courts (whether the **Court of Justice** or the **Court of First Instance**, each acting within its own jurisdiction) are called on to interpret a wide variety of legal texts, ranging from the Treaties themselves and international agreements (the later when forming part of the Community's legal order) down to administrative acts of the Community institutions and the European Central Bank (see in particular **preliminary rulings**). In itself, the task of interpretation entrusted to the European Courts is in principle no different from judicial interpretation by the courts in other jurisdictions. The methods of interpretation used by courts in different jurisdictions vary but can be grouped under a number of general headings: historical, teleological, literal, exegetical, political or sociological and so forth. Such is the variety of circumstances in which the European Courts have engaged in interpretation that the case law can usually be relied on to provide at least one possible illustration of the use of each such method. Certain particular interpretative devices (which may not necessarily be regarded as 'methods' of interpretation) may also be identified: the *eiusdem generis* rule, *generalia specialibus non derogant, in dubio pro reo* and so on.

The process of interpretation undertaken by the Court of Justice and the Court of First Instance can be analysed as proceeding in two stages. The first involves the gathering together of the raw material to be used for the task of interpretation. The second stage involves the application to that raw material of a single basic approach to interpretation encapsulated in the following formula, which is based on the dicta on the subject most frequently encountered in the case law: the Court interprets a provision of Community law in the light of its spirit, general scheme and wording as well as the overall legal context, in particular the system and objectives of the Treaties and the instrument containing the provision (Case 26/62 *Van Gend en Loos v Nederlandse Administratie der Belastingen* [1963] ECR 1 at 12; Case 283/81 *CILFIT v Ministry of Health* [1982] ECR 3415, paras 18–20).

The first stage begins with the identification of the text to be interpreted. Save in the case of an act expressed in one official language only, all the official language versions of the act in question together constitute the text to be interpreted; and each official language version constitutes a part only of that text (*CILFIT*). The remaining raw material used comprises the various aids to interpretation admitted by the European Courts. These include (where applicable): the recitals in the preamble to the act; drafts or preparatory materials or reports drawn up prior to the adoption of the act; reports or other official documents which purport to be formal and official expositions of the text, its meaning, purpose or function; the legal context in which the act was adopted and in which it is to take effect (such as the measures conferring power to adopt the act in question and the measures in company with which that act operates); the factual context in which the act takes effect. Official statements made by the persons responsible for the adoption of the act at the time of its adoption and the manner in which an act has been interpreted and applied in practice are not normally admitted as aids to interpretation; but the former may be of assistance where they have been published.

The aids to interpretation admitted by the European Courts are not always available and, when they are available, they are not of equal, far less determining, weight. Their relevance and importance varies from case to case influenced, in large part, by the degree to which the provision to be construed is or is not obscure: the primary 'aid' to interpretation remains the text itself. The text will always be preferred to any other aid to interpretation unless there is some deficiency in the text. The other aids to interpretation may be used to establish the existence of a deficiency in the text, such as where a comparison of the text with its legal context reveals that a particular interpretation of the text would produce an absurd result.

In the second stage of the process of interpretation, the objective is to arrive at an interpretation of the text which is faithful to the words used, produces a result that fully achieves the intention behind the text, and does not create any gaps or inconsistencies in the system of Community law. Where a gap is found to exist, it may be removed by a broad interpretation of an existing legal provision or by the application of such a provision by analogy.

K P E LASOK

*Recommended reading*
Schermers & Waelbroeck *Judicial Protection in the European Communities* (5th edn, 1992) Kluwer, paras 18 et seq.
Vaughan (ed) *Law of the European Communities* (1986)  Butterworths, paras 2.280 et seq.

**IOANNINA COMPROMISE** Preparing the **European Union** for the **accession** of the former EFTA States, the **European Commission** proposed a corresponding increase in the size of the voting coalition that would have blocking power in the Council of Ministers' **qualified majority voting** procedure. Claiming that this would make it harder to block the introduction of new legislation, the United Kingdom and Spain were willing to agree on such an increase only because a compromise was reached in Ioannina, Greece.

Unlike the **Luxembourg Compromise** this compromise was reduced to legal form in a Council Decision of 29 March 1994 (OJ C105 13.4.94 p 1, amendment in OJ C1 1.1.95 p 1). The essence of the Compromise is that if there are enough votes to constitute a blocking minority under the pre-accession rules but  not under the new rules, then 'the Council will do all in its power to reach, within a reasonable time' a solution which could not be blocked under the old voting rules.

It is yet doubtful whether the Ioannina Compromise has ever been invoked. Quite likely, however, its practical significance is very limited. Under present as well as previous rules only groups of Member States can block a decision. Analysing the different numbers of votes Member States have been allocated in the **Council of Ministers** some commentators have argued that the United Kingdom position implies a preference to seek coalitions with slightly larger groups of smaller Member States rather than co-operating with at least two of the other large Member States.

The Ioannina Compromise has not been judged upon by the **Court of Justice**. Considering the Compromise's essentially political nature one could also expect the Court to abstain from future involvement. One exception from this conclusion, however, is the question of what constitutes a 'reasonable time' within which efforts to reach a compromise should be pursued before recourse is had to the Treaty voting procedure.

CARL FREDRIK BERGSTRÖM

*Recommended reading*
House of Commons 'Qualified Majority Voting: The Ioannina Compromise' (1994) *European Parliament's Research Papers: National Series* 94/49.
Johnston 'The Conflict Over Qualified Majority Voting in the EU Council of Ministers: An Analysis of the UK Negotiating Stance Using Power Indices' (1995) 25 BJPolS 245.

**JUDGES** See **Court of Justice**.

**JUDICIAL REVIEW** 'Judicial review' is a term commonly used to describe the various causes of action of review of acts of institutions. The expression is used at both national and Community levels.

In the United Kingdom, by a specific procedure an application for judicial review may be made before the High Court of Justice (in England and Wales) in accordance with section 31 of the Supreme Court Act 1981 and Order 53 of the Rules of Procedure of the Supreme Court, or the Court of Session (in Scotland), for the review of acts of public bodies. Applications for judicial review which put in issue the validity of a Community act, as the basis of the national act, have formed a regular source of references for **preliminary rulings** to the Court of Justice which has the sole jurisdiction to declare such acts invalid (Case 314/85 *Foto-Frost* [1987] ECR 4199).

At the Community level, the expression judicial review covers **actions for annulment** and **actions for a failure to act**, and indirectly the **plea of illegality** (which is not a separate action but an incidental ground of invalidity). Furthermore, the Court of Justice has jurisdiction to give preliminary rulings concerning the validity of acts of the **institutions** of the Community and of the **European Central Bank**. The Court of Justice has held, in circumstances where the party's **locus standi** to bring an action for annulment was patently clear, that such a party could not seek to challenge the validity of the contested act through the preliminary ruling procedure when it had failed to initiate an action for annulment before the **Court of First Instance** (Case C-188/92 *TWD* [1994] ECR I-833).

Judicial review also covers applications for **interim measures** associated with the main judicial proceedings.

**JURISDICTION OF THE COURT OF JUSTICE** The **Court of Justice** derives its jurisdiction from the Treaties. Article L of the Treaty on European Union provides that the Court of Justice has jurisdiction over the **European Community**, the **European Coal and Steel Community** and the **European Atomic Energy Community** Treaties, Conventions adopted by the Member States under the provisions on **Co-operation in the Fields of Justice and Home Affairs** and which specifically confer such jurisdiction and the final provisions of the Treaty on European

Union (Articles L–S). Accordingly, if the Court of Justice is seized of a matter outside these competencies, it must decline jurisdiction, although it has been argued that some cases point towards an inherent jurisdiction (Case C-2/88Imm *Zwartveld* [1990] ECRI-3365).

This jurisdiction is conferred upon the Court of Justice as an **institution** of the Communities. The jurisdiction is divided, at first instance, between the Court of Justice and the **Court of First Instance**, which was established in 1989. Essentially, actions brought by natural or legal persons must be lodged with the Court of First Instance.

As to the Treaties establishing the European Communities, the role of the Court of Justice, as defined in Article 164 EC, is to 'ensure that in the application and interpretation of this Treaty the law is observed'. It therefore has jurisdiction to hear actions concerning these Treaties, as amended and in their entirety. This jurisdiction extends to all acts made by institutions acting under the powers conferred by the Treaties and includes international agreements entered into by the Community, and notably, as regards association agreements, the decisions of Association Councils (eg Case C-192/89 *Sevince* [1990] ECR I-3461). Jurisdiction has also been conferred on the Court of Justice by Conventions, notably the **Brussels Convention** and the **Rome Convention**, adopted by the Member States within the context of the Treaties.

The Court of Justice may be seized of cases within its jurisdiction in two principal ways. First, actions may be brought directly before the Court of Justice by, where applicable, a Member State, an institution or a natural or legal person. Direct actions may take the following general forms: **action for failure to fulfil an obligation** (Articles 169, 170 and 171 EC), **action for annulment** (Article 173 EC), **action for failure to act** (Article 175 EC), action for damages (contractual and **non-contractual liability** under Articles 178 and 215 EC) and staff cases (Article 179 EC).

Second, actions may be referred to the Court of Justice by national courts under the **preliminary ruling** procedure (Article 177). This procedure constitutes one step in the national procedure. Conventions which confer jurisdiction upon the Court of Justice are generally limited to the preliminary reference form of action. The Court has refused to provide responses to the questions posed by national courts in certain limited circumstances, including hypothetical cases, abuse of procedure and insufficient factual and legal information supplied by the referring court.

In addition to the direct and preliminary ruling forms of procedure, the Court of Justice may be seized of certain other specific forms of action. Two are of particular importance. First, the Council, the Commission or a Member State may obtain the opinion of the Court of Justice as to whether an agreement envisaged is compatible with the provisions of the Treaty (Article 228(6) EC). This form of procedure has been used recently regarding the World Trade Agreement (Opinion 1/94 [1994] ECR I-5267) and the potential accession of the Community to the European Convention of Human Rights (Opinion 2/94, 17 January 1996). Second, a right of appeal lies from decisions of the Court of First Instance to the Court of Justice on a point of law.

MARGOT HORSPOOL

*Recommended reading*
Brown & Kennedy *The Court of Justice of the European Communities* (4th edn, 1994) Sweet & Maxwell.
Hartley *The Foundations of European Community Law* (3rd edn, 1994) Oxford University Press.

*KECK & MITHOUARD* Joined Cases C-267/91 & C-268/91 *Keck & Mithouard* [1993] ECR I-6097 are considered under the **free movement of goods** and **precedent** of the **Court of Justice.**

**LANGUAGES** Article 217 EC declares that the rules governing the languages of the **institutions** of the Community shall be determined by the **Council**, acting unanimously. In Regulation 1 of 1958, the Council adopted the principle, still valid today, that the national languages of the Member States shall all be official languages of the European Community, with the same rank and status. The same rule applies to the operation of the **ECSC** and **Euratom** Treaties, and was extended by the **Treaty on European Union** to the 'intergovernmental Pillars' of the **European Union** (Articles J and K). As of 1 January 1995, therefore, there are 11 official languages of the European Union: Danish, Dutch, English, Finnish, French, German, Greek, Italian, Portuguese, Spanish and Swedish.

The status of official language implies that any citizens may use that language when addressing themselves to the institutions of the European Union, and representatives of the Member States in the Council and the various committees and working groups, as well as members of the **European Parliament** may express themselves in any of those languages. The language to be used in proceedings before the **Court of Justice** is decided by the applicant, subject to exceptions formulated in Articles 29–31 of the Court of Justice's Rules of Procedure.

All this means that the EU faces a heavy administrative and financial burden. Occasionally, it is suggested that the number of official languages might be reduced, but that would require an (unlikely) unanimous decision of the Council.

Official multilingualism implies that all language versions of the Treaties and of Community acts are equally authentic for the purposes of interpretation and application. As perfect translations are often impossible, discrepancies between two or more language versions may arise, but they should be reconciled without giving priority to any one of them.

VEERLE DECKMYN

*Recommended reading*
Coulmas (ed) *A Language Policy for the European Community* (1991) Mouton de Gruyter.
Lasok *The European Court of Justice: Practice and Procedure* (2nd edn, 1994) Butterworths, pp 52-57.

**LAWYERS** Lawyers receive no special mention in the EC Treaty, although there are rules on legal representation before the European Courts in the Protocol on the Statute of the **Court of Justice** attached to the Treaty ('the Protocol'). However, the Court of Justice has advanced its case law on establishment and service rights in several cases concerning lawyers.

It ruled in Case 2/74 *Reyners* [1974] ECR 631 that access to the legal profession was not excluded from the scope of Article 52 EC by the 'official authority' exception in Article 55, and in Case 33/74 *Van Binsbergen* [1974] ECR 1299 that Member States could not require otherwise unregulated lawyers to reside within their territory. The Paris Bar could not, in Case 107/83 *Klopp* [1984] ECR 2971, apply its 'single office' rules to force Klopp, a dual French-German qualified lawyer, to abandon his home or host state office.

Council Directive (EEC) 77/249 (OJ L78 26.03.77 p 17) on cross-border legal services applies to a closed list of legal professions (excluding notaries, for example). Member States' power to require visiting lawyers to act in conjunction with local lawyers was restrictively interpreted in Cases 427/85 *Commission v Germany* [1988] ECR 1123 and C-294/89 *Commission v France* [1991] ECR I-3591. Host states' deontological rules apply to court proceedings; otherwise home rules apply 'without prejudice' to objectively justified host rules which a visitor can observe.

The Diplomas Directive (Council Directive (EEC) 89/48 (OJ L19 24.01.89 p 16); see **mutual recognition of diplomas**) provides that the host state may choose between a test or an adaptation period for professions requiring knowledge of and the giving of advice on national law; in other sectors, the choice is in principle the candidate's. Most states have introduced a stiff examination, an acceptable approach when applied without discrimination: Community freedoms should not give soft entry to professions with high standards and social responsibilities.

A lighter regime should apply to those practising abroad under home state title without undertaking activities, or using titles, properly reserved to the host profession. The Court has not yet ruled specifically on such a situation: both Case 292/86 *Gullung* [1988] ECR 111 and Case C-55/94 *Gebhard* [1995] ECR I-4165 trespassed over that borderline. However, the important ruling in *Gebhard* gave the lie to the protectionists' fallacy that establishment under home state title was not establishment within Article 52 EC. The **Commission** draft Directive would limit practice under home state title to five years (COM (94) 572 final, OJ 1995 C128/6 was substantially revised following a powerful report at first reading in the European Parliament. The amended proposal (COM (96) 446 final) is currently before the Council and European Parliament and seems more in keeping with the Court's case law). Thereafter, joining the host profession would be compulsory but of course it is more difficult for those not practising host law. The draft would initially shield 'visitors' from local monopolies of legal advice, but eventually it would give rise exactly to such monopolies even in countries where they currently do not exist. This appears to lack vires under Article 57 EC as it does not 'facilitate' a freedom but restricts it, and it certainly lacks integrationist merit.

There is no EC **harmonisation** of professional ethics, which remain the province of national authorities. The Court outlined a Community concept of legal professional privilege in Case 155/79 *AM&S Europe Ltd v Commission* [1982] ECR 1575 and Case T-30/89 *Hilti AG v Commission* [1990] ECR II-163. Broadly, correspondence between client and lawyer relating to Commission proceedings is privileged if made for the client's rights of defence. The privilege applies only to a lawyer entitled to practise in an EU (and now presumably also **European Economic Area**) Member State independently, meaning that he is not bound to the client by an employment relationship. Privilege does not attach to advice from non-EC qualified or in-house lawyers, even if they belong to a regulated profession. Internal communications relaying or summarising (but not glossing) external advice are privileged (see *Hilti*).

Private litigants in direct actions before the Court of Justice or Court of First Instance must be represented by a lawyer entitled to practise before a court of an EU or EEA Member State (Article 17 of the Protocol). United Kingdom solicitors as well as barristers/advocates may therefore appear; litigation in person is precluded. In references for **preliminary rulings** under Article 177, while the ECJ must 'take account' of the referring court's rules inter alia on parties' representation (Article 104 of the ECJ's Rules of Procedure), it hears lawyers who satisfy Article 17 of the Protocol but could not appear before the referring court.

The qualifications for appointment as a member of the ECJ or CFI (Articles 167 and 168A(3) EC) may be met by non-lawyers.

JAMES FLYNN

*Recommended reading*
Adamson *Free Movement of Lawyers* (1992) Butterworths.
Lonbay 'Basic competence in European Community Law for all lawyers' (1993) 18 ELRev 408.

**LEGAL CERTAINTY** One of the most important of the **general principles of Community law** upheld by the Community judicature, the principle of legal certainty requires Community legislation to be certain and its application foreseeable, particularly where such legislation entails financial consequences (see Case 325/85 *Ireland v Commission* [1987] ECR 5041, para 18). In areas covered by Community law, legal certainty also requires national rules to be worded unequivocally so that those concerned have a clear understanding of their rights and obligations and national courts can ensure that those rights and obligations are observed (see Case 257/86 *Commission v Italy* [1988] ECR 3249, para 12).

Thus, it is no defence to an action brought by the Commission under Article 169 EC that national legislation which is inconsistent with Community law is not in practice applied (see eg Case C-58/90 *Commission v Italy* [1991] ECR I-4193, para 12) or that the provisions of Community law in question produce **direct effect** (see eg Case 104/86 *Commission v Italy* [1988] ECR 1799, para 12).

In Case 43/75 *Defrenne v SABENA* [1976] ECR 455, the Court of Justice invoked the principle of legal certainty to justify restricting the temporal effect of its decision, notwithstanding the general rule that a judgment of the Court determines the legal position with effect from the entry into force of the relevant provision of Community law. In Case 314/85 *Foto-Frost* [1987] ECR 4199, 'the fundamental requirement of legal certainty' led the Court to rule that national courts had no power to declare Community acts invalid, despite the apparently contrary indication given by Article 177 EC.

Notwithstanding its importance, the requirements of legal certainty are not absolute and may occasionally be overridden by other considerations (see eg Joined Cases 42 & 49/59 *SNUPAT v High Authority* [1961] ECR 53 at 87).

The principle of legal certainty has several important variants, such as the principle of **legitimate expectations**, **non-retroactivity** and vested rights.

ANTHONY ARNULL

*Recommended reading*
Toth *The Oxford Encyclopaedia of European Community Law* (vol I, 1990) Oxford, pp 348–350.
Vaughan (ed) *Law of the European Communities* (vol 1, 1994) Butterworths, para 2.312.

**LEGAL PERSONALITY** Article 210 EC provides that 'the Community shall have legal personality' and equivalent provisions exist in the **ECSC** Treaty (Article 6(1)) and **Euratom** (Article 184).

Within the domestic legal systems of the Member States, the three Communities 'enjoy the most extensive legal capacity accorded to legal persons under their laws' (Article 211 EC, Article 6(3) ECSC, Article 184 Euratom), and while this is expressly stated to include the acquisition and disposal of property and the capacity to be a party to legal proceedings (represented by the **Commission**), it encompasses full contractual capacity and **non-contractual liability** (Article 215 EC).

In contrast, only the ECSC Treaty contains an express reference to international legal personality – 'in international relations, the Community shall enjoy the legal capacity it requires to perform its functions and attain its objectives' (Article 6(2)) – reflecting the judgment of the International Court of Justice in the *Reparations for Injuries* case (ICJ Reports [1949] 174). Nevertheless, the **Court of Justice** has been prepared to interpret Article 210 EC to the same effect, referring to 'a Community of unlimited duration, having its own institutions, its own personality, its own legal capacity, and capacity of representation on the international plane' (Case 6/64 *Costa v ENEL* [1964] ECR 585). And this capacity was held in Case 22/70 *Commission v Council (ERTA)* [1971] ECR 263 to extend over the 'whole extent of the field of the objectives' of Part I of the EC Treaty. A similar approach has been adopted in relation to Euratom (Opinion 1/78 [1978] ECR 2151). The EC thus has Treaty-making powers (both express and implied), including the power to create new international organisations (Opinion 1/76 [1977] ECR 741); the capacity to participate in international organisations (such as the **World Trade Organization**); and to be represented in organisations such as the UN and the OECD. However its powers still flow from its constituent Treaty and are not identical to those of a state (foreign policy and defence are clearly outside the Community's current powers, for example).

The international legal personality of the Community is subject (as is that of a state) to international recognition; the USSR and Comecon, for example, did not recognise the Community until June 1988. Certain international organisations, such as the UN and its agencies such as the ILO (and Treaties concluded under their auspices) are only open to states. However, this does not affect the extent of the Community's **competence** within its own legal order and the ECJ has held that in such cases the Community's competence may be exercised on its behalf by the Member States 'acting jointly in the Community's interest' (Opinion 2/91 [1993] ECR I-1061).

If each of the three still separate Communities has legal personality, it seems clear, albeit for negative reasons, that the European Union does not, at least as yet. In spite of one of its objectives being to 'assert its identity on the international scene' (Article B TEU) there is no equivalent to Article 210 EC. Treaty-making powers and other attributes of legal personality are exercised either by the EC (Treaty making) or by the Member States jointly (as with joint action under the **Common Foreign and Security Policy**), or by a single Member State (the country holding the Presidency as representative of the Union).

MARISE CREMONA

*Recommended reading*
Lachmann 'International Legal Personality of the EC: Capacity and Competence' (1984) 1 Legal Issues of European Integration 2.
Groux & Manin *The European Communities in the International Order* (1985) European Commission.

**LEGISLATIVE ACTS** Secondary legislation in the EU takes several forms. Article 189 EC provides that the **Council** and the **Commission**

may in accordance with the necessary **decision-making** procedures, adopt Regulations, Directives, Decisions, Recommendations and Opinions.

*Regulations* are, by Article 189 EC, directly effective in the Member States (see **direct effect**). No national implementing legislation is needed to bring a regulation into force. Regulations may be issued in the following areas: conditions of the rights of workers to stay in a Member State after employment there; state aids; financial regulations on budgetary procedure; and where power to make such regulation is given by a Council Regulation to the Commission. Many Regulations relate to the **Common Agricultural Policy** (CAP). For the practitioner, the block or general exemption Regulations issued for classes of agreement under the competition rules are of principal importance. These competition law regulations exempt certain agreements falling within their terms and typically list acceptable and forbidden or 'black-listed' clauses which do not benefit from the Regulation. In practice many agreements do not fit neatly into the tidy categories of contract devised by the Commission and individual notification to the Commission for exemption under Article 85(3) EC must be made (see **competition procedure**).

*Directives* require national implementing legislation to bring them into effect. Many Directives have been issued to **harmonise** national law in the Community, such as in the areas of trademarks, **equal pay**, **technical standards** and transfer of undertakings (acquired rights). Directives leave Member States with a varying degree of latitude in relation to the terms of national law and all give a deadline usually one to two years after the date of adoption of the Directive, by which time Member States must implement the Directive. Directives were the preferred legislative act of the **Internal Market** programme. In the United Kingdom Directives are usually implemented by Statutory Instruments under the **European Communities Act**, but occasionally for major legislation by an Act of Parliament. Whilst Regulations are directly effective in the Member States, Directives are not, save in limited circumstances. The Court of Justice has enunciated the principle of direct effect, under which Directives which fulfil certain conditions may be relied upon by individuals against the state of emanations of the state (Case 152/84 *Marshall* [1986] ECR 723; Case C-188/89 *Foster* [1990] ECR I-3133; and Joined Cases C-46/93 & C-48/93 *Brasserie du Pêcheur* and *Factortame III* [1996] ECR I-1029) but not against other individuals (Case C-91/92 *Faccini Dori* [1994] ECR I-3325). In the absence of direct effect or '**indirect effect**' the duty of national courts is to interpret national law, as far as possible, in conformity with Community law, and the individual may be able to seek **damages against the Member State** where there is a failure of this duty.

*Decisions* usually relate to one Member State or one undertaking, rather than being of general application. For example, in the competition law area, once the Commission has completed an investigation it may issue a decision, effectively setting out its judgment in the case and often fining the companies who have acted in breach of the competition rules. There are at least 15 provisions of the EC Treaty which provide that Council or Commission decisions will be used, including decisions relating to state aids and decisions on the European Social Fund. Decisions are binding on those to whom they are addressed. Their binding nature before national courts, particularly in the field of directly effective competition rules remains unclear.

*Notices* are important in the competition law area. These are pronouncements of the Commission which are not binding on the Commission. The Commission does not always follow the terms of notices and is not bound to do so and some notices are later withdrawn. However, it is highly unlikely that the Commission could fine a company in relation to an agreement covered by a notice. The Commission also issues notices under Article 19 of Regulation 17, setting out the outline of agreements notified to it for exemption under the competition rules. The Commission has also issued various procedural notices affecting the competition law area and has issued guidelines on the application of the competition rules in the telecommunications sector and clarification of the activities of motor vehicle intermediaries. Under the public procurement rules, notices must be published in the Official Journal advertising contracts available for tender and stating when a contract has been awarded.

*Other measures* include recommendations and opinions. As with notices and decisions, there are a number of provisions of the Treaty which provide for recommendations and opinions to be made. Article 189 states that these have no binding force and they do not have direct effect in national courts. However, the Court of Justice held in Case C-322/88 *Grimaldi* [1989] ECR I-4407 that recommendations are not devoid of all effect. National courts may use recommendations as an aid to interpretation. Recommendations and opinions can be given in many fields including on aspects of **free movement of capital**, reduction of transport charges for crossing frontiers, reducing Government deficits, **education**, **culture** and **public health**.

The preamble to a Community legislative act should state two matters. First, Article 190 EC requires that Regulations, Directives and Decisions shall state the reasons on which they are based. Second, the act should state its legal basis as the choice of legal basis determines the decision-making procedure and is an objective factor which is subject to the judicial review by the Court of Justice.

*ECSC and EAEC* – The **European Coal and Steel Community** Treaty (ECSC) provides similar legislative measures as the EC Treaty. They are not however identical. Article 14 provides that decisions, recommendations and opinions may be adopted in accordance with the provisions of the ECSC Treaty. These legislative acts, despite their names, correspond to Regulations, Directives and opinions, respectively, under the EC Treaty.

E SUSAN SINGLETON

*Recommended reading*
Weatherill & Beaumont *EC Law – The Essential Guide to the Legal Workings of the European Community* (1993) Penguin.
Tillotson *European Community Law – Text, Cases and Materials* (1993) Cavendish Publishing.

**LEGITIMATE EXPECTATIONS** Derived originally from the German law principle of *Vertrauensschutz*, the principle of legitimate expectations constitutes an aspect of the **general principle** of **legal certainty**. In the absence of an overriding matter of public interest, businesses may legitimately expect that, for transactions into which they have entered irrevocably, no unforeseeable alteration will occur which will inevitably cause them loss.

The effect of the principle of legitimate expectations is dramatically illustrated by its impact on the Community's efforts to limit milk production. The principle was held to have been infringed by two Regulations which did not provide for the allocation of a milk quota to producers who, pursuant to undertakings given by them under Community legislation, did not deliver any milk during the year chosen for the calculation of the quota (see Case 120/86 *Mulder* [1988] ECR 2321; Case 170/86 *von Deetzen* [1988] ECR 2355). A subsequent attempt by the Council to limit the quota allocated to producers who had given non-marketing undertakings also fell foul of the principle of legitimate expectations (see Case C-189/89 *Spagl* [1990] ECR I-4539; Case C-217/89 *Pastätter* [1990] ECR I-4585). This line of cases led to a flood of claims for compensation against the Community under the second paragraph of Article 215 EC. The first to be decided were Joined Cases C-104/89 & C-37/90 *Mulder v Council and Commission* [1992] ECR I-3061, where the applicants' claims were partly upheld.

A wrongful act on the part of a Community **institution**, or a national practice which is inconsistent with Community law, is not capable of giving rise to legitimate expectations (see eg Case 316/86 *Hauptzollamt Hamburg-Jonas v Krücken* [1988] ECR 2213, para 23). Similarly, the principle of legitimate expectations cannot be invoked to challenge a Community measure if a prudent and discriminating trader would have foreseen its adoption (see eg Case 265/85 *Van den Bergh en Jurgens v Commission* [1987] ECR 1155, para 44).

ANTHONY ARNULL

*Recommended reading*
Sharpston 'Legitimate Expectations and Economic Reality' (1990) 15 ELRev 103.
Toth *The Oxford Encyclopaedia of European Community Law* (1990) Oxford University Press, vol I, pp 358-361.

**LOCUS STANDI** Courts competent to review the legality of legislative or administrative acts of a public authority will normally prescribe rules which limit the right/privilege to pursue such a legal action to those who are sufficiently affected by the act. The purpose is to ensure that the courts are not flooded by meaningless or vexatious litigation, whilst at the same time ensuring the availability of **judicial review** to persons genuinely aggrieved. In the British context such rules are commonly called standing or title and interest. In the Community context they are frequently called **locus standi**.

Requisite locus standi varies depending upon the form of action by which the **Court of Justice** is seised. Under the principal means of judicial redress before the Court provided by the EC Treaty, the **action of annulment**, it falls into three categories: an action may be raised as of right, without need to demonstrate interest, by the **Commission**, the **Council** or a Member State (Article 173(2) EC; hence, so-called 'privileged applicants'); by the **European Parliament** or the **European Central Bank** (and so provisionally the European Monetary Institute) where the act in question infringes their prerogatives (Article 173(3); 'semi-privileged applicants'); and by a natural or legal person, but only under rigorous proof of title and interest (Article 173(4); 'non-privileged applicants'). The equivalent rules for non-privileged applicants are less strict under the **ECSC** Treaty. Under present rules the privileged and semi-privileged applicants seek judicial review directly before the Court of Justice, non-privileged applicants before the **Court of First Instance**.

The privileged right of Member States to raise an action of annulment extends only to the central government of the state; even though they may be directly responsible for any obligations of the state created by a Community act, autonomous regions (such as the German Länder) and regional and local authorities are not recognised to be 'Member States' for these purposes. The prerogatives of the semi-privileged Parliament and ECB are in issue where a Community institution has purported to adopt an act in a manner which has circumvented their proper participation in its adoption (eg Case 70/88 *European Parliament v Council* (Chernobyl) [1990] ECR I-2041; Case C-295/90 *European Parliament v Council* (Students) [1992] ECR I-4193; Case C-21/94 *European Parliament v Council* [1995] ECR I-1827). A non-privileged applicant is entitled as of right to raise an action of annulment of any act of which he is personally the addressee. Given the nature of **legislative acts** provided for in Article 189 EC, this can apply only to an administrative decision adopted by the Commission and formally addressed to him. Otherwise, in order that an action of annulment be admissible he has until recently been required to show that the act in question (a) is of the legal nature of a decision even if it is embodied in some other form of act, (b) affects his interests directly, and (c) affects his interests individually (Article 173(4) EC).

As to the first of these tests, the Court always considers the substance of an act rather than its form and so will examine any type of act in order to determine whether or not it is in truth an act which produces the legal effects of, and so ought to be characterised as, a decision; this means that the act applies to a limited number of specific persons rather than categories of persons viewed objectively, abstractly and generally (Cases 16 & 17/62 *Confédération Nationale des Producteurs des Fruits et Légumes v EEC Council* [1962] ECR 471; Case 25/62 *Plaumann v EEC Commission* [1963] ECR 95; Case 26/86 *Deutz & Geldermann v Commission* [1987] ECR 941; Case T-480 & 483/93 *Antillean Rice Mills v Commission* [1995] ECR II-2305). It follows necessarily from the text of Article 173(4) that a Regulation may in truth be such an act (*Producteurs des Fruits et Légumes*), but so also may a Directive (Case 160/88R *FEDESA v Council* [1988] ECR 4121; Case C-298/89 *Government of Gibraltar v Council* [1993] ECR I-3605). As to the second and third tests, see **direct and individual concern**. The distinction between the requirement that an act be in the form of a decision and the requirement that it affect a person individually can be a fine one. Nevertheless, in the past a natural or legal person was required to show that all three elements be present, so that a person directly and individually affected by a measure none the less had no locus standi if the measure was in truth one of general application (eg Cases 789 & 790/79 *Calpak v Commission* [1980] ECR 1949; Case 307/81 *Alusuisse v Council and Commission* [1982] ECR 3463; *Deutz & Geldermann*; *Gibraltar v Council*). However, latterly the Court of Justice has found actions of annulment raised by non-privileged applicants against a measure of general application (ie one which cannot be characterised as a decision) admissible so long as they are directly and individually affected by it. It did so first in the narrow and specialised field of **anti-dumping** legislation (Case C-358/89 *Extramet Industrie v Council* [1991] ECR I-2501) but subsequently as a principle of more general application (Case C-309/89 *Codorniu v Council* [1994] ECR I-1853). The test now appears to be that a general legislative measure individually affects, and so is liable to annulment at the instance of, a non-privileged applicant where the measure adversely affects his specific rights (*Antillean Rice Mills*; Case C-10/95 P *Asocarne v Council* [1995] ECR I-4149; Case T-197/95 *Sveriges Betodlares Centralforening v Commission*, order of 19 September 1996, not yet reported).

The question of locus standi also arises in and varies with other forms of action before the Court of Justice and the Court of First Instance (see **action for failure to act**; **non-contractual liability**; **opinions**; **appeals**). Locus standi to raise an action involving Community rights before a national court, which may then be submitted to the Court of Justice by means of a reference for a **preliminary ruling**, is a matter for the rules of title and interest in national law and procedure.

ROBERT LANE

*Recommended reading*

Albors-Llorens *Private Parties in European Community Law: Challenging Community Measures* (1996) Clarendon Press.
Arnull 'Private Applicants and the Action for Annulment under Article 173 of the EC Treaty' (1995) 32 CMLRev 7.

**LOMÉ CONVENTION** Part IV of the EC Treaty provided for the association of the dependent territories of certain founding Member States with the aims of promoting their economic and social development and establishing close relations with the Community by progressive removal of obstacles to trade on a mainly reciprocal basis and the setting up of the European Development Fund (EDF) to disburse financial and technical aid. Decolonisation and political independence forced a redefinition of their relationship with the Community. The Yaoundé Convention concluded in 1963 between the Community and 18 Associated African States and Madagascar (AASM) in essence continued the pre-independence free trade and aid arrangements with the addition of a set of joint institutions. This was succeeded by a second Yaoundé Convention in force between 1969 and 1975. Implementation of the Common Agricultural Policy had started to erode the material scope of the free trade areas established between the Community and each of the AASM.

United Kingdom accession to the EC in 1973 prompted recognition of the claims of African, Caribbean and Pacific members of the Commonwealth to have their development needs treated in a similar way to those of the AASM. In 1975, Yaoundé II was replaced by the first Lomé Convention (Lomé I) a five-year agreement between the nine EC Member States and the 46 Francophone and Commonwealth countries (collectively referred to as ACP). Whereas Lomé I retained many of the basic features of its predecessor, it departed from it in several important respects. Reciprocity for trade and tariff concessions was no longer required of ACP States. Secondly, Lomé I introduced a novel scheme for the stabilisation of export earnings (STABEX) of the ACP group, which provides for compensation (repayable) to producers of certain primary products when the earnings from exports to the EC fall below an agreed reference level. Lastly, co-operation designed to diversify ACP industrial production was strengthened.

Since the expiration of Lomé I in 1980, there have been three subsequent versions of the Lomé model, each adding something new. Thus Lomé II concluded in 1980 for five years and embracing 58 ACP States, extended the range of products covered by STABEX, the principles of which were extended, *mutatis mutandis*, to a scheme to protect exporters of mineral products (SYSMIN) against price fluctuations. In addition, a special sugar Protocol guaranteed ACP exporters the sale to the EC of a fixed tonnage at a pre-determined price. Lomé III covered the period from 1985 to 1990 and extended to 65 ACP States and ten EC States. The material scope of the Convention moved into the areas of fisheries co-operation, socio-cultural co-operation, investment guarantees, and introduced the concept of policy dialogue and a concern for human rights. Lomé IV in turn differed in some important respects from its predecessors. First, it was to last for ten years. Second, if affirmed the centrality of human rights and protection of the environment to the process of sustainable development. Lomé IV also made provision for a mid-term review. This took place from May 1994 until June 1995. The outcome was the signing by 70 ACP States and 15 EU States on 4 November 1995 of an agreement amending the 1990 Convention. The revised agreement will enter into force upon ratification by all of the latter and two-thirds of the first mentioned states. Special provision is made for the accession of South Africa to the Lomé Convention. The review negotiations were influenced by a completely fresh agenda that reflected the end of the Cold War, the reduction of the role of the state in economic activity, the erosion of tariff preferences resulting from the **Uruguay Round**, and the prioritisation of democratisation and good government in trade relations between the EU and the developing world – a shift found in the new section on development co-operation in the **Treaty on Economic Union**. All these factors have left their mark on the revision to the Lomé Convention. The major changes are as follows. First, respect for human rights and democratic principles has been upgraded in the scheme of the Convention and is an essential element in the sense that alleged violations of obligations related thereto can ultimately be sanctioned by suspending the application of the Convention in full or in part to the party in default. Second, the focus on trade issues is to be shifted from preferential access to the competitiveness of ACP products and the strengthening of the role of the private sector. Programmed aid remains a cornerstone of ACP-EU co-operation and represents the largest single component of the Community's financial contribution; however, new mechanisms to ensure the efficient monitoring and implementation of programmes provide that resources are released in two tranches, a high level of commitment by the recipient country being a precondition of the release of the second tranche.

The next stage in defining the future content of EU-ACP relations will commence no later than September 1998 when negotiations resume on the successor to the Lomé Convention. The marginal economic gains of the ACP States over the past 25 years must put the continuation of Lomé seriously in doubt.

JOHN WOODLIFFE

*Recommended reading*
Babarinde 'The Lomé Convention: An Ageing Dinosaur in the European Union's Foreign Policy Enterprise' in Rhodes & Mazey (eds) *The State of the European Union – Building a European Polity?* (1995) Longman, vol 3.
Special Issue on the revised Lomé Convention *The Courier* No 155 Jan-Feb 1996.

**LUGANO CONVENTION** For the Lugano Convention on Jurisdiction and the Enforcement of Judgments in Civil and Commercial Matters signed at Lugano on 16 September 1988 (OJ L319 25.11.88 p 9 and Civil Jurisdiction and Judgments Act 1983, Schedule 3C), see the **Brussels Convention**.

**LUXEMBOURG COMPROMISE** Resulting from a French refusal to accept increased majority voting in the **Council of Ministers** the

Luxembourg Compromise was a political agreement reached in January 1966 on the use of majority voting. According to it a Member State which considered that 'a very important national interest' was at stake could insist that an attempt should be made to reach a solution which could be adopted unanimously. In effect, the Compromise created a long-lasting presumption in favour of unanimous voting in the Council of Ministers.

Having lost some of its relevance by an unsuccessful attempt of the United Kingdom to invoke it in 1982, the Luxembourg Compromise was nevertheless confirmed by the German block of a Council decision in 1985. With the former EFTA States' **accession** to the European Union and the resulting re-definition of blocking-minority in the Council of Ministers a continuous significance of the Luxembourg Compromise has been insisted on, inter alia, in the House of Lords.

Irrespectively of its formal status, it seems as if the usefulness of the Luxembourg Compromise is fading, because of the European Commission's powers to adopt interim measures (used in the case of the German blocking in 1985), but more obviously as a consequence of the **qualified majority voting** introduced by the **Single European Act** and the TEU. Being the product of unanimous decision by Member State governments and subsequent ratification by national parliaments, it will be difficult for any Member State to claim a 'very important national interest' for which the new voting procedures shall be displaced.

The Luxembourg Compromise has never been given any legally binding form. Nor has it been recognised in Community law. As held by the **Court of Justice** in Case 68/86 *United Kingdom v Council* [1988] ECR 855 **decision-making** procedures in the Treaty 'are not at the disposal of the Member States or of the institutions themselves'. Attempts have furthermore been made by the **European Parliament** to force the Council of Ministers to act in areas for which recourse to majority voting is specified (see Case 13/83 *European Parliament v Council* [1985] ECR 1513).

CARL FREDRIK BERGSTRÖM

*Recommended reading*
Nicoll 'The Luxembourg Compromise' (1984) 23 JCMS 35.
Teasdale 'The Life and Death of the Luxembourg Compromise' (1993) 31 JCMS 567.


**MAASTRICHT TREATY** See **Treaty on European Union**.


*MARLEASING* Case 106/89 *Marleasing v La Comercial Internacional de Alimentación* [1990] ECR I-435, which concerned the principle of the obligation of national courts to interpret national law as far as possible in conformity with Community law, is considered under **indirect effect**.


*MARSHALL* There have been two *Marshall* cases before the Court of Justice: Case 152/84 *Marshall v Southampton and South West Hampshire*

*Area Health Authority (No 1)* [1986] ECR 723 and Case C-271/91 *(No 2)* [1993] ECR I-4367. *Marshall (No 1)* concerned the **direct effect** of an **Equal Treatment** Directive. *Marshall (No 2)* concerned the *effet utile* of national law remedies.

**MEDITERRANEAN POLICY** The European Community's relations with its Mediterranean neighbours have evolved uneasily since 1957. The EC developed bilateral trade agreements with 17 Mediterranean countries by 1973. In 1975 the Community reorganised these into the 'Global Mediterranean Policy'. The economic results of these agreements were disappointing, and the **European Commission** admitted by 1988 that its credibility with its Mediterranean partners was low. More successful was the policy of admitting some Mediterranean countries – Greece, Spain and Portugal – into the Community during the 1980s.

Following a **European Council** decision in 1989, the EC started its 'New Mediterranean Policy'. Protocols with the Mediterranean non-Member States were signed in 1990 and 1991, incorporating the Community's free market approach to economic development. Grants and loans to the eight Mediterranean countries of Morocco, Algeria, Tunisia Mauritania, Syria, Jordan, Lebanon and Egypt rose dramatically for the years 1992–96 to over 4.4 billion ECU. But strict EU import restrictions on agricultural goods and textiles remained in place, hindering their trade.

The French and German Foreign Ministers, Alain Juppé and Klaus Kinkel, issued a joint policy statement for the **European Union** in early 1995. Deepening the Union's partnership with the Mediterranean countries was one of their top priorities. The French Presidency of the European Union (January 1995) was expected to give significant attention to Mediterranean policy for several reasons: the southern Mediterranean is seen as a potential source of political instability, unwanted immigration, terrorism and drug smuggling; furthermore France wants to develop a Franco-Mediterranean axis in the EU to balance the powerful German-Nordic axis. A comprehensive EU-Mediterranean action plan has been adopted at the issue of the Euro-Mediterranean Conference in November 1995, which provides for additional financial assistance and gradual progress towards a Euro-Mediterran free trade area.

MARJORIE LISTER

*Recommended reading*
Gillespie (ed) *Mediterranean Politics* (1994) Pinter.
Rhian 'Europe and the Mediterranean' in *European Foreign Affairs Review* (1996) vol 1, pp 79–86.

**MERGER CONTROL** The current system of merger control in the EC has been in operation since 21 September 1990, when Council Regulation (EEC) 4064/89 on the control of concentrations between undertakings ('the Merger Regulation') came into force (OJ L257 21.9.90 p 14).

The Merger Regulation applies only to concentrations which meet certain thresholds (known as concentrations with a Community dimension). Concentrations which fall below these thresholds will be subject to the control of national competition rules in the different Member States. Articles 85 and 86 EC may apply to transactions which do not come within the definition of a concentration (see below).

The term 'concentration' is defined in Article 3(1) of the Merger Regulation. A concentration will arise where two or more previously independent undertakings merge, or where one or more undertakings (or one or more persons already controlling at least one undertaking) acquire, whether by purchase of securities or assets, by contract or by any other means, direct or indirect control of the whole or parts of one or more other undertakings. 'Control' involves the possibility of exercising decisive influence on an undertaking (Article 3(3)).

Article 3(2) defines joint ventures which are concentrative in nature (and therefore subject to the Merger Regulation where they meet the thresholds), in that they perform on a lasting basis all the functions of an autonomous economic entity, without co-ordination of the competitive behaviour of the parties among themselves, or between them and the joint venture. Other joint ventures which involve the co-ordination of the competitive behaviour of independent undertakings are considered to be co-operative in nature and are not subject to the Merger Regulation (but may well be caught by Article 85(1)).

The thresholds are set out in Article 1. These currently provide that a concentration has a 'Community dimension' where the combined aggregate worldwide turnover of all the undertakings concerned is more than 5 billion ECU and the aggregate Community-wide turnover of each of at least two of the undertakings concerned is more than 250 million ECU, *unless* each of the undertakings concerned achieves more than two-thirds of its aggregate Community-wide turnover within one and the same Member State.

There are detailed rules governing the calculation of turnover (Article 5 of the Merger Regulation), in particular where joint control is being acquired.

A concentration with a Community dimension must be notified to the Commission not more than one week after the conclusion of the agreement, the announcement of the public bid, or the acquisition of a controlling interest, whichever is applicable (Article 4(1)). The Merger Task Force within DG IV of the **Commission** (the Directorate General responsible for Competition) is responsible for examining the notification. As a rule, the concentration must be suspended for three weeks following its notification (although there are special rules concerning the implementation of public bids) and a derogation will in practice only be granted in exceptional cases (Article 7).

The Commission must normally take an initial decision on the notification within one month (Article 10). It may decide that the concentration does not fall within the scope of the Merger Regulation or that although it does, it is compatible with the common market. However, if the Commission has serious doubts about the compatibility of the concentration with the common market, it must initiate an in-depth investigation involving the consultation of third parties. It has four more months to complete this detailed investigation. A decision declaring a concentration compatible will also cover ancillary restraints (see Article 8(2) concerning concentrations cleared after such in-depth investigations; the Commission has suggested in its proposal to reform the Merger Regulation (July 1996) that ancillary restraints to concentrations cleared within the one-month period should also be explicitly covered in the Merger Regulation in the interest of legal certainty).

In deciding on the compatibility of a concentration with the common market, the Commission must assess whether the concentration creates or strengthens a dominant position as a result of which effective competition would be significantly impeded in the common market or in a substantial part of it (Article 2).

The rest of the Merger Regulation concerns details of the procedure to be followed during investigations and provides for fines and penalty payments in the event of failure to notify or to co-operate. It also provides for referral of certain concentrations to a Member State authority in specified circumstances (Article 9) and for the possibility of referral of a concentration without a Community dimension from a Member State authority to the Commission (Article 22).

The Merger Regulation should be read in conjunction with Commission Regulation (EEC) 3384/94 (OJ L377 31.12.94 p 1) which contains other provisions on procedural aspects. The text of Form CO (the form on which a notification must be submitted) is annexed to this Commission Regulation. The Commission is often prepared to waive some of the information required by Form CO if approached in advance. The Commission has also published a series of notices which are a source of practical guidance (Commission Notice on the distinction between co-operative and concentrative joint ventures; Commission Notice on the notion of a concentration; Commission Notice on calculation of turnover; and Commission Notice on the notion of undertakings concerned (all in OJ C385 31.12.94 p 1)).

Non-confidential versions of Commission decisions under the Merger Regulation are only published in the Official Journal where the concentration has been subject to an in-depth investigation, although non-confidential versions of decisions taken after the initial one-month period are also available from the Commission.

A very large proportion of concentrations are cleared, with only five having been blocked as of November 1996 (although a revised version of one of these was later cleared after the initial transaction had been blocked). A small minority of concentrations are, however, only cleared after a detailed investigation has taken place, and in many cases the undertakings concerned must fulfil certain conditions in order to obtain clearance. In some cases conditions have been imposed without a detailed investigation, although this is not specifically provided for in the Merger Regulation. The **Court of Justice** and **Court of First Instance** have jurisdiction to review decisions taken under the Merger Regulation.

In its proposals to amend the Merger Regulation the Commission has suggested a lowering of the thresholds to bring more concentrations within the scope of the Merger Regulation (to 3 billion ECU and 150 million ECU respectively), as well as a procedure for allowing it to deal with certain concentrations below the revised thresholds which would otherwise have to be notified to three or more national competition authorities. The aim of the latter proposal was to relieve the heavy logistical burden which falls on undertakings involved in a concentration which falls short of having a Community dimension. Currently, they must assess whether their transaction is caught by the national competition rules applicable in the different Member States and, depending on their particular circumstances, they may be obliged to obtain clearances from several or even all the existing Member State competition authorities. However, the proposal is currently being reconsidered following an initial review by the Council.

As indicated above, Articles 85 and 86 EC may be applicable to transactions which do not constitute concentrations within the meaning of the Merger Regulation (see the judgment of the Court of Justice in Cases 142 & 156/84 *BAT and Reynolds v Commission* [1987] ECR 4487 and the Commission Decision on *Gillette* 93/252 (OJ L116 12.5.93 p 21)). National courts of the Member States technically retain jurisdiction in respect of concentrations under Article 86 EC (although not under Article 85(1) EC) but the impact of this appears to be extremely limited in practice (see also Article 22 of the Merger Regulation and Articles 88 and 89 EC).

EMER FINNEGAN

*Recommended reading*
Cook & Kerse *EC Merger Control* (1996) Sweet & Maxwell.
Freeman & Whish (eds) *Competition Law* (1996) Butterworths.

**MERGER TREATY** See **institutions**.

**MIXED AGREEMENTS** Mixed agreements, namely **international agreements** where the Community and one or more Member States are contracting parties, may be bilateral or multilateral in nature. The **Lomé agreements**, for example, are bilateral, creating relations on the international level between the African, Caribbean and Pacific States on the one hand, and Community and Member States on the other. This may be contrasted with the Law of the Sea Convention, where the Member States ratifying the Convention create international obligations inter se.

From an internal, Community point of view, mixity may lead to complications in regulating the composition of negotiating delegations. Greater difficulties arise as a matter of international law, however, where particular rights or obligations are determined by reference to the number (or size) of the contracting parties. Problems involving the Community may occur in relation to participation and entry into force of international agreements, voting, membership of institutions or organs, ratification, reservations and the delimitation of powers.

The lack of clarity as to the division of **competences** between the Community and the Member States has led third states to demand a declaration on the respective competences of the contracting parties. This may inhibit any dynamic process of transfer in defined areas of competence from the Member States to the Community. In any event, since Article 228(7) EC provides that agreements concluded by the Community are binding on the Member States, it is suggested that third states have the advantage of recourse to two international persons rather than one, should there be a breach of a treaty obligation.

PHILIP MEAD

*Recommended reading*
O'Keeffe & Schermers *Mixed Agreements* (1983) Kluwer.
Neuwahl 'Joint Participation in International Treaties and the exercise of power by the EEC and its Member States: Mixed Agreements' (1991) 26 CMLRev 717.


**MONETARY UNION** There is no simple definition of a monetary union. At its most developed, a monetary union describes an arrangement in which there is a single (common) currency that circulates across the area and is managed by a unitary central banking authority responsible for determining all aspects of monetary policy in that area (interest rates, money supply and external monetary relations). The effective authority of the central bank in conducting monetary policy varies under national different arrangements. In Germany, for example, monetary policy is the sole responsibility of the Bundesbank, which has as its main objective maintaining price stability. The independence of the Bundesbank to discharge this function is embedded in the Basic Law. Alternatively, the monetary authority can be the government itself with the central bank as an agent of government required to implement monetary policy that is consistent with the broader economic objectives of that government. This describes the situation in the United Kingdom.

Technically, the economic conditions prevailing in a monetary union can be approximated even where no common currency exists. Providing that exchange rates are irrevocably fixed, and providing that national economic policies (fiscal as well as monetary) in the participating countries are jointly managed in order that they are consistent with the declared exchange rates, then the area will be functioning *as if it were* a monetary union. The fact that currency in one participating country would not under that arrangement be legal tender in another is irrelevant (for instance, Scottish bank notes are not legal tender in England). In an economic policy sense under these conditions a monetary union would, de facto, be functioning.

As is clear from Article B of the **Treaty on European Union**, the **European Union** is committed to achieving monetary union of the conventional model. This states that the EU will aim: '. . . to promote economic and social progress which is balanced and sustainable, in particular through the creation of an area without internal frontiers, through the strengthening of economic and social cohesion and through the *establishment of economic and monetary union, ultimately including a single currency . . .*' To this end the TEU introduces a new title, Title VI, entitled `Economic and Monetary Policy'. Articles 102a–109m EC set out the institutional and policy requirements required to achieve monetary union (and a single currency) according to a stated timetable. In addition the TEU also incorporates a number of Protocols (3, 4, 5, 10, 11) which define in greater detail the institutional and policy requirements involved for monetary union, and which provide the legal basis for special arrangements such as the United Kingdom **opt-out**.

The TEU provides for monetary union to be achieved by three stages. As stage 1 was deemed to have begun on 1 July 1990 – prior to the TEU being negotiated – the detailed provisions in the Treaty relate only to stages 2 and 3. Stage 1 was essentially a preparatory stage, during which EU countries were expected to become members of the narrow band (+ / - 2.25%) of the Exchange Rate Mechanism (ERM) and all capital controls were to be removed.

Stage 2 was to begin – and did – on 1 January 1994. At that time the European Monetary Institute (EMI) was inaugurated to be the forerunner of the **European Central Bank**. The task of the EMI is to prepare the way for monetary union by strengthening co-operation between EU central banks (which are to become independent from national government during stage 2); encourage policy co-ordination; and promote the EU-wide convergence of nominal economic variables in order that Member States will be eligible for entry to stage 3. Nominal convergence is defined according to four criteria. Each criterion must be met before an individual Member State can proceed to stage 3. The 'convergence criteria' are that countries must (i) observe a high degree of price stability, with the average rate of inflation within 1.5 percentage points of the average of the three best performing countries; (ii) demonstrate a high degree of nominal exchange rate stability, with the currency having been inside the narrow ERM band for at least two years prior to entering the monetary union without being realigned; (iii) display convergence of long-term nominal interest rates, such that nominal rates are within 2 percentage points of the three best performing countries in terms of price inflation; (iv) avoid an 'excessive budget deficit' where this is defined according to two reference values, (a) a ratio of budget deficit to Gross Domestic Product (GDP) no higher than 3% and, (b) a ratio of public debt to GDP no higher than 60%.

In stage 3 monetary union will become a reality and responsibility for monetary policy in that union will be transferred from national central banks to the **European System of Central Banks** (ESCB) at the centre of which will be the ECB. The ESCB will have as its primary objective the maintenance of price stability and will be independent of EU Member States. Stage 3 will commence on 1 January 1997 only if a majority of Member States meet the convergence criteria at that time. Otherwise, it will begin on 1 January 1999 and will involve only those countries that do meet the convergence criteria. Countries not eligible to proceed to monetary union at that time will receive a derogation until such time as the convergence criteria are met and progress to stage 3 is permitted.

There are two exceptions to the general provisions of the TEU with regard to progress to stage 3. First, under Protocol 11 of the Treaty, the United Kingdom is not obliged either to implement policies leading to nominal convergence, nor to proceed to monetary union should the convergence criteria be met. Second, at the **European Council** held in Edinburgh in December 1992 it was agreed that Denmark would not participate in stage 3 of monetary union, nor be bound by the rules governing countries that did.

The currency crises during 1992-93, which witnessed the virtual demise of the ERM, threw into doubt the viability of the TEU timetable for achieving monetary union. Indeed, in some quarters it cast doubt over the entire venture. Despite this, there appears still to be considerable support for European monetary union across the EU's political establishments. What is less certain is whether this support derives from a detailed assessment of the economic benefits of creating a European monetary union (over which there is much controversy) or whether, as seems more likely, it is indicative of a desire to establish an arrangement that will represent a major step towards European political union.

ANDREW SCOTT

*Recommended reading*
Fratianni et al *The Maastricht Way to EMU* Princeton Essays in International Finance, No 187, June 1992 (International Finance Section, Princeton University).
Eichengreen 'European Monetary Union' Journal of Economic Literature, vol XXXI, No 3, pp 1321-1358.

**MONOPOLIES** Article 86 EC seeks to prevent abusive behaviour by companies with market power. To this end, it prohibits abuse by one or more undertakings of a dominant position within the common market or in a substantial part of it, in so far as this abuse may affect trade between Member States. It goes on to provide examples of behaviour which may constitute such an abuse. These include the imposition of unfair prices or other unfair trading conditions, the application of dissimilar conditions to equivalent transactions with other trading parties, and the imposition of tying clauses making the conclusion of contracts subject to acceptance of supplementary obligations unrelated to the original contracts.

When assessing conduct in relation to Article 86 it is first necessary to define the relevant market. The product market is determined by assessing the interchangeability of the product with other products, both from a demand and from a supply perspective. On the demand side, this involves an examination of the characteristics of the product; for example the **Court of Justice** has found that bananas had particular features which enabled them to be considered a separate product market in their own right, and not as part of the larger market for fresh fruit in general (Case 27/76 *United Brands v Commission* [1978] ECR 207). The **Commission** and the Court of Justice have frequently defined the product market narrowly after examining the particular conditions of competition which obtain in relation to the products in question. On the supply side, it is necessary to look at the ability of other suppliers to switch to production of equivalent products (see Case 6/72 *Europemballage and Continental Can v Commission* [1973] ECR 215). The geographical market must also be determined and this too has frequently been defined narrowly; in general terms it must consist of an area where the objective conditions of competition for the product in question are the same for all traders (*United Brands*). The market defined must also constitute a substantial part of the common market; even part of a Member State may meet this test.

Once the market has been defined, the next issue is that of dominance. The Court of Justice has defined a dominant position as one 'of economic strength enjoyed by an undertaking which enables it to hinder the maintenance of effective competition on the relevant market by allowing it to behave to an appreciable extent independently of its competitors and customers and ultimately of consumers' (see Case 322/81 *Michelin v Commission* [1983] ECR 3461; *United Brands*). Several factors are relevant in assessing whether an undertaking fulfils this test. Very large market shares (approximately 50% and upwards) are usually indicative of a dominant position where these are maintained over a period of time (see Case 85/76 *Hoffmann-La Roche v Commission* [1979] ECR 461). The position of competitors is obviously relevant; an undertaking which has a market share greatly exceeding those of all its competitors is more likely to be found to occupy a dominant position on the market. Another consideration is the extent to which it is possible for an undertaking to maintain its position; in some cases an undertaking may not be able to do so because of the ease with which new competitors can establish themselves.

It is also possible for two or more independent undertakings to hold together a position of 'collective dominance'. This is particularly relevant in the context of oligopolistic markets characterised by the presence of a few large suppliers. The **Court of First Instance** has held that there is nothing, in principle, to prevent independent undertakings from holding together a dominant position in relation to other undertakings by virtue of economic links, such as agreements or licences giving them a technological lead over their competitors (Joined Cases T-68/89, T-77/89 & T-78/89 *SIV v Commission* [1992] ECR II-1403). In an Article 177 EC reference, the Court of Justice has since held that in order for such a collective dominant position to exist, the undertakings in question 'must be linked in such a way that they adopt the same conduct on the market'. The Court of Justice went on to hold that it was for the national court to consider whether the links which existed in that case were sufficiently strong for a collective dominant position to exist (Case C-393/92 *Municipality of Almelo v Energiebedrijf Ijsselmij NV* [1994] ECR I-1477).

Once it has been established that an undertaking has a dominant position on a particular market, it must be determined whether it has abused this position and has thereby affected inter-state trade. The Court of Justice has defined abuse as relating to the behaviour of an undertaking which is 'such as to influence the structure of a market where, as a result of the very presence of the undertaking . . . the degree of competition is weakened and which, through recourse to methods different from those which condition normal competition . . . has the effect of hindering the maintenance of the degree of competition still existing in the market or the growth of that competition' (*Hoffmann-La Roche v Commission*). The Court of First Instance has recently held that conduct on markets may also be caught by Article 86 EC 'without its being necessary to establish the existence of a dominant position on those markets taken in isolation', where an undertaking had a leading position on those markets, as well as a dominant position on other markets which were closely associated with those markets. In other words, an undertaking may be found to have infringed Article 86 EC on a market in which it is not actually dominant, where it *is* dominant on a neighbouring market (Case T-83/91 *Tetra Pak v Commission* [1994] ECR II-755; confirmed by the Court of Justice by judgment of 14 November 1996, Case C-333/94P).

As indicated above, abuse may take different forms. The Court of Justice has examined various pricing practices, and has condemned excessive, discriminatory and predatory pricing policies (see *United Brands*, on discriminatory and excessive pricing; Case C-62/86 *AKZO v Commission* [1991] ECR I-3359, where predatory pricing was found; and *Tetra Pak*, involving both discriminatory and predatory pricing).

Abuse can also involve practices such as fidelity rebates (Case T-65/89 *BPB Industries and British Gypsum v Commission* [1993] ECR II-389, confirmed by the Court of Justice in Case C-310/93P [1995] ECR I-865), and turnover related discounts (*Michelin v Commission*). Tying practices have also been condemned, such as those employed by Hilti, a nail gun manufacturer, to ensure that customers bought not only the nail guns themselves, but also the cartridge strips and the nails for use with the guns (Case T-30/89 *Hilti v Commission* [1991] ECR II-1439, confirmed on appeal by the Court of Justice in Case C-53/92P [1994] ECR I-667).

The use of **intellectual property** rights may also in certain circumstances infringe Article 86 EC, although the mere ownership of an intellectual property right by an undertaking does not of itself confer a dominant position. In 1995 the Court of Justice held that certain television broadcasters had abused their dominant position over their television listings by relying on copyright law to prevent an independent undertaking from publishing a composite weekly television guide (Joined Cases C-241/91P & C-242/91P *RTE and ITP v Commission* [1995] ECR I-743; see also the **free movement of goods**).

Other examples of abusive behaviour include a refusal to supply where the dominant undertaking has no objective justification for doing so (see Joined Cases 6/73 & 7/73 *Commercial Solvents v Commission* [1974] ECR 223; *United Brands v Commission*). Similar issues have arisen in several recent Commission decisions on denial of access to essential facilities such as ports, where the Commission has found that an undertaking which both owns and uses such a facility must not grant its competitors access on terms less favourable than those which it gives its own services (see eg Commission Decision 94/19/EC *Sea Containers/Stena Sealink* (OJ L15 18.1.94 p 8).

Public undertakings and undertakings enjoying special or exclusive rights are also subject to Article 86 EC, subject to the provisions of Article 90 EC (see **state monopolies**).

It should be remembered that it is possible for both Articles 85 and 86 to apply in certain situations (see Case 66/86 *Ahmed Saeed* [1989] ECR 803). In particular, it has been held that the fact that an agreement benefits from a block exemption does not preclude the applicability of Article 86 (see Case T-51/89 *Tetra Pak v Commission* [1990] ECR II-309).

EMER FINNEGAN

*Recommended reading*
Bellamy & Child *Common Market Law of Competition* (1993) Sweet & Maxwell. Freeman & Whish (eds) *Competition Law* (1996) Butterworths.

**MULTI-SPEED** See **variable geometry**.

**MUTUAL RECOGNITION OF DIPLOMAS** Community legislative activity in the field of mutual recognition of diplomas and professional qualifications stretches back to 1964, and the Directives adopted, which intend to facilitate the **free movement of persons**, can be grouped into three categories.

The first group of Directives, the so-called 'transitional measures', apply to a wide range of activities in the skilled craft, industry and commercial sectors (for example, plumbers, travel agents, hairdressers). Where, in a Member State, access to the activity in question is made subject to the possession of a professional qualification, a migrant who produces a certificate attesting to a number of years of professional experience in a self-employed capacity must be granted an authorisation to exercise. The precise number of years of experience required varies according to the activity which the migrant wishes to exercise and to his personal circumstances (for example, possession of a professional qualification, previous experience in an employed capacity).

Second, from 1975 onwards, sectoral Directives were adopted for seven professions (doctors, nurses, dentists, veterinary surgeons, midwives, architects and pharmacists). For these professions, with the exception of architects, recognition is based on co-ordination of the national rules governing education and training. Minimum common standards have been adopted relating, inter alia, to entry requirements, the duration of education and training and course content. Diplomas which meet these standards benefit from automatic recognition in other Member States. For architects, there is no prior co-ordination as such but the relevant Directive contains criteria which a diploma must satisfy if it is to benefit from automatic recognition.

Finally, the two 'general system' Directives (Council Directives (EEC) 89/48 (OJ L19 24.1.89 p 16) and 92/51 (OJ L209 24.7.92 p 25)) apply to all those regulated professional activities which are covered neither by a transitional measure nor by a sectoral Directive. The general system is based on the principle of mutual trust and on the presumption that someone who is fully qualified to exercise their profession in one Member State should be entitled to exercise the same profession throughout the Community. Each request for recognition is examined individually and where there are substantial differences between the migrant's education and training and that required in the host Member State, a compensatory mechanism in the form of professional experience, an adaptation period or an aptitude test may be required. See also **lawyers**.

JACQUELINE MINOR

*Recommended reading*

Pertek *Free movement of Professionals and Recognition of Higher-Education Diplomas* (1992) 12 Yearbook of European Law 293.

Seché *A guide to working in a Europe without frontiers* (2nd edn, 1994) European Commission.

# NATIONALITY See **citizenship and nationality**.

**NEO-FUNCTIONALISM** See **European integration (theories of)**.


**NON-CONTRACTUAL LIABILITY OF THE COMMUNITY** The basis for the non-contractual liability of the Community is Articles 178 and 215(2) EC. The **Court of Justice**, or rather now the **Court of First Instance**, has jurisdiction in actions brought by any natural or legal person to make good damage caused by the Community **institutions** or by their servants in the performance of their duties. Actions must be brought within five years of the occurrence of the event giving rise to the damage.

Article 215(2) is a unique provision in the EC Treaty as it requires the Court of Justice to undertake the comparative law task of drawing the conditions of liability from the 'general principles common to the laws of the Member States'. The Court of Justice has not felt restricted to utilise only principles of 'public' law, but has frequently drawn on principles of 'private' law, particularly regarding remoteness, mitigation and assessing damage.

The conditions of liability which the Court of Justice has drawn from the principles common to certain Member States are: unlawful conduct on the part of the Community; damage to the applicant; and a causal link between the conduct of the institution and the alleged damage (see Case C-370/89 *SGEEM and Etroy v European Investment Bank* [1993] ECR I-2583, para 26). These three conditions formed the basis of the Court of Justice's determination of the conditions of liability of Member States under the principle laid down in Joined Cases C-6/90 & C-9/90 *Francovich* [1991] ECR I-5357 (see **damages against Member States**). The conditions of the latter 'correspond *in substance* to those defined by the Court in relation to Article 215' (Joined Cases C-46/93 & C-48/93 *Brasserie du Pêcheur and Factortame III*, [1996] ECR I-1209, para 38).

The applicant must establish that the action of the Community was contrary to law. This does not necessitate a prior action for annulment regarding the adoption of any measure by the Community, and may arise in respect of negligence (Case C-308/87 *Grifoni v Commission* [1990] ECR 1203). The damage suffered by the applicant must be proved and a direct causal link must be established with the unlawful conduct (Joined Cases 64/76 & 113/76 *Dumortier Frères v Council* [1979] ECR 3091).

The liability of Community institutions for legislative acts is subject to additional conditions. First, legislative choices of economic policy will only invoke liability if there has been a sufficiently serious breach of a superior rule of Community law for the protection of individuals (Case 5/71 *Schöppenstedt v Council* [1971] ECR 975, para 11). The Court held that the decisive test for finding that a breach of Community law is 'sufficiently serious' is whether the Community institution concerned 'manifestly and gravely disregarded the limits on its discretion' (Joined Cases C-104/89 & C-37/90 *Mulder v Council and Commission* [1992] ECR I-3061, para 12). This condition has been applied *mutatis mutandis* to the principle of damages against Member States.

Second, the damage suffered by the applicant must be beyond the bounds of the economic risks inherent in its business (Joined Cases 83 & 94/76, 4, 15 & 40/77 *HNL v Council and Commission* [1978] ECR 1209). These additional conditions significantly restrict the liability of the institutions on policy grounds in respect of legislative acts. As the Court of Justice has indicated that the conditions of liability of the Member States and the Community are intertwined, it remains to be seen whether the developments in the liability of Member States in damages for breaches of Community law will relax the stringent conditions under Article 215(2).

WILLIAM ROBINSON

*Recommended reading*
Brealey & Hoskins *Remedies in EC Law* (1994) Longman, ch 15.
Heukels & McDonnell *The Action for Damages against the European Communities* (forthcoming) Kluwer.

**NON-RETROACTIVITY** This principle is closely linked to the principle of the protection of vested rights. Both principles may be regarded as aspects of the broader principle of **legal certainty**, which the Court upholds as a **general principle of Community law.** As a matter of interpretation, Community acts are presumed not to be retroactive (see Joined Cases 212 to 217/80 *Amministrazione delle Finanze dello Stato v Salumi* [1981] ECR 2735, paras 8 to 12). Where it is clear that a Community act was intended to have retroactive effect, its validity may thereby be cast into doubt. In Case 98/78 *Racke v Hauptzollamt Mainz* [1979] ECR 69, para 20, the Court stated: 'Although in general the principle of **legal certainty** precludes a Community measure from taking effect from a point in time before its publication, it may exceptionally be otherwise where the purpose to be achieved so demands and where the **legitimate expectations** of those concerned are duly respected.' In that case, the Court accepted that a Regulation extending the system of monetary compensatory amounts with effect from a date which preceded the regulation's adoption (and *a fortiori* its publication) was valid. By contrast, in Case 224/82 *Meiko-Konservenfabrik v Germany* [1983] ECR 2539, the Court held that the **Commission** had acted unlawfully in retroactively imposing a fixed deadline by which contracts between producers and processors of fruit and vegetables had to be forwarded to the competent national agency in order to qualify for aid.

These rules apply only to cases of retroactivity *stricto sensu*. The application of new legislation to transactions which have not yet been completed is regarded as less objectionable (see eg Case 246/87 *Continentale Produkten-Gesellschaft v Hauptzollamt München-West* [1989] ECR 1151, para 17).

*Non-retroactivity*

The principle of non-retroactivity is applied with particular strictness in the field of criminal law (see Case 63/83 *Regina v Kirk* [1984] ECR 2689, para 22).

ANTHONY ARNULL

*Recommended reading*
Lamoureux 'The Retroactivity of Community Acts in the Case Law of the Court of Justice' (1983) 20 CMLRev 269.
Toth *The Oxford Encyclopaedia of European Community Law* (1990) Oxford University Press, vol I, pp 469-474.


**NORMAL VALUE** See **anti-dumping**.


**NOTIFICATIONS** See, generally, **competition policy** and **competition procedure**, and more specifically, **merger control**, **state aid** and **complaints to the Commission**.


**OBLIGATION OF INTERPRETATION** See **indirect effect**.


**OFFICIAL JOURNAL** See **publications of the EU**.


**OFFICIALS OF THE EUROPEAN UNION** EC officials who make up the staff of the Community **institutions** all form part of the European public service and are employed on the basis of the same set of legal rules. The statute for the officials of the EC, published as Council Regulation 259/68 (OJ Sp Ed 1968 p 30) and amended and consolidated in 1982 (OJ L329 25.11.82 p 31), is based applicable legal principles prevalent in the Member States. A distinction is made between temporary agents and officials. The rules are regularly amended by the **Council of Ministers** following a proposal by the **Commission** and after having obtained the opinion of the **European Parliament**, so that they now reflect a wider range of traditions.

Much personnel administration is a matter of legal administration and the **Court of First Instance** now handles these cases. The Community made a fundamental choice in recruiting its own officials rather than having staff from national administrations seconded to it for short periods. Because of the need to guarantee the officials' independence, the structure which also exists in most Member States was adopted and officials are obliged to carry out their duties with only the interest of the Community in mind. Recruitment must be conducted in as objective a manner as possible and is organised through periodic open competitions. No discrimination is allowed on the basis of race, sex or creed, but there are different age limits set for different types of posts. Competitions generally involve written and oral tests.

Pay scales are laid down and reviewed at least annually by the Council of Ministers. A common career structure is laid down for all officials, with categories of staff corresponding to the minimum educational qualifications required for entry to each category, from category D, requiring a primary education certificate, to category A (LA for linguistic staff), requiring a university degree. Each category is divided into grades, corresponding to different levels of responsibility. The total Commission staff in December 1995 was about 15,000; the total staff of all the other Community bodies taken together is about 12,000.

MARGOT HORSPOOL

*Recommended reading*
Lasok & Bridge *Law and Institutions of the European Union* (6th edn, 1994) Butterworths, pp 46–47.
The European Commission and the Administration of the Community, Periodical 3 / 1989, Office for Publications of the European Communities.

**OLIGOPOLY** See **monopolies.**

**OMBUDSMAN** The office of Ombudsman was established for the first time in Sweden in 1809 as a means for people to defend themselves against administrative abuse.

At supranational level the idea for establishing an Ombudsman of the European Union was introduced by Spain in the framework of the 1990/91 **Intergovernmental Conference** on Political Union.

The Ombudsman is appointed by the **European Parliament** for the duration of the latter's mandate. He must have Union **citizenship,** full civil and political rights, offer every guarantee of independence and meet the conditions required for the exercise of the highest judicial office in his country or have the acknowledged competence to undertake the duties of Ombudsman.

According to Article 8d EC, every citizen of the Union may apply to the Ombudsman established in accordance with Article 138e EC. The latter empowers the Ombudsman to receive complaints concerning instances of maladministration in the activities of the Community institutions or bodies with the exception of the **Court of Justice** and the **Court of First Instance** acting in their judicial role.

The following persons are eligible to submit complaints: any citizen of the Union; any natural person residing in a Member State; and any legal person having its registered office in a Member State.

Should the Ombudsman find that there has been maladministration, he must inform the **institution** or the body concerned and may suggest ways of remedying the matter. In this case the institution thus informed is obliged to send the Ombudsman a reasoned opinion within three months.

For each case of maladministration found, the Ombudsman must send a report to the European Parliament and to the institution concerned. The Ombudsman may propose solutions and measures to be taken in the future.

At the end of each annual session, the Ombudsman has to submit to the European Parliament a report on the outcome of his inquiries.

EPAMINONDAS A MARIAS

*Recommended reading*
Marias (ed) *The European Ombudsman* (1994) European Institute of Public Administration, Maastricht.
Marias 'Mechanisms of protection of Union Citizen's rights' in Rosas & Antola (eds) *A Citizen's Europe* (1995) Sage.


**OPINIONS** Opinions may refer to the opinion of the **Court of Justice** under Article 228(6) EC as part of its **jurisdiction** or to the opinion of an **Advocate General** in his role of assisting the Court of Justice. Alternatively, an opinion is a non-binding **legislative act** under Article 189 EC and Article 14 ECSC. Opinions are also issued by the **European Parliament** under the Community legislative procedures and the **Court of Auditors**.


**OPT-OUT** In the context of the **Treaty on European Union** the term 'opt-out' refers to the decision of one or more Member States not to participate in a certain area of Community (or Union) policy. In the Treaty on European Union opt-outs were created in a number of policy fields.

In the field of **economic and monetary union** the United Kingdom and Denmark are not obliged to enter the third stage of EMU, even if they fulfil the objective requirements of Article 109j EC. In a Protocol annexed to the Treaty on European Union the Member States 'recognise' that the United Kingdom shall not be obliged or committed to move to the third stage of EMU without a separate decision to do so by its government and Parliament. Thus the United Kingdom opted out, with a possibility of opting in. With regard to Denmark, another Protocol enables the Danish government to notify the **Council** of its position concerning participation in the third stage. Thus Denmark reserved the possibility of opting out of the third stage. Denmark subsequently activated this possibility, albeit prematurely: at the Edinburgh **Intergovernmental Conference** in December 1992, Denmark gave notice that it will not participate in the third stage of EMU.

In the field of **social policy** the United Kingdom opted out, at least as far as the **Social Policy Protocol and Agreement** are concerned. It will not take part in the deliberations and the adoption by the **Council** or **Commission** proposals made on the basis of this Protocol and the Agreement on Social Policy. Acts adopted by the Council (of the other Member States) shall not be applicable to the United Kingdom.

A third possibility of opting out exists in the field of the **Common Foreign and Security Policy**. The **Western European Union** (WEU) is 'requested' to implement decisions and actions of the Union which have defence implications (Article J.4 TEU). However, according to a Declaration on WEU – as interpreted by the European Council of Edinburgh – there is no obligation to become a member of WEU (which is currently of relevance to Denmark and Ireland).

The present opt-outs in certain areas of Union policy raise the fundamental question whether a so-called multi-speed Europe (as well as **'variable geometry'**) should be given preference over the maintenance of the uniform applicability of Union law. This is one of the major issues of the 1996 Intergovernmental Conference.

RONALD H VAN OOIK

*Recommended reading*
Curtin 'The Shaping of a European Constitution and the 1996 IGC: "Flexibility" as a Key Paradigm?' (1995) *Aussenwirtschaft*.
Curtin & Van Ooik 'Denmark and the Edinburgh Summit: Maastricht without Tears' in O'Keeffe & Twomey (eds) *Legal Issues of the Maastricht Treaty* (1994) Chancery Law Publishing, p 349.


**ORAL PROCEDURE (ECJ)** The oral procedure is the final stage of the inter-party procedure before the **Court of Justice** (and the **Court of First Instance**). Its essential purpose is to focus argument on the key issues, highlighting the strong points and answering the counter-arguments.

Beforehand, the Court circulates a draft Report for the Hearing, setting out the issues and principal arguments from the **written procedure**. The parties may submit comments and suggested corrections.

Most hearings are concluded within half a day, and usually within an hour or two. Hearings are normally in two parts. First, there are set-piece speeches from the parties, starting with the applicant and any supporting interveners, then the defendant and any other interveners. In **preliminary rulings**, the parties are followed by any intervening states and the Commission. Advocates are encouraged to keep speeches short, 30 minutes or less, though exceptionally an hour or longer may be allowed. The Court provides simultaneous interpretation. Reading from prepared texts is discouraged, though common; extempore speaking from notes is preferred. Advocates should not merely repeat arguments already made and summarised in the Report for the Hearing. Production of further evidence (written or oral) at the hearing is not permitted; but the Court may exceptionally allow informal presentations by experts – and even slide shows or a short film – to aid presentation of a complex case.

The second part involves questions from the Court. Occasionally, parties are given prior notice of questions (eg with the draft Report for the Hearing). Questions normally seek clarification rather than debate, the judges generally being reluctant to disclose any provisional views they may have formed. The parties are allowed a short closing statement (usually not more than five minutes) in which to reply and sum up.

Successful oral argument relies on simplicity, speaking slowly and clearly, and the ability to define the issues and reduce argument to its essentials.

NICHOLAS FORWOOD

*Recommended reading*
Lasok *The European Court of Justice: Practice and Procedure* (2nd edn, 1994) Butterworths.
*Notes For the Guidance of Counsel at Oral Hearings*, ECJ, Luxembourg.

**PARLIAMENT** See the **European Parliament**.

**PENSIONS** Community law's involvement with occupational pensions has been through Article 119 EC, which requires that women and men receive **equal pay** for equal work. The definition of pay for these purposes has been expanded by the **Court of Justice** to cover 'any consideration, whether in cash or in kind, whether immediate or future, provided that the worker receives it, albeit indirectly, in respect of his employment from his employer' (Case C-262/88 *Barber* [1990] ECR I-1889, para 12) and therefore includes occupational pensions paid by employers to their ex-employees. It does not, however, cover pensions paid pursuant to statutory schemes of **social security** (Case 80/79 *Defrenne v Belgium* [1971] ECR 445). Both the (ex-)employer and the (ex-)employee fall within the scope of Article 119, as do the employees' survivors and those to whom the employer entrusts the administration of his pension scheme. It is irrelevant whether the employer is active in the public or private sector (Case C-7/93 *ABP v Beune* [1994] ECR I-4471).

The employer is obliged to grant women and men, part-time and full-time employees, equal access to occupational pension schemes and has been so obliged since April 1976, the date from which Article 119 enjoys **direct effect** (Case C-57/93 *Vroege* [1994] ECR I-4541). Equal access must lead to equal benefits (Case C-435/93 *Dietz*, judgment of 24 October 1996, not yet reported). Where access has wrongly been denied, an employee can claim retroactive membership, although where the scheme is contributory (s)he can be required to make good those contributions which (s)he has not previously been given the opportunity to make. The employer is similarly obliged (Case C-128/93 *Fisscher* [1994] ECR I-4583). National time-limits for bringing actions can be applied to limit the volume of claims.

The levels of contribution required from male and female employees must be equal (Case C-15/91 *Neath* [1993] ECR I-6935). Nevertheless, employer contributions to money purchase and final salary schemes may differentiate between women and men where the objective is to ensure that the benefits received by women and men are more equal (Article 6(1)(i) of Council Directive (EEC) 83/378 (OJ L225 12.8.86 p 40)).

The benefits provided by occupational pension schemes must be equal for women and men. Only in relation to benefits under money purchase schemes may different amounts be paid out where this is a consequence of the use of actuarial tables which distinguish between women and men.

In relation to survivors' pensions and pensionable age, Article 119 has direct effect only *vis-à-vis* benefits corresponding to periods of employment lying after 17 May 1990 (Case C-57/93 *Vroege*). That is, **equality** need only be introduced for the future in relation to these matters. This temporal limitation on the effect of Article 119 was prompted by the Court's respect for the **legitimate expectations** of pension schemes, which had been led by exceptions to Directive 86/378 to consider that some forms of differentiation between women and men were still compatible with EC law. Despite its clear position that secondary EC law cannot limit the scope of primary Community law (Case C-110/91 *Moroni* [1993] ECR-I6591), the Court demonstrated sympathy for the predicament of pension funds. In formulating the temporal limitation, the Court's language was vague, allowing a number of conflicting interpretations to be put forward. In recent judgments the Court confirmed that the temporal limitation only applies to those subjects for which EC law provides temporary derogations, in other words, the exceptions to Directive 86/378. The Protocol on Article 119 which had been appended to the Treaty on European Union by the Heads of State or Government to settle the controversy provides the same statement of the law (Case C-7/93 *ABP*).

ELAINE A WHITEFORD

*Recommended reading*
McCrudden 'Equal Treatment and Occupational Pensions: Implementing European Community Law in the United Kingdom following the post-*Barber* judgments of the European Court of Justice' (1995) 46 NILQ 376.
Whiteford ' Lost in the Mists of Time: The ECJ and Occupational Pensions' (1995) 32 CMLRev 801.

**PERMANENT REPRESENTATIONS** Permanent Representations are the Brussels based embassies of the Member States to the **European Union**. A typical Permanent Representation has 30-40 staff (more during a Presidency) usually composed of officials of the Member States with diplomatic status, plus support staff who are either members of the national diplomatic service and/or who seconded to it from national ministries. The Permanent Representatives receive instructions from their respective governments where the different agencies co-ordinate national positions, and they advise their governments on proposals by the **European Commission** and on views of other Member States. They benefit from the usual immunities and privileges of diplomats.

The Permanent Representatives are often referred to as 'Ambassadors', although their role is somewhat different from that of an Ambassador to a country, and are sometimes replaced by 'visitors' from home, often referred to as 'experts'.

An 'Attachés Group' consisting exclusively of members of Permanent Representations can be convened at short notice and is sometimes used to resolve problems encountered by 'experts'. There is also a special kind of Attachés Group, known as 'The Friends of the President', consisting of members from the Permanent Representations who know a subject particularly well, or who can spend longer on difficult points than the Permanent Representatives themselves.

The so-called 'Antici Group' of Ambassadors' assistants, which sits in the ante-room to each meeting, is normally responsible for the detailed timing and organisation of **COREPER** and **Council** meetings under the direction of the Presidency and COREPER. Its members act as a channel of communication between the Heads of Government and their advisers at the **European Council**.

PHILIP BASTOS MARTIN

*Recommended reading*
Butler *Europe: More than a Continent* (1986) Heinemann.
Hayes-Renshaw, Lequesne & Mayor Lopez 'The Permanent Representations of the Member States to the European Communities' (1989) Journal of Common Market Studies 119.

**PETITION (RIGHT TO)** The right to petition the **European Parliament** acquired a formal legal status in the **Treaty on European Union**. Until that time it was a purely customary right which, although provided for by the Parliament itself in its rules of procedure, was dependent on the co-operation of the **Commission** for its effective exercise.

Article 8d EC provides that every **citizen** of the Union has the right to address a petition to the European Parliament in accordance with Article 138d EC. However, Article 138d EC extends the right beyond citizens of the Union to 'any natural or legal person residing in or having its registered office in a Member State'.

The petition must be both formally and substantively admissible. Substantive admissibility has three facets: *rationae personae; rationae materiae;* and locus standi.

The *rationae personae* requirement is satisfied by four categories of person: (i) citizens of the European Union; (ii) residents of a Member

State; (iii) legal persons with their registered office in a Member State; and (iv) non-resident citizens of third countries and legal persons with their registered office outside the Community. It remains to be seen whether the Committee on Petitions will extend the second category, residents of a Member State, to illegal residents. The fourth category is extremely broad and does not derive from the TEU, but from the amended rules of procedure of the European Parliament.

The *rationae materiae* test is laid down in Article 138d EC, which requires that the subject matter of the petition 'comes within the Community's field of activity'. However, Article 156 of the Parliament's rules of procedure provides that the Committee must ascertain whether the subject matter of the petition falls within the sphere of activity of the Union. This is important because the Union's field of activities is much wider than that of the Community. It is not yet clear how the Committee will resolve this discrepancy.

Article 138d EC also imposes a locus standi test which requires that the petitioner be directly affected. No such requirement featured in the customary right. Previously, petitions could equally be requests that the Parliament take a position in relation to a general problem. Neither the Treaty nor the rules of procedure of the European Parliament define 'affected directly'; however, it is clear that a petitioner does not have to have an exclusive interest.

Once declared admissible, the petition may be referred to a parliamentary service or committee for information, opinion or referral elsewhere, or to the national authorities of the state concerned for an amicable solution. It may also be referred to the Commission with a request for action or information. If the Commission considers that the Member State concerned has breached its Treaty obligations, it can institute proceedings under Article 169 EC. The Committee on Petitions has already decided that it may intervene in favour of the petitioner in negotiations between Member States and the Commission, but will not interfere once a matter goes to the **Court of Justice**.

SUNDHYA PAHUJA

*Recommended reading*
Marias 'The Right to Petition the European Parliament after Maastricht' (1994) 19 ELRev 169.
Rosas & Antola (eds) *A Citizen's Europe: in Search of a New Order* (1995) Sage.

**PILLARS** The **Treaty on European Union** comprises three elements which have become known as 'Pillars'. The Union is based upon the Treaties establishing the **European Community**, the **European Coal and Steel Community** and the **European Atomic Energy Community** (the First Pillar). The intergovernmental provisions on a **Common Foreign and Security Policy** and on **Co-operation in the Fields of Justice and Home Affairs** have been termed the Second and Third Pillars, respectively. The structure of the Union is fully discussed under **European Union**.

**PLEA OF ILLEGALITY** Whilst the EC Treaty provides a framework of judicial review whereby the legality of an act of a Community institution may be challenged before the Court of Justice (see **action of annulment**), it is very difficult for natural or legal persons to show the necessary title and interest to raise the matter directly before the Court (see **locus standi; direct and individual concern**). To mitigate this restricted access to the Court, the Treaty provides alternative avenues of judicial review. One such is Article 184 EC, which provides that where a Community act is subsequently 'in issue' before the Court, that is in most cases where a question arises in the context of its direct application by means of a subsequent Community measure, a person may seek annulment of the latter and in so doing plead the 'inapplicability' of the former. The availability of this ancillary plea, recognised early on by the Court to be a **general principle of Community law** (Case 9/56 *Meroni v High Authority* [1958] ECR 133), is most refined in French administrative law where it is known as the *exception d'illégalité*, and so is usually called the 'plea of illegality'.

The plea of illegality is not an independent form of action; it can be raised only as an ancillary plea as a means of challenging indirectly the application of a previous act in a case properly raised before, usually, the **Court of First Instance**, under some other head of jurisdiction (Cases 31 & 33/62 *Wöhrmann v EEC Commission* [1962] ECR 501). Whilst the text of Article 184 limits its application to the indirect challenge of Regulations, the Court has said that it may be invoked to question the legality of any Community act which produces like effects, ie an act which can serve as a legal basis for a subsequent act of a Community **institution** (Case 92/78 *Simmenthal v Commission* [1979] ECR 777). There is no time-bar for this indirect challenge, but there must be a sufficient link or connection between the general enabling act and the administrative act based upon it. The grounds for challenging the legality of the enabling act are the same as those in an action of annulment.

The purpose of the plea of illegality is to protect the rights of persons who lack title and interest to challenge a legislative measure when it is adopted, so enabling them to challenge it subsequently when the measure is applied to them in a manner which directly affects their interests (*Simmenthal*). It may therefore not be invoked to challenge an act by its addressee, whether a Member State or a natural or legal person, for they had the opportunity of raising an action of annulment as of right; having failed to do so, the interests of legal certainty override those of legality and the act becomes definitive for them (eg Case 156/77 *Commission v Belgium* [1978] ECR 1881; Case C-183/91 *Commission v Greece* [1993] ECR I-3131 (decisions); Case C-74/91 *Commission v Germany* [1992] ECR I-5437 (Directives)). It can be deduced from the judgment in Case C-188/92 *TWD Textilwerke Deggendorf v Germany* [1994] ECR I-833 that this applies also to any person who clearly had sufficient locus standi to raise an action of annulment. Whether or not the plea may be invoked as a means of challenging indirectly a Regulation (which is addressed to no one) by those with title and interest (Member States; Community institutions; other persons with sufficient locus standi), and so could directly have raised, but did not, an action of annulment, has not yet authoritatively been established (on this point see the opinion of **Advocate General** Slynn in Case 181/85 *France v Commission* [1987] ECR 689). It might also be possible for a Member State to invoke the plea of illegality as a defence in enforcement proceedings under Article 169 EC for failure to comply with obligations imposed upon it by a Regulation on the ground that the Regulation, which is 'in issue' in the proceedings, is unlawful; but this too remains untested.

Where a plea of illegality is successful, the parent act is rendered 'inapplicable' in the case and the subsequent administrative act therefore annulled because it is deprived of its legal foundation. However, the parent act is not annulled (it being immune from annulment) and continues to exist. In theory, it could be applied in other proceedings. But the institution which adopted it is under an obligation to take all necessary measures to comply with a judgment of the Court (Article 176(1) EC) and so is under a duty to repeal or amend it in the light of the Court's judgment.

ROBERT LANE

*Recommended reading*
Barav 'The Exception of Illegality in Community Law: A Critical Analysis' (1974) 11 CMLRev 366.
Van Rijn *Exceptie van onwettigheid en prejudiciële procedure inzake geldigheid van gemeenschapshandelingen* (1978) Kluwer.


**POLICE CO-OPERATION** The **Treaty on European Union** has integrated previous law enforcement initiatives between members of the EC as a matter of common interest (Article K.1(9)) in Title VI on **Co-operation in the Field of Justice and Home Affairs**. Improvement of police co-operation was primarily a call in reaction to the abolition of internal **border controls** flowing from Article 8A of the **Single European Act**, which led to expectations that cross-border crime would increase. Concerted international police co-operation was considered to be an adequate response to this problem. The rise of serious, international organised crime, such as systemic· drug-trafficking, money laundering and vehicle theft, also acted as a catalyst.

Title VI has linked the various working groups of Trevi and the Ad Hoc Group on Immigration together under the Co-ordinating Committee (or K.4 Committee). Trevi, which predominantly functioned as a policy forum for the exchange of expertise and strategies between senior civil servants of the interior ministries of the Member States, covered interests such as anti-terrorism, police tactics and public order issues, internal security consequences of the abolition of the internal border controls, serious organised international crime and the creation of Europol. Most policy issues were transferred to Steering Group II (Security, Police and Customs Co-operation) of the Co-ordinating Committee. Police co-operation is also an element in the two other steering groups, Immigration and **Asylum** (I) and Judicial Co-operation (III), as they deal with forged entry documents and with international organised crime. Although Trevi's former accountability deficit has been slightly compensated by Article K.6, which states that the Presidency shall consult the **European Parliament** on the principal aspects of Title VI activities, the negotiations and legislative procedures remain non-communautarian. Nor does the creation of the Co-ordinating Committee offer a solution to the low participation of law enforcement professionals.

This criticism seems less applicable to the Europol Drugs Unit (EDU), which was instituted in The Hague in January 1994 as a consequence of Article K.1(9) of Title VI. The Unit, which is the predecessor of the more mature European Police Office (Europol), derives its status from the June 1993 Copenhagen Ministerial Agreement, which says that it should only engage itself with international drug trafficking and that it cannot operate its own (intelligence) database. Officially, its remit can only be extended after ratification of the Convention on the Establishment of Europol, which is subject to negotiation, but its remit was extended by the **Council** in December 1994 to include money laundering, vehicle trafficking and illegal immigrant smuggling, and in December 1996 to include trade in human beings. The creation of Europol has not been without controversy. Difficult negotiation issues concerned judicial and parliamentary control, access to Europol's intelligence, executive powers, and the inclusion of terrorism. Europol's most important function will be to complement the national police forces, and to offer them information, assistance, strategic analysis and expertise. Europol will only be involved when collective action is required and when the targeted criminal organisation is internationally active (principle of **subsidiarity**). The organisation occupies a hierarchical position as contact runs via the national criminal intelligence services in the Member States.

In contrast, the provisions on police co-operation in the **Schengen Agreements** have more significance for the 'vertical' co-operation between police forces. Title III of the Schengen Implementation Agreement covers police and security matters, and includes measures on police co-operation, drugs and firearms. More concretely, the Chapter provides rules on the cross-border exchange of written information and evidence (Article 39), cross-border surveillance (Article 40), the right of cross-border pursuit (Article 41) and controlled deliveries of illegal drugs (Article 73). Police co-operation between EU Member States is furthermore shaped by numerous other bilateral and multilateral initiatives, such as Benelux and the so-called NEBEDEACPol network between Germany, Belgium and the Netherlands.

MONICA DEN BOER

*Recommended reading*
Anderson et al *Policing the European Union* (1995) Oxford, Clarendon Press.
den Boer & Walker 'European Policing after 1992' (1993) 31 JCMS 1, 3–28.

**POLLUTER PAYS PRINCIPLE** The polluter pays principle is defined as a principle of European Community **environmental policy** under Article 130r(2) EC. The principle essentially means that the producers of goods should be responsible for the costs of preventing or dealing with any pollution which a process causes. This includes environmental costs as well as costs to people and property. According to this principle, the costs of pollution control should therefore be reflected in the cost of goods and services which cause pollution in production and/or consumption. The principle is closely related to the idea that prevention is better than cure. The principle was developed as a method of allocating the costs of pollution control. At an international level, the OECD member countries agreed in 1972 that subsidies should not be provided to cover pollution control costs; these costs instead should be borne by polluters, who could generally pass them on to consumers. The objectives of the principle are to ensure that the generators of pollution bear the costs of measures taken to ensure that the environment is in an acceptable state, and to avoid disruption of trade or unfair competitive advantage for the industry of one country over that of another. The principle has commonly been invoked in support of applying economic incentives and disincentives.

JANE HOLDER

*Recommended reading*
Ball & Bell *The Law and Policy Relating to the Protection of the Environment* (2nd edn, 1994) Blackstone Press, ch 4.
Kramer *Focus on European Environmental Law* (1992) Sweet & Maxwell, ch 11.

**PRE-ACCESSION STRATEGY** See **enlargement**.

**PRECAUTIONARY PRINCIPLE** The precautionary principle is defined as a principle of the European Community's **environmental policy** in Article 130r(2) EC. The precautionary principle reverses the traditional understanding that environmental damage must be proved before action is taken; instead, only when there is sufficient proof that no environmental damage will occur should there be failure to take action. The principle provides a basis for determining policy in the face of scientific uncertainty about whether preventive measures are necessary, based on an appreciation that many environmental processes and changes can be irreversible. The principle clearly applies to the promulgation of anticipatory measures, as confirmed by the **Court of Justice** in Case C-2/90 *Commission v Belgium* (Wallonian Waste) [1992] ECR I-4431, in which it was decided that wastes should be disposed of as close to their place of origin as possible in order to reduce the possibility of harm occurring. Its essence, that the lack of full scientific certainty shall not be used as a reason for not taking action to protect the environment, suggests that it might also be applied in a number of different respects, for example, in justifying provisions providing for strict liability or an alteration of the rules of evidence in environmental liability cases.

The precautionary principle was first enunciated internationally by the OECD in 1987. Since then it has been cited frequently in the context of marine pollution, climate change, dangerous wastes, and hazardous products.

JANE HOLDER

*Recommended reading*
Birnie & Boyle *International Law and the Environment* (1993) Clarendon, ch 3.
Hession & Macrory 'Maastricht and the Environmental Policy of the Community: Legal Issues of a New Environmental Policy' in O'Keeffe & Twomey (eds) *Legal Issues of the Maastricht Treaty* (1994) Wiley Chancery.

**PRECEDENT** All courts strive for consistency in their decisions. The **Court of Justice** is no exception in this regard. To ignore the need for consistency would be to violate two principles to which the Court is deeply attached, namely, the principle of **equality**, which requires that like situations must be treated in like manner, and the principle of **legal certainty**, which requires that the law must be reasonably predictable so that **citizens** may arrange their affairs in full knowledge of the legal consequences.

In considering the Court of Justice's attitude to precedent it must be remembered that the Court's work often represents a fusion between the diverse legal traditions of the Member States. Although differences between the common law and the civil law in relation to precedent should not be exaggerated, it is probably true to say that civil law courts have a more flexible attitude and generally manage without some of the sophisticated tools developed by the common law (such as the distinction between ratio decidendi and obiter dicta). In general, it may be said that the Court of Justice, like the supreme courts in the Member States, does not regard itself as strictly bound by its previous judgments but is reluctant to depart from a precedent and will only do so exceptionally.

As Koopmans points out, the Court has from its earliest years cited its previous judgments. None the less, in the 1960s and 1970s it often preferred vague references to 'the settled case law of the Court' and disguised quotations from previous judgments. In the 1980s, the citation of previous cases becomes more systematic and there is evidence of a conscious attempt to build up a coherent body of case law. Some would regard this as due in part to the advent of lawyers drawn from the common law tradition.

In the first 35 years of its existence the Court carefully avoided expressly overruling any of its earlier decisions, perhaps feeling that such a practice would damage the credibility of a newly established judicial body. From that point of view, the judgment in *HAG II* (Case C-10/89 *CNL SUCAL v HAG GF* [1990] ECR I-3711) can be regarded as a coming of age for the Court. There the Court declared the need to 'reconsider' a precedent established 16 years earlier in *HAG I* (Case 192/73 *Van Zuylen v HAG* [1974] ECR 731) and went on to indicate that the previous case had been wrongly decided.

Prior to 1990 the Court had occasionally given judgments which were difficult or impossible to reconcile with earlier decisions (eg Joined Cases 115 & 116/81 *Adoui and Cornuaille v Belgium* [1982] ECR 1665 in relation to Case 41/74 *Van Duyn v Home Office* [1974] ECR 1337) but whatever overruling there was in that period was implicit and may sometimes have been accidental, the earlier case law simply being passed over in silence.

In 1989, in the 'Chernobyl' case (Case 70/88 *Parliament v Council* [1990] ECR I-2041), the Court had come very close to expressly overruling a judgment given 15 months before in the 'Comitology' case (Case 302/87 *Parliament v Council* [1988] ECR 5615) concerning the capacity of the European Parliament to bring an **action of annulment** under Article 173 EC.

The area in which the Court has had the greatest difficulty in achieving consistency is the **free movement of goods**. Between 1980 and 1993 the Court gave a series of conflicting judgments on the scope of Article 30 EC, which prohibits quantitative restrictions on imports and measures having equivalent effect. The various strains in the case law are identified in **Advocate General** Tesauro's opinion in Case C-292/92 *Hünermund v Landesapothekerkammer Baden-Wuerttemberg* [1993] ECR I-6787. If the judgment in Joined Cases C-267/91 & C-268/91 *Keck and Mithouard* [1993] ECR I-6097 was an attempt to clear up the resulting confusion, it was not entirely successful because the Court, while expressly indicating that some of its previous rulings could no longer be considered good law, failed to state which judgments were being overruled.

Since the establishment of the **Court of First Instance** in 1989, the question arises whether that body is bound by the previous judgments of the Court of Justice. Apart from the special situations covered by Articles 47 and 54 of the Statute of the Court of Justice, the prevailing view is that the Court of First Instance is not bound by decisions of the Court of Justice (see Arnull, cited below, at p 262), though it will not of course disregard such precedents lightly. In Case T-586/93 *Kotzonis v Economic and Social Committee* [1995] ECR II-665 the Court of First

Instance expressly indicated (in paragraphs 91 to 99 of the judgment) that it was departing from a precedent established by the Court of Justice 21 years earlier.

The question remains whether and to what extent national courts are bound to follow precedents established by the Court of Justice. A preliminary ruling given under Article 177 EC is, of course, binding on the referring court in the proceedings which led it to request a ruling. Preliminary rulings are also considered to produce effects *erga omnes*, in the sense that they must be taken into account by other national courts in subsequent proceedings. For courts in the United Kingdom that is made clear by section 3(1) of the **European Communities Act** 1972. It is, however, always open to a national court to resubmit to the Court of Justice a question on which the latter has already ruled, suggesting, where appropriate, grounds for answering the question differently.

DAVID T KEELING

*Recommended reading*
Arnull 'Owning up to Fallibility: precedent and the Court of Justice' (1993) CML Rev 247–266.
Koopmans '*Stare decisis* in European Law' in O'Keeffe & Schermers (eds) *Essays in European Law and Integration* (1982) Kluwer, pp 11–27.

**PRELIMINARY RULING** Preliminary ruling is a procedural term to describe proceedings in the **Court of Justice** arising under Article 41 ECSC, Article 150 Euratom and Article 177 EC. This account is confined to Article 177 EC: Article 150 Euratom has never been invoked and Article 41 ECSC, although the forerunner of Article 177 EC, is more limited in scope and has been used only rarely: Articles 150 and 41 have become virtually dead letters.

Article 177 EC confers jurisdiction on the ECJ to give preliminary rulings concerning (1) the *interpretation* of the EC Treaty (and amending Treaties) and of acts of the Community **institutions**, such as Regulations and Directives, and (2) the *validity* of such acts.

The jurisdiction under Article 177 reflects the fact that most disputes involving **Community law** never come directly before the ECJ but commence before the courts and tribunals of the Member States. The Article empowers the ECJ, at the request of the national judge, to rule on questions of Community law which have arisen in the national forum. It is a kind of switching mechanism, whereby the national proceedings then stand adjourned, to be resumed when the ruling has been given by the ECJ. The term *renvoi préjudiciel* in the French text of Article 177 is clearer, denoting the submission of an issue for prior judgment before a decision on the principal issue, a procedure for which the French legal system provided a model.

Article 177 distinguishes between those national courts which have a discretion to refer and those which are obliged to do so. The latter are those courts from which in their national system no appeal would lie in the instant case to a higher court: such a 'final' court must refer a question of Community law whenever this is necessary to resolve the issue before it. A narrow exception is admitted where the answer to the question of interpretation is clear, as where the ECJ has already ruled on the same question in a previous decision. Where, however, the question is one of the validity of the Community measure (eg a regulation) a reference must always be made if the measure is to be declared invalid: only the ECJ has power to do this (Case 314/85 *Foto-Frost* [1987] ECR 4199).

Non-final courts have a discretion to refer: this is the discretion of the judge, not the parties. Again, a national judge, faced with a challenge to the validity of a Community measure, should refer that question under Article 177, unless he concludes there are no grounds to doubt the validity of the measure.

Article 177 speaks (in the English version) of 'courts or tribunals' of the Member States. These two terms are intended to embrace any body which exercises judicial functions under state authority: an arbitrator has been excluded on this test (Case 102/81 *Nordsee* [1982] ECR 1095).

The ECJ will generally accept to rule on whatever questions are referred to it. It reserves, however, the power to declare a reference inadmissible where the referring court has not provided sufficient factual and legal background in its reference (see Case C-343/90 *Dias* [1992] ECR I-4673). It may also decline to rule in plainly collusive proceedings (see Case C-83/91 *Meilicke* [1992] ECR I-4871).

Preliminary rulings have proved of great importance for the development of Community law. Thus, in Case 26/62 *Van Gend en Loos* [1963] ECR 1, on a reference from a Dutch court, the ECJ first propounded the doctrine of **direct effect** of the Treaty Article in issue. The protection in this way of rights claimed under Community law was extended to a Regulation in Case 93/71 *Leonesio* [1972] ECR 287 and to a Directive in Case 41/74 *Van Duyn* [1974] ECR 1377.

Again, preliminary rulings have affirmed the principle of the **supremacy** of Community law whenever the law of a Member State is found to be in conflict with Community law (Case 6/64 *Costa v ENEL* [1964] ECR 585). Where there is such conflict, even an Act of Parliament cannot be applied by the British judge (Case C-213/89 *Factortame* [1990] ECR I-495 followed by the House of Lords in *Equal Opportunities Commission v Secretary of State for Employment* [1994] 1 All ER 910).

Jurisdiction to give preliminary rulings is confined to the Court of Justice: the **Court of First Instance** cannot give preliminary rulings. The ECJ, however, is not obliged to sit *in pleno*: a ruling may be given by a Chamber. Preliminary rulings make up well over a third of the caseload of the ECJ.

In the absence of a federal structure, under which a Community court might be given appellate jurisdiction over national courts, the preliminary ruling is an example of judicial co-operation between Community judges and national judges as equals. It is also the only procedure whereby uniform application of Community law in all official **languages** (now 12) can be secured: only such uniformity can provide a level playing field for competitors in the single market.

L NEVILLE BROWN

*Recommended reading*
Anderson *References to the European Court* (1995) Sweet & Maxwell.
Schermers et al *Article 177 EEC: Experience and Problems* (1987) Asser Institute.

**PRINCIPLE OF SOLIDARITY** Solidarity as a notion was used for the first time in the Declaration of Robert Schuman in 1950, where it was stated that Europe will not be built all at once or according to a single plan but through concrete achievements which will create a de facto solidarity.

Solidarity as a binding principle of **Community law** was established by the case law of the **Court of Justice**. According to the ECJ, solidarity is founded on mutual trust among the Member States. It creates an equilibrium for the Member States between rights and obligations and comprises the notions of **Community preference** and Community loyalty (Article 5 EC).

Solidarity has acquired a central role after the Treaty on European Union. It has become a legally binding objective of the **European Union** and the European Community.

In the framework of the Community it denotes solidarity among the Member States while, in the context of the Union, it extends also to the relations between the peoples of the Member States. The deepening of solidarity between the peoples and the Member States is envisaged by the TEU in a manner that should respect their history, culture and traditions as well as the national identities of the Member States and their national and regional diversity.

The TEU establishes a direct link between economic and social **cohesion** on the one hand and solidarity of Member States on the other.

To this extent solidarity is not restricted only to the development of regions lagging behind or to the conversion of declining industrial areas or to reducing disparities between Community's North and South and backwardness of the least-favoured regions. It is also extended to rural areas, local communities and to the citizens of the Union. Furthermore, the establishment of the Cohesion Fund will provide financial assistance to Member States with a per capita Gross National Product of less than 90% of the Community average.

EPAMINONDAS A MARIAS

*Recommended reading*
Marchal *L'Europe Solidaire* (1964) Cujas.

Marias 'Solidarity as an objective of the European Union and the European Community' (1994) 2 LIEI 85-114.

**PROPORTIONALITY** Derived from the German principle of *Verhältnismässigkeit,* the principle of proportionality was described in Case 8/55 *Fédération Charbonnière Belgique v High Authority* [1954-56] ECR 245, 299, as 'a generally accepted rule of law', although in *Brind v Secretary of State* [1991] 1 All ER 720 the House of Lords refused to accept that it was applicable as a separate head of review in English law.

In Case C-331/88 *Fedesa* [1990] ECR I-4023, para 13, the Court explained that it had 'consistently held that the principle of proportionality is one of the **general principles of Community law**. By virtue of that principle, the lawfulness of the prohibition of an economic activity is subject to the condition that the prohibitory measures are appropriate and necessary in order to achieve the objectives legitimately pursued by the legislation in question; when there is a choice between several appropriate measures recourse must be had to the least onerous, and the disadvantages caused must not be disproportionate to the aims pursued'. As Lord Diplock put it in *R v Goldstein* [1983] 1 WLR 151 at 155, 'you must not use a steam hammer to crack a nut, if a nutcracker would do'.

Thus, in Case 261/81 *Rau v De Smedt* [1982] ECR 3961, the Court held that national legislation requiring margarine to be packaged in cube-shaped blocks in order to prevent it from being confused with butter constituted an unlawful restriction on trade. Although legislation designed to avoid confusion in the mind of the **consumer** was in principle legitimate, the Court took the view that 'Consumers may in fact be protected just as effectively by other measures, for example by rules on labelling, which hinder the free movement of goods less' (para 17).

The importance of the principle of proportionality is underlined by the third paragraph of Article 3b EC, introduced by the TEU, according to which 'Any action by the Community shall not go beyond what is necessary to achieve the objectives of this Treaty'.

ANTHONY ARNULL

*Recommended reading*
de Búrca 'The Principle of Proportionality and its Application in EC law' (1993) 13 Yearbook of European Law 105.
Herdegen 'The Relation Between the Principles of Equality and Proportionality' (1985) 22 CMLRev 683.

## PUBLIC POLICY, PUBLIC SECURITY AND PUBLIC HEALTH
Articles 48(3), 56(1) and 66 EC permit domestic law exceptions on the three stated grounds to the **free movement of persons**, the right to

**freedom of establishment** and the right to provide **services** respectively. The **free movement of goods** may be similarly restricted under Article 36 EC, though the list of grounds there is longer.

Essentially, as exceptions to fundamental principles of the Treaty, these grounds are construed narrowly by the Court of Justice and are subject to the proportionality principle. The exceptions cannot be invoked to service economic needs. It is, however, recognised that in relation to grounds such as public policy or public morality, each national government has a degree of discretion to set its own standards.

In relation to goods, the exceptions can be used to justify general barriers to trade and its operation should be viewed alongside the doctrine of mandatory requirements and relevant harmonisation measures. Whereas the doctrine of mandatory requirements should only be invoked in relation to indistinctly applicable measures, Article 36 EC can be used to justify distinctly applicable measures (Case 34/79 *R v Henn* and *Darby* [1979] ECR 3795). In *Oberkreisdirektor v Moorman BV* (Case 190/87 [1988] ECR 4689) the ECJ held that Article 36 cannot be invoked once the subject matter has been dealt with in a harmonisation measure, though this will not be the case if it is clear that the measure was intended only to supplement, not replace, national standards (Case 4/75 *Rewe-Zentralfinanz GmbH v Landwirtschaftskammer* [1975] ECR 843).

In relation to persons, the restrictions are amplified in Council Directive (EEC) 64/221 (OJ Sp Ed 1963-64 p 117), which is applied to the employed, the self-employed and recipients of services, and to such of their families as have acquired free movement rights under the Treaty. However, it extends only to natural persons, not to companies. The Directive imposes both substantive and procedural limitations on the use of these exceptions. The public policy and public security exceptions can be used only where the conduct of a particular individual causes concern (Article 3(1)), and cannot justify the existence of more general barriers to movement (Case 157/79 *R v Pieck* [1980] ECR 2171). Criminal convictions cannot of themselves constitute a sufficient basis for limiting entry or movement (Article 3(2)). The ECJ has stated that a 'genuine and sufficiently serious threat . . . affecting one of the fundamental interests of society' must be shown (Case 30/77 *R v Bouchereau* [1977] ECR 1999). In determining the proportionality of the restriction, the ECJ will consider what measure the Member State takes to suppress similar conduct on the part of its own nationals. While it is recognised that there may be differences (a state cannot, for instance, deport its own nationals), repressive measures or other 'genuine and effective' restrictions should be in place (Cases 115 & 116/81 *Adoui* and *Cornuaille v Belgian State* [1982] ECR 1665).

Public health is covered in some details in Article 4, Directive 64/221 and the Annex thereto, with the result that only a limited range of health grounds can be invoked and these only to restrict entry or the issue of a first residence permit. Thus, health problems arising after a person has settled in another Member State cannot be used to justify removal or expulsion.

The procedural restrictions contained in the Directive are largely matters relating to 'due process'. Article 5 lays down time-limits for the determination of an application for a residence permit, whilst Articles 6 and 7 concern the right to be given grounds, where a permit is refused and the right to receive adequate notice of refusal. Articles 8 and 9 deal with the rights of appeal; Article 8 attempts to ensure that nationals of other Member States are treated at least as favourably as nationals in similar circumstances, though there are of course no direct parallels in such cases; hence Article 9 establishes a minimum 'due process' framework of a right to appeal and adequate time and assistance to prepare a defence, subject to national security constraints where applicable.

FIONA C BEVERIDGE

*Recommended reading*
Hall 'The ECHR and the public policy exceptions to the free movement of workers under the EEC Treaty' (1991) 16 ELRev 446.
O'Keeffe 'Practical Difficulties in the Application of Article 48 of the EEC Treaty' (1982) 19 CMLRev 35.

**PUBLIC PROCUREMENT** Public procurement refers to the acquisition of goods, works or services by public authorities and utilities.

The public procurement rules set out procedures for the award of contracts above certain values throughout the **European Union**. The purpose of these rules is to establish greater **transparency** and improve competition in the public procurement market. Under the **GATT**, the **European Economic Area** Agreement and various other multilateral and bilateral agreements, the benefits of the EC rules, or their equivalent, may be extended to suppliers and contractors from non-member countries.

Council Directives lay down a legal framework to which public authorities must adapt their procedures for the award of public works contracts, public supply contracts and public service contracts which are for a value in excess of specified thresholds (Council Directives (EEC) 93/37 (OJ L199 14.6.93 p 54), 93/36 (OJ L199 14.6.93 p 1) and 92/50 (OJ L209 18.6.92 p 1) respectively). For service contracts, the rules apply in full only to contracts for certain categories of services such as, for example, maintenance and repair services and certain transport, telecommunication, financial, computer and accounting services. Furthermore, certain contracts may be excluded from the application of procurement rules, for example on grounds of secrecy.

Public authorities are defined as the state, regional or local authorities, bodies governed by public law, associations formed by one or several of such authorities or bodies governed by public law.

A separate Council Directive co-ordinates the procurement procedures for entities operating in the water, energy, transport, and telecommunications sectors ('the excluded sectors') (see Council Directive (EEC) 93/38 (OJ L199 14.6.93 p 84)).

Generally, contracts which are governed by the Directives must be subject to a call for competition by publishing a contract notice in the Official Journal of the EC (see **publications of the EU**) and the Tenders Electronic Daily. In most cases, the time allowed for responses or tenders must be no less than a specified period. Entities operating in the excluded sectors can alternatively call for competition either by publishing sufficiently specific periodic indicative notices or by publishing a notice of a qualification system.

The Directives set out criteria for the rejection or selection of tenderers based on evidence of their personal position, their economic and financial standing, their technical capacity, and, for services, their ability. The Directives also set out criteria for determining the award of contracts based on which offer is 'the most economically advantageous' for the purchaser of 'the lowest price'. The criteria are designed to avoid discrimination on the grounds of origin in a particular Member State and to ensure that all suppliers or contractors established in the Member States are treated on equal terms. However, entities operating in the excluded sectors may reject any tenders made for the award of a supply contract where the proportion of the products originating in non-member countries, which do not provide comparable and effective access for Community undertakings, exceeds 50% of the total of the products constituting the tender.

The Directives provide for three award procedures. Under the open procedure, all interested persons may tender for the contract. Under the restricted procedure, only selected persons may submit tenders for the contract. Under the negotiated procedure, a purchaser may negotiate the terms of the contract with one or more persons selected by it.

Public authorities have a free choice between the open and restricted procedures but may only use the negotiated procedure in limited circumstances. Utilities have a free choice between the open, restricted, and competitive negotiated procedures, ie those where a call for competition is required. Under restricted and competitive negotiated procedures, there must be a sufficient number of participants to ensure general competition. Normally, a minimum will be three, but where a public authority specifies the range in which the number of participants will fall, the minimum will be five.

The Commission completed the legislative framework by adopting Directives under which Member States must provide national review or control bodies with the power, inter alia, to adopt interim measures to suspend the award procedure or the implementation of any decision taken by the contracting authority, to quash decisions unlawfully taken and to award damages to persons harmed by them (see the

Remedies Directives (Council Directives (EEC) 89/665 (OJ L395 21.12.89 p 33) and EC 92/13 (OJ L76 25.2.92 p 14)).

PAULETTE VANDER SCHUEREN

*Recommended reading*
Trepte *Public Procurement in the EC* (1993) CCH Editions.
Weiss *Public Procurement in European Community Law* (1993) Athlone Press.

**PUBLICATION OF ACTS** Publication is the procedure whereby certain acts of the institutions are brought into force. Thus, Article 15 ECSC provides that general decisions and recommendations 'shall take effect by the mere fact of publication'. Article 191 EC requires that Regulations, Directives and Decisions adopted in accordance with the co-decision procedure laid down in Article 189b EC, as well as all other Regulations and Directives addressed to all Member States must be published in the Official Journal of the Communities. The same applies to Regulations adopted under the Euratom Treaty (Article 163). All these acts enter into force on the date specified in them or, in the absence thereof, on the twentieth day following their publication. In the case of these acts, publication is thus an essential formal/procedural requirement and has a constitutive effect in the sense that through publication only and exclusively can such acts acquire binding force and become applicable (Case 39/72 *Commission v Italy* [1973] ECR 101 at 114; Case 185/73 *König* [1974] ECR 607 at 616–617). It would therefore seem that lack of publication entails not merely voidability but absolute nullity (non-existence) of the act concerned (although this has not so far been definitively decided by the **Court of Justice**).

The precise date of publication is of importance in two different respects. First, it may determine the date on which the act enters into force (which may be the date of publication itself). Second, it makes time run for the bringing of an action for the annulment of the act before the Court of Justice. There is a rebuttable presumption that the date of publication is in fact the date appearing on each issue of the Official Journal. Therefore, in the absence of evidence to the contrary, a Regulation is to be regarded as published throughout the Community on the date borne by the issue of the Official Journal containing the text of that Regulation (Case 98/78 *Racke* [1979] ECR 69 at 84–85; but see also Case 88/76 *Exportation des Sucres v Commission* [1977] ECR 709 at 726). In some cases, eg in the field of competition law, the publication of certain acts not listed above (eg Decisions) has been, or may be, made compulsory (see eg Article 21 of Council Regulation (EEC) 17/62 (OJ Sp Ed (1959–62) p 87)).

AKOS G TOTH

*Recommended reading*
Hartley *The Foundations of European Community Law* (3rd edn, 1994) Oxford University Press, p 135.

Toth *The Oxford Encyclopaedia of European Community Law*, vol I *Institutional Law* (1990) Oxford University Press, p 435.


**PUBLICATIONS OF THE EU**   According to Article 191 EC, Regulations and Directives must be published in the *Official Journal of the European Communities* (OJ). There is no such obligation for Decisions, although they generally are published as well. Acts adopted within the framework of the 'Second and Third **Pillars**' of the **European Union** (Articles J and K of the **Treaty on European Union**) must not be published, although there is an incipient practice to publish any binding acts agreed within those areas. The name of the OJ has accordingly been changed into *Official Journal of the European Communities*

The OJ is published on most weekdays simultaneously in each of the 11 official **languages** of the European Union, each language version having the same pagination. It is divided into an 'L' series (containing legislation, treaties, the budgets and binding acts in general), the 'C' series (containing miscellaneous information and notices, such as **Commission** proposals for legislation, common positions adopted by the **Council** and minutes of the plenary sessions of the **European Parliament**). The 'S' series is for the specialised use of firms competing for public contracts. Finally, the *Debates of the European Parliament* are published, under that title, as an Annex to the OJ.

In addition to the OJ, important publications emanate from the single institutions, mainly from the Commission. It publishes every year the *General Report on the Activities of the Union*, which describes the development of all policies of the EU. More detailed than the General Report is the monthly *Bulletin of the EU*, which gives a full survey of EU activities. It provides easy access to EU publications, because it carries references to the pages of the OJ (or other sources) where Community acts and other material can be found. There is also a *Supplement to the Bulletin*, published at irregular intervals and devoted each time to a single subject of special importance.

The Commission's working documents or *COM.DOCs* are used for proposing legislation, describing a first approach to a policy document, or for reporting on the implementation of a policy. Regular bulletins are published on single policies (for example, *Social Europe, European Economy* and *Green Europe*), and all Directorates General of the European Commission can supply information on demand about matters coming within their remit.

The operative part of European Court rulings is published in the OJ(C), but their full text is to be found in separate *Reports of Cases before the Court of Justice and the Court of First Instance* (ECR). **Court of Justice** judgments and the Opinions of **Advocates General** appear in part I. Judgments of the **Court of First Instance** appear in part II. Judgments concerning disputes between officials and the institutions are published in the Reports of European Community Staff Cases.

The European Parliament produces *session documents* containing opinions on draft legislation and other committee reports.

In order to disseminate all the above documents, various channels are used including the *Information Offices* of the European Commission and of the European Parliament in each Member State, the *European Documentation Centres* (*EDCs*) (comprehensive collections of publications and documentation on the European Union, usually located in universities or other institutions providing education or carrying out research in European integration, and which can freely be consulted by the public) and the *Office for Official Publications* (*EUR-OP*) in Luxembourg (which publishes, distributes and supplies virtually all material emanating from the institutions of the European Union through a network of sales agents in the Member States and worldwide). This Office makes several useful compilations of EU documents such as the *Directory of Community Legislation in Force and Other Acts of the Community Institutions* (twice a year) and the *SCAD Bulletin*, a weekly catalogue of EU publications and documents.

VEERLE DECKMYN

*Recommended reading*
Deckmyn *Guide to Official Information of the European Union* (1996) European Institute of Public Administration.
Thompson *The Documentation of the European Communities* (1989) Mansell.


**QUALIFIED MAJORITY VOTING (QMV)** See **decision making** and **European Commission**.


**REASONED OPINION** See, for the administrative procedure under Article 169 EC, **action for failure to fulfil an obligation**, and, for competition matters, **competition procedure**.


**RECOMMENDATIONS** See **legislative acts**.


**REGIONAL POLICY** The Community's regional policy has evolved considerably since its inception in 1975, with the establishment of the European Regional Development Fund (ERDF, Article 130c EC) and the setting up of a Regional Policy Committee. Today it is but one dimension of a broader Community strategy of ensuring economic and social cohesion. In seeking to redress regional imbalances in the Community the ERDF is assisted by two other structural funds (the **European Social Fund** and the Guidance Section of the European Agricultural Guidance and Guarantee Fund), the newly established Financial Instrument of Fisheries Guidance (FIFG) and, where appropriate, loans from the **European Investment Bank**. The

261

**Cohesion** Fund, set up pursuant to Article 130d EC, though not strictly a part of the Community's regional policy, provides further financial assistance in respect of investment in transport and environmental infrastructure in those Member States (Greece, Spain, Portugal and Ireland) which are characterised by a high concentration of 'lagging' regions. The existence of a separate EC regional policy has been justified in terms of efficiency relative to national intervention, and in the light of the negative regional impact which, in the short and medium term at least, **Internal Market** integration and progress towards **economic and monetary union** can be anticipated to generate.

The Community's regional policy provides a framework for the granting of financial assistance in three categories of regions: those whose development is lagging behind, as evidenced by their exceptionally low (less than 75% of the Community average) per capita Gross Domestic Product (GDP) ('Objective 1' regions); those seriously affected by industrial decline ('Objective 2' regions); and those rural areas exhibiting a low level of socio-economic development ('Objective 5(b)' regions). A fourth category of region was added following the recent accession of the two Nordic States in order to facilitate assistance to sparsely populated areas, such as the Arctic regions of these new Member States ('Objective 6' regions). During the years 1994–99 almost 70% of total assistance from the structural funds and the FIFG will accrue to 'Objective 1' regions.

The Community's regional policy provides part-financing for a wide range of activities, including investment in basic infra-structure, such as communications, energy and water equipment and to a lesser extent social infrastructure, investment in productive enterprise and in the development of local and human resources. The proportion of the total cost met by Community assistance is variable according to the gravity of the specific problem to be addressed, the financial capacity of the Member States concerned, and the special importance attaching to the measure to be funded. In 'Objective 1' regions Community assistance shall only exceptionally exceed 75% of the total cost of the measure but shall, as a general rule, comprise at least 50% of public expenditure. In the case of revenue bearing investments the Community's contribution shall not exceed 50% of the total cost in 'Objective 1' regions, and 30% in other regions. The principle of additionality applies to the granting of Community assistance in order to ensure that it achieves a genuine economic impact. To this end the **Commission** and the Member States are to ensure that national regional policy expenditure is maintained at a level which is equal to that employed during the previous reference period. Account may, however, be taken of the macroeconomic circumstances in which national funding occurs.

During each programming period Member States shall submit to the Commission regional plans. These may include applications for assistance for specific measures. In the light of these the Commission shall, in consultation with the Member States, draw up Community Support Frameworks or, where the regional plan includes specific applications for assistance, a Single Programming Document. These should identify, inter alia, the objectives to be pursued, the priorities adopted for Community assistance and an indicative financial plan which includes details of the amount of assistance sought and its source and duration. The Commission may also simultaneously approve applications for assistance submitted by the Member States as an integral part of their regional plans. Measures will be eligible for funding only if they fall within the scope of the relevant Community Support Framework or Single Programming Document. The planning process is to be conducted in accordance with the principle of partnership. This implies the close involvement of regional and local bodies, together with the 'social partners', in the planning and implementation of regional development measures. Assistance is granted primarily by way of investment in large-scale infrastructure projects and increasingly through the continuous funding of operational programmes. Such operational programmes are intended to comprise coherent, multi-annual, packages of co-ordinated measures and may be undertaken upon the initiative of either the Member States or the Commission (Commission initiatives). They may be regional or multi-regional in their scope, and may draw upon one or more of the structural funds, the FIFG and loans from the EIB.

Measures part-funded by the Community are subject to prior appraisal, monitoring and *ex post* evaluation. Whereas monitoring essentially implies a check on the financial and physical implementation of measures, appraisal and evaluation are designed to measure the socio-economic impact of operations and their effectiveness in terms both of the general objectives laid down in Article 130a EC and the specific goals identified. Measures financed by the Community are, moreover, to be in conformity with the provisions of the Treaties, instruments adopted thereunder and with Community policies, including those concerning the rules on competition, the award of public contracts, environmental protection and the application of the principle of equal opportunities for men and women. Member States are required, where appropriate, to supply the Commission with the information required to verify compliance with this principle of compatibility. This notwithstanding, the **Court of Auditors** has voiced criticism of the Community's regional policy from the perspective of environmental law and policy (see *Special Report No 3/92 Concerning the Environment* (OJ C245 23.9.92 p 1) and Case T-461/93 *An Taisce* [1994] ECR II-733 and Case T-585/93 *Stichting Greenpeace Council* [1995] ECR II-2205).

JOANNE SCOTT

*Recommended reading*
Armstrong, Taylor & Williams 'Regional Policy' in Artis & Lee (eds) *The Economics of the European Union* (1994) Oxford University Press.

Scott 'Regional Policy' in Vaughan *Law of the European Communities* (1996) Butterworths.


**REGULATIONS** See **legislative acts.**


**RESEARCH AND DEVELOPMENT POLICY** The initial stimulus for European common research and development activities was taken under the **Euratom Treaty** with the creation of the Joint Research Centre (JRC) in 1959. In 1972, at the Paris Summit, it was accepted that the JRC could be involved in non-nuclear research as well. This reform represents a first step towards a wide-ranging research policy.

During 1982-83 attempts were made to reorganise the Member States' research and development activities. To include them into a framework programme, which would last over several years and co-ordinate Community and national activities, would provide the Community with a means of selecting scientific and technological aims. The First Framework Programme (1984-87) was approved by the **Council** in 1983.

With the **Single European Act** Research and Technological Development (R&TD) was formally declared to be a responsibility of the Community. Article 130f, amended by the Treaty on European Union, added the idea originally giving rise to the Framework Programme, that the Community's R&TD policy should be, first and foremost, at the service of other Community policies. More obvious legitimacy was hereby given those research activities initiated on the basis of Article 235 EEC, which were not directly concerned with the competitiveness of European industry.

Further, the desire to respond to the social needs of European citizens and strengthen economic and social cohesion between various European regions was added by the TEU. This field supplements the two concerns traditionally directing Community R&TD policy, the conservation and improvement of human and material resources, and the need for autonomy and competitiveness *vis-à-vis the* USA and Japan.

The Fourth Framework Programme (1994-98) covers four spheres of activity. The first sphere includes research programmes divided into the following headings: (i) information and communications technologies; (ii) industrial technologies; (iii) environment; (iv) life sciences and technologies; (v) energy; (vi) transport; and (vii) targeted socio-economic research. This first sphere is allocated more than four-fifths of the total funding of 12.3 billion ECU, to which a further 700 million might be added in 1996. The second sphere concerns co-operation with non-EU countries and international organisations. The third sphere concerns disseminating and exploiting the results of research and the fourth includes activities of training and mobility.

Two specific programmes are assigned to the JRC, which will also continue to offer its expertise to the departments of the Commission as well as to third parties. A new aspect is that the Centre will be involved in other Community programmes and will here compete on equal terms with other European research centres, including undertakings and universities. A second new aspect concerns assessment processes. These will, together with an annual report, provide a complete assessment on which proposals for the following Framework Programme can be based. In implementing the Framework Programmes, supplementary programmes may be adopted, which, however, seem to be a purely intergovernmental matter (Article 130o).

It has always been hard to co-ordinate national policies within these fields. Today, various attempts are being made to co-ordinate the policies of the Union and of the Member States (Article 130h). The established Community co-operation can also serve as a basis for co-ordination with other forms of European scientific co-operation. Further, the recognition of the European 'added value' on the part of the Member States can be seen in the increased funding of the Fourth Framework Programme. This at the same time as most governments are making cuts in their budgets for science and technology.

Research and development policy requires unanimous approval by the Council. The replacement of unanimous voting for the adoption of framework programmes by a qualified majority vote might, however, be the outcome of the 1996 **Intergovernmental Conference**.

MARIA BYSTRÖM

*Recommended reading*
Guzzetti European Commission Directorate General XII, Science Research, Development *A brief history of European Union research policy* (1995) Office for Official Publications of the EC.
Willke, Krück & Thorn *Benevolent Conspiracies, The Role of Enabling Technologies in the Welfare of Nations, The Cases of SDI, SEMATECH, and EUREKA* (1995) Walter de Gruyter.

**REVERSE DISCRIMINATION** The provisions in Articles 48, 52 and 59 EC can only be invoked by those individuals who move from one Member State to another. This is very clear from the wording of Article 52, which refers to 'the **freedom of establishment** of nationals of a Member State *in the territory of another Member State*' (emphasis added). This requirement of movement within the Community means that, in principle, nationals cannot invoke these Community provisions against their own Member States, since this is a purely internal situation. This may well mean that migrant workers enjoy more favourable treatment than nationals because migrant workers can rely on their Community law rights which may be more favourable than the provisions of national law. Nationals in an otherwise identical position can only rely on national law. This situation is referred to as reverse discrimination.

Consequently, in Cases 35 & 36/82 *Morson and Jhanjhan* [1982] ECR 3723, two women of Surinamese origin wishing to join their children, who were Dutch nationals living in the Netherlands, wanted to rely on Community law rights to enable them to stay in The Netherlands. The **Court of Justice** found that since the children had never exercised their right of free movement within the Community, the situation was wholly internal to the Member State and Community law did not apply. By contrast, in Case C-370/90 *Surinder Singh* [1992] ECR I-4265 the Court found a sufficient Community element to enable the parties to invoke Community law rights. Mr Surinder Singh, an Indian national, married a British citizen in England in 1982. From 1983 to 1985 Mr and Mrs Singh lived and worked in Germany. In 1985 they returned to the United Kingdom to run a business which they had bought. The Court of Justice found that nationals who have gone to work in another Member State in order to exercise their Community law rights under Articles 48 and 52 EC were entitled to benefit from Community law. However, it also ruled that the provisions of the Treaty cannot be used as a means of evading the application of national legislation and as a means of prohibiting Member States from taking the necessary measures to prevent such abuse.

CATHERINE BARNARD

*Recommended reading*
Greenwood 'Nationality and the Limits of Free Movement of Persons in Community Law' (1987) 7 Yearbook of European Law 185.
Pickup 'Reverse Discrimination and Freedom of Movement for Workers' (1986) 23 CMLRev 135.

**RIGHT OF INITIATIVE** The right of initiative within the framework of the European Community belongs exclusively to the **Commission**. The **Court of Justice** has emphasised in Joined Cases 88-90/75 *Sadam* [1976] ECR 338 that the Treaty itself entrusts the Commission with the general task of initiation of measures.

According to Articles 189a and 189c EC on the one hand, and Article 189b EC on the other, the **Council** in the former case or the **European Parliament** and the Council in the latter case legislate upon a proposal submitted by the Commission.

Furthermore, Article 189a EC provides that as long as the Council has not acted, the Commission may alter its proposal at any time during the procedures leading to the adoption of a Community act.

The right of initiative was extended to the European Parliament by the **Treaty on European Union**. According to Article 138b EC, the European Parliament may request the Commission to submit any appropriate proposal on matters on which it considers that a Community act is required for the purpose of implementing the EC Treaty.

The European Parliament's request takes the form of a Resolution adopted by a majority of the component Members of Parliament on an own-initiative report from a EP Committee responsible and authorised pursuant to Rule 148 of the Parliament's Rules of Procedure.

The EP Resolution may at the same time fix a deadline for the submission of the legislative proposal of the Commission.

The Parliament Resolution must indicate the appropriate legal base and be accompanied by detailed recommendations as to the content of the required proposals, which must respect the principle of **subsidiarity** and the fundamental rights of the **citizens**.

Should the proposal have financial implications, Parliament is obliged to indicate how sufficient financial resources can be provided.

The progress of preparation of any legislative proposal drawn up following a particular request by Parliament is monitored by the Committee responsible.

EPAMINONDAS A MARIAS

*Recommemded reading*
Lasok & Bridge *Law and Institutions of the European Union* (6th edn, 1994) Butterworths.
Wyatt & Dashwood *European Community Law* (3rd edn, 1993) Sweet & Maxwell.


**ROME CONVENTION** The Rome Convention provides for a harmonised regime of choice of law rules to determine the law applicable to contractual obligations. Although the Convention is inspired by the perceived need for a common approach to contracts in the Member States of the European Community, its making was not an obligation under the Treaty of Rome. Nevertheless, in common with the **Brussels Convention** on Jurisdiction and Judgments, provision was made for the **Court of Justice** to have jurisdiction upon preliminary reference to interpret the Rome Convention by the Brussels Protocol and the Second Protocol which confers the required extension of jurisdiction on the Court.

The Convention came into force with British ratification in 1990, and was implemented into the law of the United Kingdom by the Contracts (Applicable Law) Act 1990. Although exempt under the terms of the Convention (see Article 19(2)), the United Kingdom chose to regulate internal choice of law issues in contracts (eg between English law and Scots law) according to the Convention's rules. The United Kingdom did exercise permitted derogations in respect of the consequences of nullity of contract and the application of certain foreign policy rules which might be considered to be only indirectly connected to the issues.

The Convention gives effect to the choice of law made by the parties, whether express or demonstrated with reasonable certainty. This principle does not differ materially from the previous English law. Where party choice cannot be ascertained, the contract is governed by the law of the country with which it is most closely connected. Here there is an innovative and not universally popular approach: closest connection is presumed to exist with the habitual residence or place of business of the party providing the characteristic performance. Separate choice of law rules, intended to guarantee the continued protection of certain special groups, apply to consumer contracts and employment contracts.

T ANTHONY DOWNES

*Recommended reading*
Kaye *The new private international law of contract of the European Community* (1993) Dartmouth.
Plender *The European Contracts Convention* (1991) Sweet & Maxwell.

**RULES ON ORIGIN** The distinction between the origins of goods is a vital element of the functioning of the **Internal Market**. Whereas goods originating from the Community are subject to the principle of free movement, goods originating from third countries are subject to the rules of the **Common Customs Tariff** and the **Common Commercial Policy**. By virtue of Article 10(1) EC, the latter can only be considered to be in free circulation within the Community after import formalities have been complied with and any applicable customs duties or charges having equivalent effect have been paid. The common EC rules on origin, laid down in Council Regulation (EEC) 2913/92 (OJ L303 19.10.92 p 1), apply to both EC internal trade and EC non-preferential trade with third countries. Goods produced or obtained in one country or its territorial sea are regarded as originating in that country. Goods produced in two or more countries are regarded as originating in the country in which 'the last substantial process or operation' was performed. The term 'substantial' is of central importance because importers from third countries have frequently tried to circumvent EC customs duties or anti-dumping duties by applying a merely symbolic processing or working to their products within the Community. In Case 49/76 *Überseehandel* [1977] ECR 41 the Court held that a process or operation is only to be regarded as 'substantial' if it results in 'properties and a composition' which the product did not possess before. Besides qualitative change, however, the commercial value added to a product by its last processing can also be a decisive criterion in determining the origin of goods (Case C-26/88 *Brother* [1989] ECR 4253).

JÖRG MONAR

*Recommended reading*
Zairnis *EC Rules on Origin* (1992) Wiley Chancery.
Waer 'European Community rules on origin' in Vermulst (ed) *Rules of Origin in International Trade* (1994) University of Michigan Press, p 85.

**SCHENGEN AGREEMENTS** The Schengen Agreement on the gradual abolition of checks at the common borders of France, the

Federal Republic of Germany, and the Benelux countries of 14 June 1985 (Schengen I) was the result of a symbolic Franco-German move to relax the checks at their common border (see also **border controls**). This agreement was implemented by the Convention Applying the Schengen Agreement of 19 June 1990 between the same five contracting parties (Schengen II). This last Convention came into force on 1 September 1993 and was finally being applied as from 26 March 1995 among the five founding Member States as well as Spain and Portugal, which have acceded to both instruments. Italy and Greece, although also having acceded to the Schengen instruments, are excluded from the application until these parties have met certain conditions concerning the control of their external borders and administrative infrastructures. Austria has acceded to Schengen II by Agreement of 20 April 1995. Protocols of accession will presumably be signed by Denmark, Sweden and Finland in December 1996. An Agreement on Co-operation with Norway and Iceland (the other partners in the Nordic Council) is in the making, thus ensuring a uniform position of all Nordic States, notwithstanding Article 140 Schengen II, which allows only EC Member States to become a party to the Schengen Agreements.

Although the instruments state as their objectives as being to bring about the abolition of checks on the movement of persons at their common borders and facilitating the transport and movement of goods, in line with the establishment of an **Internal Market** characterised by an area without internal frontiers, they have actually increased checks and controls, especially at the external borders of the 'Schengen area'.

Schengen II consists of eight titles, concerning respectively Definitions (Title I); the Abolition of Checks at Internal Borders and Movement of Persons (Title II); Policy and Security (Title III); the Schengen Information System (Title IV); Transport and Movement of Goods (Title V); Protection of Personal Data (Title VI); the Establishment of an Executive Committee (Title VII); and Final Provisions (Title VIII).

Certain topics are dealt with at the same time and in a similar way in other 'paracommunitarian' Conventions: the Convention Determining the State Responsible for Examining Applications for **Asylum**, Dublin, 15 June 1990 (in force as per 1 November 1996), covers the same ground as Chapter 7 of Title II of Schengen II. According to a Protocol of 26 April 1994, concluded in Bonn, the Chapter on asylum in Schengen II is replaced by the Dublin Convention as from its entry into force. Similarly, the Draft Convention on Checks at the External Borders of the EC Member States more or less duplicates large parts of Schengen II, but its passage towards formal conclusion was blocked by a controversy between Great Britain and Spain about Gibraltar.

Several Readmission Agreements have been concluded between the Schengen countries and states at the external borders of the 'Schengenland', obliging these states, such as Poland, to readmit persons who have crossed the common border in an irregular way. Thus, a *'cordon sanitaire'* as it is commonly called, is built around the Schengen area.

Problems concerning the Schengen instruments include: the secrecy surrounding their drafting; the uneasy relationship with the Geneva Refugees Convention of 1951; the lack of **harmonised** substantive rules on asylum in the Member States; the lack of democratic and judicial control over official activity in pursuance of Schengen II; and the uncertain status of decisions of the Executive Committee and their place in democratic societies. France reintroduced systematic checks at all borders, including all airports for intra-Schengen flights, following terrorist activity in Paris in the summer of 1995; this measure was also intended as a warning towards The Netherlands, which is seen by the French government as a drug state.

HANS ULRICH JESSURUN D'OLIVEIRA

*Recommended reading*
Meijers et al *Schengen: Internationalisation of Central Chapters of the Law of Aliens, Refugees, Privacy, Security and the Police* (1992) NJCM boekerij, Leiden.
Schermers et al (eds) *Free Movement of Persons in Europe. Legal Problems and Experiences* (1993) Asser Institute Colloquium on European Law, Session XXI, Martinus Nijhoff.

**SEAT OF THE INSTITUTIONS** The Treaties establishing the **European Community**, the **European Coal and Steel Community** and the **European Atomic Energy Community** each provide that the seat of the institutions 'shall be determined by common accord of the Governments of the Member States' (Articles 216 EC, 77 ECSC and 189 Euratom). Three decisions have been adopted to give effect to the compromises on political and linguistic grounds which the Member States have agreed.

The Decision of 8 April 1965 (OJ 152 13.7.67 p 18) sets out an interim compromise, by which the seat of none of the institutions was allocated to a Member State or city. However, the Decision of 12 December 1992 (OJ C341 23.12.92 p 1) adopted the 1965 solutions and gave effect to the agreement reached at the Edinburgh European Council on 12 December 1992. It states that the **Council**, the **Commission** and the **Economic and Social Committee** shall have their seats in Brussels. However, the Council shall hold its meetings in Luxembourg during the months of April, June and October. Similarly, the Commission shall locate certain ECSC and Euratom departments, the Office for Official Publications and the Statistical Office in Luxembourg. The **Court of Justice** and the **Court of First Instance**, the **Court of Auditors** and the **European Investment Bank** shall have their seats in Luxembourg.

The **European Parliament** has its seat in Strasbourg, where it is required to hold 12 periods of monthly plenary sessions. Additional plenary sessions and its committees meet in Brussels, whilst its secretariat remains in Luxembourg. The delicate nature of this costly compromise is highlighted by the recent introduction of an **action of**

**annulment** by France of the European Parliament's calendar for 1996 (Case C-345/95 *France v European Parliament* OJ C351 30.12.95 p 7). France argues that by providing for only 11 sessions in Strasbourg, the 1996 calendar is invalid.

As to other bodies and departments, the Decision of 1992 provided for priority to be given to Member States who did not provide the sites for Community institutions. Accordingly, the locations for the seat of the following institutions were allocated by a decision of 29 October 1993 (OJ C323 30.12.93 p 1): the European Environmental Agency in Copenhagen; the European Training Foundation in Turin; the Office for Veterinary and Plant Health Inspection and Control in Ireland (Dublin); the European Monitoring Centre for Drugs and Drug Addiction in Lisbon; the European Agency for the Evaluation of Medicinal Products in London; the Agency for Health and Safety at Work in Spain (Bilbao); the European Monetary Institute and the future European Central Bank in Frankfurt; the Office for Harmonization in the Internal Market (Trade Marks, Designs and Models) in Spain (Alicante); and Europol and the Europol Drugs Unit in The Hague. Further to a declaration in annex to this decision, the European Centre for the Development of Vocational Training was moved to Thessaloniki (Council Regulation (EEC) 1131/94 (OJ L127 19.5.94 p 1)).

WILLIAM ROBINSON

*Recommended reading*
Lasok & Bridge *Law and Institutions of the European Union* (6th edn, 1994) Butterworths.
Weatherill & Beaumont *EC Law* (1993) Penguin.


**SERVICES** See **free movement of services**.


**SEX EQUALITY** See **equal pay, equal treatment, social security, discrimination** and **equality**.


**SINGLE EUROPEAN ACT** This is the Treaty signed by the 12 Member States of the European Communities on 17 and 28 February 1986, amending the **ECSC**, EEC and **Euratom** Treaties and laying down provisions on European political co-operation. The Act entered into force on 1 July 1987 (OJ L169 29.6.87 p 1). In substance, it deals with the following four matters.

*Institutional reform* Provisions are laid down with a view to making the institutional structure of the Communities more efficient and more democratic. For the first time, Treaty status was conferred on the **European Council** and the use of the title '**European Parliament**' was officially recognised. A new co-operation procedure was introduced in specified cases giving the European Parliament increased influence in the legislative process, although not a real power of co-decision, except with regard to the conclusion of accession Treaties and association agreements. **Qualified majority voting** was extended within the **Council**, particularly in respect of measures necessary for the establishment and functioning of the Internal Market. The Council is to confer implementing powers on the Commission. A new **Court of First Instance** was to be attached to the Court of Justice to relieve it of some of its increased workload. All the institutional changes except those relating to the Court of Justice affect the E(E)C Treaty alone.

*An Internal Market* comprising an area without internal frontiers, was to be progressively established by 31 December 1992. To this end, a number of provisions are amended in the EEC Treaty.

*Five new policies* and areas of activity are formally included in the EEC Treaty, such as: co-operation in economic and monetary policy; **social policy**; economic and social **cohesion**; common research and technological development policy; and action on the protection of the **environment**.

*European political co-operation* was given, for the first time, a Treaty basis, although it was not made an integral part of Community law.

AKOS G TOTH

*Recommended reading*
Glaesner 'The Single European Act' (1986) 6 Yearbook of European Law 283.
Toth *The Oxford Encyclopaedia of European Community Law* vol I, *Institutional Law* (1990) Oxford University Press, p 480.

**SINGLE INSTITUTIONAL FRAMEWORK** See **institutions**.

**SINGLE MARKET** See **Internal Market**.

**SOCIAL POLICY** European social policy is a unique synthesis of the national laws of the Member States. Proposals inspired by national experience are channelled through the EU legislative process and undergo transformation to adapt them to different national systems.

The **ECSC** Treaty included social provisions to mitigate the effects of the reorganisation of the coal and steel industries. The EEC Treaty, however, reflected the view that the benefits of the common market would provide the desired improvement in living and working conditions without the need for active intervention by the EC institutions.

The common market's mandatory freedom of movement for workers led to measures providing for equal treatment of migrant workers and their families with regard to education, housing and social security, but otherwise, the development of European social policy was haphazard. It reflected exceptional Treaty provisions, such as Article 119 E(E)C, guaranteeing **equal pay** for men and women, or spasmodic political interventions, such as the First Social Action Programme of 1974.

On these narrow bases, the Community did construct an impressive edifice of law and social policy. In particular, the concept of equal opportunities in the EC Treaty expanded from the original concept of direct and intentional **discrimination** in the form of less favourable treatment of women by reason of their sex, to include, among others, indirect discrimination, positive action, critical review of protective legislation, pregnancy, maternity and childcare and sexual harassment. The scope of the concept expanded beyond pay to include discrimination in access to work, conditions of work, vocational training, **pensions**, both public and private, and social welfare.

Pressures to develop a coherent European social policy began to emerge alongside the adoption of the **Internal Market** programme, and the momentum it generated towards further European integration. The **Single European Act** inserted a new Article 118a EC, which allowed for Directives on the working environment to be approved by qualified majority voting. A Framework Directive (Council Directive (EEC) 89/391 (OJ L183 29.6.89 p 1)) on **health and safety** laid the foundations of a European social policy based on prevention (obligatory risk assessments) and participation by workers and their representatives.

The **Community Charter of Fundamental Social Rights of Workers** of December 1989, approved by 11 Member States, excepting the United Kingdom, led to a variety of new social policy measures. But the constraints of the EC Treaty's narrow social competences and requirement of unanimous voting continued to frustrate progress.

The 11 Member States signatory to the Community Charter persisted in the attempt to develop a European social policy during the negotiations preceding the Maastricht Summit of December 1991. A crucial intervention was made by the social partners, organisations of labour and management at European level. During 1991 negotiations led to an Agreement of 31 October 1991 between the social partners proposing new Articles of the Treaty. These were adopted almost entirely by the 11 Member States as the Agreement annexed to the **Social Policy Protocol** to the **Treaty on European Union**.

As a result, there are currently two legal frameworks for European social policy. The first is the EC Treaty, which applies to all Member States. The second is the TEU, which includes a Protocol on Social Policy by which all the Member States but one, the United Kingdom, are authorised to use a different legal framework embodied in the Agreement annexed to the Protocol. This differs from the EC Treaty in two fundamental respects.

273

First, the new social competences in the Agreement are much wider than those of the EC Treaty. For example, they provide the legal basis for adoption of measures by **qualified majority voting** in the field of 'working conditions', and by unanimous voting in such fields as 'protection of workers where their employment contract is terminated', and 'representation and collective defence of the interests of workers and employers, including co-determination'. The Member States, excluding the United Kingdom, now have the legal **competence** to create a European social policy at EU level which goes beyond the confines of sex equality and health and safety.

Second, a role for the social partners at EU level in formulating EU labour law is introduced. The **Commission** is obliged to consult labour and management 'on the possible direction of Community action' and 'on the content of [any] envisaged proposal'. On the occasion of such consultation, the social partners may initiate the process of social dialogue which may lead to contractual relations, including agreements.

The procedure is that of 'bargaining in the shadow of the law'. Negotiations between the social partners will be influenced by the prospect of legislative action.

If the social partners at EC level reach agreements, Member States are obliged to implement these agreements within their national legal orders. This may be by articulation with national procedures and practices, or by virtue of a **Council** decision on a proposal from the Commission embodying the agreement. The first such European collective agreement is given legal effect in Council Directive (EC) 96/34 (OJ L145 19.6.96 p 1) on parental leave.

The **Court of Justice** has also been a dynamic force through a 'spillover' effect: legislative measures constrained by narrow competences to specific issues tend to spill over into related areas. For example, the requirement in Council Directives (EEC) 75/129 (OJ L48 22.2.75 p 29) and 77/187 (OJ L61 5.3.77 p 26) to consult workers' representatives in specific circumstances (collective dismissals, transfers of undertakings; see **employment protection**) was interpreted to imply the existence of workers' representatives and hence legislation to that effect (Cases C-382/92 & C-383/92 *Commission v UK* [1994] ECR I-2435, 2479). The protection in the Working Time Directive (Council Directive (EEC) 93/104 (OJ L307 13.12.93 p 18)) from disadvantage of an individual employee refusing to work more than an average 48 hours weekly is likely to spill over to influence the law concerned with discipline and dismissal at work (see Case C-84/94 *UK v Council*, judgment of 12 November 1996 (not yet reported)).

The future of European social policy is likely to be along the path indicated by the Maastricht Protocol. The other Member States clearly wish the United Kingdom to join the new social policy initiatives. The United Kingdom retains the right to refuse to take part. Until it joins, however, European social policy will develop along the path dictated by the cumulative experience of the other Member States.

BRIAN BERCUSSON

*Recommended reading*
Kennor (ed) *Trends in European Social Policy* (1995) Dartmouth.
Bercusson *European Labour Law* (1996) Butterworths.


**SOCIAL POLICY PROTOCOL AND AGREEMENT** Unable to agree on a new 'Social Chapter' for the EC at the negotiations culminating in the **Treaty on European Union**, all the Member States at that time agreed, in the Social Policy Protocol, to annex a Social Policy Agreement (to which the United Kingdom is not a party) to the EC Treaty. The Protocol authorises the Member States, with the exception of the United Kingdom, to utilise the Community's institutions, procedures and mechanisms in order to enact provisions of **social policy**.

The Agreement builds upon the **Community Charter of Fundamental Social Rights of Workers** (1989). The objectives of the Agreement are the promotion of **employment**, including development of human resources, improvements to living and working conditions, sex equality at work and the combating of social exclusion. The Agreement provides a legal basis for action, by means of Directives, in those areas, in accordance with either the co-decision procedure or unanimity in **Council** (excluding the relevant Minister of the United Kingdom). A central role is given to dialogue between the social partners, who may be entrusted with the implementation of Directives adopted pursuant to the Agreement.

The Protocol is 'an integral part' of the Treaty (Article 239 EC). The Agreement, as an Annex to, or integral part of, the Protocol, appears to share its status. Consequently, the Agreement is not open to **judicial review**, and provisions enacted under the Agreement are not intergovernmental action, but constitute part of **Community law**, albeit inapplicable in one of the Member States. The Protocol and Agreement are expressly stated to be without prejudice to the *acquis communautaire*: their provisions supplement, rather than replace, the Treaty's social policy provisions. It has been the practice for the Commission to proceed initially according to the Treaty's social policy provisions, resorting to the Agreement only where the requisite majority is not otherwise available in Council.

TAMARA K HERVEY

*Recommended reading*
Watson 'Social Policy after Maastricht' (1993) 30 CMLRev 481–513.
Whiteford 'Social Policy after Maastricht' (1993) 18 ELRev 202–222.


**SOCIAL SECURITY** The principle of **free movement of persons** would be of little practical utility without co-ordination of the social security systems of the Member States. People would be reluctant to work in other Member States if their entitlement, or that of their dependants, to benefits in respect for example of sickness or unemployment were to be thereby jeopardised, or if they were to be precluded from exporting benefits on return to their home state after paying contributions in a host state.

Article 51 EC therefore empowers the **Council** to adopt such measures in the field of social security as are necessary to secure freedom of movement, in particular to ensure the 'aggregation, for the purpose of acquiring and retaining the right to benefit and of calculating the amount of benefit, of all periods taken into account under the laws of the several countries' and the 'payment of benefits to persons resident in the territories of Member States'. Council Regulation (EEC) 1408/71 (OJ Sp Ed 1971 (II) p 416, as amended by Council Regulation (EEC) 2001/83 (OJ L230 22.8.83 p 6) and Council Regulation (EEC) 1249/92 (OJ L136 19.5.92 p 28)), enacted in pursuance of this power, contains complex provisions designed to achieve these aims. It does not attempt the enormous task of **harmonising** the laws of the Member States, but rather co-ordinates their provisions so that nationality and residence do not adversely affect the rights of migrants. The cost of funding benefits is apportioned equitably amongst the states in which the migrant has paid contributions. The Regulation covers employed and self-employed persons who are or have been subject to the legislation of a Member State and who are nationals of a Member State, stateless persons and refugees residing within the territory of a Member State, and the families and survivors of such persons (Article 2(1)); the category of 'employed' persons is wider than that of 'workers' for the purposes of Article 48 since the Regulation extends to persons 'insured, compulsorily or on an optional continued basis, for one or more of the contingencies covered by the branches of a social security scheme for employed or self-employed persons' (Article 1(a)); it can therefore extend to those in the territory of other Member States for non-work purposes, such as holidays (Case 44/65 *Maison Singer* [1965] ECR 965). It applies to benefits, whether contributory or non-contributory, in respect of sickness, maternity, invalidity, old age, survivors, accidents at work, occupational diseases, death, unemployment; and family (Article 4(1)). The Regulation prohibits all **discrimination**, both direct and indirect (see **equal treatment**), in relation to nationality or residence (Article 3).

Council Directive (EEC) 79/7 (OJ L6 10.1.79 p 24) applies the principle of sex equality in social security provision to 'the working population, including self-employed persons, workers and self-employed persons whose activity is interrupted by illness, accident or involuntary unemployment', 'persons seeking employment' and 'retired or invalided workers and self-employed persons' (Article 2). Provided that the claimant's work is interrupted by one of the risks specified, it does not matter that that risk did not materialise in relation specifically to the claimant (Case 150/85 *Drake* [1986] ECR 1995). However, if work is not 'interrupted' by one of these risks, the provision is inapplicable, even if the claimant is in fact unable to work (Cases 48/88, 106/88 & 107/88 *Acteberg* [1989] ECR 1963). The instrument applies to statutory schemes protecting against sickness, invalidity, old age, accidents at work, occupational diseases, unemployment and social assistance (so far as the last is intended to supplement or replace the other schemes referred to) (Article 3). An exception is provided in relation to state pensionable age (Article 7(1)(a)) and occupational schemes are the subject of separate provision (Council Directive (EEC) 86/378 (OJ L225 12.8.86 p 40)).

EVELYN ELLIS

*Recommended reading*
Bonner, Hooker & White *Non-Means Tested Benefits: the Legislation* (1994) Sweet & Maxwell.
Wyatt & Dashwood *European Community Law* (3rd edn, 1993) Sweet & Maxwell, ch 11.

**SOFT LAW** 'Soft law' refers to rules of conduct which, in principle, have no legally binding force but which nevertheless may have practical effects. It is used frequently by all EU and EC **institutions**, which in this respect resemble national administrative authorities or international organisations. Community soft law also includes numerous joint declarations and **interinstitutional agreements**, usually between the **Council**, the **Commission** and the **European Parliament**.

Some types of soft law are provided by the EC Treaty: for example, Article 189 EC refers to recommendations and opinions. Though not legally binding, recommendations have been given legal effect by the Court of Justice, to the extent that national courts must take them into account when they cast light on the interpretation of national measures adopted in order to implement them, or where they are designed to supplement binding EC provisions (Case C-322/88 *Grimaldi* [1989] ECR 4407).

Other types of soft law have been elaborated by the EC institutions, particularly the Commission. They may be used in matters concerning which the Community has legal authority to act, within the limits of the discretion of the institution concerned, and so long as the soft law does not impose any new obligations on Member States (Case C-366/88 *France v Commission* [1990] ECR I-3571; Case C-303/90 *France v Commission* [1991] ECR I-5315).

Soft law is also used, more problematically, to express views or issue guidelines on matters concerning which the division of powers between the EC and the Member States is not entirely clear, or which, strictly speaking, may lie outside the power of a specific institution to take binding legislation. Examples include the Commission codes of conduct with regard to **state aid,** motor vehicles or synthetic fibres (see Case C-313/90 *Comité international de la rayonne et des fibres synthétiques (CIRFS) v Commission* [1993] ECR I-1125). The continued efficacy of such soft law depends on a measure of consensus among the Member States not to contest the EC institution's position.

FRANCIS SNYDER

*Recommended reading*
Snyder 'The Effectiveness of European Community Law: Institutions, Processes, Tools and Techniques' (1993) 56 MLR 19.
Wellens & Borchardt 'Soft Law in European Community Law' (1989) 14 ELRev 267.

**SOVEREIGNTY** Sovereignty refers to the independence and autonomy of a nation state and its right to self-government within its own jurisdiction. From sovereignty, legal validity flows and the sovereign legal power is usually represented in a basic law taking the form of a written constitution. In the United Kingdom, the sovereign legal power is historically represented by the legal omnicompetence of the Crown in Parliament: that no law is above parliamentary legislation and that Parliament can make or unmake any law whatsoever. Furthermore, obligations flowing from international treaties cannot *ipso facto* become part of domestic law unless implemented by legislation or other legislative instrument approved by Parliament. In the European Community, the **Court of Justice** has interpreted sovereignty to mean the supremacy of the Community Treaties, as amended, and the sovereignty of the institutions created under the Treaties over the governing institutions of Member States in matters covered by Communities. The ECJ is sovereign in the interpretation of Community law and the Community itself is 'supranational' – an entity above the Contracting States.

In Case 26/62 *Van Gend en Loos* [1963] ECR 1 the ECJ stated that the objectives of the E(E)C Treaty imply that the Treaty is more than an agreement which 'merely creates obligations between Member States'. The Treaty concerns governments *and* people and creates institutions endowed with sovereign rights whose exercise affects both Member States *and* people. The Community was a 'new legal order of international law for the benefit of which states have limited their sovereign rights'. The ECJ believed that such limitations took place within limited fields, although it has subsequently expressed the opinion they took place in 'ever wider fields'. In Case 6/64 *Costa v ENEL* [1964] ECR 585 the Community was described as one of 'unlimited duration' having its own **institutions,** its own personality, its own legal capacity and power of legal representation on the international plane and, more particularly, real powers stemming from a limitation of sovereignty or a transfer of powers from the Member States to the Community the former of which have created a body of law which is binding over both their nationals and themselves in rights and obligations arising under the Treaty. Such a transfer, the ECJ held, 'carries with it a permanent limitation of sovereign rights'.

It follows from this that Community law overrides the basic constitutional law of a Member State. This has presented problems to those states who feel that their constitutions afford special and fuller **human rights protection** than does the EC Treaty or which give protection to democratic forms of government that cannot be overridden by Treaties. The ECJ has argued that 'respect for fundamental rights forms an integral part of the **general principles** of law protected by the Court of Justice'. 'The protection of such rights . . . must be ensured within the structures and objectives of the EC' (Case 11/70 *Internationale Handelsgesellschaft* [1970] ECR 1125).

On joining the Community, a Member State is obliged to make provision for the application of EC law over national law. In states following a monist tradition appropriate provisions of EC law become part of national law. Or, powers may be transferred to the EC under constitutional provisions or legal measures as in those states that follow a dualist tradition. In the United Kingdom, transfer of sovereignty was achieved by the **European Communities Act** 1972, as amended.

However, ambiguity may be present in the manner of transfer because it is not always clear whether there has been a complete transfer of sovereignty which is absolute within limited but ever widening spheres, or whether there has been a delegation which may be conferred for a potentially limited duration and even withdrawn. Community law stipulates that only a complete transfer satisfies the terms of membership. In the United Kingdom the courts have acknowledged that Parliament retains the right to repudiate the Treaty or any of its provisions – 'a prospect growing ever fainter as time passes' (per Lord Denning in *Macarthys v Smith* [1979] 3 All ER 325). And in *R v Secretary of State, ex p Rees Mogg* [1994] 1 All ER 457, concerning an unsuccessful challenge to the ratification of the Maastricht Treaty, Lloyd LJ stated (at 467) that it was under section 2(1) of the European Communities Act 1972 'by which alone Community treaties have force in domestic law'. Here as elsewhere, however, abstract legal theory must give way to political realities.

PATRICK BIRKINSHAW

*Recommended reading*
Hartley *Foundations of European Community Law* (3rd edn, 1994) Oxford University Press, ch 8.
Weatherill & Beaumont *EC Law* (1993) Penguin, ch 12.

**STATE AID** The EC Treaty rules on state aid complement those concerning the creation of an **Internal Market** and the protection of effective competition between private undertakings. They do not seek to abolish the provision of aid by Member States to undertakings altogether, but to ensure that such aid is granted under Community supervision.

Article 92(1) EC provides that aid 'granted by a Member State or through state resources' which affects trade between Member States and which distorts or threatens to distort competition 'by favouring certain undertakings or the production of certain goods' is prohibited unless authorised in accordance with the specific EC Treaty rules governing such aid.

The concept of aid has been interpreted very widely and can include loans on favourable terms, guarantees, tax write-offs, equity injections and subsidies. The 'private investor test' has been developed by the **Commission** in deciding whether aid is involved with respect to Member State assistance to publicly-owned undertakings in particular, by comparing the behaviour of the Member State in question with that which a private investor would find acceptable. The reference to 'state resources' has also been interpreted widely to include public bodies established by the state as well as private bodies through whom state resources are administered. With respect to the distortion of competition, the **Court of Justice** has held that where state aid strengthens the position of an undertaking compared with other undertakings competing in intra-Community trade, this has an effect on competition (Case 730/79 *Philip Morris v Commission* [1980] ECR 2671, para 11).

Article 92(2) EC sets out some limited mandatory exceptions to the general prohibition in Article 92(1) EC, such as aid to repair damage caused by natural disasters. Aid falling within these exceptions is deemed to be automatically compatible with the common market, although it is generally considered that such aid must still be notified to the Commission to enable it to verify whether the aid meets the criteria of Article 92(2) EC. Article 92(3) EC is far more significant in practice, as it sets out certain types of aid, in particular regional aid and aid to specific sectors of the economy, which *may* be considered compatible with the common market but which may only be granted by Member States if duly authorised.

To this end, the Member States are obliged to inform the Commission of any plans to grant or alter aid (Article 93(3) EC). The Court of Justice has confirmed on a number of occasions that Article 93(3) is directly effective (see, for example, Case 120/73 *Lorenz v Germany* [1973] ECR 1471). The Commission undertakes a preliminary investigation, which lasts approximately two months (although some aid is dealt with more quickly under an accelerated procedure). If the Commission has concerns about the aid, it initiates an in-depth investigation, which includes the consultation of third parties. It may eventually decide to prohibit the aid altogether, or to allow it subject to conditions. In recent years, litigation before the **Court of First Instance** and the Court of Justice over state aid decisions has become increasingly common, as potential beneficiaries and Member States challenge Commission decisions prohibiting aid, and third parties challenge the granting of aid to their competitors.

New aid which is not notified to the Commission is invalid (see Case C-354/90 *FNCEPA v France* [1991] ECR I-5505). The Commission investigates many instances of unnotified aid every year, and where it decides that the aid is incompatible with the common market, it may take a decision requiring repayment of the aid already disbursed, together with interest. Beneficiaries of aid should satisfy themselves beforehand as to the lawfulness of the aid received, as they do not, in principle, have a legitimate expectation that aid granted illegally will not be recovered (Case C-5/89 *BUG-Alutechnik* [1990] ECR I-3437). While the Commission is examining the unnotified aid, after giving the Member State concerned an opportunity to comment, it may also take an interim decision requiring suspension of further aid payments pending its final decision. If the Member State fails to comply, the Commission may bring the matter directly before the Court of Justice by applying for a declaration that such payment amounts to an infringement of the EC Treaty (see Article 93(2) EC and Case C-301/87 *Boussac* [1990] ECR I-307).

The Commission also keeps existing aid schemes under review in co-operation with the Member States (Article 93(1)). Existing aid constitutes pre-Treaty or pre-accession aid measures, as well as schemes which have been approved by the Commission. The Commission may still require the alteration or abolition of such schemes, but any decision taken will have prospective effect only.

National courts also have certain powers with respect to state aid; although they cannot decide on the compatibility of an aid with the common market, they can decide whether or not a measure constitutes an aid and they must provide appropriate remedies where aid has been granted in breach of a Member State's notification obligation under Article 93(3) EC (see *FNCEPA*).

Article 94 EC empowers the **Council of Ministers**, inter alia, to make appropriate Regulations for the application of Articles 92 and 93. To date, there has been very little formal legislation, although the Commission has published a series of notices and communications in order to provide guidance on its authorisation procedures, as well as its policies concerning specific types of aid.

EMER FINNEGAN

*Recommended reading*
Bellamy & Child *Common Market Law of Competition* (1993) Sweet & Maxwell.
Freeman & Whish (eds) *Competition Law* (1996) Butterworths.

**STATE MONOPOLIES** The EC Treaty contains two specific provisions regarding the operation of public monopolies. Article 37 EC concerns the progressive adjustment of state monopolies of a commercial character so as to ensure that there exists no discrimination between nationals of Member States regarding the conditions under which goods are procured and marketed. Article 90 EC concerns the balanced application of the Treaty's non-**discrimination** and **competition** rules to undertakings to which Member States grant special or exclusive rights.

Article 37 refers specifically to the **free movement of goods**. It can not be applied, for example, to the **free movement of services** (Case C-17/94 *Gervais* [1995] ECR I-4353). It applies widely to 'any body through which a Member State, in law or in fact, either directly or indirectly supervises, determines or appreciably influences imports or exports between Member States' and includes bodies with an exclusive right to import or export a particular good (Case 59/75 *Manghera* [1976] ECR 91). It is clear that such bodies are capable of obstructing the free movement of goods. Article 37 requires Member States to eliminate discrimination on the grounds of nationality, prohibits any new national measures which are contrary to this principle and is directly effective (see **direct effect**). Finally, the Commission has power under Article 37(6) to adopt recommendations as to the achievement of the adjustments required by the Article.

Article 37 is of particular interest in the field of state monopolies of a commercial character in the tobacco and alcohol markets. No judgment of the **Court of Justice** has, to date, found such markets incompatible with Article 37, particularly due to the exercise of monopoly rights not being in issue. However, two cases pending before the Court of Justice are of special interest. First, the Swedish alcohol retail authorisation monopoly has been challenged solely on the grounds of Articles 30 and 37 EC (Case C-189/95 *Franzén* OJ C208 12.8.95 p 14). Second, the Spanish tobacco monopoly is alleged to be contrary to, inter alia, Articles 37 and 90 EC in Case C-145/94 *Rubio* (OJ C202 23.7.94 p 7).

Article 90 EC forms the pivot between several competing policies, including **competition**, **social** and **industrial** policies. Member State management or direction of certain economic entities, particularly in the fields of 'natural monopolies', and the grant of monopolistic or special powers to such entities are at first glance at odds with the Treaty's competition policy. Article 90 exists to provide a balance between these competing interests, and provides legislative power to the Commission in this area.

Article 90 consists of three paragraphs which must be read as a whole. Article 90(1) deals with public undertakings and undertakings to which Member States grant special or exclusive rights and requires the Member States, in granting such rights, to comply with the rules on non-discrimination and competition. Article 90(2) deals with undertakings, whether public or private, entrusted with the operation of services of general economic interest or having the character of a revenue producing monopoly. These undertakings are to be subject to the rules in the Treaty, in particular the rules on competition, but only in so far as the application of such rules does not obstruct the performance of the particular public interest tasks assigned to them. Article 90(3) provides the power for Commission legislation (decisions or Directives addressed to the Member States) to ensure the application of the article.

The approach of the Court of Justice when interpreting Article 90 has not been entirely consistent. Two extreme interpretations of the Article have been advocated before it. The first interpretation, argued by France in Case C-202/88 *France v Commission* [1991] ECR I-1223, is that Member States have exclusive competence in relation to the grant of legal monopolies. The Court of Justice firmly rejected this approach (para 22). The second interpretation approaches Article 90 from a diametrically opposed position. According to this interpretation, the mere creation of a legal monopoly is sufficient to breach Article 90(1). Although glimpses of this approach may be found in Case C-260/89 *ERT* [1991] ECR I-2925 and Case C-179/90 *Merci* [1991] ECR I-5889, it would deprive Article 90 of any useful effect and for that reason should be rejected.

Although these extreme positions may be rejected, the Court of Justice has not conclusively determined from which fundamental premise it should start its analysis under Article 90. In certain cases (Cases C-41/90 *Höfner v Macrotron* [1991] ECR I-1979; C-323/93 *La Crespelle* [1994] ECR I-5077; and C-387/93 *Banchero* [1995] I-4663) the Court held that Member States may grant legal monopolies but they must not create a situation in which operation of the monopoly has the *necessary* consequence of contravening the competition rules. The point of departure was therefore the legality of Member State action, which must be tempered by consideration for the competition rules. On the other hand, in certain other cases (Case C-230/91, *Corbeau* [1993] ECR I-2533; Case 155/73 *Sacchi* [1974] ECR 409), the Court found that Member States may create legal monopolies only where this is justified by a legitimate national objective and where the consequent restriction of competition is limited to what is necessary and proportional to achieve this objective. In these cases, the very grant of monopoly powers is itself conditional upon an evaluation of the potential restrictions on competition.

The Court has clearly established that the restrictive effect on competition resulting from the grant of a monopoly or special or exclusive rights must be proportional and necessary to the objective pursued by the Member State, whether that objective is social, industrial or economic. The theoretical approach of the Court of Justice is imprecise, although this may result from the sporadic and piecemeal nature by which such complex questions of sectoral policy arise before the Court.

In order that a wider Community approach could be adopted to the balance to be achieved between these competing policies, Article 90(3) provides the Commission with a specific but limited legislative power. As the power is limited, its use as a legal basis has been a source of continued litigation before the Court of Justice. Member States have argued that the correct legal basis should be either Article 100 EC, Article 100a EC or Article 87 EC. The Commission first adopted on the basis of Article 90(3) Commission Directive (EEC) 80/723 on the transparency of financial relations between Member States and public undertakings (OJ L195 29.7.80 p 35). France, Italy and the United Kingdom unsuccessfully challenged this Directive in Joined Cases 188-190/80 *France, Italy and the United Kingdom v Commission* [1982] ECR 2545.

The Commission has been particularly active in legislating in the **telecommunications** sector. It adopted Commission Directive (EEC) 88/301 on competition in the markets in telecommunications terminal equipment (OJ L131 27.5.88 p 73) and Commission Directive (EEC) 90/388 on competition in the markets for telecommunications services (OJ L192 24.7.90 p 10) as amended by Commission Directive (EC) 95/51 which extended its provisions to cable television networks (OJ L256 26.10.95 p 49). Each of these Directives has, or is, being challenged.

In *France v Commission* the Court struck down Article 7 of Directive 88/301 as the Commission had legislated in respect of anti-competitive behaviour by undertakings at their own initiative, rather than solely in respect of state measures. The Court, however, rejected in their entirety the challenges by Spain, Belgium and Italy to Directive 90/388 (Joined Cases C-271, 281, 289/90 *Spain, Belgium, Italy v Commission* [1992] ECR I-5833) and the actions brought by Spain and Portugal seeking the annulment of Directive 95/51 remain pending (Case C-11/96 *Spain v Commission* and C-12/96 *Portugal v Commission*, both at OJ C95 30.3.96 p 5). The Court of Justice therefore remains embroiled in the predominantly policy sphere of the treatment of state monopolies in the Member States.

WILLIAM ROBINSON

*Recommended reading*
Edward & Hoskins 'Article 90: Deregulation and EC Law. Reflections arising from the XVI FIDE Conference' (1995) 32 CMLRev 157.
Gardner 'The Velvet Revolution: Article 90 and the Triumph of the Free Market in Europe's Regulated Sectors' (1995) 16 ECLR 78.

**STUDENTS** Under the original Treaty of Rome it appeared that the rights of students to choose to study outside their countries within Europe was dependent on the goodwill of recipient states and their higher education institutions. This resulted from their lack of status in **Community law**, not being workers as such (ie not economically active), nor recipients of services (Case 263/86 *Humbel* [1988] ECR 5365) (see **education policy**).

As the Community expanded its horizons generally, and especially in the sphere of educational policy, significantly aided by the **Court of Justice**, so students were granted rights of mobility by the Court of Justice (Case 66/85 *Lawrie Blum* [1986] ECR 2121; Case C-357/89 *Raulin* [1992] ECR I-1027), rights now enshrined in Council Directive (EEC) 93/96 (OJ L317 18.12.93 p 59) on the right of residence for students (see **free movement of persons**). Some of the conditions of this Directive are arguably contrary to Article 6 EC, for example the requirement of an adequate income, or medical insurance, if these conditions are not required also of nationals.

Certain categories of students (migrant workers and their offspring) were granted rights of residence and rights of access to educational institutions as well as supplementary rights to educational grants (Case 9/74 *Donato Casagrande v Landeshaupt München* [1974] ECR 773; Joined Cases 389 & 390/87 *Echternach and Moritz v Netherlands Minister for Education and Science* [1989] ECR 723; Council Regulation (EEC) 1612/68 (OJ Sp Ed 1968 II p 475), Articles 7, 12; Council Directive (EEC) 77/486 (OJ L199 6.8.77 p 32). A less favoured category of students (Case 197/86 *Brown* [1988] ECR 3205) could migrate to study without the right to full educational benefits. The basis of this right prior to the Residence for Students Directive arose from Articles 7 and 128 EEC. Article 3 of Directive 93/96 maintains the *Brown* case law.

The key role played by the Court of Justice in increasing the rights of those studying is not in doubt. In the *Gravier, Barra, Blaizot* and *Humbel* cases (Case 293/83 *Gravier* [1985] ECR 593; Case 309/85 *Barra* [1988] ECR 355; Case 24/86 *Blaizot* [1988] ECR 379; Case 263/86 *Humbel* [1988] ECR 5365) the Court's broad interpretation of 'vocational training' in Article 128 EEC made the issue of access fall within Article 6 EC (then Article 7 EEC) thus disallowing any discrimination, whether direct or indirect, on grounds of nationality in admitting students. The assessment of academic credentials prior to admission to a course of study was certainly a national competence, and it is unlikely that the new Article 126 EC alters this conclusion (see **mutual recognition of diplomas**).

Students can benefit from many EC-supported activities such as cross-border access to courses or linguistic training (SOCRATES, Leonardo de Vinci; see also **education policy**). The fruits of their cross-border studies will enhance their ability to transfer professions across countries under the EC's provisions for the mutual recognition of qualifications.

JULIAN LONBAY

*Recommended reading*
Lonbay 'Education and the Law: the Community context' (1989) 14 ELRev 363.
Hartley 'Equal Treatment in Education' in Green, Hartley & Usher *Legal Foundations of the Single European Market* (1991) Oxford University Press.

**SUBSIDIARITY** The origins of subsidiarity lie in Catholic doctrine and in some national constitutional traditions such as the German Basic Law. However, it first overtly appeared in EC law in the Single European Act in relation to environmental matters. The TEU then introduced subsidiarity in Article B and established it as a general principle by inserting Article 3b into the EC Treaty:

> 'The Community shall act within the limits of the powers conferred upon it by the Treaty and of the objectives assigned to it therein.
>
> In areas which do not fall within its exclusive competence, the Community shall take action, in accordance with the principle of subsidiarity, only if and in so far as the objectives of the proposed action cannot be sufficiently achieved by the Member States and can therefore, by reason of the scale or effects of the proposed action, be better achieved by the Community.
>
> Any action by the Community shall not go beyond what is necessary to achieve the objectives of this Treaty.'

The first and last sentences of this provision appear merely to confirm existing principles, ie that the Community can only act within the powers attributed to it and that the general principle of proportionality applies to its acts.

The nub of subsidiarity is to be found in the second sentence of Article 3b, which betrays the tension between its political origins and functions and its precariousness as a legal principle. The political debates during the Maastricht negotiations about federalism and the relations between the centre and periphery led to the enactment of Article 3b. In the areas in which it applies, subsidiarity operates politically as a decentralising force and as a principle to be addressed in the law-making process.

Legally, subsidiarity must be applied in fields where the Community does not have exclusive competence. As a principle appearing in the body of the EC Treaty it binds Community **institutions** and is capable of giving rise to Article 173 **actions of annulment** where it is disregarded. However, the precise scope of Article 3b remains a matter of doubt because of the way in which it combines notions of both efficiency and effectiveness in establishing whether an activity should be undertaken by the Community or by the Member States.

The 1993 Interinstitutional Agreement on Procedures for Implementing the Principle of Subsidiarity requires that the Commission provides a justification for a proposed legislative measure in its explanatory memorandum in terms of subsidiarity. So too must any amendment by Council or Parliament if it involves more extensive Community action. The choice of legal instrument is also subject to the subsidiarity requirement.

The Court of Justice has yet to provide a detailed exposition of the scope and meaning of Article 3b. Uncertainty thus remains as to the extent of the review of law making that is possible by recourse to the subsidiarity principle. In other areas of the EC Treaty, such as Article 215, the Court has not intervened without there being some manifest error on the part of the Community institution. However, Article 3b may be interpreted as an invitation to consider whether a particular course of legislative action is necessary or the best one. The extent to which the Court takes up this type of inquiry will determine how intrusive subsidiarity is as a general legal principle.

Subsidiarity has made an impact in the practices within the legislative machinery. The paradox of the concept is that its looseness and fluidity are at once its political advantages and its legal complications.

MALCOLM ROSS

*Recommended reading*
Emiliou 'Subsidiarity: an effective barrier against the "enterprises of ambition"?' (1992) 17 ELRev 383.
Toth 'A legal analysis of subsidiarity' in O'Keeffe and Twomey (eds) *Legal Issues of the Maastricht Treaty* (1994) Wiley Chancery.

**SUPREMACY** The Treaty of Rome did not provide explicitly for the supremacy of Community law over the law of Member States. Such a doctrine flows from Community **sovereignty** and the limitation of Member States' sovereign rights.

Under Article 164 EC, the Court of Justice is charged with ensuring that 'in the interpretation and application of this Treaty the law is observed'. Under Article 177 EC, which provides for the reference by national courts to the Court of Justice of points of law in **preliminary rulings**, the Court of Justice shall have jurisdiction to interpret, inter alia, the Treaty and acts of relevant **institutions**, ie **Community law**. Under Articles 169 and 170 EC a Member State may be brought before the Court of Justice by the **Commission** or another Member State when it is alleged that it has breached Community law. Article 189 EC provides that Regulations are directly applicable in Member States. From this background the Court of Justice has fashioned a remarkable jurisprudence which has extended and makes more effective the scope of Community law, not only *vis-à-vis* Member States but also in relation to individuals.

In holding that Community law was supreme and that Treaty provisions may have **direct effect** in Member States' legal systems which national courts must respect, the Court of Justice invoked 'the spirit, the general scheme and the wording of those provisions' (Case 26/62 *Van Gend en Loos* [1963] ECR 1). The Court of Justice concluded that the Community constitutes a 'new legal order of international law' which 'not only imposes obligations on individuals but is also intended to confer upon them rights which become part of their legal heritage'. Such rights may arise not only expressly from the Treaty, but also 'by reason of obligations which the Treaty imposes in a clearly defined way upon individuals as well as upon Member States and upon the Institutions of the EC'. In other words, Treaty provisions will be directly effective when they are clear and unconditional and require no further action by the Member State. In Case 6/64 *Costa v ENEL* [1964] ECR 585 the Court of Justice affirmed that the Member States have created 'a body of law which binds both their nationals and themselves'. Community law made it impossible therefore for Member States to adopt a contradictory measure taking precedence over a legal system 'accepted by them on a basis of reciprocity'. To allow such would be to subvert the 'executive force' of Community law which cannot vary from one Member State to another. Treaty conditions would be contingent and not unconditional if a subsequent legal measure of a Member State could challenge their authority. 'The law stemming from the Treaty, an independent source of law, could not, because of its special and original nature, be overridden by domestic legal provisions, however framed, without being deprived of its character as Community law and without the legal basis of the Community being called into question.' It followed *Van Gend en Loos* in holding that under specified conditions, Articles of the Treaty could be directly effective in national legal systems and their courts.

In Case 11/70 *Internationale Handelsgesellschaft* [1970] ECR 1125 the Court of Justice emphasised that Community law by virtue of its independent nature, cannot be overridden by national law adding that not even an appeal to 'fundamental rights' could override Community law which itself respects such rights and which form an 'integral part of the general principles of law' and whose protection 'must be ensured within the structure and objectives of the Community' (see **human rights protection**).

From this it follows that national courts must enforce Community law and give full effect to it and they should not wait for annulment or repeal of inconsistent legal measures by domestic legislatures or constitutional organs (Case 106/77 *Simmenthal* [1978] ECR 629).

This was illustrated with dramatic effect in the United Kingdom when British legislation was in conflict with the Common **Fisheries Policy**. The House of Lords, after an initial refusal, issued an interim injunction against the Crown (the British government) disapplying an Act of Parliament which prima facie appeared to be in breach of Community law (*Factortame (No 2)* [1991] AC 603). The episode constituted a blow to the doctrine of parliamentary legislative supremacy. The creative attitude of the Court of Justice was exemplified when it held that Directives could be directly effective and invoked by individuals in national courts when the appropriate conditions were met despite Article 189's silence on this point and the existence of Article 169 (Case 41/74 *Van Duyn v Home Office* [1974] ECR 1337). However, Directives are only effective against the state or organs of the state and not against other individuals.

This qualification has been circumscribed to a large measure by rulings from the Court of Justice that statutes in a Member State –

whether enacted before or after the date of the Directive and even before the founding Treaty – have to be interpreted in the light of relevant Directives (Case C-106/89 *Marleasing* [1990] ECR I-4135; Case C-91/92 *Faccini Dori* [1994] I-3325) (see **indirect effect**). In perhaps one of the most far-reaching developments to date, the Court of Justice ruled in Cases C- 6/90 & 9/90 *Francovich* [1991] ECR I-5357 that where a Member State has failed to implement a Directive into the national legal order and where it is not directly effective, then, upon certain conditions, those injured by the non-implementation may sue the Member State for breach of Community law and the loss suffered (see **damages against Member States**). To hold otherwise would be to impair the full effectiveness of Community law (see *effet utile*) and would allow states to breach Article 5 EC, under which Member States are required to take all appropriate measures to ensure fulfilment of Community legal obligations. Serious breaches of Community law will result in successful actions by those injured by the breach where the laws that were broken were meant to protect individuals and the necessary causal link between breach and injury is established. In the case of laws conferring a legislative discretion, a Member State will itself be liable for breaches of law by its legislature which are in 'grave and manifest' disregard of its own discretion (Cases C-46/93 & 48/93 *Brasserie du Pêcheur and Factortame III* [1996] ECR I-1029).

On a variety of occasions the Court of Justice has held that a Member State must not obstruct the full realisation of Community rights whether by allowing domestic limitation periods to bar Community claims, by providing inadequate remedies for Community rights or by seeking to prevent a plaintiff invoking judicial remedies by ministerial *fiat* concerning national security (Case C-208/90 *Emmot* [1991] ECR I-4269; Case C-271/91 *Marshall (No 2)* [1993] ECR I-4367; and Case 222/84 *Johnston v Chief Constable of RUC* [1986] ECR 1651).

The jurisprudence of the Court of Justice has shown a vibrant and remarkable development in its articulation of the supremacy of Community law.

PATRICK BIRKINSHAW

*Recommended reading*
Cragi & de Búrca *EC Law* (1995) Oxford University Press, ch 6.
Weatherill & Beaumont *EC Law* (1993) Penguin, ch 12.

**TAXATION (DIRECT)** Unlike Article 99 TEU in the field of indirect tax, there is no legislative mandate for the **harmonisation** of direct taxes within the **European Union**. Such legislative activity as there has been derives its vires from the general mandate in Article 100, which permits the issue of Directives for the approximation of the laws of Members States which 'directly affect the establishment or functioning of the common market'. Despite the clear potential of tax as an area in which barriers to cross-border trade could be eliminated, attempts to reach agreement between the Member States on a policy of general harmonisation have failed. The Commission has been forced to withdraw no fewer than 30 legislative proposals after they stalled in the Council of Ministers due to the unanimity rule. Although the EC Treaty provides that such legislation may now be passed by way of a majority vote of the Council, fiscal measures were specifically excluded. By the time of the publication of the Ruding Report in 1992 the ideal of universal harmonisation had already given way to a more pragmatic approach on the part of the Commission.

The harmonisation of tax regimes has appeared on the Commission's political agenda at intervals since the establishment of the Community. The Neumark Report, published in 1962, elicited little in the way of legislative action. It was not until 1990 that ideals came to fruition in the form of Finance Ministers agreeing to implement two Directives and a Convention.

Council Directive (EEC) 90/434 concerns transactions associated with cross-border mergers and Council Directive (EEC) 90/435 deals with cross-border parents and subsidiaries. The former sets out to standardise tax reliefs available for certain forms of corporate reorganisation, while the latter requires that dividends paid between parent companies and subsidiaries in different Member States must be free from withholding taxes on payment and either tax exempt in the hands of the recipient or with credit for the tax paid by the subsidiary on its profits. These Directives became law on 1 January 1992. The Convention, adopted in 1990, obliges Member States to establish an arbitration procedure for transfer pricing. The Transfer Pricing Arbitration Convention came into force on 1 January 1995.

Two further Directives, the Interest and Royalties Directives and the Losses Directive, existed in draft. The former, which sought to abolish withholding tax on interest and royalties paid between Member States, was withdrawn because agreement could not be reached between the Member States. The Losses Directive aimed to allow the losses of a subsidiary in one Member State to be offset against the profits of a parent in another. While not yet formally withdrawn, the Directive has not proceeded beyond draft form and there is no indication that it will do so in the foreseeable future.

These measures are indicative of a more pragmatic approach to harmonisation, addressing specific distortions at national frontiers rather than seeking to impose a common system of direct taxation across the Union. This approach has been confirmed in a Commission working document published on 20 March 1996, in which the word 'harmonisation' is replaced by fiscal 'co-operation' and 'consultation'. The rather modest ambitions of the paper are to improve the transparency of European and national taxation measures (which means that such measures should be considered in the context of the EC Treaty's competition rules) and the definition of joint codes of conduct relating to the introduction of tax incentives in the Member

States. In the recent case *Finanzamt Köln-Altstadt v Schumacher* (Case C-279/93 [1995] ECR I-225) Advocate General Leger remarked that 'unlike VAT, direct taxation is at a purely embryonic stage of harmonization'. Given the clear reluctance of Finance Ministers to compromise national sovereignty in this arena, it is likely to remain so for some time.

Against this backdrop of legislative inertia, the **Court of Justice** has demonstrated that fundamental principles of EC law can override domestic tax rules where the latter conflict with the former. The case law is based on the fundamental principle of non-discrimination between Community nationals set out in Article 6 EC as applied to the so-called 'four freedoms': free circulation of goods, free movement of persons and right of establishment, freedom to provide services and free movement of capital (see **free movement of capital, goods, persons** and **services** and **freedom of establishment**).

There have been a number of important tax cases in recent years, the majority of which have concerned personal income tax. The Court has, in dealing with cases which concern the taxation of corporate entities, equated the concept of 'corporate seat' with that of the residence of natural persons. In Case 270/83 *Commission v France* [1986] ECR 273 the Court of Justice held that rules denying tax credits on dividends on shares held by branches or agencies of insurance companies based in other Member States were incompatible with Article 52 of the Treaty where such credits were available to French companies or French subsidiaries of non-French companies. It was unlawful for differential tax treatment to interfere with the right to choose to establish a business as either a branch or an agency. Yet the Court did concede that distinctions based on the location of a company or the place of residence of a natural person might be justifiable in an area such as tax law under certain conditions. Unfortunately, the Court did not go on to specify what those conditions were.

There was no equivocation in the decisions in Case C-330/91 *R v Commissioners of Inland Revenue, ex p Commerzbank AG* [1993] ECR I-4017 and Case C-1/93 *Halliburton Services BV v Staatsssecretaris van Financiën* [1994] ECR I-1137. In *Commerzbank* the Court held that the concept of the 'seat' of a company could be equated with the concept of nationality as regards individuals and on that basis found that the use of the criterion of residence for granting interest on refunded tax could lead to indirect discrimination and was thus in contravention of EC law. Similarly, in *Halliburton*, The Netherlands was found to be discriminatory in levying property transfer tax on a Dutch branch of a German company where, in the same circumstances, relief would have been available to a Dutch company.

In certain cases, the Court is prepared to treat a discriminatory rule as compatible with the Treaty if it is necessary to reserve the coherence of a tax system. In Case C-204/90 *Bachmann v Belgian State* [1992] ECR I-249 the Court found the Belgian rule which made pension and insurance contributions deductible only if they were paid in Belgium to be in contravention of Articles 48 and 59 of the EC Treaty. Yet here they looked at the rationale behind the rule which in this case was that in Belgium deductibility is inextricably linked with the ability to tax the ultimate proceeds of such policies in the hands of the recipient. Notwithstanding the fact that it was discriminatory, the restriction did not infringe EC law on the basis that it was the least restrictive way of preserving the coherence of the system.

*Commerzbank* and *Halliburton* were decided after *Bachmann* and it may be that the Court is moving to a position where the non-discrimination principle will be applied to direct taxation without qualification. Indeed, in the most recently decided case, *Schumacher*, a number of Member States argued that discrimination was justified (this case concerned the availability of personal allowances and reliefs to a non-resident) by the need for tax regimes to adopt a cohesive approach to all non-residents worldwide. Significantly, this reasoning was rejected by the Court. These decisions and the judicial trend they display suggest that the most significant developments in the harmonisation of direct taxes will be found in the enforcement by the Court of Justice of the principles of non-discrimination rather than by legislative activity.

MARK BALDWIN

*Recommended reading*
Famer & Lyal *EC Tax Law* (1995) Oxford University Press.
Lyons 'Discrimination Against Individuals and Enterprises on Grounds of Nationality, Direct Taxation and the European Court of Justice' (1994) British Tax Review 554.

**TAXATION (INDIRECT)** One of the fundamental prerequisites for the establishment of a common market without internal frontiers was the removal of fiscal barriers to intra-Community trade. Consequently, the EC Treaty provided for the abolition of customs duties on imports and exports between Member States and national turnover tax systems which discriminated in favour of domestic products. Furthermore, Article 99 EC instructed the Commission to consider how the legislation of the Member States concerning turnover taxes could be **harmonised** in the interests of the **Internal Market**. In 1958 only France applied a value added tax. The other Member States operated multi-stage turnover taxes. Thus, when the findings of a Commission working party and the Neumark Report both advocated the adoption across the Community of a common system of value added tax it was clear that such a harmonisation would take time. The harmonisation proposals required by Article 99 were submitted to the Council of Ministers in 1962. On 11 April 1967 the Council adopted the First and Second Directive (Council Directive (EEC) 67/227 (OJ (1967) Sp Ed p 14) and Council Directive (EEC) 67/228 (OJ (1967) Sp Ed p 16) respectively). Member States were obliged to introduce a common system of value added tax to replace their turnover tax system.

The common system of value added tax is based on the application to goods and services of a general tax on consumption. The First Directive established the basic scheme of value added tax as a tax on the value which traders add to their purchases of materials, goods and services. The tax levied is to be exactly proportional to the price of the goods or services, irrespective of the number of transactions which take place in the production and distribution process before the stage at which the tax is charged. On each transaction, value added tax – calculated as a percentage of the price of the goods or services – is chargeable after deduction of the amount of value added tax borne directly by the various cost components. The system is applied up to and including the retail stage.

The Second Directive imposed the legal requirement for Member States to put in place the structure described in the First Directive. It also dealt with procedural matters and required the Commission look at common procedures for applying value added tax to transactions related to agricultural products and for completing the harmonisation of a common system of value added tax. The result of their endeavours was contained in the Sixth Directive, which was adopted by the Council on 17 May 1977 (Council Directive (EEC) 77/388 (OJ L145 13.6.77 p 1)). The Sixth Directive incorporates and replaces the provisions of the Second Directive. It takes account of the fact that contributions to the Community **finances** were to be funded from value added tax and that a Community-wide calculation was required which applied a uniform rate to a uniform assessment basis. The Sixth Directive clarified the uniform basis of assessment, the fundamental components of which were a clear statement of those transactions which are chargeable to tax, an extension of the tax to retail transactions, the establishment of common exemptions and the abolition of certain derogations previously permitted under the Second Directive.

The Sixth Directive was subject to major amendment prior to the introduction of the Internal Market on 1 January 1993. These amendments reflected the views of the Commission as to what changes should be made to the common system of value added tax in order to complete the Internal Market. In their proposal set out in 1985, the Commission envisaged charging value added tax on supplies of goods between Member States in the country in which the goods originated and at the prevailing rate in that country. The Council took the view that the origin system of taxation required the harmonisation of rates of value added tax across the Community. For reasons of practical exigency, the Council adopted a transitional system to take effect from 1 January 1993. This was contained in Council Directive (EEC) 91/680 (OJ L376 31.12.91 p 1), which amends the Sixth Directive. Supplies of goods between Member States are taxed on the basis that intra-EC supplies of goods between registered trades are zero-rated, with the tax charge being levied on the acquisition of the goods by the ultimate consumer. The transitional system also abolished the movement procedures in force prior to 1 January 1993 for movements of goods between Member States. The transitional system will remain in operation until 31 December 1996 or the date on which a definitive system based on the origin principle is established, whichever is the later. Progress towards a fully harmonised origin system has been slow and it will clearly be well beyond 31 December 1996 before the transitional system is superseded.

The completion of the Internal Market also precipitated a number of changes to the regulations concerning customs duties. Unlike the transitional system of value added tax, these changes do not concern the abolition of internal frontiers but seek to develop a consistent tax treatment of imports from outside the Community. Rates of duty and the scope of exemptions from tax were already harmonised. Changes introduced on 1 January 1992 were aimed at fine tuning systems of customs bonded warehouses and free zones across the community. The EC Community Customs Code (which became fully applicable in all Member States as of 1 January 1994) pulled together the diverse strands of EC customs legislation into a coherent and accessible form.

Excise duties are consumption taxes on special products generally levied according to the destination principle. In this field, the harmonisation process is not as far advanced as is the case for value added tax and customs duties. Member States still apply different rates of duty and the tax base differs. The only Directive adopted so far concerns the intra-Community transport of excise products (Council Directive (EEC) 92/12 (OJ L76 23.2.92 p 1)). The scope of the new rules is limited to measures which are essential for the abolition of customs formalities in the intra-EC transactions. Given the moves towards the abolition of such frontiers in the fields of value added tax and customs duty, the existence of formalities in respect of excise products would be wholly inconsistent with the principles of the Internal Market.

MARK BALDWIN

*Recommended reading*
Farmer & Lyal *EC Tax Law* (1994) Oxford University Press.
Raponi 'Recent EC Developments in the Field of Indirect Taxation' (1995) 2 EC Tax Review 105.

**TECHNICAL STANDARDS** Technical standards serve traditionally several main purposes, in particular: rationalisation of production and application, compatibility of products, promotion of safety of products. In terms of their authority, technical standards are 'norms', in that they are created and widely accepted to guide conduct, but can be distinguished from a rule of law by the fact that they lack direct binding effectiveness. Rather, in order to exert legal force they need to be transposed by a legal provision into the legal system.

Seen from the point of view of the **European Union**, technical standards that are established in a specific national framework on a national level are regularly capable of impeding the **free movement of goods** in the **Internal Market**, thereby driving up the costs for a Union-wide marketable production and distorting competition. Partially, such accession barriers of a state for products manufactured according to the standards of another Member State can violate **directly effective** prohibitions of the EC Treaty, in particular Article 30, and can henceforth be quashed if they are not capable to be justified by exception rules such as Article 36 EC or the *Cassis de Dijon* jurisprudence. However, in all cases in which this remedy is not available or sufficient (eg lack of technical compatibility) positive measures have to be taken.

Consequently, numerous initiatives have been developed to remove the impediments that result from different national technical standards for the trade between Member States, in particular: (a) the establishment of a system of early information of national standardisation projects (Council Directive (EEC) 83/189 (OJ L109 15.2.89 p 8)) that is designed to make national activities more transparent and to spot possible fields for European standardisation; (b) the setting up of special organisations for the development of European technical standards such as CEN and CENELEC that are constituted as private bodies, composed of national standardisation organisations and charged with the development of **harmonised** European standards; (c) the adoption of technical harmonisation Directives by the **Council** which have been based consecutively on different concepts, starting in the first case with a connection between Directive and CENELEC standards (OJ L77 26.3.73 p 29), developing later on into forms of technically very detailed Directives and favouring presently the 'new concept' of harmonisation Directives that are restricted to the fixation of cogent requirements of **health and safety** in order to enable the free movement of a product (OJ C136 4.6.85 p 1) and leave the definition of technical specifications with standardisation bodies such as CEN and others; (d) the encouragement of **mutual recognition** of different national technical standards as long as European standards do not exist.

PETER-CHRISTIAN MÜLLER-GRAFF

*Recommended reading*
Anselmann 'Die Rolle der europäischen Normung bei der Schaffung des europäischen Binnenmarktes' (1986) RIW 936.
Müller-Graff (ed) *Technische Regeln im Binnenmarkt* (1991) Nomos.

**TELECOMMUNICATIONS** The foundations of the Community's extensive telecommunications policy (which currently consists of over 100 legislative measures) are to be found in the Commission's

1987 Green Paper on the development of the Common Market for Telecommunications Services and Equipment (COM(87) 290) which called for the progressive liberalisation and **harmonisation** of the telecommunications services and equipments markets.

The Commission acted by adopting two key Directives in 1988 and 1990 based on **Article 90** EC (see **state monopolies**), aimed respectively at liberalising the telecommunications equipments and the telecommunications services markets by requiring the abolition of the exclusive rights held by the national telecommunications organisations, subject only to certain permissible restrictions aimed at ensuring conformance with what are termed the 'essential requirements' (being requirements relating to the security of network operations, user safety, maintenance of network integrity, interoperability of terminal equipment and services, and, in certain cases, data protection). An additional fundamental feature of both Directives was the requirement that the regulatory and operational functions of national telecommunications organisations be separated so as to prevent potential infringement of Article 86 and Article 90 EC. Challenges to the legal basis of these Directives by certain Member States resulted in the **Court of Justice** confirming the Commission's competence in using Article 90 EC (Case C-202/88 *France v Commission* [1991] ECR 1223 and Joined Cases C-271, 281 & 289/90 *Spain v Commission* [1992] ECR I-5833).

The 1988 Directive, known as the Terminal Equipment Directive (Commission Directive (EEC) 88/301 (OJ L131 27.5.88 p 73)) specifically required Member States to publish technical requirements and approval procedures for the marketing and interconnection of terminal equipment so that private suppliers have the information necessary to operate in the market. The Directive is accompanied by a package of harmonisation measures concerning standards and national type approval (principally, Council Directive (EEC) 86/361 (OJ L 217 5.8.86 p 21) and Council Directive (EEC) 91/263 (OJ L 128 23.5.91 p 1)).

The 1990 so-called 'Services Directive' in its original form required the introduction of competition in data and voice services, with an exception for public voice telephony and related infrastructure, justified by the need to ensure the financial viability of the national telecommunications organisations entrusted with universal service obligations. The definition of 'voice telephony' contained in the Directive, however, means that many voice services – such as voice messaging services, closed user group telephony, voice refining/least cost routing, and intelligent network functions ought to have been liberalised.

Following a major review in 1992 (1992 Review of the Situation in the Telecommunications Services Sector (SEC (92) 1048)) and the adoption of a landmark Council Resolution in 1993 (Council Resolution (EEC) 93/C 213/01 (OJ C213 6.8.93 p 1)), a programme of legislative action aimed at the full liberalisation of the EU's telecommunications sector by 1998 was agreed. As a result, Member States have been required to liberalise satellite and mobile services (both excluded from the original scope of the Services Directive) by Directives adopted in 1994 and 1996, respectively (Commission Directive 94/96 (OJ L268 19.10.94 p 15) and Commission Directive 96/2 (OJ L20 21.6.96 p 59)).

The first step towards infrastructure liberalisation was introduced by a Directive lifting all restrictions, as from 1 January 1996, on the use of cable TV networks throughout the EU for the provision of those telecommunications services which have, to date, been liberalised (Commission Directive (EC) 95/51 (OJ L256 26.10.95 p 49)). In order to achieve this, Member States are required to allow cable TV networks to interconnect with the public telcommunications network.

Further infrastructure liberalisation is provided for in the Directive adopted in April 1996, known as the 'Full Competition Directive' which requires Member States to lift restrictions by July 1996 on the self-provision of all liberalised services. The Directive, moreover, requires Member States to take all necessary steps by 1 January 1998 to ensure that the provision of voice telephony and related infrastructure are fully open (Ireland, Spain, Greece, Luxembourg and Portugal are eligible for certain transitional derogations, subject to the Commission's approval by the end of 1996).

Underlying the Commission's liberalisation of telecommunications is its Open Network Provision (ONP) policy, which has its origins in the 1987 Green Paper and the ONP Framework Directive (Council Directive (EEC) 90/387 (OJ L192 24.07.90 p 1)). ONP is a regulatory framework designed to complement the EU's competition rules as applied to the telecommunications market (in particular the Commission's guidelines on the application of EEC competition rules in the telecommunications sector (OJ C233 6.9.91 p 2)). Its overall aim is to ensure that all users have access to a system of interconnected public networks throughout the Community. The ONP Framework Directive identifies three main areas to which ONP harmonised conditions should apply, based on objective transparent and non-discriminatory conditions: technical interfaces, including network termination points; usage and supply conditions (eg delivery time, repair time, conditions for resale of capacity); and tariff principles (in particular cost-orientation and unbundling). Specific ONP measures have been developed for particular areas, including leased lines, integrated services digital networks and public packet switched data services. Existing ONP rules relating to voice telephony are due to be replaced by a pending proposal dealing with the application of ONP in a fully liberalised environment (COM (96) 419).

Building on the basic ONP principles, the Commission has proposed a Directive on interconnection which provides for a harmonised framework for regulation by National Regulatory Authorities of interconnection between network operators (OJ L220 29.7.96 p 13).

A draft Directive dealing with the harmonisation of licensing and authorisation regimes, which proposes that the use of licences be limited to certain circumstances, such as the need to ensure the provision of universal service (OJ L291 4.10.96 p 12).

The Commission has established criteria for assessing national schemes for financing the provision of universal service for telecommunications (COM (96) 608).

The emerging multimedia and superhighways technologies have been the subject of in-depth study at Community level (Europe and the Global Information Society, Recommendations to the European Council by the Bangemann Group 26.05.94) and a work programme of regulatory measures and research and development initiatives are in progress (Communication from the Commission, Europe's way to the Information Society: An Action Plan (COM (94) 347)).

PATRICIA BOYLE

*Recommended reading*
Ungerer 'EU Competition Law in the Telecommunications, Media and Information Technology Sectors' (1996) Annual Proceedings of Fordham Corporate Law Institute 465.
Ravaioli & Sandler 'The European Union and Telecommunications Recent Developments in the Field of Competition (Part I) and (Part II)' vol 2, no 4 (April 1994), vol 2, no 5, May 1995, The International Computer Lawyer.

**TRANS-EUROPEAN NETWORKS** The **Treaty on European Union** inserted Title XII, Articles 129b–129d, into the EC Treaty. Title XII conferred upon the Community new **competencies** in the field of 'Trans-European Networks'. Article 129b(1) states that to help achieve the objectives of the **Internal Market** and economic and social **cohesion** and to enable citizens, economic operators and localities to derive full benefit from an area without internal frontiers, the Community shall contribute to the establishment and development of trans-European networks in the areas of transport, telecommunications and energy infrastructures. In particular, the Community shall aim at promoting the interconnection and interoperability of national networks, as well as access to such networks.

In order to achieve these objectives, the Community shall establish guidelines of action, implement necessary measures to ensure the interoperability of networks and may provide financial support for projects of common interest (Article 129c(1)). The **Council** and the **European Parliament** have adopted a Decision laying down guidelines for trans-European energy networks (Decision (EC) 1254/96 (OJ L161 29.6.96 p 147)) and will shortly adopt a similar Decision in respect of transport (COM (94) 106 final), its second reading before the European Parliament having been completed (OJ C17 22.1.96 p 58). The guidelines set out the objectives, scope, Community measures and priorities in each of the sectors, as well as listing projects of common interest. Community funding for projects in the transport sector are to be granted through the **Cohesion** Fund.

The **Court of Justice** has handed down one judgment in the field of trans-European networks (Case C-271/94 *European Parliament v Council* [1996] ECR I-1689) regarding the legal basis of Council Decision (EC) 94/445 (OJ L183 19.7.94 p 42) on the inter-administration by automatic and electronic transmission of data relating to the trading of goods between Member States. The European Parliament argued that the legal base of this measure should have been trans-European networks. The judgment is important in two respects.

First, the Court stated that the 'guidelines' referred to in Article 129c(1) are not a necessary prerequisite to legislative measures in this field. Second, it found in favour of the Parliament's application, and held that Article 129c(1) constituted a more specific provision than Article 100a, for the achievement of the Internal Market. The Court's decision strengthens the autonomy of trans-European networks provisions of the TEU, although the Commission has not, to date, produced its approach to general implementation of the Title.

WILLIAM ROBINSON

*Recommended reading*:
Obernesser 'Trans-European Telecommunications Networks' (1993) Computer and Telecommunications Law Review 16.


**TRANSFER OF UNDERTAKINGS** See **employment protection**.


**TRANSPARENCY** The term 'transparency' is used in two distinct ways in Community law. First, it refers to the openness of economic activities, particularly in the fields of **competition policy, energy policy, public procurement** and the dealings of public entities (Article 90 EC). Second, it refers to the openness of the Community decision-making process, which is discussed below.

In the TEU, the Member States incorporated a Declaration (No 17) on the right of access to information, in response to perceived public concern about the opacity of the Community decision-making process.

In response to the Declaration, the **Commission** and **Council** jointly approved a Code of Conduct ('the Code') concerning public access to Commission and Council documents on 6 December 1993. The Code sets out the general principle that the public will have the widest possible access to documents held by the Commission and the Council. The term 'document' is defined as meaning 'any written text, whatever its medium, which contains existing data . . . .'.

The Code sets out rules governing the lodging and processing of requests for documents, as well as the procedure to be followed where it is intended to reject a request.

The Code specifies that the institutions *must* refuse access to a document where disclosure could undermine the protection of the public interest, of the individual and of privacy, of commercial and industrial secrecy, of the Community's financial interests and of confidentiality. An institution *may* also refuse access in order to protect its interest in the confidentiality of its proceedings.

The Council adopted its own decision on public access to Council documents on 20 December 1993 (Council Decision (EC) 93/731 (OJ L340 31.12.93 p 43)) ('the Council Decision'). This implements the principles of the Code. The Commission adopted its decision on public access to Commission documents on 8 February 1994, Article 1 of which adopts the Code directly (Commission Decision (ECSC, EC, Euratom) 94/90 (OJ L46 18.2.94 p 58)).

The **Court of Justice** has dismissed an application by the Netherlands for annulment of the Council Decision and of the Code (in so far as the latter has legal effects). The application was dismissed as inadmissible in so far as it was directed against the Code. On the Council Decision, the Court of Justice rejected the arguments that the Council had used the wrong legal basis and that it had infringed the institutional balance required by the EC Treaty by failing to involve the **European Parliament**. Notably, the Court of Justice did not rule on the argument made by the European Parliament in its intervention that the requirement for openness and the right to information (of which access to documents is the corollary) constituted a **general principle of Community law**, respect for which should be ensured by the Court (Case C-58/94 *Netherlands v Council,* judgment of 30 April 1996).

In 1995 the **Court of First Instance** annulled two decisions of the Council refusing John Carvel access to certain preparatory reports, minutes and attendance and voting records of various Council meetings. It found that, when refusing access to the documents in order to protect its interest in the confidentiality of its proceedings, the Council had failed to balance the interest of citizens in gaining access to its documents against its own interest, and had therefore failed to exercise its discretion in compliance with Article 4(2) of the Council Decision (Case T-194/94 *Carvel and Guardian Newspapers v Council* [1995] ECR II-2765).

EMER FINNEGAN

*Recommended reading*
Curtin & Meijers 'Access to European Union Information: an element of citizenship and a neglected constitutional right' in Neuwahl & Rosas *The European Union and human rights* (1995) Nijhoff.
Michael 'Freedom of Information comes to the European Union' (1996) Public Law 31.

**TRANSPORT** See **Common Transport Policy.**

**TREATY ON EUROPEAN UNION (TEU)** The Treaty on European Union, which was signed in Maastricht on 7 February 1992 and

entered into force on 1 November 1993, is discussed fully under
**European Union**.


**URUGUAY ROUND** The Uruguay Round of Multilateral Trade
Negotiations was launched on 22 September 1986, at Punta del Este,
Uruguay, by the Trade Ministers of 100 countries. The negotiations
were held under the general supervision of the **GATT**. The Round
itself was unquestionably the most complex and ambitious programme
of negotiations ever undertaken by that organisation.

The Uruguay Round was the eighth round of international trade
negotiations to take place within the framework of the GATT, and by
the time the negotiations were formally concluded in Marrakesh,
Morocco, there were 125 participating countries.

The mandate for the Uruguay Round negotiations was contained in
the Declaration of Punta del Este, and it was very broad. It included
subjects such as tariffs, non-tariff measures, tropical products, natural
resource-based products, textile and clothing, agriculture, GATT
articles and the functioning of the GATT system, safeguards measures,
subsidies and countervailing measures, dispute settlement, trade-
related aspects of intellectual property rights, trade-related investment
measures and, most importantly, trade in services. The GATT
contracting parties established 14 negotiating groups to work on the
problems of trade in goods, and a separate structure was set up for
negotiations on trade in services.

In fact, the Uruguay Round negotiations also led to the demise of
the organisation under which the discussions were held. The
institutional and structural aspects of GATT have been replaced by a
new body, the **World Trade Organization**. The original GATT was
modified and became GATT 1994 and then subsumed under the
general umbrella of the WTO Agreement. To this was joined a host of
new undertakings and this system in turn is linked to the organisational
structures for the General Agreement on Trade in Services and to the
Agreement on Trade-Related Aspects of Intellectual Property Rights
(TRIPS).

The Final Act Embodying the Results of the Uruguay Round of
Multilateral Trade Negotiations, informally agreed in an almost final
form on 15 December 1993, was signed by the participating
representatives of governments and the European Community on
15 April 1994 in Marrakesh. One hundred and eleven countries
signed the Final Act and 104 signed the WTO Agreement (to which all
the other Agreements were annexed).

PAOLO VERGANO

*Recommended reading*
McGovern *International Trade Regulation* (1995) Globefield Press.
Stewart *The GATT Uruguay Round: a negotiating history (1986-1992)* (1993) Kluwer.

**VARIABLE GEOMETRY** The EU does not have a homogeneous structure or entity, particularly since the TEU has been marked by provision for differentiated integration. Variable geometry is one such model, and permits integrative development to take place to different degrees among clusters of countries. It thus acknowledges that the diversity of traditions, perspectives and cultures within Europe makes homogeneous patterns of integration undesirable or impossible.

The concept of differentiated integration has spawned many terms and metaphors. These may usefully be reduced to three broad types: multi-speed, variable geometry and *à la carte*. 'Multi-speed' Europe permits some states to progress on particular objectives at a slower rate than others. Article 7c EC, for example, allows for temporary derogations to take account of differences in economic development in relation to the achievement of single market aims. However, the key feature of a multi-speed approach is that there remains commonality in the agreed objective. 'Variable geometry' assumes from the outset that, in addition to the core activities undertaken by all members, there will be certain projects which will only be undertaken by certain participants. This facility may permit greater levels of integration to develop for those groups, sometimes referred to as the 'opt-in' approach. However, variable geometry is distinct from the concept of Europe '*à la carte*', which allows Member States to pick and choose which areas of policy they wish to adopt, ie an '**opt-out**' arrangement, such as that made in relation to the United Kingdom regarding social policy.

These models are not always easily distinguishable, and indeed some areas of activity may display characteristics of more than one. The programme for **economic and monetary union**, for example, has a timetable in keeping with multi-speed differentiation, whilst the reservation of Danish and United Kingdom opt-outs belongs to the *à la carte* scenario. The latter are permanent rights to remain outside the EMU, not just temporary derogations from it.

Institutionally, the perceived risk of variable geometry is that it may create separate structures, usually based on intergovernmental agreement, which could undermine the normal decision-making processes of the Union. Illustrations of variable geometry can be seen in the collaboration over particular projects, such as JET, or in policy development such as the **Schengen Agreements**, and in particular elements of the Second and Third Pillars of the TEU. In the field of foreign and security policy for example, Article J.4(5) allows for closer co-operation between two or more Member States on a bilateral level in the framework of the **Western European Union** and the Atlantic Alliance. Article K.7 permits similar closer **co-operation in the fields of justice and home affairs**. Variable geometry is less evident in the EC Treaty, although Article 130K envisages supplementary **research and development** programmes being undertaken by some Member States only.

Differentiated integration represents the response to the tension between the widening and deepening of integrative activity and the interests and commitment of individual Member States. The constitutional problem that it raises is whether, and how, the different units and rates of integration can be co-ordinated and remain compatible. The single institutional framework aspired to by the TEU is one example of the attempt to maintain at least the appearance of a common approach. However, the 'borrowing' of Community institutions under the Second and Third Pillars to reach intergovernmental decisions has been roundly criticised. The removal of certain aspects of Union activity from review by the **Court of Justice** (Article L TEU) raises similar controversies as to the coherence of variable geometry. Greater use of differentiated integration models has also been seen as a threat to the *acquis communautaire*. Such principles as might be developed to operate as co-ordinating mechanisms, such as the expressed need for consistency and solidarity (Article A TEU), remain immature.

The Reflection Group Reports prepared for the 1996 **Intergovernmental Conference** expressly rejected the idea of *à la carte* Europe. Instead, it considered that flexibility should only be allowed where it would be possible for the Union to manage diversity without jeopardising the *acquis communautaire* and the common objectives. In particular, there was a large majority view in the Report that differences in the degree of integration should be temporary and that flexibility should only be permitted if all other solutions have been ruled out and on a case-by-case basis. The Report also stressed the need for a single institutional framework to be respected, irrespective of the structure of the Treaty. These suggestions thus run closer to multi-speed models, rather than variable geometry. Nevertheless, the Report acknowledged that there could still be greater flexibility in the foreign and security policy and justice and home affairs Pillars than under the EC Treaty.

The extension or curtailment of variable geometry is susceptible to the general pressures shaping the evolving architecture of the Union. The prospect of significant further enlargement of membership heightens the probability that the greater user might be made of institutionalised space between the levels of integration demanded of and accepted by groupings of states within an overall looser framework.

MALCOLM ROSS

*Recommended reading*
Curtin 'The constitutional structure of the Union: a Europe of bits and pieces' (1993) 30 CMLRev 17.
Subb 'A categorisation of differentiated integration' (1996) 34 Journal of Common Market Studies 283.

**VISA POLICY** See **immigration policy**.

**WESTERN EUROPEAN UNION (WEU)** The Western European Union developed out of the 1948 Brussels Treaty which was designed to convince the United States that its European allies were willing to assist in the defence of the continent. When attempts to construct an integrated defence system, the European Defence Community, failed in 1954, the Brussels Treaty was enlarged into a Western European Union and Germany and Italy were allowed to join. The WEU was responsible for monitoring the process of German rearmament.

From that period onwards, the WEU played a relatively minor role in European security, subordinate to NATO. It acted as a discussion forum for European States but by the 1970s was of little utility. However, the WEU was revitalised in 1984 at a time when tensions over security issues between the Europeans and the United States were increasing. The WEU provided a mechanism for bringing France into discussions about security and developing a common European perspective. The WEU saw its first operational role in 1987 with the co-ordination of European naval forces in the Persian Gulf during the Iran–Iraq War.

The importance of the WEU increased markedly with the ending of the Cold War. It appeared to offer an alternative security framework to NATO and it had the potential to deal with crises outside the borders of Europe. Furthermore, the WEU was identified as a mechanism that could contribute to the process of European integration. When France and Germany called for political union in April 1990, the WEU was seen as a way to bring defence issues into the EC.

The Treaty on European Union (TEU) achieved a careful balancing act in the case of the WEU, designed to satisfy the varying demands of Member States. Title V, Article J of the Treaty established a **Common Foreign and Security Policy** and Article J.4 declared that a common defence policy would be a long-term ambition for the EU. Under Article J.4 the **European Council** would be the body that would 'request' the WEU to act on behalf of the EU. In the 'Declaration on WEU' that accompanied the Treaty, it was stated that the WEU would serve as the defence component of the European Union and as a mechanism for strengthening the European Pillar within NATO.

The period since the signing of the TEU has seen the implications of these decisions being explored. At Petersberg, in June 1992, it was agreed that the WEU would perform tasks at the lower end of the conflict spectrum, such as humanitarian and peacekeeping actions, whilst the territorial defence of Europe would continue to be assured by NATO. In order to undertake such military tasks, the WEU will be able to request the use of NATO assets under an agreement signed in June 1996, removing the need for duplicate forces. It has also become accepted that the enlargement of NATO to include states from Central Europe will take place before any enlargement of the WEU.

With the ending of the Cold War there was speculation that the WEU might grow into a competitor with the Alliance. This has not come to pass and the primacy of NATO continues. Nevertheless, the Intergovernmental Conference on the reform of the TEU has provided an opportunity to review the role of the WEU. All the members of the WEU, except for the United Kingdom, wish to see the WEU integrated into the EU to create a clearer identity in the defence field. Although such a development appears unlikely for some time, it is possible that the European Council will be accorded greater influence over the WEU's actions. For the foreseeable future, the WEU will continue to serve as both the defence arm of the EU and the European Pillar within NATO.

G WYN REES

*Recommended reading*
Jopp 'The Strategic Implications of European Integration' Adelphi Paper 290, Brassey's for the Institute for Strategic Studies, London, July 1994.
The Federal Trust 'Security of the Union: The Intergovernmental Conference of the European Union 1996' Federal Trust Papers No 4, London, October 1995.

**WEU** See **Western European Union**.

**WORKS COUNCIL DIRECTIVE** The Works Council Directive (Council Directive (EEC) 95/45 (OJ L254 22.11.94 p 64) creates a legal framework for the establishment of a European Works Council or alternative information and consultation procedure (hereinafter known collectively as EWCs) in Community-scale undertakings and groups of undertakings. Such procedures will provide a mechanism for over 1,000 European companies to inform and consult employees on transnational issues concerning the interests of those employees. The Directive was influenced by previous unsuccessful, similar initiatives, in particular the **European Company Statute**, the Fifth Company Directive and the Vredeling Directive (see **company law**).

In accordance with the principle of **subsidiarity**, the Directive leaves existing national EWC structures intact and does not lay down detailed regulations. Instead it provides for a Special Negotiating Body composed of management and employee representatives, which determines the existence, scope, composition and functions of EWCs. Negotiations may be initiated either by central management or at the request of at least 100 employees. Subsidiary requirements apply only if a voluntary agreement cannot be reached.

The Directive's legal basis is Article 1 of the **Social Policy Agreement**, which has the objective of the promotion of dialogue between management and labour. For the first time the social partners were consulted in the formation of the proposal with a view to their concluding an agreement in place of binding legislation, consistent with Article 3(4) of the Social Policy Agreement. However, no such agreement was reached.

Due to the United Kingdom opt-out of the Social Policy Agreement, the Directive does not directly apply to United Kingdom companies or their employees. However, approximately 100 United Kingdom companies will be affected due to the size of their operations elsewhere in the EU and many non-United Kingdom companies are expected to include United Kingdom representatives voluntarily in EWCs on practical and political grounds.

ELINOR CAMPBELL

*Recommended reading*
Carlin 'The European Works Council Directive' (1995) 20 ELRev 96.
McGlynn 'European Works Councils: Towards Industrial Democracy?' (1995) 24 ILJ 78.


**WORLD TRADE ORGANIZATION (WTO)** The World Trade Organization is the international trade body that has replaced the General Agreement on Tariffs and Trade (**GATT**) in its organisational and institutional aspects.

The WTO started operating on 1 January 1995, and is formally established by the first Article of the WTO Agreement. This Article provides a 'common institutional framework' for the conduct of trade relations among its members (now up to 119) in matters related to the WTO agreements and the associated legal instruments. The Organization also co-ordinates international policy with the International Monetary Fund and the World Bank. The WTO represents, in fact, the Third Pillar of the intended post-war 'economic world order' conceived at Bretton Woods but which was never achieved after the ill-fated International Trade Organization failed to get off the ground.

The WTO is considered a 'single undertaking', meaning that each member must accept all parts of the WTO Agreement which includes a revised General Agreement (GATT 1994). On the other side, the Plurilateral Trade Agreements have independent status and need only to be accepted by those countries willing to be bound by them.

The WTO is headed by a Ministerial Conference, made up of all members of the WTO, which meets at least once every two years. Beneath the Ministerial Conference sits the General Council, which is also made up of all members. It also oversees the operation of the Agreement acting as the head of the WTO between the ministerial meetings. The General Council also convenes as the Dispute Settlement Body (DSB) administering the Dispute Settlement Understanding (DSU) and as the Trade Policy Review Body administering the Trade Policy Review Mechanism.

Subsidiary specialised councils include the Council for Trade in Goods, the Council for Trade in Services and the Council for Trade-Related Aspects of Intellectual Property Rights. Various committees have also been established by the Ministerial Conference in specific areas and with particular competencies and functions. The daily work and administration of the Organization is carried out by the WTO Secretariat, headed by a Director General and based in Geneva. All countries which are signatories to the WTO Agreement are required to ensure that their laws, regulations and administrative procedures comply with the principles and provisions provided for by the WTO Agreement. A new and more stringent dispute settlement mechanism has been agreed and disputes between countries participating in the WTO are referred to the DSB. The DSU establishes a detailed system of dispute settlement and specific working procedures. This system is now a compulsory and binding one based on stringent deadlines and complete with the possibility of a legal appeal to a Standing Appellate Body, which can review panel reports and amend legal errors. This 'second degree of jurisdiction' was inevitable to balance the now binding nature of the final rulings or recommendations, which are automatically adopted unless the DSB decides by consensus not to adopt them ('negative consensus'). Detailed rules on surveillance of implementation of panel recommendations and rulings, along with precise and binding prescriptions on compensation and suspension of concessions, are also provided for by the new mechanism.

The WTO is to continue the practice of decision making by consensus whereby consensus is achieved if no member formally objects. Certain amendments require, however, unanimity (formal acceptance by all members), while various decisions need specific majorities. Financial regulations and budget estimates need a two-thirds majority comprising more than half of the members; the entry into force of amendments and the approval of terms of accession require a two-thirds majority of members; waivers of obligations, amendments effective for all members and adoption of interpretations need a three-quarters majority of members.

PAOLO VERGANO

*Recommended reading*
Bourgeois *The Uruguay Round Results A European Lawyers' Perspective* (1995) European Inter-University Press.
McGovern *International Trade Regulation* (1995) Globefield Press.


**WRITTEN PROCEDURE (ECJ)** Written procedure is the most important phase of proceedings before the **Court of Justice** (and **Court of First Instance**). In direct actions it comprises the application and defence, followed usually by reply and rejoinder. The application defines the issues, and must specify the relief sought (including any claim for costs) and contain all arguments of law relied on (Rules of Procedure of the Court of Justice Article 38.1); all supporting documentary evidence must be annexed (RP Article 37.4). Oral evidence may be offered (though rarely taken). New claims and issues may not be introduced later unless they are based on matters of law or fact emerging in the course of procedure (RP Article 42.2). Further evidence may be introduced in reply, but the delay must be explained.

After close of pleadings, the Court may make preparatory inquiries or proceed directly to the **oral procedure**. Preparatory inquiries include appearance of the parties, requests for information or documents, oral testimony, the commissioning by the Court of its own expert's report or the inspection of a place or thing. Oral testimony involves the witness making a statement in his own words, followed by questions from the Court and only then from the parties' lawyers.

In **preliminary ruling** proceedings there is one round of written pleadings, in which all parties and any Community **institution** or Member State may simultaneously file written observations on the questions referred. Written observations are not obligatory, and failure to file them does not preclude attendance at the oral hearing.

Written pleadings require a careful balance of explanation and argument. Their primary purpose is to inform and persuade. Although commonly divided into sections dealing with procedural issues, facts and law, overlap is inevitable. The best written advocacy is understated; presentation influences perception of the issues and their resolution. Familiarity with the Court's thinking is also valuable.

NICHOLAS FORWOOD

*Recommended reading*
Lasok *The European Court of Justice: Practice and Procedure* (2nd edn, 1994) Butterworths.
Plender *European Court Practice and Procedures* (1996) Sweet & Maxwell.